O9-BHK-381

# *Yesterday's Faces*

# Yesterday's Faces Volume 6

## Violent Lives

## Robert Sampson

MIDDLEBURY COLLEGE LIBRARY

Bowling Green State University Popular Press
Bowling Green, OH 43403

Copyright © 1993 by Bowling Green State University Popular Press

Library of Congress Catalogue Card No.: 82-73597

ISBN: 0-87972-614-8 Clothbound
0-87972-615-6 Paperback

Cover design by Gary Dumm

To Diggs Latouche, Steve Miller, and Leonard Robbins,

incredibly patient and well-informed, for all their help, all

these years — as this book testifies.

# Contents

# Acknowledgements

To Richard Bleiler, whose index to *Adventure*, finally opened that particular enigma for close study.

To George Hocutt for all those photographs of air war covers.

To Diggs LaTouche for sharing the results of years of note taking and finally unraveling both the intricate story of the Freelances and John Solomon's more obscure appearances.

To Cynthia Lindsey and John Gunnison for all their labors to provide cover photographs.

To Walker Martin, who obliged with a whole new batch of answers, himself, as usual, patient, accurate, endlessly informed.

To Steve Miller for those priceless xeroxes when everything else had failed.

To Will Murray for the stack of Jimgrim books that revealed so much about the narrative continuity and character evolution in that remarkable series.

To Frank Robinson who provided the material essential to understanding the Khlit series.

To Howard Snively for his help, so many years ago, with Khlit and other Lamb ferocities.

And to Earl Kussman, shrewd, quiet, tough minded, and much mourned.

Certain material in this volume has appeared in somewhat different form, as follows:

"The Avenging Aces," *Echoes*, Vol. 3, #3 (June 1984).

"By the Nine Red Gods of Battle," *Echoes*, Vol. 9, #1 (February 1990).

"End of a Strange Series," *Echoes*, Vol. 10, #4 (August 1991, #56).

"A Peculiar Gift," *Echoes*, Vol. 5, #3 (June 1986, #25).

"Shadow on the Wind," *Age of the Unicorn*, Vol II, No. 2 (Undated, [1979], Whole #8).

"Still Another Master Criminal," *Echoes*, Vol. 5, #1 (February 1986, #24)

"'Tis I, The Wonderful O'Leary of Medal Fame," *The Pulp Collector*, Vol. 4, #4 (Summer 1989).

"'Tis I, Th' Immazin' Terence X. O'Leary, Sky Hawk," *The Pulp Collector*, Vol. 5, #1 (Winter 1990).

i

Covers from *Argosy, Battle Aces, and Detective Fiction Weekly*, reprinted by permission of *Argosy* Communications, Inc. Argosy, December 2, 1933 and September 21, 1935; copyright © 1933 and 1935, respectively, by The Frank A. Munsey Company; copyright renewed © 1961 and 1963, respectively, by Popular Publications, Inc., and assigned to Argosy Communications, Inc. All Rights Reserved. *Battle Aces,* September 1931, copyright © 1931 by Popular Publications, Inc.; copyright renewed © 1959 by Popular Publications, Inc., and assigned to Argosy Communications, Inc. All Rights Reserved. *Black Mask,* September 1931; copyright © Pro Distributors Publishing Company, Inc.; copyright renewed © 1959 by Popular Publications, and assigned to Argosy Communications, Inc. All Rights Reserved. *Detective Fiction Weekly,* March 14, 1934; copyright © 1931 by The Red Star News Company; copyright renewed © 1959 by Popular Publications, Inc., and assigned to Argosy Communications, Inc. All Rights Reserved. *Blue Book,* July 1928; copyright © 1928 by the Consolidated Magazines Corp; copyright renewed © 1956 by the McCall Co. *Complete Stories,* Second February 1931, and *The Popular Magazine,* October 7, 1925; copyright © 1931 and 1925, respectively, by Street & Smith Publications, renewed 1959 and 1953 by Conde Nast Publications. *Everybody's,* November 1917; copyright © 1917 by the Ridgeway Company; *Triple X,* March 1929; copyright © 1929 by the Fawcett Publications. *War Stories,* November 1931, copyright © 1931 by Dell Publishing Company. *Wings,* July 1934, copyright © by Wings Publishing Co., Inc.

# To the Curious Reader

The Jurassic forests, webbed by shallow streams, dense with curiously branched conifers and cycads as scaly as a carp, are irretrievably vanished. The camptosaur herds are extinct. Allosaurs no longer stalk the scrub growth. Nor do flying reptiles still circle ceaselessly, skeletal shapes against the intense sky. Of all the rich fire of life that once blazed across the visible world, only traces now remain: a coal field, a scattering of stony bones, a startling three-toed footprint huge in rock.

The Jurassic has passed. And, rather closer to us, so has the time of the pulp magazines. Once as common as air, these magazines filled homes, packed newsstands, piled second-hand stores in proliferating numbers. So common were they, so much a part of life, that who could believe them ephemeral. As well believe that the streets would melt away.

But although it seemed as impossible as a jade green sun, the magazines proved, after all, ephemeral. Like the Jurassic and its creatures, they melted in time's wind. *All Story Weekly, The Cavalier, Dime Detective, .44 Western, Love Story Magazine:* bones all, coal traces, footprints in stone.

Not quite one hundred years ago, in 1896, *The Argosy*, a ten-cent magazine printed on cheap pulp paper, abandoned articles and halftones to concentrate on fiction; by this simple transformation, it became the first all-fiction pulp magazine. Turn from that point and stride forward through time. Roughly thirty-five years ago, at the end of the 1950s, pulps, as a genre, became extinct. Between creation and extinction was about sixty-five years, including a slow beginning and an agonizingly extended demise. During that period, the pulps marched gaudily along, drums pulsing, trumpets sassy, banners vivid in the wind.

All gone now. Even the echoes of that long parade grow silent.

Still something is left. Something is always left. Fiction from the pulps still flares to sudden heat in anthologies of stories collected from *Black Mask, Weird Tales, Famous Fantastic Mysteries*, or selections from the early work of Erle Stanley Gardner or reprints of *The Shadow, the Spider*, and *Doc Savage*.

Other traces remain. These, more subtle, are more difficult to observe. Unlike fossil bones and coal measures such traces remain

1

viable in living literature, expressing themselves in terms of the present, rather than of the past. Like particularly shy ghosts, they whisper behind the text of a modern paperback. They mutter faintly within the dialogue of a television program or the latest motion picture. Today's fiction still vibrates with the conventions, story forms, and character types that were widely popularized and disseminated through generations of pulp magazines.

Particularly this is true of character types. We have with us still the quick-gun western hero, the hardboiled private investigator, the somewhat crooked hero, the crime-fighting hero using the latest technology, the clever heroine and her dumbly admiring boy friend, the adventurer to far lands and distant planets....

Previous volumes of *Yesterday's Faces* have examined many of these characters and conventions. In this, the sixth volume of the series, we continue, rummaging like children in some benign attic among the enchantments of adventure fiction.

We will consider a fine selection of rogues and bent heroes, all outside the law for one reason or another, in costume or with alternate identities, or merely trifling with the staid forces of law and order. Then we will meet spies of amazing skill and equally amazing eccentricities, whose influence shaped the world, whether you realized it or not. And we will visit professional fighting men, armed with sword or machine gun, scattered across the world and through time like so many fiery coals. And we will meet a few World War I aviators whose exploits ignited an industry of air war magazines.

From these old fictions, modern faces seem to grin out at us—men manipulating national destinies, Irish pilots with the right stuff, laughing cavaliers, teasing thieves of improbable originality, accomplished swordsmen, taciturn adventurers, hired soldiers.

Today's characters, today's conventions, sparkling up from pages closed sixty years ago. As if beyond that Mall, past that complex of condominiums, waited the dazzle of the Jurassic, quite unchanged, waiting for you to step among the conifers and cycads.

# Chapter One
## Still More Rogues and Bent Heroes

Long, long ago, in that distant lobe of time before World War I, when civilization reached its peak, they say, and gracious living meant something more than a frozen dinner—before the television—in 1912, that is, the slightly crooked hero was slowly forming in pulp magazine fiction.

Criminal heroes were no novelty to fiction. Such vivid characters as Raffles, Colonel Clay, and Romney Pringle trampled casually on the law through turn-of-the-century English publications. Similar characters found warm welcome in America, particularly from 1915 on, after Street & Smith launched *Detective Story Magazine.*

Slightly crooked heroes, bent heroes, were not quite the same as criminal heroes. To begin with, a bent hero was not really a criminal. Not really. More exactly, he was an adventurer with an elastic conscience. He bent the law for fun and frolic; and also to turn an occasional $10,000. Most often, he was involved in crime only to do a favor for someone badly in need of a favor.

A bent hero would not swindle a widow or an orphan. His prey was other crooks. With great relish he skinned the shady lawyer, the greedy banker, the con man—to the reader's intense gratification. A great many of these gentlemen of fortune, and a few equally artful ladies, exercised their peculiar gifts during the 1920s. In their ranks you could find The Avenging Twins, several of Edgar Wallace's blithesome brigands, and The Saint. For most of them, a delightful woman lurked just off stage, trembling a little at the hero's peril. He would marry her soon enough.

Well, The Saint didn't. But that was his own fault.

In 1912, this delightful, if slightly criminal, fellowship was just forming. And prominent among its charter members was Mr. John T. Laxworthy, who was about as untypical a hero as ever adventured through his own series.

In appearance he was both unremarkable and undistinguished. He was of somewhat less than medium height, of unathletic, almost frail physique. His head was thrust a little forward, as though he were afflicted with a chronic stoop. He wore steel-rimmed spectacles with the air of one who has taken to them too late in life to have escaped the constant habit of peering, which had given to his neck an almost storklike appearance. His hair and thin mustache were iron-gray, his fingers long and delicate.... (Oppenheim, "The Secret of the Magnifique" 67)

To this unprepossessing description, it might be added that the glasses are thick and that he customarily wears a shawl to ward off drafts. Moreover, he is fussy. His fearsomely methodical manner, precise to the finest detail, is reflected in his method of preparing an apple for eating. During this elaborate and time-consuming procedure, he slowly peels the fruit with a small, silver knife, neatly dissects out the core, then slices the subdued remainder into exact sections. Precise, exact, demanding. The attributes are those of an old man. But that feeble body conceals astounding physical strength. His grip is unbreakable. His reactions are those of a man in his teens.

Nor does his intelligence show any signs of age. He sees everything. Reasons with electronic efficiency. Is informed in crushing detail. His mental processes, swift and shining, are untouched by age. It is decidedly an open question whether his age is assumed or actual. Laxworthy describes himself in the following manner:

I am a man of over middle-age and I am moderately wealthy. Of my principles I will not speak, but such as they are, although I claim myself a considerable latitude of action, I am on the side of the law. (Oppenheim, *Mr. Laxworthy* 248)

He appeared in a twelve-part series, "The Peculiar Gifts of Mr. John T. Laxworthy," published bi-weekly in *The Popular Magazine* from May 15 through November 1, 1912. The stories were later collected in the book *Mr. Laxworthy's Adventures* (1913), most of the chapters retaining their magazine titles.

The series begins amid the literary equivalent of violins, trumpets and drums jittering up an atmosphere of complexity and suspense. Such elaborate preparations suggest that a major gentleman criminal and his cronies are about to be loosed upon society. And so it appeared for the first episode. But immediately afterward, the series veered abruptly from crime exploit to mystery-adventure at the fringes of upper-class wealth. Then it reversed like a frightened rabbit and plunged headlong into seedy London back streets filled by even seedier crooks.

In spite of these frequent changes of direction, the series contains a sprightly lot of adventures that end improbably in a June-December romance. Here is offered something for every taste. But if the series is inconsistent, it is also charming and well worth an evening or so of your time.

Since there is no reason to keep the series authorship a secret, it may be revealed that Mr. John T. Laxworthy was the invention of E(dward) Phillips Oppenheim (1866-1946). Over a period of 60 years, Oppenheim wrote 116 novels and 39 short story collections. The total could have been increased, but he wasted nearly 20 years growing up and being educated. Born in London, he left school at age 17 to assist his father, whose business—he was a leather merchant—was then in financial shoals. The boy worked a full day, then wrote until 2 am. His literary work received strong support from his father, who helped revise Oppenheim's first novel and afterward published it at his own expense.

In 1898, Oppenheim published "the first of my long series of stories dealing with that shadowy and mysterious world of diplomacy," *The Mysterious Mr. Sabin.* ("Diplomacy," in that context, refers less to the world of the State Department than to the world of the CIA. We will meet a few practitioners of this noble art in a later chapter.)

About 1906, Oppenheim sold the leather business, although he remained a salaried director, and turned to full-time writing. He was hugely successful, becoming one of the great shapers of the novel of international intrigue. Over the years he accumulated wealth, a yacht, a reputation for lechery, a passion for golf and homes on the East Coast of England and in France. From that continental home he barely escaped the Nazis as they occupied France during World War II.

Through Oppenheim's fiction move glittering crowds of the wealthy, curiously insecure within their opulence. Plots web the Riviera's gleam. That meltingly beautiful woman is a strand in a dark design. The security of immense wealth is not enough; at its fringes prowls something with fangs, impatient, terrible.... Here, in this world, begin Mr. Laxworthy's adventures: *The Popular Magazine*, May 15, 1912, "The Secret of the *Magnifique*." As the story opens, Mr. Laxworthy, in the leisurely way of 1912, is meeting his pupils, Mr. W. Forrest Anderson and Mr. Sidney Wing. For six months, Laxworthy has been coaching the pair in the roles they will use while working with him. The implication is that adventure, strongly smoked with criminality, is about to burst forth. For as the gentlemen-adventurers prepare for action, it is obvious that they are none too particular about how they earn their daily truffle. Laxworthy remarks in one instance, "Society is divided into two classes, those who have and those who desire to have. The one must always prey on the other" (69). Elsewhere he remarks:

My chief aim—I have no objection to telling you this—is to make life tolerable for ourselves, to escape the dull monotony of idleness, and, incidentally, to embrace any opportunity which may present itself to enrich our exchequer. (71)

It is the classic theme that echoes through a thousand magazine stories of the period: Since we are a little bored, a touch of crime will brighten us up. Late in the series, another explanation is trotted out:

Mr. Laxworthy, I know about your mania for adventure. I know that you go about the world looking always for new things, new adventures, new interests. (Oppenheim, *Mr. Laxworthy* 278)

The world here defined as a few watering places in France and London. But not to quibble.

In the first story, Mr. Laxworthy arranges to have a lady's apartment broken into and her purse robbed. Nothing valuable is taken—only a pass to board the French battleship in the harbor. Using this pass, Laxworthy intercepts a German spy in the act of stealing The Plans for the Macharin Torpedo "Which is to make warfare in the future impossible." The spy, frustrated, relinquishes the plans and pays Laxworthy ten thousand pounds for his silence. They ride together back to the hotel, chatting in a well-bred manner, as gentlemen do.

Breaking and entry, purse robbing, and blackmail are about the last direct crimes Laxworthy commits. From this point, the crooked hero theme recedes gracefully into the background.

"The Tragedy of the Flower Farm" (June 1, 1912) tells how Laxworthy solves a murder. In "The House of the Woman of Death" (June 15) and "The Strange Meeting At the Villa De Cap Frinet" (July 1), he spoils the plotting of some vigorously lethal anarchists who have turned their angers from society to each other. Laxworthy and friends manage to hand most of these fiends over to the police, although the leader succeeds in exploding a bomb that blasts away his wife, his confederate and himself.

In "The Vagaries of the Prince of Liguria" (July 15), Laxworthy exposes a German imposter masquerading as a Prince, a role permitting him to cheat at baccarat. "Mystery House" (August 1) tells of the foiling of an insane clergyman who has kidnapped a millionaire in order to extort money for London's poor. In "The Flowers of Death" (August 15), he saves the reputation of a Monte Carlo restaurant whose customers have been tumbling down with the green cramps. And in "The Deserted Hotel" (September 1) he saves a girl abducted by an egotistic violinist.

The next four stories concern the affairs of Mr. Dan Greenlaw, an accomplished murderer, disguise artist, and master criminal. "The Stetson Affair" (September 15) tells how Mr. Greenlaw murders and escapes, tweaking Mr. Laxworthy's self-esteem so painfully that he applies Holmes-like reasoning to the problem of Greenlaw's disguise. Resulting in that gentleman's arrest in London.

Greenlaw promptly escapes from the Bobbies and threatens Laxworth with nothing less extraordinary than death. Since, however, nothing in an Oppenheimer series remains fixed for long, the master criminal promptly forgets his threats. Instead, in "A Little Matter of Forty Thousand Pounds" (October 1), he sends his sister, Paula Garesworthy, to ask Laxworthy's help in recovering that sum of money. The cash had been entrusted to a pair of Jewish sterotypes. Now that Greenlaw is a hunted man, they have clamped tight to the funds. Laxworthy pries them loose without apparent effort.

Miss Greenlaw/Garesworthy is more fascinating than the adventure. She is a young lady of intense beauty and originality of opinion. "The greater part of my life," she remarks, "has been spent in Bohemian circles, not only from necessity, but because I prefer their society to any other" (249-250). This lady of unorthodox tastes is

...tall, slim, and exceedingly dark. Her complexion was absolutely colorless, but it seemed to be more the natural pallor of a woman from some southern race than any evidence of ill health...She walked with a natural grace which was entirely un-Saxon. (241)

Her eyes are large and black and she is an accomplished liar. Mr. Laxworthy greatly admires her, without being in the slightest influenced by her beauty. His unique mental apparatus never falls to dissarray in the presence of large black eyes and other weapons of the sex.

Paula returns during the events of "The Disappearance of Mr. Colshaw" (October 15). On this occasion Laxworthy prevents the murder of a man falsely believed to have betrayed Greenlaw and company. Following this adventure, Paula vanishes for some months of story time and two weeks in the world where *The Popular Magazine* was published.

When we meet Paula again in the final story of the series, "The Debt Collector" (November 1), she is in a dreadful fix. Her brother has cast her off. She is penniless. Her jewels long sold, she is reduced to dining in places smelling strongly of cabbage. To Oppenheim, this is equivalent to living in the town dump.

At this time, Mr. Laxworthy is also having problems—although for different reasons. Perhaps scenting the imminent end of the series, Sidney Wing has married. Anderson has received a small legacy and is touring the world. Mr. Laxworthy is left alone, his elaborate plans for adventure, or whatever they were, entirely scotched. To seek excitement, he is reduced to tramping the streets of Soho, where he meets Paula and undertakes to collect one hundred pounds owed to her by an ex-crony of her brother. Since the crony has babbled all to the police, he now cowers in remote shadows, sure that Greenlaw is out to kill him. Laxworthy locates the fellow snivelling in a room crusted with indecent pictures. Ruthlessly skillful, Laxworthy extorts from the informer all of Paula's money, plus 100 pounds extra. "To tell the truth, I am proud of that hundred pounds," he tells Paula, as he hands all the money over to her. "So far as I can remember, it is the first money I ever really stole" (Oppenheimer, "The Debt" 166). He has, perhaps, forgotten the 10,000 pounds blackmailed from the German spy. But no matter, no matter.

Laxworthy is determined to save Paula from her unfortunate life among the cabbage fumes. But she will not accept charity, and he can think of no ready way of employing her talents. So he proposes marriage to her—and is accepted. At this point, the series ends. Although there was the strong promise of further adventures, whatever these were, we have not been advised of them.

Mr. Laxworthy and his peculiar gifts, Paula and her peculiar gifts, vanished like figures passing through a crowded airport. Their influence on subsequent fiction seems negligible, although occasionally, in later years, you meet a few seemingly elderly men with lightning minds and grips of steel. What is certain is that Paula and Laxworthy are forever and eternally part of the Pre-War scene—the first Pre-War scene. After World War I swept that bubble away, nothing was ever again the same. Only memories linger in such magazines as the 1910 *Blue Book*, 1912 *Popular*, and such series as *Norroy, Freelances in Diplomacy*, and *Mr. Laxworthy*. From their pages rises a wan perfume, the whisper of a time long past that never quite was, except in fiction, when adventurers were gentlemen and good manners were at least as important as a hand gun.

You begin to see times changing in the mystery-adventure fiction published around 1914. In that year, Louis Joseph Vance had created the Lone Wolf, who was featured in a long series of vigorous and remarkably unsentimental action novels. The Lone Wolf adventures influenced mystery—adventure fiction as powerfully as did Frank Packard's Jimmie Dale serials of the same period. Both began with criminal heroes—talented safecrackers who were diverted by love into reform and the more perilous ways of fighting crime.[1] As a criminal, Dale was a dilettante, turning to safe-cracking for the thrill of it. But the Lone Wolf was the real thing, a criminal in life and practice until love got him by the nose and dragged him to spiritual rebirth.

Anthony Trent followed ever so closely in the Lone Wolf's literary footsteps. Another master criminal from the Post-War period, Trent was one of those cracksmen who worked alone, staggered the police, and made a fabulous success of stealing things. All this, and how he gave it all up, is recorded in his first appearance, *Anthony Trent, Master Criminal* (1918). Thereafter he spent his life atoning for his grubby past, and, as a privately-wealthy adventurer, helping his friends, performing amateur detection with conspicuous success.

Trent appeared in about 25 novels published between 1918 and 1950. These were written by Wyndham Martyn, one of those literary fellows. Martyn is not his pen name—that was William Grenvil. Born in London, 1875, Martyn graduated from the London and Brucelles School of Mines. In 1904, he moved to the United States, eventually becoming a citizen. In 1915 he became the editor of *Pearson's Magazine*, and, during the early 1920s, was the associate editor of *The Smart Set*. As usual with literary men of the period, he published hugely: one-act plays, verse, short stories, and novels—most of these mysteries. His first novel appeared in 1910. He published fiction of all lengths in the slick magazines (*Red Book, Liberty, Cosmopolitan*), in *Munsey's* and *Everybody's* (both of them a cross between a slick and a pulp) and in *Flynn's, Detective Fiction Weekly*, and *Clues*. Five Trent novels were serialized in the pulps, where they fit in neatly. The pulps thoroughly appreciated stories about reformed master criminals who enjoyed long series of violent adventures.

As explained in *Anthony Trent, Master Criminal* (1918), Trent's father was a country doctor. He put his boy through Dartmouth, where he became a famous athlete. Graduating with a Bachelor of Arts, Trent promptly emigrated to New York City and became a reporter. Although he showed immense ability, he left reporting in a couple of years. The explanation was that he had received a legacy and would, henceforth, amuse himself writing fiction.

That was partly true. He did write mystery stories, which sold briskly. But he had also taken to slipping out nights and stealing jewels. He struck only for major stakes. He collected the great Takawaja emerald, the Mount Aubyn ruby, the Edgcumb sapphire, the hundred-caret Nizam's diamond.

The police, baffled, shuffled about in their shoes. So it went for eight years.

*The Great Ling Plot* (1933) gives a glimpse of his adventures in 1913. To begin with, he steals a half-million dollar diamond necklace from an American bounder nestled in an out-of-the-way castle. No sooner has the necklace vanished than four people at the castle are murdered, and Trent finds evidence that he is being closely stalked by all-knowing adversaries.

Immediately afterward, he makes a second raid—this one upon General Ling, a Chinese diplomat and soldier. Ling is the front man for some higher power, never identified, who is preparing a world uprising against the white races. No sooner does Trent break into the fortress that is Ling's home, than he accidentally overhears details of the conspiracy. Before gliding away, he manages to steal the huge ruby that everyone has been fervently worshipping.

Two thefts; two successes. And, less fortunately, two major adversaries come raging on his trail. Before long he has been identified, captured, and imprisoned in a cave part way down an unscalable peak. His guards are a pair of murdering sadists. After some hair-raising maneuvering, he knocks out one of them, a professional prize fighter, and captures the other. Then he lights off to save Sir Elliott Coutts, a famous police detective whose reputation gleams as brightly as that of Sherlock Holmes. Sir Elliott has infiltrated Ling's outfit and, in the way of these things, has been captured. Trent saves him by crashing a truck and trailer loaded with stone through Ling's guarded house. Ling dies. Elliott is restored to his grateful country, and Trent slips away to Antwerp to rid himself of stolen jewelry.

Even for a master criminal, Trent seems blithely incautious. He thrusts himself into situations which almost certainly will snap back at him. "He was headstrong, ready to see the point of an argument but not to be talked into caution when his mind was made up to take a risk" (Martyn, *The Great Ling Plot* 205).

He acts for all the world like a man trying to be caught and punished. Too slick for his own good, he slides out of trouble every time; but always his rashness plunges him into avoidable difficulties. The strain on his nervous system is considerable.

Then came the First World War. Trent fought overseas and was decorated for valor. And disaster struck: while in France, his criminal past was uncovered by an ex-lieutenant of the New York police. Only by a fluke, at the last instant, was Trent's secret protected.

But that secret, like a bad odor, proved impossible to keep hidden. In The Secret of the Silver Car (1920) someone else has learned of that past. Trent is on his trail, willing to do heaven's knows what to protect himself. But then he falls in love with the fellow's sister, recovers The Stolen Papers for her father, and is all set to marry her and become very very respectable.

At this point, the usual doom descends. His betrothed is killed while jumping a horse over a wall. Reeling from this blow, Trent reforms, "I shall never again tread the old paths because the woman I loved died believing in my uprightness" (Martyn, *The Return of Anthony Trent* 129).

Back to New York he goes. What to do? To this point, he has few friends, none close, for "if men outside the law would have no intimates, and write no letters, and let the social side of life go, they might keep out of jail more often than they do."

Which is precisely what the Lone Wolf had observed back in 1914.

So what was Trent to do? He played piano reasonably well, but no more than that. He loved literature. He was a golfer of nearly professional skill. Later in life he would dabble in real estate. By means we shall not consider too closely, he had accumulated enough money to maintain a luxurious standard of living.

But what to do, personally, with the rest of his life?

The problem solves itself in "The Baited Trap" (*Flynn's*, four-part serial, April 11 through May 2, 1925). This had been previously published as *The Return of Anthony Trent* (1923).

A friend has been framed to prison. The friend's brother, Campbell Sutton, has learned of that open secret, Trent's black past. (The brother served in the Army with Trent and was present, supposedly unconscious, at the near exposure in France.) Sutton applies a little gentle blackmail. Trent is to force a confession from Payson Grant, the man who framed Sutton's brother. Otherwise....

Most reluctantly, Trent agrees to do what he can. It is difficult. Grant has married Sutton's ex-wife. They live in what amounts to a fortified mansion by the sea, guarded by toughs and killer dogs.

When all ways seem closed, Trent works up an elaborate charade. Grant is led to believe that he has murdered Sutton. Drugged, he is hustled into a carefully designed movie set, full of actors looking like convicts, actors looking like guards, iron bars, and a depressing air of verisimilitude. Chemicals are used to roughen Grant's hands. He is given to understand that he has had amnesia for the period of his trial.

Grant is hustled into believing that he can get his sentence lightened by confessing the Sutton matter. He does so. And isn't he upset when the true situation is revealed.

In performing this little miracle, Trent has dipped into kidnapping, personal assault, unlawful restraint, and assorted other minor crimes. Perfectly normal for a hero who isn't all that far removed from the shadows, himself. But justice has been served. And if you serve justice, what difference are a few little laws?

Trent's technique for breaking a man psychologically proved singularly attractive to other writers. Whether Martyn originated the idea, or borrowed it from another source, isn't known. But similar situations appeared during the adventures of the Just Men, The Saint, and, deep into the 1930s, a couple of Doc Savage novels.

While busy with "The Baited Trap," Trent falls in love with Madame de Beaulieu, a brilliant adventuress whose long, almond-shaped green eyes ignite his soul.

Once The Countess had been a convent girl. However, before she was 18, her regrettable guardian lured her into crime. Thereafter she married the Count for money. Turns out that he had none. He left her, conveniently died, leaving her hating men, reveling in crime, luring men to destruction, her scarlet lips curving provocatively.

Then she met Trent. Their hearts touched and, after the close of "The Baited Trap," they are married. Then follows a miracle. For one of the few times in mystery-adventure fiction, marriage doesn't kill the wife. But a wife is an awkward impediment to an adventuring ex-master criminal. So Martyn gets her out of the way, in subsequent novels, by having her travelling in Europe, New Jersey, and other far places.

Now well launched, the Trent series sails briskly along, about a book a year. "Trent of the Lone Hand" (*Flynn's Weekly,* four-part serial, December 11, 1926, through January 1, 1927) gets him closed into an isolated castle in England. There a crazy genius holds a handful of men and women prisoners for the duration of their lives. The place is staffed with bad Malays bristling with knives. In the moat swims a tremendous shark. Beyond the moat rise electrical fences, backed by legions of fierce dogs and hardboiled guards. It is just the place for a long rest. And how does Trent escape and save the prisoners? Really, it was quite simple.

"The Death Dread" (*Detective Fiction Weekly*, five-part serial, September 7 through October 5, 1929) features Trent as the complete amateur detective. The book was published under the title of *The Death Fear* (1929).

We begin with this rich fellow who stays locked up in his expensive mansion. He is terrified. Why? No one knows. Then he disappears. Trent, harassed by incompetent police officials, must find the reason, through one of the dullest stories published in the English language.

There would be many later Trents—later and better. All adhered to this general pattern: Trent, the millionaire sportsman with a past he would much rather keep concealed, and a wife rarely mentioned, finds himself in isolated places. Danger springs up, arfing horribly. Menacing problems rumble at every side. All these he handles in his cool, softly incisive, extra-legal way.

In the 1939 *Trent Fights Again*, he has renounced his violent life. "He had been a solver of mysterious things long enough." Now wealthy from oil royalties, he wants only to grow roses in his New York City penthouse and travel to distant places in the manner of Somerset Maugham.

Instead, he finds himself flung head first into danger: from a womanizing bad hat and from a concealed enemy grunting for revenge. Through a long, leisurely novel, Trent investigates much, finds little, avoids several death traps more or less by accident, gets captured, and escapes by sheer luck and personality. Through 284 pages, he is tied, slugged, beaten, bruised, bashed, and bloodied. He ends the novel in an inferior state of repair. His concealed enemy gets a broken arm instead of the Trent millions, and a tough thug gets killed by accident. The consequences of crime are ill distributed.

Through the personal chaos of his days, Trent glides onward, his manner calm, even a trifle remote. Trent, himself, never changed much. He was a tall man, erect, rather hawk-faced and stern, who carefully cultivated the impassive face of all such men with a past. At the opening of "The Baited Trap," he was 34. In later books, he was 45 and looked 35. It is a comfortable age; he lingered close to it for some decades.

Under his easy veneer of manners, he might have been high-strung, as his friends believe, but he masked it well. He was endlessly flexible. When it was master criminal time, he was a master crook. When readers' tastes shifted to millionaire amateur detectives, there stood Trent detecting away. When *Black Mask* toughness saturated the field, the prose around Trent became hard as a drug lord's smile.

His changing character reflected his changing times. Therefore he survived. Admittedly, this means that the earlier Trent books, while packed with detail and character drawing, reflect times long past and are laboriously obsolete.

A man works all his life and ends up as a museum artifact. It hardly seems fair.

It did not quite happen to Bulldog Drummond.

Drummond had his own cross. As a character he was so highly successful that he soon became a fixture of low-budget moving pictures. Huge numbers of these were released, giving a new dimension to the word "trash." As usual with Hollywood adaptations of pulp fiction heroes, no effort was spared to make films that were an insult to the character. But what did the misguided dupes, who paid ten cents for admission, know about a book character? Or care?

From all these films, the character of Hugh Drummond was conspicuously absent. But his style was not one the moving pictures could comfortably reproduce, although they kept trying, if sporadically, into the 1970s.

But to begin at the beginning.

Herman Cyril McNeile (1888-1937), author of the series, wrote under the pen name of "Sapper"—military slang for a combat engineer.

His background was formidably military. The son of a Royal Navy captain, he studied at the Royal Military Academy, enlisted in the Army, and served twelve years in the Royal Engineers, retiring as a Lieutenant Colonel at the end of World War I. His military background marked his mind and his prose style. A year after his retirement from the military, in 1919, he published his first novel about Bulldog Drummond, his best known character. Nine additional Drummond novels appeared through 1937, plus a scattering of short stories.

McNeile died in 1937. His close friend, Gerald Fairlie, took over the series. By mid-July 1938, a new Drummond serial began in *Detective Fiction Weekly*. It was the same exuberant Drummond, as always—heavily jocular, massive of fist, a superb fighting man. Fairlie would write six more Drummond novels, the final one appearing in 1954.

So the character persisted, 1920 through 1954. Unlike Trent, who occupied about the same slice of time, Drummond does not alter a great deal. His more blatant mannerisms smoothed out, slightly. But he remained essentially as he had first appeared—a huge man built on the lines of a truck, massive shoulders, vast hands, the agility of a fencer.

He may be said to have outlived his own influence.

Drummond was assimilated directly into the literary bloodstream. He became part of the convention of the Post-War adventure hero. For the following ten or fifteen years, his appearance, behavior, abilities, and background were all mined by other novelists. In some measure, great or small, Drummond echoes in the work of Lester Dent, Norvel Page, and D.L. Champion, all series novelists of the 1930s pulp magazines. And Drummond directly influenced the early years of such a major character as The Saint.[2]

Not that Drummond, himself, plunged from the sky, all white flame and thunder. Partly he was drawn from McNeil's own character, partly from other big, tough men who stormed through English adventure fiction. And partly he reflected that curious English convention of a competent, weighty man blathering iridescent humorous drivel in the style of the clever young men of A. A. Milne's 1907 Punch sketches, or, somewhat later, Wodehouse's Bertie Wooster and Dorothy Sayers' Lord Peter Wimsey.

*Drummond*: said, You priceless old bean, I gathered from the female bird punching the what-not outside that the great brain was heaving....

What a way for a hulking combat captain to go on. His voice roars out these mannered imbecilities. They are half teasing, half a deliberate mask. He waves a huge mug of beer in one great paw and booms with laughter.

This is the man who delighted in silent glides through No Man's Land, leaving behind a string of silently slaughtered Germans. This is the man, worshipped by his friends, who conducted private, personal, unsanctioned, bloody warfare against enemies of England, and similar doers of evil, for more than thirty years.

He is pleasantly ugly. Frequently he gets tight. If someone needs killing, Drummond will obligingly kill him. He deals death as immediately as The Just Men.

First and always, he is a man of action. Not complex. Not subtle at all. "...my strong point is pushing a bloke's face in."

So taking these characteristics altogether, what was it that Captain Hugh Drummond brought to the mystery adventure and the legion of the bent hero?

a military background,and friends who found peace intolerably dull, so that they sought adventure in civil life, using techniques learned on the battle field, applying military discipline and craft in murderous battles with enemies of society, conducting these private wars outside the law, under the assumption that the Law is to be honored but not allowed to interfere with Duty, although close ties are maintained with important law enforcement officials, who may be called in to approve the smoking ruins, since Drummond and friends are respectable representatives of the best social class and have deep roots within the Establishment, together with sufficient money to support their merry pranks.

Beer, adventure and a paste in the face for the Ungodly. For sport and for England. And warm damnation to all Germans, Russians, anarchists, master criminals and sniffling thieves. A punch in the head corrects all.

...something that felt like a pile driver hit him straight in the mouth, so that he staggered back, spitting blood....

*Bulldog Drummond* (1920) tells how he bands together a group of friends to take on an assortment of Bolsheviks, traitorous Englishmen, and that devilish arch-criminal Carl Peterson. This troika of evil plans to overthrow the English government and create a new social system. To demonstrate their social consciousness, they tend to dip enemies in a vat of acid.

Drummond and friends go after this infamous company and strike them head and heel. The conspiracy is shattered in a glare of melodrama.

Peterson escapes to plot again—he will return three more times before the law of averages snares him. At this point, Drummond marries the beautiful Phyllis.

*The Black Gang* (1922) continues similar adventure. To clean up England, Drummond is collecting left-wingers, anarchists, and Communists—vermin of that type—and imprisoning them on an island off the English coast. At the end of the book, Scotland Yard Inspector McIver gets a glimpse of this place. McIver, who will become a series regular and work closely with Drummond, accepts this private concentration camp with professional stoicism. He seems to object neither to kidnapping nor infringement of civil liberties, nor to Drummond's magnificent indifference to the common law. All these deviations are excused by patriotic motives. British patriotic motives. Had the Germans taken such actions, they might have been called Fascists.

(Several related establishments cropped up in the 1930s Doc Savage and Shadow novels. Savage maintained a surgical clinic in the wilds of up-state New York where criminals were made honest men by operations on their "crime glands." At one time, The Shadow depopulated New York's underworld by kidnapping criminals to an island where they were given work, education, and, possibly, psychotherapy. After a few years, he seems to have dropped the whole idea and returned to shooting down transgressors.)

Carl Peterson's last appearance is in the novel *The Final Count* (1926), published in *The Popular Magazine*, October 7, 1925, under the title of "The Nameless Terror." The story is of engaging improbability, filled with scenes that, ten years later, would crackle through the single-character pulp magazines.

A virulent poison, developed as a weapon to end war, has been stolen and its inventor kidnapped. Both are in the hands of international crooks, led by Carl Peterson. Masterfully disguised, Peterson plans to use the poison to rob and steal and kill and make a grand nuisance of himself.

The hordes of Scotland Yard achieve nothing. It remains for Drummond to convene the original Black Gang. Off they march, a disciplined military unit fighting a brutal patrol action across England.

Immediately, all of them get captured and tied up tightly. After that false start, they manage to secure an antidote to the poison. It is difficult. Traps wait cocked on every side—gigantic spiders, poison squirters, deadly rooms, all the gadgets employed by Dr. Fu Manchu with such success. But all traps fail.

The trail leads Drummond to a cave in the coastal cliffs. There the inventor, now quite crazy, brews tons of liquid death. Peterson has equipped a hydrogen-filled air ship to rain poison from the sky. For practice he attacks a yacht filled with wealthy folks, killing them all and looting the vessel. It is a dress rehearsal for greater things.

Like so many of the villains Drummond faced, Peterson is the perfect psychopath, sketched in incisive black lines and colored black. Blood death agony leave his cool serenity unmarred. Like mountain ranges, his plans rear up, enormous concepts uneroded by conscience.

His immediate goal is 30 million in bullion aboard an ocean liner. To secure this, he plans to murder all thousand of its passengers. And also 150 more who have been invited for dinner aboard his dirigible. After collecting the bullion, he also intends to murder his accomplices, then retire to enjoy his leisure years. For an instant, he teeters at the lip of success. But then Drummond thrusts aside the poisoned cocktail and whips out a pistol. Poison sears into Peterson's wrist. He dies. After which the dirigible flares up like the Hindenberg. The innocent escape, but everyone else dies who deserved to.

Following Peterson's death, matters continue as intensely as before. *The Female of the Species* (1928) relates how Peterson's mistress kidnaps Drummond's wife, Phyllis, in an attempt to bring Bulldog to an unsatisfactory end. She doesn't manage it.

Phyllis does not take kindly to these activities. She is unsettled by gigantic spiders, murderous kidnappers and other aspects of adventuring. With razor tongue, she urges her husband to settle for a quieter life.

He does not. Nor do his friends—the aristocratic Algie Longworth, who wears a monocle and talks like a character from Wodehouse; or Drummond's useful valet Denny. Or Peter Darrell and others who occasionally look into the adventures—Toby Sinclair, Ted Jerningham, *et al.*

By 1933, Drummond's island has been discontinued. In deference to Depression tastes, his speech mannerisms have been toned down. But he is as ready as ever to defend England against the plots of the Ungodly. *Bulldog Drummond Strikes Back* (1933)—the English title is *Knockout*—features another batch of conspirators. These plan to break the English pound, thus reaping millions. Men die as a mystery weapon blasts a pellet through the eye into the brain. Here creeps a tricky doctor; there glides his sadistic blond moving-picture charmer. And behind it all, grins an evil little bald-headed genius.

Drummond copes cheerfully with drugged drinks, blazing houses, a hand-to-hand fight with a giant wearing spiked gloves, and terrorist attacks against the English rail system. By the end, he has been shot in the shoulder. None of the evil gang survive. The pound is saved.

England is saved. And Drummond, roaring for beer, feels boredom creeping in again.

In 1929 and 1931, the *Detective Fiction Weekly* had published Drummond serials, and, in 1939, brought out Sapper's final novel, *Bulldog Drummond's Challenge*, as a seven-part serial, March 13 through April 24. That same year, the magazine published four Drummond short stories. McNeile had begun writing a series of these, perhaps expecting to bring them out in book form. Only five were completed before his death.[3] The fifth story, "The Mystery Tour," was published in the July 1937 issue of *Popular Detective*.

That story is typical of the group. The general format is that Drummond happens by just as an elaborate crime is fermenting. Seeing through the scheme, he foils it, and pounds the criminal with very hard fists. Thus in "Mystery Tour," Drummond foils the robbery of a batch of rich Americans, conned into taking a "mystery tour"—a sight- seeing trip by bus to an undisclosed location.

"Lonely Inn" (*Detective Fiction Weekly,* September 4, 1937), is in much the same vein. A crooked lawyer lures a young woman and her father to the lonely inn. The lawyer has been dipping into her funds and plans to cover himself by arranging that she die by apparent accident. Drummond, fog-bound at the inn, is bothered by various inconsistencies in remarks by the bribed inn keeper and the lawyer. He is able to save the girl from drowning in an open well. After which the lawyer gets pounded to Steak Tartare. It's a crisp little story that flies along, not bothering much with characterization.

"Wheels Within Wheels" (*Detective Fiction Weekly,* November 20, 1937) described the destruction of a cocaine smuggling ring. Drummond—who makes his initial appearance very tight and wearing a false nose—meets a man about to be murdered. Presently he is. Shortly afterward, Drummond, Algy, and Inspector McIver track the gang to a resort. Observing some peculiar manipulation of automobile tires, Drummond deduces where the cocaine is concealed and the gang is collected, with the help of a lot of sugar in their gasoline tank.

"The Oriental Mind" (December 25, 1937) involves another kill-the-girl-for-money. The murder weapon is to be a madman with a crowbar. Drummond stops that, although the rest of the plot has to be explained to him by a Chinese servant.

"Thirteen Lead Soldiers" (January 1, 1938) is a bright little piece using mosquitoes boiling with yellow fever as the murder weapon. (The idea was not that new, having been used at least once, back in 1928, in a Dr. Bentiron serial for *Detective Story Magazine*.) Drummond sees through the murder plot early and makes a few judicious rearrangements, the would-be murderer dying in his own trap. Rough justice. But effective.

The first Drummond story signed by Gerald Fairlie is "Bulldog Drummond on Dartmoor" (*Detective Fiction Weekly,* six-part serial, June 11 through July 16, 1938). This recounts strange doings at Moreland Hall, once a fine old home, now an inn. Algy and Phyllis stop in for a beer, find themselves in a complex confusion of sullen landlords, escaped convicts, and sinister cross-purposes.

No sooner does Drummond rumble through the front door than the flash point of violence is reached. It's always that way. Immediately guns blaze in the darkness, and a hulking great thing, like King Kong, only less intelligent, stalks the night. Drummond conducts himself in the grand tradition, grinning, roaring, bashing his way through a scalding story. Phyllis, on the other hand, is a continuing pain in the neck. You wouldn't be surprised to learn that she is frigid.

No point in coming to a Bulldog Drummond adventure for perfumed subtleties. Action is his forte, not significant thought. Does he imprison agitators on an island, it is because they deserve it. If they weren't fools, they wouldn't be agitators, messing around trying to spoil society. After all, England fought a war to teach the Germans their place. Not helped by the Russians, of course. They had no spunk; simply gave up. Nothing in them. Whimpering lunatics, on the whole. A solid punch in the mouth might buck them up.

Such familiar sentiments:

-My religious group was founded by God's direction. Therefore it speaks for God and those speaking against church policies are speaking against God. Such heretics must be punished.

-This political state is perfect, containing no error or contradiction. Therefore an individual speaking against state policies is insane and must be confined in an asylum.

-Blessed Old England. Its society is the grandest conceived by the mind of man and, therefore, those who want to change it should be punched square in the face.

-My position is the only possible position to be taken seriously. It must be adhered to as an article of faith because I am right, and, therefore, if anyone takes a different position, it is because they are insolent fools, morally corrupt and generally despicable. Because of this, it is my duty to punish them.

To these effete vaporings, Drummond would roar with laughter, slam your back with one huge paw, and shove a quart of beer into your hand: "You brainy chaps need a bit of action to set you up."

Maybe so. The only difference between a popular hero and a criminal is that the hero strikes on the side of the right.

There is no question, is there, which side that is?

Many of yesterday's rogues and bent heroes enjoyed a long series of magazine stories, later reprinted as books. Zorro, Drummond, White Wolf, Trent and Don Everhard were among them. As were Black Star, Bluejean Billy, the Gray Phantom, Mr. Chang, Sanderson, the Avenging Twins, Rafferty and John Doe—all these later characters from the *Detective Story Magazine*, which specialized in the adventures of criminal heroes, whether mildly bent or fiends of crime.[4]

All were above life-size, glittering like images of jade and gold. They were accompanied through the magazine pages by less notable series characters, sparrows in a flight of rocs. As a group, these minor characters are usually not so successful. The writing is a shade more pedestrian, the characters a trifle less idiosyncratic and interesting, the stories generally more derivative. Yet these lesser series are of interest, too. For they demonstrate the same conventions of character and incident, the same assumptions of the period in which they were published. And they offer useful clues as to how character types and literary styles altered and changed like snowmen in the blast furnace of commercial fiction.

"The Doings of Dion," for example, which ran in the 1922 *Detective Story Magazine*. "Dion" is influenced by Sanderson, The Noiseless Cracksman (also a *Detective Story* regular), Raffles, Trent, and the Lone Wolf—a heady combination. With all these distinguished grandfathers, you wonder that the series, written by John D. Swaim, isn't better.

"The Doings of Dion" consists of six closely connected stories running chronologically. Looks, however, are deceiving. "The Doings" are not short stories. Not in the sense that anyone recognizes a short story. They are actually chapters of a very short book. For reasons best known to *Detective Story*, these sections were offered to readers as a series, not a serial.

The truth is that the stories have no more content than the inside of a ping-pong ball. Consider Part I, "The Nest Egg" (March 18, 1922). The scene is a Paris jazz joint. Our hero, the nearly penniless John Dion, is gavotting with a scented creature, black haired and depraved. Dion observes unwashed types slipping things under the table to a ritzy young man. Smelling illegal cash, he trails the young man to a lair in the Latin Quarter. There the young man conceals something in a sundial.

Shortly afterward, Dion opens the secret compartment. Extracting a diamond necklace and other valuables, he slips away into the night. For

Dion is an American jewel thief, quite wicked and unreformed. He was not always such a monster of evil.

Once he was a bookkeeper. At that far-off time, his name was not Dion, either; he rechristened himself later. At the trust company where he worked, one of the executives had been "indiscreet." Which seems to mean he tapped the till or carried home paperclips or something scandalous. There was a cover up. Dion was blamed. He was cast out, blackballed. No bank or trust would employ him. He attempted to break into vaudeville. But vaudeville managers scoffed at his magic tricks. Starvation loomed.

Then one evening at the movies, he found himself sitting behind a pudgy woman, wife of the executive who had ruined Dion. Around her fat neck glowed a sapphire necklace. And in a moment, Dion had it. (Explaining why the shrewd author gave Dion ability at parlor magic, for magicians have notoriously deft fingers.) Stealing the necklace of the over-stuffed woman in the seat ahead was an acknowledged way of beginning a criminal career. Maxwell Sanderson, began his career in a 1925 *Detective Story Magazine* by doing exactly the same thing.

Dion was avenged. True, he had become a criminal. But it wasn't actually his fault. Society made him a criminal. Society refused him food and opportunity and laughed ha! ha! when he tried to support himself. It's no wonder he turned to crime. And so would you, if you had any spirit at all, instead of being satisfied with a six-year-old car and all those kids and a bunch of pulp magazines flaking onto the carpet.

Soon Dion became one of the world's great jewel robbers. He lived in a snazzy hotel wearing white spats and oiling his hair. A success.

One day came Old Inspector Callahan and told him to leave the country. Dion had caused too much of an uproar by stealing this gem and that. If he didn't cut out, the cops would frame him up the river.

There had been no hard feelings. They (Dion and Callahan) had even shaken hands. Between crooks and policemen a great game, the most exciting game in the world, is being played out all the time. It is not unusual to find mutual esteem among the contestants. Provided a yegg has not assaulted an officer, or shown a yellow streak, and if the bulls win out without the use of stool pigeons, or brutal third-degree methods, there is no more animosity than exists between great Wall Street operators, who set out to raid one another's holdings. (Swaim, "The Doing of Dion" 124)

This business of crime being "a great game" is probably an English conceit. The idea kept cropping up in those American magazines that published a lot of English-influenced crime fiction: the early Flynn's,

Detective Story and, very early, in The Black Mask, and the much later Scotland Yard. The more warmly a magazine embraced English detective fiction of the period, the more frequently "the great game" got mentioned. The realistic school, as represented by flashes in the Jimmie Dale stories, and the hardboiled fiction of Gordon Young, Carroll John Daly, and Dashiell Hammett, finally shoved crime back into social pathology. But it took a while.

Dion came to Paris with little money, little French, no knowledge of local conditions, and proceeded to live by his wits. The author has already remarked that Dion was nearly broke. Now he has this fine diamond necklace. But he hasn't the faintest idea where he can sell it for cash.

Worse follows. In "Hiding the Shells" (March 25, 1922), Dion is visited by a representative of the local crook's union. They offer him a place in the Paris mob. But he refuses to join them. He does not realize that they have already learned a great deal about him—that, in a few hours, they will connect him, by some form of mental telepathy, with the theft of the necklace from the sundial.

Hiding the loot in the hollow leg of his bed, Dion goes forth to eat. Later, in a dark little dive, he is jumped by three Apaches and nearly gets whomped. But an Englishman helps him whip them. You expect something to come of this. But it doesn't. That's all the excitement for this installment.

In "Counting the Chickens" (April 8, 1922), Dion feels invisible currents of crime swirl all around him. He answers an ad in the newspaper columns about a certain necklace. Immediately he receives a letter from Madame X.Z. describing the necklace he has liberated. Going to the address, he meets Madame Delyce—that divinely beautiful sexpot he'd seen in the jazz joint.

They bandy words. She wants the necklace back without payment. He wants money. Suddenly....

Suddenly the earth opened under him; or, at least, the little prayer rug on which he stood ceased to caress his feet, and his body shot like a plummet down through the flooring. His last glimpse was an absurd view of the tiny gold slippers of Madame Delyce and the proud arch of her silken instep. (Swain 124)

Drops into a big mess of straw. Scares some rats. Finds himself, gun, and flashlight OK. Discovers a concealed bottle and drinks some wine. Escapes up a fireplace to a rooftop. End of Part III.

It is extraordinary how these pages roll by and nothing happens. Part III consists of eight double-column pages of rather small type—

roughly about 5,000 words. It's simply amazing how you can use so many words and end up with so little.

There is no particular need to examine every last feather in the next few stories. To summarize Parts IV through VII, Dion escapes from the roof. Runs into menace. Loses the necklace. Has a terrific fight. Recovers the necklace. Loses the necklace. Meets a quaint sort named Arizona Pete who does not carry six-guns but a matched pair of throwing knives.

Finally recovering the necklace, Dion is off to the Chateau Yquem, several hours from Paris. A fabulous treasure is there, and he wishes to steal it before Madame Delyce and her fancy man, Boss of the Apaches, do so. The necklace, he learns, actually belongs to the Countess d'Yquem, a warm-eyed doll of a darling. Dion suddenly finds himself protecting her interests. She needs help, for Madame Delyce is on the spot, disguised as a nurse. Suddenly....

In the night, the crooks strike. They open the Countess' personal safe. They have her jewels! Then Dion leaps upon them.

Big fight. The robbery is frustrated, the jewels recovered. But Dion is clubbed unconscious.

While he lies helpless, Madame Delyce lifts the diamond necklace from his money belt. This is about the fourth time that the necklace has changed hands. It's been handled so much, you wonder that the stones still shine.

Now we come to the final chapter, "Au Revoir" (May 27, 1922). Dion, the hero of the battle, is carried to bed in the chateau. Madame Delyce gives him drugged medicine. But he spits it out and slips away into the night. After bumming a ride to Paris, he looks up Arizona Pete. Together they prepare to raid the crooks' headquarters and carry off all their francs.

They get inside the place so easily, you'd think they were in a story. Arizona Pete acts as look-out. Dion begins searching the rooms. Immediately he finds a sackfull of English sovereigns and a passport for England. As he is stuffing these into his pockets, suddenly....

A shot rings out. Arizona Pete is down. From a trapdoor, five men leap. They corner Dion. Big fight. Fists, blackjack, chair legs—just terrible.

Dion licks four of them. But the Big Boss, the number one crook, takes dead aim at him with an automatic.

At this moment, Arizona Pete comes crawling down the hallway, leaving a dramatic trail of blood. (He has been shot through the shoulder.) At the last possible second, he hurls a knife into the Boss's heart.

Actually it happens a little slower than that. Swaim takes about 250 words to describe how Arizona Pete whips out the knife, how he throws it, how the Boss sees it float slowly toward him, how he feels the spot on his shirt where the blade will hit, how the blade hits. About 250 words. Don't let people tell you that all the pulps were invariably filled with hard, constant, concentrated action.

"Let's get out of this!" Dion says to Pete. "There are too many dead men here!"

They exit. And that is the last we see of them.

But the story continues as if the principal has not exited. Madame Delyce has discovered that Dion is gone and she prepares to return to Paris at daybreak.

Meanwhile—two Paris police officers sit in consultation. They will arrest Madame Delyce on her return to the city. But they will let the Boss leave France and go to England, although he will be shadowed by a plainclothes man. (As we know, the person leaving France will be Dion, traveling on the Boss's passport.) Once in England, the French officer will advise Scotland Yard. Likely the English police will be interested in Dion as a supposed French Criminal King-pin. So, already, new adventure fluffs up on the horizon.

Only it doesn't.

At this precise point, the series ends.

Just like that. Like a road going over a cliff. Like the light when you snap a switch. Like a kiss when you have to sneeze. Gone.

Who finally gets the diamond necklace? Does Arizona Pete bleed to death? Won't the police detective recognize that Dion isn't the Boss? Will Madame Delyce be arrested? If so, what for? Will she care? Will the Countess d'Yquem care? And what about Dion? Does it ever dawn on him that he is too inept for this kind of fiction?

After seven parts and about 35,000 words, the story has just begun to develop. And the moment it does, it gets cut off. Nothing is resolved. Nothing is clarified. You stand gaping, fumbling for Part VIII. But there is no Part VIII—not now, not later.

What happened? All we really know is that Dion's Doings did for seven parts and then stopped like an egg hitting a brick wall.

However John D. Swain continued merrily onward through the 1920s and into the 1930s. Many of his stories and novels appeared in *The Popular Magazine*. He published stories in *Adventure* and the 1921 *Black Mask*. He also appeared in *Detective Tales, Mystery Stories, Cabaret Stories*, and *Detective Fiction Weekly,* as well as *Detective Action Stories, Complete Underworld Novelettes*, and *The Underworld*.

And his fiction continued to appear in *Detective Story Magazine* week after incredible week. Likely a lot more of it appeared under names that would have amazed his mother.

Apparently he never got back to Dion. Which is just as well. Doctor Frankenstein revived a bunch of dead parts. But neither Swain nor anybody else has managed the trick since.

Dion was reasonably typical of the short-run series characters. Hundreds of them appeared during the years of the pulp magazines. They sparkled briefly, candles of hope against the world's dark indifference. Two stories or a dozen. Then gone, leaving a few readers grieving, and all the others unaware that anything had been missed.

Let us honor a few of all those who departed without a ripple, if only to show our respect to the tradition of the bent hero.

Consider the peculiar instance of Peter Wright, the Amateur Millionaire. Peter adventured in *Flynn's* during 1925. It is stretching courtesy to consider him a bent hero.

Understand, he did steal. Once. He stole 53 pounds, 17 shillings, and 6 pence from the Isaac Dinwoodie Sons & Co., wholesale provision merchants. They employed Peter for two pounds a week, far too little to marry the lovely Dolly Munro of the flashing dark eyes and curly dark hair.

He proposes. She refuses him. So staggered is he by this rejection that he snatches a handful of money from I. Dinwoodie Sons & Co. and hies off to America. He gets about twenty-five miles. Then he is found out by that eccentric millionaire, Japhet Drabble, also known as The Golden Gambler.

Drabble hands our feckless hero a check for 10,000 pounds.

*Drabble*: You've got to spend it within a month.... If by the thirty-first, you have a penny of this check left, I shall see that you go to jail for today's folly. Spend, mind you! No giving away. But spend on— what you like. Report to me on the thirty-first, with detailed notes of your expenditure.

That's the premise, as laid out in "The Golden Gambler" (Flynn's, January 3, 1925). The story is signed S. Andrew Wood, who was obviously aware of the book, Brewster's Millions, or the popular play by the same title.

Drabble, you see, has wagered with a friend that a man cannot spend 100,000 pounds a year without killing himself. Peter is the test case.

He does not kill himself. But it is a near thing. His adventures begin shortly after he returns to his office (replacing the money with no incident). There he discovers that Dolly has become engaged to Mr. Goosetree, the chief cashier.

Pierced to the heart, Peter takes to the road with his friend, Alf Bumby. Immediately they are drugged and tied up by crooks who want every scrap of that 10,000 pounds. Just before doom lowers its fearsome curtain, Dolly manages to save them.

Dolly, it should be noted, spends all her waking hours saving Peter and Alf. She does it over and over.

But she can never be Peter's. For she is engaged to another.

The rest of the series, six more stories, concerns Peter's efforts to rid himself of all that money, each and every issue. He meets a mighty river of people eager to help him, by feeding him drugs, swindling him, threatening his life.... Between financial spasms, he moons about Dolly.

Eventually, after idiotic episodes have piled high, we reach "Peter Makes Good" (February 12, 1925). Dolly can become Mrs. Peter, after all. Goosetree is discomfited. The Golden Gambler loses his bet—although in every story there is a moment when he seems about to win.

Most of the English local color in the series seems fraudulent. Either the stories were rewritten from an English series or S. Andrew Wood (a probable pseudonym) was an American faking a British manner, for *Flynn's* was heavily seasoned with reprints from Edgar Wallace, Anthony Wynne, and other genial writers of English popular mystery fiction. However it is hardly to be believed that any sane English writer would name a character Japhet Drabble. Moreover, the story line bears a certain kinship to the light romantic serials being published at that time in *Argosy All-Story Weekly*. An American author is entirely possible.

Peter is a wimp. Captain Jim Clavering, on the other hand, reflects the glory that was Bulldog Drummond. The 1926 *Flynn's* featured Clavering in a short series titled "The Admirable Crimes of Captain Clavering," by Walter Archer Frost. They ran for ten installments in *Flynn's* and *Flynn's Weekly* from April 17 through June 19, 1926.

The crimes are admirable because Clavering is intensely busy returning an assortment of stolen jewels to their owners. The task is not quite that simple, because everything must be returned in secrecy. Secrecy is essential. Helen Armistead, whose smiles fry Clavering's heart, was somehow involved in the theft.

These are tightly knit stories, resounding with violent action and not indigestible amounts of the posturing common to minor series fiction of the 1920s. It is the Prohibition era, with gangsters, speakeasies, and jazz music. Clavering, himself, is a huge man, caked all over with muscles. He wears a mustache and faultlessly tailored tuxedos, a thoroughly conventional moving picture image. When necessary, he is also tough, quick, and violent.

The stories are prickly with action and suspense, which gradually build as detectives, or perhaps crooks, slowly close in on Clavering and Helen. "The Ashford Necklace" (*Flynn's*, June 12, 1926) is reasonably typical of the group.

Clavering visits a beach club to restore a stolen pearl necklace to its owner, Carol Ashford. The club is raided by Prohibition agents. Not wishing to be caught with a stolen necklace in his pocket, Clavering shorts the lights. From that point it is Hurrah, Slug, Bash around in the darkness. The Prohibition agents turn out to be hold-up men. After they are captured and Clavering has punched the lead crook simple, he slips the necklace in among their loot. And another jewel is silently returned.

The final story of the series, "Mrs. Amory's Diamond" (*Flynn's Weekly*, June 19, 1926), dangles the reader over crocodiles as Clavering attempts to evade the detectives and shield Helen. Guns flare in the final pages. The men causing all the trouble (and having all that bothersome knowledge about Clavering's activities) are shot dead. They deserve it. And Helen is proved innocent. Did you ever doubt it? She was merely trying to shield a girl friend who had taken revenge on society in unwise ways.

On the whole, Drummond would have been heartier and louder, with more cheerfully lunatic dialogue, but Clavering continues the tradition admirably.

As did Simon Templar, The Saint. His affairs properly belong to a discussion of 1930s adventure fiction, for he is one of the major figures of that era. But no commentary on bent heros could possibly be complete without touching, however briefly, on The Saint's lustrous career.

It has long been apparent that orderly intellectual maturation requires the reading of quantities of The Saint's adventures. He appeared in novels, novelettes, and short stories, and later moving pictures, comic books, and television series. His sobriquet appeared monthly on the masthead of *The Saint Mystery Magazine.*

His adventures are a continuous joy. The Saint foams with gaiety and youth. For generations, magazines had featured athletic young heroes, bronzed and blue-eyed, some of them capable of laughter. None had the fleetness of wit or radiated the infectious charm and polished mockery that makes The Saint so special a figure.

He is the essence of the Spanish Main, stripped of capricious cruelty, brought glittering into the present crazy century. As any good buccaneer, The Saint does not scorn the good things of life. His clothing is from Saville Row, worn with taste and personal flair. His apartment is splendidly austere; his automobile offensively expensive.

All this has been earned by his wits. He started poor.

At the beginning of his career, he carried two neat little throwing knives and a gun. These saw use, for Templar is an admirable justice figure in the original tradition. Unlike most justice figures, he has no objection to making a profit. No thief is safe from him. Nor any con man or promoter. Some of his most joyous exploits are recorded when swindling cheats. While he strikes for justice, he manages, at the same time, to transfer a substantial quantity of material goods to his pockets.

It is only sensible. Buccaneering must pay its way.

His first appearance was in *Meet the Tiger* (1928), the blithe young adventurer pitted against the master criminal. Co-starring with him was the extraordinary Patricia Holm, honored above all women. Patricia remained devoted to The Saint for years, their relationship thoroughly irregular but glorious.

Around him gathered a small groups of friends, dedicated and intense. Through the years they included the indispensable 'Orace, Monty Hayward (named after the editor of *The Thriller*), Peter Quentin, Norman Kent (who sacrificed his life for The Saint and Patricia in *The Last Hero*, 1930), Hoppy Uniatz, an iron-headed gangster with an endless capacity for whiskey, and much later on, Hamilton, an FBI man.

He also collected a few continuing adversaries on the law's side. Notably Claude Eustace Teal of Scotland Yard, a tubby, methodical man with a taste for chewing gum; and Inspector John Henry Furnack of the New York Police. They were enraged by Templar, admired and respected him, had their lives made miserable by him, and would have regretted jailing him, although they rarely stopped trying.

At the beginning, The Saint's adventures resonate with echoes of Sapper and whispers from the prose of Edgar Wallace. Even at this early stage, Templar was brilliant, although not yet sublime. Shortly, he would rise even to that height. The miracle began during 1929 in the British magazine, *The Thriller*, first issue dated February of that year. Shortly the publication became the vehicle for an extended series of Saint novelettes.

The author was Leslie Charles Bowyer Yin, born in Singapore, 1907, of an English mother and Chinese father. Brought to England at the age of twelve, he attended King's College at Cambridge for a year. About this time, he changed his name to Leslie Charles Charteris Bowyer-Ian, which seems hardly an improvement. After acceptance of his first novel, *X Esquire* (1927), he dropped out of Cambridge to pursue a writer's career. This caused his father, a surgeon, to withdraw support. Unable to keep himself by writing short fiction for English magazines, Charteris passed through an extraordinary collection of jobs in England

and Malaya, including such notable positions as an auxiliary policeman, sailor, gold prospector, pearl fisher, and professional bridge player.

Moving to the United States in 1932, he became a naturalized citizen in 1946. Between those dates he wrote for Hollywood, poured out perhaps fifty books.

Some of the early novels as *The Last Hero* (1930) and *The Avenging Saint* (1930), now show the grooves and creases of advancing age, exciting as they still are. The action has become faintly mannered and the subjects reflect the Post-War disenchantment with international politics.

The short stories and novelettes are quite another thing. One by one they emerged, an impudent cavalcade, collected in *Enter the Saint* (1930), *Wanted for Murder* (1931), *The Saint vs. Scotland Yard* (1932), *The Brighter Buccaneer* (1933), *The Saint Goes On* (1934). Down through the years they pranced to the 1964 *Vendetta For the Saint*. After that still more Saint books emerged, although written by others, and given a final golden brushing by Charteris.

Even in the later books, when The Saint has become a trifle more sedate, aged past that magic boundary of forty, he retains a jaunty impishness.

He is a specific for the spirit. If times are heavy, if politicians make hoggish sounds, if glum government agencies reduce the world's bright spice to printed forms, then it is time to return to The Saint.

He floats above it all, a bright spark, reveling in blood and melodrama. Through the urban jungle he pursues adventure. Always there are new beautiful girls to be rescued, Mr. Teal to be teased, and fresh ranks of the Ungodly begging to be punched on the nose.

For all his merry criminality, Simon Templar openly strolled the streets of London and New York, gloomily regarded by the police, always hovering a trifle beyond their reach.

Other series characters were not so fortunate. Through bad luck, the malice of others, or a natural wish to disguise their illegal activities, characters often found themselves outlaws. Some were framed, others misunderstood; all found themselves hunted men, every hand against them, every eye needling out their secret.

We will meet several of these explosive individuals in the next chapter.

# Chapter Two
# Outlaws for Justice

In the Summer of 1912, Frederic Van Rennselaer Dey wrote his final Nick Carter story. These fields he had worked since 1891. It had been a rather odd profession for a man trained to the law. But then Dey, himself, was more than a rather odd man.[1]

If we may judge from this distance in time, he felt the urge toward more substantial attainments than the writing of dime novels. What man is content doing what he does supremely well? The perfumed promise of the formal novel beckoned him, like a saucy girl skipping ahead, just beyond reach.

He reached, therefore. He yearned. Novels formed under his fingertips, serials handwritten, pen across paper, page after rapid page. These appeared in *The Cavalier* and *All-Story Weekly*. When published as books, they contained 315 pages and a pencil-sketch frontispiece. Their titles have a certain brazen ring—*The Two-Faced Man, The Girl By the Roadside, Alias the Night Wind*. They were what we may call mystery-adventure stories. The scene was contemporary. The characters toyed with emotions too profound for words. Or perhaps it only seemed that way. They were nice bland people confronted by the intrigues of men with oily hair and faces lit by evil.

Too long had Mr. Dey tarried over the adventures of Nick Carter. Across his style flared the gaudy emblem of the dime novel. His serials, for all their contemporary emoting, remained dime novels still. They were dime novels tamed and saddened, wearing straw hats and lacy dresses. Under the splendid clothing are recognizable situations and characters from the *New Nick Carter Weekly*. And, if you listen intently, you can hear old-style melodrama booming in the deeps.

Consider the adventures of Bingham Harvard, known to the police as The Night Wind.

Harvard, a clerk in his foster-father's bank, is framed for theft by the unscrupulous detective, Rodney Rushton. Intent on proving his innocence, Harvard becomes a fugitive. Harried by the police, he turns ferociously upon them, using his supernormal strength to break their bones and dislocate their limbs. He escapes repeated police traps. So strong, agile, and elusive is Harvard that the police refer to him as The

Night Wind. Lady Kate Maxwilton (Maxwell in the book), a nurse become special police detective, is brought in to snare him. She will swiftly accept Harvard's innocence. Severely wounded in a police trap, Harvard escapes through the help of Lady Kate, her black servant Julius, and Tom Clancy, a close friend from college days. Rushton spreads his snares for them all. After numerous adventures, Kate and Harvard marry and escape overseas from New York City. Thus the four-part serial, "Alias the Night Wind," published weekly in *The Cavalier*, May 10 through 31, 1913.

The story is developed in three main sections: first, the false accusation, Harvard's subsequent outlawing, and his struggle alone against the police. Next, the progressive involvement of Lady Kate and Tom Clancy, both of whom come to support him, and Harvard's decision to kill Rushton. Finally, Harvard's wounding at police hands, the tightening of suspicion around Lady Kate and Clancy, and exploitation of The Night Wind's resolution to kill Rushton, until, at the last moment, his murderous intention melts beneath love's fragrant breath.

Much of interest crowds the first part of the novel. The serial begins with a flash-forward a scene several weeks into the story and filled with perfectly splendid gratuitous violence and excitement. A young police patrolman sees an attempted robbery foiled under his nose. As he charges up, he recognizes the rescuer as that wanted criminal, The Night Wind:

[The Patrolman] sprang forward to grapple with the man—and found himself in a grasp that he could not shake off or loosen.

He felt himself whirled around so that his back was toward the man he would have fought. His night-stick was torn from his grasp and tossed into the middle of the street, and a sharp pain followed by a pipe-stem snap at the middle joint of his right hand maddened and startled him. Then his gun was taken from him and he was sent spinning after the night-stick; and the gun, broken and emptied, fell upon him an instant later and clattered to the pavement.

[The patrolman] felt as if he had been run through a threshing machine. He was dazed and lamed and half paralyzed. as if all the bolts of electricity that his system would withstand had been shot through him. He thought that both shoulders were dislocated—only they were not; nor were any important bones broken, although the sensation was the same as if many of them might be. Only that one finger had paid the penalty for his daring. (Vanardy 13-14)

The Patrolman has unfortunately tried to arrest the 1913 equivalent of Superman. Bingham Harvard is perhaps four times as strong and six times as agile as mortal man. Why, he does not know. He was a foundling, adopted and brought up by bank president Chester for reasons which appear to be extraneous to the narrative, since they are never given. Harvard's astonishing physical abilities, well known to his college friends, are coupled with a flaring violent temper. Self discipline has been difficult. But Harvard realizes that the combination of phenomenal strength and temper is too deadly to toy with. He must discipline himself. And he does. But for all his self control, the outwardly mild and accommodating bank clerk is a tiger wearing a pink bow.

This is the man that police detective Rodney Rushton elected to frame for bank robbery. Rushton's reasons were not complex: to build his reputation, he needed to produce the thief before the other investigators; Harvard looked as if he could be handled; the bank president looked as if he could be bluffed; and Mr. Dey required the frame-up for his plot. Simple, straightforward, overwhelming reasons.

Reasons that hardly give you confidence in the police or the integrity of the prose.

Dey's Nick Carter novels approved enthusiastically of the New York City police and lavished endless praise on Chief of Police Thomas Byrnes. A far different picture was seen by Algernon Blackwood, at this time a reporter in New York City:

Most of my work on the *Evening Sun*, at any rate, took me among the criminal and outcast sections of the underworld. In those days the police, as a whole, were corrupt, brutal, heartless; I saw innocent men against whom they had a grudge, or whom they wanted out of the way for some reason, `railroaded to gaol' on cooked-up evidence; sickening and dreadful scenes I witnessed.... Tammany had its slimy tentacles everywhere and graft was the essence of success in every branch of public life. A police captain had his town and country house, perhaps his yacht as well...." (121-122)

This is far from Nick Carter. The hateful reality noted by Blackwood only whispers through "Alias The North Wind." The novel is not otherwise over-stressed by realism. Harvard's foster-father rigidly denies his innocence, for no better reason than plot requirements. The Police Chief refuses to doubt Rushton's accusation, filmy as it is and bolstered by a single faked clue. These people are rigidly brainless. They have to be that the mechanism of the story continues to click and whir.

These plot-driven characters are balanced by two excellent secondary characters. Julius, Lady Kate's black driver and co-conspirator, conceals an astute mind under a deliberately assumed dialect; a responsible person of superior integrity, he carries major responsibility in the novels as a man, not a black caricature. A character of nearly equal interest is Redhead, chief of a private detective agency. (His formal name is never given.) Untouched by corruption, he is in the already familiar vein of the private investigator more intelligent and more professional than the police. Redhead plays an important role in the next serial, "The Return of the Night Wind" (five-part serial, *The Cavalier*, October 4 through November 1, 1913).

In this sequel, the Harvards return to New York City to clear Bingham's name. He begins a crusade to shake out corrupt officials in the police department. Kate works with the private investigator, Redhead, to study the bank theft. While much harassed by Rushton, she is aided by "The Society of Crippled Cops," police who have been injured by The Night Wind but have come to believe in his innocence. Ultimately Kate and Redhead expose a complex plot to rob the bank. Harvard is vindicated. Rushton and the other criminals are arrested and sent to prison.

The story gallops merrily. Yet almost none of Harvard's special abilities are used. While Dey has provided his hero with a superb physique, he has also faced Harvard with a problem unsolvable by physical strength. Harvard requires physical challenges, obstacles to battle, feats of agility and endurance to perform. A few such opportunities are provided him. But only a few. They are quite insufficient.

Perhaps, at last, Dey sensed this difficulty. In *The Night Wind's Promise* (serialized in *The Cavalier*, 1914), the story is built around Kate and the action focused upon her problems.

In *Promise*, Harvard, now become bank president, is tricked into paying a confidence man $325,000. Immediately the scoundrel rips away his disguise and returns, attempting to win Kate from Harvard.

A sort of semi-hypnosis grips Kate, a condition common to dime novel heroines. The villain's personality both fascinates and repels her. At one time, her father, a U.S. senator, wished her to marry this man. Then she fled from home to become a police woman. Can she again resist this man's dreadful charm? Good gracious, we do hope so.

All of which may have a certain familiarity to readers of the *New Nick Carter Weekly*. The insistently clever criminal and his slippery plots dominate the first action. Through the last part of the book, the plotter's effectiveness dwindles. His meticulous psychological plot degenerates to raw violence. He attempts to shoot Clancy; he kidnaps Kate. These brainless acts suggest that Dey was at his wit's end to keep the story moving. Action is a commodity more accessible to description than involved psychological states.

The story ends in a long chase, the criminal racing ahead of The Night Wind and his friends. Finally, trapped at an abandoned farm house, the rascal is killed by accident. *Sic transient* menace. The stolen money is recovered. Kate is recovered. Rushton, parolled from prison to help Harvard, is pardoned. Clancy gets a wife. The story closes on page 320, invincibly optimistic in this essentially good world.

For some reason, Dey did nothing more with these characters for four years. Then he published "The Lady of the Night Wind" (six-part serial, *All-Story Weekly*, October 5 through November 9, 1919).[2] Once again, the story focuses on Kate and her problems.

They are troublesome. A clever blackmailer threatens to reveal to her parents that her black-sheep brother is not dead, as believed. There follow complexities of purpose, identity, character, and alliance. Ultimately Kate traps the blackmailer in a secret room, constructed for her private amusement. This steel-sheathed place is an amazement of trap doors and panels, restraining arms, shutters, drops—all powered by electro-pneumatic energy and controlled by dozens of concealed switches. After elaborate negotiations, the blackmailer is allowed to leave and, later, is accidentally killed while attempting to escape from The Night Wind. Accidental death leaves the hero blameless of blood guilt.

The novel struggles hard to depict real people facing crime. But those dime novel flames will not be damped. Dey wishes to avoid melodrama, action scenes, improbable events. Yet his story demands improbable events, action scenes, and melodrama, black lightning ripping a scarlet sky. Complex character interaction is sought. But his characters never mature, never expand to three dimensions, and they interact only in the simplicities of action. Decades of writing first draft dime novels had left their imperishable mark.

It was a mark more terrible than anyone realized. In 1922, Dey was sixty-one years old, without money or future. Unable to keep up payments, he had lost his home. He drank too much, too often, and that helped no more than it usually does. And perhaps he realized, more bitterly than we may know, the distance separating the writing he could do and the writing he wished to do. Incapacity is endurable only when not comprehended.

A Street & Smith editor, C.A. MacLean, received a letter from Dey saying "...I'm just tired out and I want to try the long sleep...I can't stand the thought of growing old and becoming a burden" (Godfrey 22).

MacLean hurried to the East Side New York hotel where Dey had taken a room. With the manager, he broke open the door. Dey lay dead on the bed. He had shot himself with a .32 automatic. All series were ended.

Superhuman strength, the good man falsely accused, the smiling villain carrying off the maiden, even trapdoors actuated by switches, all were recognizable parts of the dime novel scene. All transferred gracefully into the fiction of the popular magazines. All continued, variously painted and caparisoned, through the single-character action magazines of the 1930s and into our own enlightened time of television and motion pictures featuring foul-mouthed women.

The hero made criminal by the malice of others became a favored theme of detective fiction during the late 1930s and 1940s. It seemed that no private investigator managed to struggle through a novel without waking, as from a nightmare, to find a corpse, his own gun as the murder weapon, and the police hammering down the door. Dashiell Hammett may have been at the root of this—The Continental Op, himself, was framed in *Red Harvest* (1930)—and Hammett's scenes and character types profoundly penetrated magazine mystery fiction. But even in 1930, the framed hero was a recognized convention. Bingham Harvard had been there earlier, and before him, decades of dime novels had exploited the idea of the false accusation, the hero shamed and hunted, the forces of darkness, like an obsidian wall, closing around him.

Other heroes contrived to get into trouble with the law by other paths. Some went out of their way to get themselves outlawed and hunted. For a seeker of justice, the side of the law is not always the right side.

In the Zorro series, the side of the right was that of the peons and natives.

Zorro, as you may recall, defended justice for Walt Disney through an extended series of 1950s television programs. Early scripts were by Johnston McCulley, who had given the world Zorro in 1919 and was now reaping the reward of his sagacity.[3]

Zorro was the second, and most successful, of McCulley's costumed leading men. (Black Star, the superior master criminal, had appeared in 1916.) McCulley reveled in costumed melodrama. He is the spiritual father of all 1930s avengers who administered bushwhack justice from the night and strewed the scene of their exploits with scarlet spiders and paste-on bat decals.

From the figure of Zorro sprang innumerable other masked men riding horses of unnatural learning and shooting with that accuracy obtainable only in fiction. All adventured in the shadow of Zorro. At one point in his history, he was even aided by a faithful Indian companion.

Not that the Zorro adventures are westerns. Call them, instead, historical adventures. For they are set during those interesting years of 1775 to 1800. Thus Zorro rode during the Revolutionary War and the presidencies of Washington and Adams.

He rode El Camino Real, a 650-mile trail that linked 21 Spanish missions from San Diego de Alcala to Sonoma, north of San Francisco de Aris. Out of the night, Zorro would materialize—black cloak, black clothing, his face black- masked to the chin, thin black silk gloves on his hands, astride a huge black horse. Coiled on the black saddle, a rope and whip. In his sash, a single-shot pistol. At his side a sword.

His purpose was to punish oppressors. He was "friend of the oppressed! Giving punishment where punishment was most needed! Dealing it out when the authorities would not...."

Most usually the oppressed were peons and the native Cocopah Indians. Less frequently, a Spanish grandee trapped in plots or a beautiful woman haunted by greedy tricksters.

Some oppressors, Zorro whipped and terrorized. Others met him at sword point, their inaccurate appraisal of their fencing ability earning them a "Z" slashed across the cheek:

The mark of Zorro was made with a single stroke of the blade, a quick twisting of the point that seemed like a flash of fire. (McCulley, *Zorro Rides Again* 296)

For those meriting exceptional humiliation, the mark was etched in three strokes. When the crime was great, the mark was placed on the forehead. The slashes cut to the bone and scarred. All cuts were administered during the blood dance of the duel, swords flickering in the candlelight, the sing of blade on blade, the supple figure of Zorro twisting, graceful as death. One hand grips a pistol, primed and cocked. This discourages spectator participation in a two- man sport. In his other hand dances that blade that so rarely killed, so often humiliated. Avengers rise from the circumstances of their society. The circumstances creating Zorro were approximately these:

Along El Camino Real, small towns grew up around each mission. The population, a mixture of Mexicans and Indians, comprised the work force. The masters were the Spanish.

In Southern California, the Spanish created a modified feudal society. Aristocrats brimming with noble blood administered vast estates. To lessen their load, the aristocrats were served by the peons and natives, thus pleasing God, who is nice about these social distinctions.

The regional Governor administered Spanish policy. From California, Spain sucked wealth as a child sucks candy. Of all the wealth gathered for Spain, a certain amount remained to console the Governor for his hours of dedication. A lesser amount remained stuck to the hands of officials, cronies, hangers-on, a brazen horde.

The law of the land was the law of Spain, modified for distant places.

The law was enforced by military detachments, answering to the Governor. Military posts bloomed at each major town. The wine shops bloomed also.

The missions would appear to introduce another factor. In the Zorro stories, McCulley did not explore this. Barely did he mention the Church's role in the exploitation of California; and the Church, as a political entity, plays no significant part in the action. History and historical fiction travel parallel but incompatible paths.

"These are turbulent times," sighs Don Diego Vega. Across his nostrils he draws a perfumed handkerchief, edged with lace. Foul odors make him come all over faint.

"Violence. Violence. It is something I cannot understand."

He does not appear to understand that his world reeks of corruption and the abuse of power. It quite escapes him that between the Governor and the aristocrats thrills constant tension, concealed by smiling ceremony. Each group maneuvers for position. Those long links between California and Spain tingle with concealed animosity.

The Governor squeezes. The aristocrats resist. The peons and natives ignore politics, the harshness of their own reality being more than enough.

Of all this, the limp fop, Don Diego Vega sees nothing. He is lifeless, that one. Son of that old fire-eater, Don Alejandro Vega, you would expect better of him. But no. He deplores effort. Blood and sword play offend him. Let others swill wine and dice loudly at the inn. From all that his fastidious stomach recoils.

Poetry and philosophy sing in his brain. He yawns daintily, as does one saturated with poetry and philosophy.

So the story opens. Don Diego, twenty-four years old and exhausted by it all. He yawns and yawns again. His noble blood protects him from physical harm, if not from the sniggered scorn of those living in Reina de Los Angeles.

On occasional nights, Don Diego is also Senor Zorro, The Fox. Has been since he was seventeen. Which makes sense, for Zorro is the stuff of seventeen, a daydream grown real.

He has become more real than Don Diego Vega. Zorro exists; Don Diego is only an artifice.

But who could imagine? Don Diego's voice is listless, thin; Zorro's, deep and rich. Don Diego wears an ornamental sword, full of jewels, never drawn; Zorro's sword is plainly functional and bathed in blood (it hangs on Don Diego's wall, concealed in the open). Don Diego must be assisted to mount a horse and is fatigued to ride four miles; Zorro pounds scores of miles through the night at a full gallop.

Who would suspect?

Various people at various times.

Bernardo, the personal servant of Don Diego. At first he does not know, but McCulley cannot sustain such a situation long. A big hulking fellow, Bernardo begins as a deaf-mute. To assist the narrative, his afflictions are silently altered and he becomes merely mute. By the 1941 "The Sign of Zorro," it seems that he is not even that. With the correction of a speech impediment, he can now talk, if with difficulty.

Fray Felipe also knows. He is Don Diego's confessor, a massive man, over sixty years old, still more than six feet tall. He directs the Los Angeles chapel; by the 1941 stories, he will be transferred to the Mission de Santa Barbara.

And there are others who know the truth about Don Diego and his alternate identity.

One of these is Bardoso, the ex-pirate, an evil-smelling old drunk, his left eye cut out during battle on the high seas. Now retired, he lounges before a filthy hut near the Los Angeles town square. He notices everything. The secret identity of Don Diego Vega, for example. He is a staunch ally.

So is Jose, Chief of the Cocopahs. And Don Carlos Cassara, saved from ruin and suicide by Zorro ("Zorro Saves a Friend," *Argosy*, November 12, 1932.) Eventually even Don Alejandro Vega, Don Diego's father, learns the truth.

As does the lovely Senorita Lolita Pulido (Don Diego will marry her), Sergeant Pedro Gonzales (pitted against Zorro in so many stories), the townspeople of Los Angeles, the soldiers, the Governor, the readers of *Argosy* and *West*.

Later most of them forgot. But that is another matter.

Zorro's adventures fall into three loose groupings.

"The Curse of Capistrano" (1919), "The Further Adventures of Zorro" (1922), "Zorro Rides Again" (1931), and "The Sign of Zorro" (1941) more or less represent the main story line, spread across about twenty years, with large gaps. The central root from which this foliage springs is "The Curse of Capistrano." It provides prototype scenes and characters which busily repeat for the remainder of the series.

A second group of material, published in the 1932-1935 *Argosy*, introduces such continuing characters as Bardoso, the ex-pirate; Don Carlos Cassara; and Jose, Chief of the Cocopahs. All these know the Zorro secret, as do Fray Felipe and Bernardo. As yet, Don Diego's father does not. Nor do those dozens of people who witness the revelation of Zorro's true identity in the final part of "Capistrano," way back in 1919.

The matter of identity is not the only inconsistency in this group. During the 1935 "Mysterious Don Miguel" (*Argosy*, two-part serial, September 21 and 28, 1935), Don Diego pays court to a woman other than Senorita Lolita. Has the naughty fellow forgotten that he wed her? Or has he not yet met her? And finally the political influence of the Vega family is diminished from its towering 1919 peaks.

In the final story group, published 1944 and after in *West* and a few other magazines, still another variation is offered. Now the Zorro secret is known only to Don Diego's father, Fray Felipe, and Bernardo. Now the military suspects that Don Diego might be Zorro and plot and scheme to trap him. They forever fail through stories of brief, shallow, cheerful formula.

Let us grant that these story groups are inconsistent and move on. The dedicated reader must ignore his urge to arrange fictional events in rational order. No such order exists. Fortunately no need presses to unify the series. Each story may be read independently with nearly no mental anguish.

If taken in small doses, like rhubarb extract, the stories are charming. Across them flicker familiar scenes from "Capistrano," blended in like bits from an old movie. The characters are vividly painted shells. The stories, bland simplicities, string together direct confrontations, crafty menace, immediate action. It is all as predictable as eggs in a carton.

Don Diego, that spineless lounger, learns of wicked doings. Often these are military traps to capture Zorro—who appears where least expected to punish this issue's villain, carving him with a "Z," sticking him through the shoulder, then flitting into the night. Pursuing soldiers find only young Don Diego yawning over a book of poems in his father's house.

Johnston McCulley, as you may recall, wrote nearly one hundred stories about Thubway Tham stealing wallets. McCulley's ability to wring new stories from a simple plot line is staggering.

The first Zorro novel is not only the richest of the series, but it sparkles with a joyous sort of light foolery. "The Curse of Capistrano" (five-part serial, *All-Story Weekly*, August 9 through September 6, 1919) opens with Sergeant Pedro Gonzales, that huge and evil-tempered man, lounging half-full of wine before the inn fire. Outside, the night roars with rain. Inside Sgt. Gonzales roars boasts to yawning Don Diego of how he shall defeat and capture the infamous Zorro. "Meal mush and goat's milk," he shall collect the reward on Zorro's head.

Don Diego buys a pot of honey and departs. No sooner has he gone than Zorro materializes from the storm.

Zorro: "I am the friend of the oppressed, senor, and I have come to punish you."

[Gonzales] attacked furiously, hoping to drive Senor Zorro off his feet and make an end of it. But he found that his attack ended as if against a stone wall, his blade was turned aside, his breast crashed against that of his antagonist, and Senor Zorro merely threw out his chest and hurled him back half a dozen steps....

And suddenly [Zorro] began to press the fighting, taking step after step, slowly and methodically going forward and forcing Gonzales backward. The tip of his blade seemed to be a serpent's head with a thousand tongues. Gonzales felt himself at the other's mercy...(18-19)

Gonzales is disarmed. Zorro does not run the sergeant through or slash his face. Merely slaps him. In public. The shame!

After which Zorro vanishes into the night, leaving Gonzales sputtering alibis into disbelieving ears.

So begins the novel. And so it continues, full of courtly gestures, simple characters, simple comedy, action in an irresistible flow.

Don Diego, the languid, has taken a fancy to Senorita Lolita Pulido. With permission of her family, he pays a formal call, conducting his courtship with all the enthusiasm of a sleeping oyster.

After he shuffles away, drooping with fatigue, Zorro enters, full of passion, wooing Lolita with word sorcery, glowing her heart. Her father, Don Carlos, seeks to detain the notorious highwayman until the soldiers arrive.

But as Captain Ramon and his men rush in, Zorro's horse thunders away. The Captain does not follow, being struck by Lolita's beauty. He remains to brag and leer, only to find himself confronted by Zorro, whose horse had galloped off alone. Zorro, himself, remained behind, comfortably listening inside a cupboard.

He does not like what he heard and Captain Ramon finds himself in another duel. Down he goes, pinked through the shoulder. Zorro bows gracefully into the night, and the novel, now charged with motivation and conflict, rears high and gallops after him.

From this situation evolve complications of love, pursuit, and swordplay. Zorro and Don Diego press their suits in their respective ways. Captain Ramon is determined to secure Lolita's hand by means foul, since no one expects a nice villain. Which is to say that he attempts to have the Governor declare Don Carlos disloyal, thus ruining the family, thus forcing them to yield up Lolita to Ramon's dark passions. At every turn, however, Zorro blocks the Captain's intrigues, melts from his traps, whips his minions.

Aware that the story is building to a climax, Zorro persuades the individualistic caballeros to unite in resisting the Governor's troops. But Ramon has succeeded in having Don Carlos and family jailed. Zorro frees them and escapes into the darkness with Lolita. Loses her. Confronts Ramon in the presence of the Governor. Forces Ramon to admit his crimes and lies.

The Governor's eyes narrow meaningfully.

Down goes Ramon, a "Z" slashed across his forehead.

Zorro flees, closely chased by soldiers. He finds Lolita, herself fleeing from the soldiers. They barricade themselves into the tavern. In the wine-smelling dimness, they battle yelling hordes.

All is lost. But well lost, of course, for love.

As troopers batter down the door, the town square fills with fresh young caballeros eager for battle. They charge the soldiers and beat them back in wild free-for-all.

The Governor's power has been blunted and concessions wrung from him. Zorro is pardoned. After all these miracles, he emerges from the tavern to reveal to the assembled population of Southern California, the face beneath Zorro's mask.

Don Diego: "And now Senor Zorro shall ride no more, for there will be no need" (191).

He was wrong about that.

Zorro rides and again rides and again. To recount each adventure would send you stumbling off for wine. On the other hand....

"The Further Adventures of Zorro" (six-part serial, *Argosy All-Story Weekly*, May 6 through June 10, 1922): Don Diego rouses Zorro from retirement to battle hordes of pirates and the convoluted plots of Captain Ramon. (Ramon seems to have risen from the dead, since he was left a branded corpse at the end of "Capistrano.") After Lolita is kidnapped, Zorro surmounts perils innumerable (including imprisonment in a strait jacket) before the pirates are threshed and Captain Ramon killed for the final time.

"Zorro Rides Again" (four-part serial, *Argosy,* October 3 through 24, 1931): A Zorro imposter commits outrages against the people. Outlawed, Don Diego must flee to clear his name, a hero falsely accused. Shades of the Night Wind.

The Zorro imposter is part of a plot to avenge Captain Ramon. Another military man, Captain Rocha, has thought up the scheme and continues in Ramon's unwholesome tracks by having Don Carlos and family again jailed. That incautious act earned him a "Z" on the face, severely eroding his pride.

(In passing, note that Senorita Lolita has not yet married Don Diego. She took sick before the wedding, poor thing, and went to Spain for several years to recover her health. Serial heros must endure long courtships.)

Rocha plans still more outrages, with the help of the Governor's secretary, the powerful Don Esteban. Now comes unexpected failure. Aided by Jose, Chief of the Cocophas and Fray Felipe, Zorro traps the false Zorro. They battle in the public square and the imposter is killed.

Unmasked he is revealed as Roche. But now Don Esteban and soldiers storm forward to seize Zorro.

Once again, as in "Capistrano," the young bloods resist the soldiers. Esteban gets a large initial carved on his forehead; love, plus good Toledo steel, has conquered all.

"Zorro Saves A Friend" (*Argosy*, November 12, 1932), offers twenty pages of non-stop heroics, as Zorro unsnares his fool friend, Don Carlos Cassara from ruin and suicide. The Don has been thoroughly fleeced by a crooked gambler, a secret agent of the Governor, that fountain of evil.

"Zorro Deals With Treason" (*Argosy*, August 18, 1934) sticks closely to the plot of "Zorro Rides Again," the serial being reduced to a short story by striking it with a cleaver. The villain's name has been changed. The story, as usual, is cheerfully energetic. But the constant Zorro impersonators take their toll of your temper. Unfortunately for your temper, there will be more impersonators.

"The Sign of Zorro" (five-part serial, *Argosy*, January 25 through February 22, 1941) opens in September of 1800. Don Diego's wife has died of fever and he languishes. Zorro has not appeared for years and rumor relates that he was killed in a fight in Monterey.

Now the exquisite Senorita Panchita Canchola comes secretly to the drunken Bardoso. She is seeking Zorro's help. Her headstrong younger brother, master of the estate, is being ruined by unscrupulous men. The vile Don Pedro Moreolos is behind it all, seeking revenge because Panchita's father once shamed him.

Soon the languid Don Diego, limply boring, ambles over to call on her. Thereafter the world explodes as Don Pedro and his ill-washed legions attempt to kidnap Panchita, and Zorro, dodging, slashing, evading, tricking, laughing, risks his life for her.

They make such a lovely couple at the end. And isn't she surprised when the mask is removed.

About three years later, an extended series of Zorro short stories began in *West*, a magazine of uncomplicated western action adventures. The series includes two long episodes that were enthusiastically called novels, although a less fevered definition would classify them as novelettes. These are titled "A Task For Zorro" (June 1947) and "Zorro's Fight For Life" (July 1951). The rest of the series are slender short stories, economically built to formula. The primary suspense technique is to have someone suspect that Don Diego is Zorro and almost catch him. Zorro impersonators abound.

As in the September 1944 "Zorro Upsets a Plot." In this, a peon's daughter is stolen by Zorro, who isn't Zorro, and is recovered by Zorro, who is Zorro.

"Zorro Lays a Ghost" (December 1945) features a plotter all dressed in white so that he looks exactly like a ghost. He attempts to turn the superstitious natives against Zorro. He does not.

"Zorro's Masquerade" (March 1946) features three Zorros, two of them whirling at a costume ball, while the original spoils another crafty plot to sour his reputation. "Zorro Shears Some Wolves" (September 1948) features a new trap by agents of the Governor. They abuse the natives, expecting to lure Zorro into their clutches. For all their pains, they get frightfully whipped.

"Hangnoose Reward" (March 1949) is a welcome relief from McCulley's thread-bare plotting. A slick-talking fellow has persuaded this dim-witted peon to dress up as Zorro and allow himself to be captured. Then he will share the reward with the slick talker. It does not dawn on the peon that he will not be around to split anything. Zorro saves him. You wonder why.

"Zorro's Stolen Steed" (March 1950) tells how horse thieves lift Zorro's horse. After soldiers nab the thieves, they recognize the horse and cock the usual trap. Zorro, that fox, recovers the horse anyway and whips two wicked men most dreadfully.

These pot-boilers do not seem to have engaged McCulley's mind or imagination very deeply. Since the early 1940s, he had written a number of westerns in a less improbable vein that were filled with realistic patches and characters whose boots occasionally touched the ground. By this time, the Zorro story lay rigid with rigor mortis. As a concept, it had been charming in its day, if limited; McCulley never really developed the idea, but only played his casual variations until squeezing from it the ultimate final drop of life.

Then he began scripting Zorro stories for Disney.

Like all McCulley's major series heroes, Zorro gleefully broke the law. That it was law protecting the privileged is possibly no excuse. For a popular adventure character, it was, if no excuse, his immediate justification. Selective obedience to law is a familiar game in popular fiction.

To the exploited and unprotected, Zorro provided spotty assistance. He could avenge only those crimes he knew about. Perhaps fear of his coming might deter other criminals. Unfortunate as it may be, the scope of a masked avenger is limited. That is why law, imperfect though it is, remains preferable to individual action in any social organization larger than your thumb.

Even the fear inspired by Zorro faded when he became inactive. And there you are again. At best, an avenger provides a short-term cure, not a long-term solution.

It is curious to note that Zorro could not be effective against broader, although no less representative, social problems. Since Don Diego Vega was, himself, an aristocrat, we have the interesting spectacle of the hero maintaining a paralyzing status quo. Zorro's constant message to the natives is "Don't rise up. Don't revolt. You will be protected."

And protected they often were.

Protected, at least, from the greedy Governor and his avaricious minions.

But still the peons remain fixed within that monolithic Spanish-fuedal system which cemented society to immobility. The many supported the noble few and so the years crept on.

But all this was long ago in the country of the popular magazine. The story is of one brave man dealing justice, extending the legend of Robin Hood another century. If Zorro's means were imperfect and his aims self-limiting, we can celebrate the glory of his intent. If nothing more, we can do that.

In the instance of The Jailbird's Club, the glorious intent is the whole point. The series aims to present the experiences of a group of modern saints whose example will set golden music ringing in your heart. What it manages to offer is a monument to the more obvious forms of sentimentality.

The Jailbird's Club, that exclusive English organization, appeared briefly in *Flynn's* during 1924-1925, the stories signed T.A. O'Keeffe. To become a club member, each individual must have served jail sentences "that reflected honor on [him]."

Which is to say that members had served time to shield a friend, to save a loved one, to do a good deed, or merely to demonstrate the lengths altruism will go in making a point.

Among the Jailbirds may be found a church dignitary, a Scotland Yard Inspector, a famous actor. These are continuing characters. Other members contribute only their names and flicker pallidly at the story rim, peering in at the action.

The original idea seems to have been a sequence of short tales told within the frame of the Club. Each story would illustrate the nobility of self-sacrifice.

In practice, the idea worked out rather differently, since the Club, as a formal group, never really comes to focus. In the first story, "The Seesaw" (*Flynn's*, December 6, 1924) we meet the Club and its new president, Carleton, a surgeon who had briefly gone to prison to protect his partner, Drummond. To the meeting comes a wreck of a man requesting membership. He is in terrible shape. He can hardly babble out a story of how his partner went to prison for him, then was released; and he, in turn was arrested. "I, an innocent man — as innocent as the unborn infant."

After gasping out these touching words, he drops dead. Carleton recognizes his old partner Drummond and goes insane, setting a record for brevity as President. This rather incoherent tale sets the standard for the rest of the series.

"The Six-Fingered Man" (December 13, 1924) tells how ex-Inspector Courtenay (the spelling is Mr. O'Keeffe's) manage to demonstrate the innocence of a man imprisoned for murder. This fellow was shielding a six-fingered retardee who rather casually murdered and left his prints—all six of them—on the murder weapon. How the courts managed to send a five-fingered man to prison is hard to understand.

By mid-1925, the series seems to melt away. The honorable felons nibble at the edges of other people's mysteries: Is this man suitable for membership? What is going on in that man's life? The dialogue is as sentimental as an 1891 valentine, and the characters, given to spectacular emotional detonations, wring their hearts as if they were wet sponges:

"... thank God, I am not the murderer of the one being that ever loved me and gave up her life to me.

"God, I thank you," and he lifted his arms and eyes to heaven. "My fight is now over, and I commit myself into Your hands!"

There was a tense silence after he had finished, broken only by the sobbing of highly strung women. (O'Keefee 546)

The series flies to Limbo on superheated wings. At its dissolution, the Club likely had a membership of 20,000 or more. You have no idea how many noble souls suffer, innocent as the unborn infant, within their prison cages.

Quite frequently, the guilty suffered outside their prison cages, too. One of the constant themes found in pulp magazine pages is that of the criminal who attempts to reform and is so nagged by former associates and the police that he cannot do so. Jimmie Dale, the Lone Wolf, The Gray Phantom, Anthony Trent, and a hundred others following bright-eyed in their tracks, found the path of reformation difficult indeed. They had the will to live in quiet honesty, but their authors had other plans.

Think of Jim Allen, for example. Otherwise known as Jim-twin Allen, the Killer Wolf, or more fetchingly, The White Wolf.

All Jim Allen wanted to do was wander amiably around the Old West during the 1880s and eat pie. He was a great pie eater, Jim was. So were his gray horses, Princess and Honey Boy, who ate all the pie he could beg for them. Jim is a short little pug-nosed kid, slender, freckled, and boyish, with a grin as big as the Arizona sky. He looks about eighteen and is ten years older. Even for a wandering horseman, he dresses casually. His clothing is usually worn out, often tattered, occasionally so ragged he must hold the fragments together with pins. Unlike most saddle tramps, he wears two heavy revolvers, tied down. And his eyes are not the usual eyes. Big and round, faintly slanted at the corners, they are brown flecked with bits of yellow.

On occasion, this innocuous little ragged figure becomes Death.

Then the inconsequential boyishness vanishes. He might have torn away a mask. In its place a taut figure moves on the stiff legs of a fighting wolf:

Allen had become a relentless force of destruction. His face was drawn in a thousand little wrinkles; the corners of his lips were drawn in a taut, mirthless smile; his eyes flamed with a yellow, dancing light. There was no hate or passion in that face. It was expressionless, impersonal, deadly.

Then he began to laugh...mocking laughter—mirthless, dry, metallic.... (Dunning, "The Killer and the Kid" 42)

At this point, the killing starts. Always against odds, it is as theatrical as a Rossini overture:

A continuous stream of fire came from his guns. The reports were blended into one, and the five [killers] melted as if caught by a machine gun.
34
Blue smoke swirled in rings; the glasses and bottles on the bar danced and crashed to the floor from the heavy concussions of many Colts. The roar of the reports was deafening. (Dunning, White Wolf's Law 163)

*Spectator:* "[Jim] ain't human. He was laughin' horrible jumpin' about like a grasshopper, and his guns goin' so fast I couldn't see 'em. No, sir, he ain't man, nor wolf, neither, 'cause he ain't like nothin' possible. (Dunning, *White Wolf's Law* 249-250)

Traveling alone on the outlaw trail has shaped Jim Allen. He is wanted in every state west of the Mississippi. A fifteen thousand dollars reward weighs on his head. He is, it is said, a bandit, killer, and universal menace. Yet he is none of these things. Well, he does shoot people. But only if they deserve to be shot.

He is the son of "Give-'em-hell" Allen of Mosby's Raiders. Having fought through the Civil War with a pistol in each hand, Allen came west to the Arizona Territory, presumably with his wife and his two small sons, twins, named Jim and Jack.

Shortly afterward, Allen was killed in a Pecus County feud that began over a horse race and ended after two families were wiped out—all but the two Allen boys. Then more bad luck struck.

When Jim was eighteen, he shot and killed a captain of the US Army. "That the killing had been deserved and had prevented an Indian uprising made no difference."

Jim became an outlaw. Jack, his twin, grew a beard and eventually became a Wyoming sheriff and US marshal. He believed in the letter of the law, Jack did, a fine, up-standing man, rather rigid about right and wrong. Perhaps he would have arrested his own brother. Or perhaps not. He comes from great distances to support Jim-twin whenever called and they laugh and scuffle together, fine young animals, raucous and joyous. Then there is no question of right or wrong or which side of the law each man represents. Sometimes, when the need is great, Jack impersonates Jim. Sometimes Jim passes himself off as Jack.

As in "The Outlaw Sheriff" (*Complete Stories*, May 1927), when Jack breaks his leg and Jim assumes his identity to clean out a town simply packed with horse thieves.

The brothers love each other. But when Jack makes up a list of undesirables, Jim's name heads the list. The situation is interesting and the series writer, Hal Dunning, revived it whenever it seemed things were becoming too easy for Jim-twin Allen, The White Wolf.

The series began in *Complete Stories* with "The White Wolf" (February 1927) and ran until late 1934, totalling nearly one hundred stories. From these six books were compiled: *The Outlaw Sheriff* (1928), *White Wolf's Law* (1928), *White Wolf's Pack* (1929), *White Wolf's Feud* (1930), *The Wolf Deputy* (1930), and *White Wolf's Outlaw Legion* (1933).

The series was so popular that it survived even Dunning's death. In 1938, the adventures of White Wolf resumed in *Wild West Weekly*. These, signed Hal Dunning, were written by Walker A. Tompkins through an arrangement with Dunning's widow.

The deadly little figure of Jim Allen, forever hunted, regarding his fate with an regretful eye, uncorrupted by the savagery of his life, is of considerable interest. It makes a pretty myth—the good man crucified on an undeserved reputation. The sentimental elements are pumped up grandly. To the reader, White Wolf is noble. Self-sacrificing. Half Robin Hood, certainly.

The other half continues the legend of Jesse James, the noble martyr, harassed by self-seeking lawmen. As additional spice, there are hints of the Billy the Kid legend—the deadly young man ambling through a gun-quick West.

The grimmer aspects of all these legends are ignored. Dunning is interested in picturesque characters and violent action, not character complexity nor historical authenticity. You do not expect White Wolf to show any of those shrewd ambivalences that Max Brand drew in the character of Whistling Dan Barry. And your expectations are not disappointed.

White Wolf is a sentimental character embedded in fiction of considerable casual violence. His peculiar position as a hunted savior sustains the stories. They are about gun fights, blood, and the crushing of evil, again and again and again. Lots of western stories were that. What makes the White Wolf series special is the dimly shamed figure of Jim-twin Allen, self-obligated to defend those unable to defend themselves, while he is forever and eternally hunted by the law. A romantic hero avid for pie.

"The Killer and the Kid" (July 1927): The son of an old couple has been framed for murder. The real killers have forced a neighbor woman to perjure herself and swear the boy did it. Allen forces her to confess in court, then shoots down the gang members responsible in a long rage of gunfire. Four men dead in the dirt of a cowtown street. And Jim Allen slowly leads his grays out of town, through the gray mists of powder smoke, toward other savage adventures.

After about five years of such stories, the series took another twist. The governor of an unidentified state, Texas, perhaps, or Arizona, appoints Jim Allen captain of an irregular group of rangers. This unorthodox step is because the governor has lost control of a three-county area to a massive and entrenched gang. These people control the courts and the sheriffs; they have deep political ties in the state capital. Those they can't terrorize, they kill. Through the three counties, the gang runs dope, steals cattle, steals entire ranches, operates with the impunity of the Mafia.

The governor provided Allen immunity in the state by first having him arrested, then released on bail. Thus protected from the law by the law, Allen was then made a Ranger captain. To fight the gang, Allen collected about twenty known outlaws and gunmen. Together with ten regular rangers, this group, The Outlaw Legion, will pit itself against the gang until Dunning's death terminated the series.

"With His Own Weapons" (March 15, 1931): One of the Wolf's men, named Silent, has taken to rustling a few cattle to support the extravagant tastes of his wife. Jim catches him in the act, gives him the chance to reform. Silent tries it one more time and is caught. But Jim has been tracking down a bunch of drug smugglers and manages to save Silent's neck from a rope by blaming the rustling on them. Might as well. The smugglers have all been shot dead anyway.

The May 1, 1931, "Outlaws Ain't So Bad," involves conflict between a crooked sheriff and an ex-outlaw now married and reformed. The sheriff merrily crimes along, shooting Jim-twin with a shotgun, framing the ex-outlaw, and doing a little stealing and murder on his own. Then he stirs up a lynch mob. But Jim Allen has been playing tricks with evidence, himself, and the sheriff ends as the lynch party's guest of honor.

"Hangman's Hickory" (July 1, 1932) introduces a Citizen's Committee that feels Jim Allen is not moving against the gang fast enough. They collect some ropes to speed matters up, not realizing that the sheriff is a double-faced trickster and charter member of the gang. From there matters escalate to murder. For which Jim-twin is promptly framed. At this point, Jack-twin comes riding down to give Jim a hand and is nearly hung. By a last second exercise of reason, Jim demonstrates to the Committee how wrong they were and the sheriff gets hung instead. It keeps happening to sheriffs in this series.

During the activities of "Once An Outlaw" (August 15, 1932), Jim nearly loses control of the Legion, a hard-headed and unruly bunch. They wear little golden wolves on their collar to give them team spirit, but they are too quarrelsome to be disciplined and too independent to be organized. The Confederate States had much the same problem. During the story, Jim must control his men and, at the same time, clean up the reputation of Bad Bill who has got himself suspected of rustling, murder, and several more serious crimes.

The final White Wolf story to appear in *Complete Stories* was "Hard To Hit" (September 24, 1934). Three years later, the magazine, itself, was terminated, having lasted slightly more than a decade.

The magazine had begun as *Complete Story Magazine* (July 1924) and continued for somewhat more than two years before being retitled *Complete Stories* (November 1926).[4] In early 1931, the magazine received a mild retitling to *Street & Smith's Complete Stories.* Late that year it had the equivalent of a small stroke and for about seven months was called *The Popular Complete Stories* before reverting to the *Street & Smith's Complete Stories* once more.

Through all these title changes, the magazine remained much the same — a concentrated explosion of action, adventure, mystery, and a large amount of western fiction. Featured were such artists as Jerome Rozen and Modest Stein, and such writers as Dunning, C.S. Montayne, Oscar Schisgall, Bertrand Sinclair, Raoul Whitfield, Frederick C. Davis, J. Allan Dunn, Anthony Rud, H. Bedford Jones, and some dozens of others, less celebrated, who have sunk silently into the sub-soil.

The final issue of *Complete Stories* seems to have been September/October 1937. By then, the White Wolf series had begun again in Street & Smith's *Wild West Weekly*, a magazine of odd history and an incredible number of issues.

Originally a dime novel, first issued by Frank Tousey in 1902, the *Wild West Weekly* ran for 1294 issues through August 5, 1927. Sold to Street & Smith, it was converted to a pulp magazine and continued through a reeling dazzle of series characters until 1943, the final issue being dated November.

*Wild West Weekly* fiction was a single seamless strand of captures, escapes, desperate struggles, and nearly continuous shooting, fighting, riding. It was aimed at readers somewhat younger than those believed to be buying Street & Smith's companion magazine, *Western Story*, in which so much of Max Brand's work appeared. The White Wolf series in *Wild West Weekly* had a distinctly different texture than those of *Complete Stories*. The tone of the magazine was different, certainly. But also Walker Tompkins' touch differed from that of Hal Denning.

*Walker Tompkins*: "Hal Dunning was a real author.... After his death, Editor Oliphant had me take over the character, paying a royalty to Dunning's widow, resulting in the White Wolf being reduced to a thud and blunder hero from 1938 to 1943." (13)

Thompkins did a far better job with the character than that, but all his published remarks carry a tinge of lightly humorous self-depreciation. Walker A. Thompkins (1909-1988) was born on a small ranch in the Washington Yakima Valley. After working as a newspaper reporter from the age of fourteen, he began his twenty-seven year career in western pulp fiction by accident. "Chancing to read a Western pulp magazine some hobo had tossed out of a box car, I said to myself, 'Hell, I can do that good!' So I batted out an 11,500-word cowboy story in four afternoons." (13)

On second submission, the novelette, featuring the cowboy-detective Tommy Rockford, sold to *Wild West Weekly*. Tompkins' professional writing career, and Rockford's strenuous life, were mutually under way. In addition to writing and selling a weekly story, he sold a novel before entering the University of Washington. After a year, he dropped out to write fiction until he joined the Army during World War II. He served as a correspondent and writer at General Eisenhower's Headquarters in England. After the war, Tompkins returned to pulp western fiction until the final magazines folded. Later he wrote "lending-library novels in hard cover," and western television scripts for Hollywood, before turning to biographies, histories of corporations, a daily radio program ("Santa Barbara Yesterdays"), and works on California regional history.

In Tompkins' hands, the White Wolf series streamlined and accelerated. Peril comes immediately and every page introduces new danger. The hero, never in control, reels wildly along the lip of an abyss that crumbles under his feet.

Crouched at bay behind the bullet-pitted boulder where the Nevada posse had held him since sunrise, Jim-twin Allen rubbed exploring fingertips around the double cartridge belts which looped his wiry body.

"Down to my last two loads," the outlaw clipped tonelessly through cracked and blood-threaded lips. "An' a plumb slim chance o' crashin' in on 'em, at that" (9).

The Wolf is less boyish now, harder and less engaging. His clothing is less ragged. His pie-eating is diminished. No longer does he stalk stiff-legged to battle, eyes flaring yellow, a human wolf. The reward on his head has shrunk to $5,000. His wolf dog has vanished into the limbo of lost pets, and his grays are now named Princess and Gray Comet.

A few old characters remain from the former series. His old friend, Toothpick Jarrick, blabber-mouthed as ever, wanders in and out. And that skinny shred of a girl, Snippets Macpherson, who once cared for Jim-twin when he was exhausted and hurt, has grown into a lean woman of twenty. The lights in her eyes are for the Wolf.

He feels warmth toward her, too. But what is a hunted man to do? Love and marriage is not for him. He must ride on, heart breaking, head bowed, through the deadly turmoils of his life.

"Fangs of the White Wolf" (November 19, 1938) began the *Wild West Weekly* series. Slightly more than twenty stories would appear, the final one, "Trigger Twins" (June 19, 1943), being published a few months before the magazine terminated.

In "The White Wolf Leads a Pack" (December 17, 1938), the leader of a gang of killers claims to be White Wolf and does dreadful things. A posse chasing them blunders into the real Jim-twin, disguised as a prospector. He leads the posse to the gang, which get chopped up.

But the false White Wolf escapes. After Jim-twin's real identity is accidentally revealed, he is forced to flee, unarmed, and capture the White Wolf imposter with his bare hands. Which he manages to do—and escapes with the sheriff's blessing.

"White Wolf Reaches Cactus Country" (July 1, 1939). Jim-twin is captured by a Nevada posse. But then a pair of hardcase riders, hot for the $5,000 reward on Allen's head, steals him from the sheriff. They leave the sheriff dangling by his hands from a tree. Handcuffed, weaponless, alone, Jim-twin must escape, punish the evil, and save the sheriff. Which he does, no wonder being beyond his abilities.

In an afternote to this story, written in the strange patois reserved for such communications, the Wild West Weekly editor remarked:

That's the sort of hombre Jim-twin Allen is—fair an' square to friend an' enemy alike, an' not afraid to back any play Fate hands out. Yuh'll meet up with 'im ag'in soon in Street & Smith's Wild West Weekly. (34)

In "Hot-Lead Homecoming" (October 31, 1942), White Wolf returns to the Macpherson Bar L L Bar ranch, to celebrate the birthday of the adorable Snippets. There he is taken prisoner by that crooked lawyer, Judge Calhoun, who has bought up the ranch mortgage and pitched the Macphersons out. The Wolf is jailed. And promptly blamed for the theft of $10,000 from a stage and murder of the drivers and a passenger.

To the amazement of all, White Wolf confesses to these crimes. He offers to reveal where he buried the loot. But it's all a trick to escape, as the sheriff soon discovers. Before long, White Wolf has ferreted out the real thief and killer. Judge Calhoun obviously. The sheriff gets a charge of buckshot in the legs. The judge gets twelve .45 slugs in his chest. The Macphersons get back their ranch. And Jim-twin gets long gone.

How satisfactory it all is, this extended ballet of danger and violence. How sleekly the formula works. How powerfully the narrative drags you along, gold flecks of action glinting in the bright flow of the prose. And the action so exhausting that you need to rest after reading. Hal Dunning's original character, the goblin Jim Allen, half boy, half demon, has faded out. A more familiar figure remains, the outlaw hero, admired by a few, hunted by the world, whose personal goodness and decency brings admiration to the sheriff's eyes by the end of the story.

Society created these outlaws. By malice, as in the Night Wind series. By oppression, as in the Zorro adventures. By altruism, as the Jailbirds' series would have it. Society is relentless. It punishes with mechanical fervor, dreadful to face. Nor can this punishment be predicted, for an accident, a single misunderstanding, an action, however well justified, is sufficient to distort a man's life. White Wolf kills a villain; for this he is savagely punished, according to the logic dictating these fictional matters. Forever afterward he ranges outside society, forever pursued, forever peering from sleety darkness toward the hearth-glow forbidden him.

Not all criminal heroes are created by accident. It was will, not misadventure, that made criminals of such disparate figures as Ed Jenkins and Lester Leith. Both chose the delights of a life in crime. Jenkins immediately regretted his choice; as usual, it was too late, then. Leith never repented. He had no need. His life was joy, glowing total joy, and he had nothing whatsoever to regret.

These gentlemen, both creations of Erle Stanley Gardner, are unique. Their rather different stories sing like high bells through the halls of adventure fiction.

## Chapter Three
## Crime by Gardner

Erle Stanley Gardner (1889-1970) was a lawyer, writer, professional maverick, outdoorsman, traveler, and a phenomenon as hard to capture as the sky. Largely self-trained in law, he was admitted to the California bar at the age of twenty-one. Thereafter, he became the official lawyer for the Chinese community of a small California town— the echoes of that experience ringing through much of his published fiction. After his marriage in 1912, he briefly practiced law in Ventura, California, then spent four years as salesman. When the Depression of 1920 wiped out his company, Gardner returned to the law and, on the side, during 1921, began writing fiction for the pulp magazines then beginning to appear in astonishing numbers. After two initial sales to *Breezy Stories* and an extended struggle to learn the basics of commercial fiction writing, Gardner began selling to *Black Mask*, then *Droll Stories, Mystery Magazine, Top Notch, Triple X, Brief Stories,* and *Argosy.* Later came pieces in the *Smart Set, Sunset Magazine, Short Stories, Detective Fiction Weekly, Clues, Dime Detective,* and a reeling array of other detective, gangster, and western action magazines.

"Under my own name, and a dozen others," he remarked, "I [averaged] a full novelette every third day.... For ten years I kept up this pace of a hundred thousand words a month."[1]

The writing took place at night, for he was a working lawyer by day. Although inconvenienced by a need to sleep at least three hours a night, he poured out millions of words, hundreds of stories, dozens of series characters for the magazines. In 1933 he created Perry Mason, shaping the character from an earlier lawyer-detective he had used in *Black Mask.* Mason rapidly rose to the status of an American myth figure, appearing in moving pictures, radio programs, television, and about eighty-five novels and short stories.

During his later life, Gardner relinquished the daily practice of law. As the pulp magazines slowly shriveled, he continued to pour out novels. He found himself in the slick pages of the *Saturday Evening Post,* began to travel and to publish books on his experiences. His ferocious energy continued unabated, writing, arguing, directing the destinies of his television production company, adding to the properties he owned, and marrying for the second time, two years before his death from cancer. He had enjoyed a richly realized life.

It is likely that Gardner created more series characters than any other writer for the pulps. For each magazine, he created special characters, providing them with elaborately devised backgrounds and remarkable talents. For *Top Notch*, Speed Dash, the human fly; For *Black Mask*, Bob Larkin, a juggler in the action detection business, and Black Barr, a two-gun western avenger, and Ed Jenkins, the Phantom Crook; for *Double Detective*, Ed Migrane, who gave crooks headaches; for *Argosy*, El Paisano, the White Rings, Bob Zane of the Whispering Sands series, and Major Brane; for *Gang World*, Paul Pry, an adventurer preying on criminals; for *Detective Fiction Weekly*, Lester Leith, Senor Lobo, Sidney Zoom, and the Patent Leather kid; for *Detective Action Stories*, Rex Kane and Mr. Manse; for *Dime Detective*, Dane Skarle and the firm of Small, Weston and Burke. And others for *West, Clue, Brief Stories, Short Stories, All Detective*. Numerous others. Each character was outrageous, fantastic, endlessly inventive, moved through stories astonishing in their complexity.

Many characters appeared only briefly, two stories or five, then vanished without explanation. With so many characters demanding attention, the less popular or, perhaps, the less interesting to the author, quietly disappeared. Other characters returned repeatedly, amassing enormous runs. Of these, a number floated lightly on the wrong side of the law. Criminals, in the technical sense of the word, certainly. But criminals of decency, wit, high personal integrity. Call them instead adventurers, somehow elevated from the normal laws that bind lesser spirits to society's rules. Supremely free agents, these characters blithely let off guns, cracked safes, astounded the police. Although exceptionally casual of the law's commandments, each character lived by moral codes as inflexible as iron underwear. Their personal standards of honor redeemed their transgressions, which were frequent and spectacular.

One of the most illustrious names of this group is Edward Gordon Jenkins, better known to readers of the *Black Mask* as Ed Jenkins, the Phantom Crook. For thirty-six years (published time), Jenkins sought a life of quiet obscurity. What he got was altogether different:

> I went through the door and took the steps two at a time. I was halfway up the first flight when a gun roared from a top floor. I heard the scream of a woman and the roar of other guns, the stamp of feet, shouting....
> I looked up in time to see a man come plunging down the stairs, his face white, his hair disheveled, his eyes wide and staring. There was a gun in his hand. He flung up the gun, stared for a moment over the sights with glassy eyes, and pulled the trigger.

I ducked as the gun roared.... My hands caught him around the knees and I flung him, with every ounce of strength that I had, over to one side. His head caught on the side of the banister, the gun flew from his hand, and he lay still. (Gardner, "Red Jade" 27-28)

How the guns do talk in these adventures. The action begins immediately, urgently, progresses through intricate double and triple crosses, with every man a liar and nearly every woman. And at the end, death, that great cleanser, purges the final paragraphs with a scald of gunfire:

... it was a searing blast of gunfire which came from the interior of the office and caught Dorcus full in the forehead. I saw his head jerk back, as though some invisible sledge-hammer had smashed him squarely in the face. Then there was another burst of fire. Once more, the head jerked. [His]... great torso thudded to the floor with a jar that shook the walls. (Gardner, "Cop Killers" 70)

The survivor of these savage episodes, Ed Jenkins, enjoyed one of the longest runs of any popular magazine character. His series continued for eighteen years and seventy-three stories, all but one published in *Black Mask*. Jenkins' first adventure, "Beyond the Law," appeared in January 1925, in the heart of Prohibition and the gangster era, the year of the Charleston, cloche hats, and the Scopes monkey trial in Tennessee. Jenkins' final adventure in *Black Mask*, "The Gong of Vengeance," appeared September 1943, in the heart of the Second World War, two years before atom bombs struck Japan. There followed an absence of eighteen years, before Jenkins made a final appearance in "The Blond in Lower Six," a novel published in the September 1961 *Argosy*. By then Kennedy was president and the Russians had placed a man in orbit.

From Prohibition to space flight. It was an extraordinary career for a character who was, to begin with:

a crook that's known to three nations, wanted in six states, but enjoying immunity from extradition from the State of California because of a technicality.... I'm not a 'fugitive from justice' within the meaning of the law, but every crook in the state feels licensed to pick on me, and the cops are just waiting to get a chance to hang something on me. (Gardner, *Laugh That Off* 49)

The Phantom Crook he was called. The name was given to him in a Sunday supplement article, which also published his picture, mentioned his dog Bobo, and lingered over the fact that he glided through the hands of the police like a phantom. Thus the name. Jenkins was sheepishly proud of the article, although it cost him his valuable anonymity and an incredible amount of trouble over the years.

His adventures are written in the first person. Slangy, colloquial, self-consciously tough, he has a low tolerance for cant or liars. "I've got a brittle disposition," he remarks. What infuriates him is to be double crossed or, worst of all, to have someone shift blame for a crime to The Phantom Crook:

I was just beginning to get that cold rage that comes up within me at intervals when someone is trying to pull a dirty double cross. For two pins he would have been my meat right then. Not murder, for I don't care for murder, but I'd match wits with him, outguess him at the finish, and leave him in the tolls of the law, fast in the trap he'd laid for me. (Gardner, "Laugh That Off" 72)

There, in miniature, is a summary of the Ed Jenkins' stories. He is drawn into a situation by someone planning to use his skills, then double cross him. Too wary to accept any proposition at face value, Jenkins checks, discovers much of the true situation. Most usually this involves a young woman in great trouble. Her problems wind tightly with those of Jenkins, for by this time, he has worked out why a double cross was planned. He strikes first, causing vast consternation. Then an unforeseeable accident threatens his plans. He must plunge into intense personal peril before the girl is saved and evil shattered.

These proceedings are symphonies of violence. The stories bristle with hard physical danger often laced with sadism. But Jenkins floats through all savageries without being contaminated by them. His method of operation is not that of the usual hardboiled herowhich is to say, swift gun action and the ability to absorb physical punishment. Jenkins does not carry a gun. And, while he can endure pain when he must, he is so intellectually agile that this uncomfortable circumstance is rarely forced on him.

He is extraordinarily quick. This characteristic he shares in common with such other of Erle Stanley Gardner's series characters as Perry Mason and Lester Leith. First of all Jenkins is a thinking man. Ingenuous, careful, coolly dispassionate, he remains unconfused by the corruption and self interest of that ferocious world slashing around him.

In that world, criminality swarms. Secret contracts tie the social leader to the crooked politician. The police commissioner kisses the crime boss's fingers. The police chief belongs to the crime syndicate. Gangsters murder openly. Bribed judges deliver directed verdicts. The world is a sewer and through it evil stalks on reptilian legs:

Those people are above the law. They've corrupted the law. There isn't any punishment for them. God's asleep in heaven, or he wouldn't let them do the things they've done. (Gardner, "Promise To Pay" 102)

"Laugh That Off" (*Black Mask*, September 1926): A crooked politician devises an elaborate crime involving blackmail of the socially prominent Chadwick family and theft of a simply stunning gem the size of a Hadrosaur egg. Jenkins is brought in to crack the safe, for he is the most famous of all safecrackers—the man who can open anything. To interest Jenkins, the politician offers to negotiate a pardon for him in all those states where he is wanted. Better yet, as an extra reward, he can have as his bride, Miss Helen Chadwick, a slender little flapper in waistless dress and raspberry lipstick.

Immediately detecting the usual double cross, Jenkins moves with habitual speed. Entering the politician's house long before his scheduled appointment, he overhears the man offering to sell Helen a set of ten promissory notes. These tie her deceased father to a crooked concrete contract. (The struggle to possess these notes will spill over into half a dozen later stories.)

From this point, Jenkins invisibly joins the girl's side. For the balance of the story he dodges one frame-up after the other, while committing a wonderful series of crimes for justice—opening safes, stealing fist-sized jewels to save them from thieves, forging documents. His greatest triumph is moral: as a gentleman should, he flatly refuses to marry Helen, although that was part of the blackmail scheme. Even if she rather likes the idea. Even though they sort of become engaged through no fault of his own.

For no sooner does Helen know him than she adores him. But marriage? Appalling! Helen is too far above him. She is an aristocrat, one of the first families of San Francisco. And what is he? A notorious low-down crook. It can never be. Never!

Never turns out to be two and a half years. Helen finally manipulates him into marriage at the end of "Bracelets for Two" (February 1929).

Before taking to his heart a singularly accommodating and helpful wife, Jenkins is a solitary adventurer in the tradition of Michael Lanyard and Anthony Trent.

I'm a funny bird. I don't run with a pack and I won't play in a gang. I'm a lone wolf, and I'm my own law, my own judge and jury. I've been a legal outcast for many years and I've grown to depend on myself. If any bird tries to hang anything on me, I'm my own court of equity, my own judge. (Gardner, *Money, Marble* 100)

Being a loner, Jenkins relies on his wits, a few special skills, and a couple of useful devices. One such device, rarely used, is a walking stick containing a burglar's kit and a blade. Another gadget, used for special jobs, is a radio amplifying apparatus designed to magnify the clicks of safe tumblers as they fall into position.

On a less mechanical level, he has the assistance of Bobo, his dog, a huge, tawny animal of vague breed. More intelligent than most of the characters, Bobo performs astonishing feats of tracking and surveillance in the luminous tradition of Rin Tin Tin. The animal does everything but write and sing.

Jenkins is wonderfully proud of his pet. But Gardner soon finds that even a gifted dog impedes a story moving at near light speeds. Before long, Bobo gets shot ("Dead Men's Letters," December 1926); in the following story, "The Cat-Woman" (February 1927), he lingers in the animal hospital. He plays no role in subsequent stories.

Which is as you expect. Series heroes rarely carried more responsibilities than could they tuck into their pocket. Their rootlessness and lack of permanent emotional ties made it easy for the author to dance them through long series of violent adventures. For adventure is not tied to marriage's regular hours. Nor does the adventurous life tolerate such routine social obligations as returning a book to the library, buying a birthday card for Aunt Maunette, or appearing at the dentist's office promptly at 9:15 a.m.

Adventurers lead shallow lives, if busy ones. The reader understands these silent constraints. And, understanding, has little confidence that Bobo will survive the hospital or that Jenkins' marriage will long endure.

In addition to mechanical devices and the help of a loyal dog, Jenkins relies heavily upon disguise. It is a remarkable skill to find in a magazine of such gritty fiction as *Black Mask*. Disguise was a convention born of the dime novel era, when every detective and every criminal could instantly transform his appearance. As the dime novels faded, the convention slowly grew less acceptable. After World War I, a more skeptical wind blew. Although a few characters periodically disguised themselves in the pages of the early *Detective Story Magazine,* the convention languished until a slow revival began in mid-1920s. By the early 1930s, disguise again flared to a major convention. The Shadow, Doc Savage, The Phantom Detective, the Spider, Secret Agent X, G-8, Operator 5, The Avenger—indeed most of the single—series magazine characters—again turned to disguising themselves with little more effort than combing their hair.

Jenkins is not a disguise artist in the sense that he impersonates others. He merely wishes to obliterate his own identity. In person he seems to be rather small, wiry, and with an unusually youthful face. Upon this unassuming foundation, he uses false hair and grease paint skillfully enough to pass as an elderly man, a Chinese, or some average fellow no one would bother to notice. The Chinese disguises are the most demanding. He has learned to speak Cantonese like a native and Chinatown is one of his favorite retreats when police officials howl for his blood.

Disguise, a safe-opening kit, a trained dog, a solitary disposition, the ability to speak a Chinese dialect, a few hideouts scattered around San Francisco—these things seem little enough to shield a man from the outrage of the world. Still Jenkins made do quite successfully.

"Money, Marbles and Chalk" (November 1926) is a wild hurrah about a misplaced gold mine and a pack of murderers trying to snatch the claim from a sweet Eastern girl. Or they would snatch the claim if they could find it. Jenkins is brought in to open the safe containing the map. And so he does, but long before he is scheduled to do so. From this, he learns of the plot, the planned double-cross, and the dire need of the girl who has inherited the mine. All these are usual plot elements. As usual they flow as if bathed in hot oil.

Soon the story rages into the desert. There Jenkins faces an extended deadly struggle against thirst, a murderous gang, and a tempest of rifle bullets. But even in the blazing waste, Jenkins, the trickster supreme, cons the criminals out of $10,000 and their freedom. The girl ends up with the fortune, as is right and proper.

"The Cat-Woman" (February 1927) offers another symphony of lies and treachery. Jenkins is offered $10,000 if he will steal a necklace and kidnap a girl—with the written permission of the necklace owner and girl's guardian. Free money, obviously. To protect Jenkins, he is handed a full statement of complicity signed by the Cat-Woman herself, the girl's aunt. Unfortunately for her, Jenkins is familiar with Gardner's habit of using false confessions as a plot element. When the pretended kidnapping explodes as a calculated murder trap, Jenkins is unsurprised. The heiress works with him for the balance of the story, to the severe discomfiture of her aunt.

The following three stories are so closely linked as to constitute a form of serial. "This Way Out" (March 1927), "Come and Get It" (April), and "In Full of Account" (May) are individual stories, reasonably complete in themselves, but each a portion of the larger story of The Girl with the Mole.

We have already seen in the Dion and Laxworthy series how chains of loosely associated stories gradually flesh out a larger tale. *Black Mask* was particularly partial to this form and used it to great effect. Dashiell

Hammett, Paul Cain, Carroll John Daly, and Raoul Whitfield, among others, all wrote loosely sequential stories later polished (to varying degrees) into novels.[2]

Gardner wrote similar story groups. Much of the Ed Jenkins series consists of lightly linked stories unified by a single problem and a single villain. For some reason, these were never published as novels; only a few of the stories, themselves, have ever been reissued.

In the three-part story concerning The Girl with the Mole, Jenkins again attempts to retrieve the Chadwick papers. He had recovered these in "Laugh That Off." But they are again floating around the underworld in "This Way Out" (March 1927). The mysterious Maude Enders, the girl with a mole on the back of her hand, abducts Jenkins. She takes him to an interview with Icy-Eyes, head of San Francisco crime. This master criminal offers Jenkins $2,000 and all the Chadwick papers if he will open an impregnable safe, remove one will, and substitute another.

As you might expect, there is a hidden agenda. Witnesses of the real will are to be murdered and Jenkins framed for their killing. It doesn't happen. A criminal is murdered instead, and the killer is shotgunned instead of Jenkins. Maude helped some, her true purpose unknown. But the deft lethality of the finish is pure Jenkins.

In the following story, "Come and Get It" (April 1927), Jenkins attempts to force Icy-Eyes to disgorge those infernal papers. He hopes to do this by making a major nuisance of himself, spoiling the master criminal's crimes, one after another. Again we meet Maude, enigmatic as ever. Helen Chadwick reappears; as usual, she is being blackmailed by criminals, their hands full of her father's indiscreet papers. They demand that she sponsor a society jewelry show. Icy-Eyes plans to steal the whole show by vanishing the armored truck in which the gems are being transported. Jenkins spoils that lovely scheme and retrieves eight of the ten Chadwick papers.

In the next part, "In Full of Account" (May 1927), Icy-Eyes is out to murder Jenkins; Ed is out to recover the remaining papers. The story leaps from violence to violence, glittering with intrigue, complex deceptions, and savagery like a rising wall. Maude, The Girl with the Mole, is revealed as a police agent. Trapped in Icy-Eyes' headquarters, exposed as a spy, she is to be swabbed with acid until blind and seared. Outside an army of fierce police grip their machine guns. Inside malignant killers watch every shadow. Jenkins must slip through them all to rescue Maude and get his hands on those remaining papers.

All that's going for him is his knowledge of criminal psychology and a fake Russian crown that conceals a pair of hypodermics filled with fake poison. Little enough. But enough to end Icy-Eyes' career. Jenkins is able to save the girl, burn the papers, and get a nice sticky kiss from a policewoman. He is even permitted to stroll out through police lines, recognized but unarrested.

That truce does not last. Gardner never relents. If at story end, the police recognize the contributions of The Phantom Crook, if society people admire his qualities, if his Chinese friends honor him, if the current lady views him with passionate delight, all comes to dust. By the following story, Jenkins is again the outcast, hunted and alone.

The next story group contains six episodes, from "The Wax Dragon" (November 1927) to "Out of the Shadows" (May 1928). This describes an extended struggle against Paul Boardman, the malignant power behind city politics. Immediately (in "The Wax Dragon") there is a plot to frame and blackmail Helen, so that Boardman can get his hands on Jenkins and murder him. With some difficulty, Ed twists their plot around. As a result, a crooked police detective gets himself killed in a shotgun trap set for Jenkins. Blamed for the murder, Jenkins loses his California immunity and is now hunted by the combined civil and criminal powers of the city. Not until the coming of the Spider in 1933 will a hero be so alone and so intensely hunted.

Not only must Jenkins stay alive, but he must also protect Helen. Now allies arrive unexpectedly. While hiding out in Chinatown, disguised as a Chinese, Jenkins defends a young girl against a pair of foul-mouthed whites. (Grinning Gods" December 1927.) The girl is Ngat T'oy, "Little Sun," the pert, Americanized daughter of Soo Hoo Duck, uncrowned king of Chinatown.

Fragile, elderly, bearded, intelligent as a god, Soo Hoo Duck first appears in "The Wax Dragon." He commands the loyalty of tong killers and political factions, as well as the people of that closed community. On his finger gleams a jade ring, carved into a dragon, and this ring, the sign of Soo Hoo Duck and honored by all Chinese, eventually gravitates to Jenkins, who uses it to secure refuge when the wolves howl just behind. Both Soo Hoo Duck and Ngat T'oy will remain to the end of the series. They play important roles in the final *Argosy* novel.

Jenkins is able to earn their lasting gratitude during "Snow Bird" (April 1928). Boardman, the crooked politician, and Mansfield, a crooked cop, come to Soo Hoo Duck to demand a heavy political donation and the Chinese votes—for they have papers that would cause Ngat T'oy's immediate deportation. Jenkins must crack the police commissioner's safe to destroy those papers and collect the information that will wreck Boardman's bid for re-election.

Jenkins' struggle with Boardman continues to "Out of the Shadows" (May 1928). No rest is granted the weary series hero.

Immediately begins a desperate, three-part battle with The King of Bootleggers, Big Bill Delano, January through March, 1929. The plot, convoluted nearly beyond recounting, involves the repeated thefts of a diamond necklace. Somehow or other, Helen Chadwick is mixed up in the stealings, killings, and violence stamping bloodily across San Francisco. Jenkins has his hands full keeping both of them alive. At the end of the final story, "Bracelets for Two," he marries Helen.

It lasts nine stories. Marriage caused immediate trouble for Gardner, who learned that such homey details as Helen ironing her dress in the same room with Ed, were not for the squeamish readers of *Black Mask*.

"So," wrote Gardner, "I got mad and killed Helen off. It was a horrible thing to do. My daughter wouldn't speak to me for a month. Readers wrote in quivering with indignation."[3]

It happened in "Big Shot" (July 1930). Machine gunners ambush Jenkins. To save him, Helen hurls herself in front of the bullets and so dies. Jenkins ends up in the hospital, has a breakdown, and is in terrible shape for a while. Then those responsible end up in even worse shape.

The adventures continue, violent as a blast furnace, until the Depression wipes Jenkins out. Escaping from pressures of the police and the underworld, he slips away to the desert. There he creates the new identity of Bob Sabin, a tough private detective who knows more than he says. Sabin is Jenkins with sun tan and mustache.

As Sabin, Jenkins faces all the usual violence, peril, and murderous intrigue. "The Hour of the Rat" (February 1933) tells how crooks learn of a murder personally planned by a big crime boss. They come to Sabin, asking for help to shake the boss down. But the boss smells betrayal and promptly kills one of the conspirators. Since there is a dope connection, Jenkins/Sabin turns to Hoo Soo Duck and Ngat T'oy for help, only to learn that they are in peril from the crime boss. With not much difficulty, Jenkins arranges that the boss is convicted of murder; with somewhat more difficulty, he saves Hoo Soo Duck's life.

By the end of the story, it is evident that Ngat T'oy is in love with Jenkins. Behind her expressionless Chinese face and her slangy Americanized sauciness pounds an adoring heart. And perhaps Jenkins is not insensitive to her charms.

But the story is told in the first person. Any affection Jenkins might feel is ruthlessly ripped from the prose. He would march barefoot through scorpions to help her. But his private feelings are not permitted on the page.

Nor could they be. Bad enough that he was once saddled with a wife—an intelligent, competent, adorable, wealthy wife. All those qualities could not save her from the doom that regularly visits wives and sweethearts of pulp magazine series characters. Men must suffer;

women must die. Not for long can the hero remain married and responsible to someone other than himself. There are safes to crack, gunmen to outwit, death traps to dodge, crooked lawyers and politicians to destroy. To do this requires more time than any marriage can tolerate.

Worse even than being married is to contract an inter-racial marriage. A minor character might do so, providing that he ends up badly. But no major series character may do so. Doc Savage will never marry Princess Monja. Ed Jenkins will never marry an exquisitely lovely, highly Americanized Chinese woman. She is permitted to love him. At the end of "The Blond in Lower Six" (*Argosy*, September 1961) she cries: "Oh, Ed. Oh, my *darling!*"

Women are permitted weakness.

As for men:

It is not well that a woman should mention the name of The Phantom Crook in her sleep. Our ways are different. Hers is the way of light and life and laughter. My feet take me through the dark alleys. I travel in the ways of stealth. Better to let her go her own way that to encourage her eyes to see the dark shadows of life. (Gardner, *The Blond in Lower Ten* 143)

Still their lives twine tightly. "Red Jade" (March 1933): Ngat T'oy is framed for murder while trying to buy back a collection of ancestral jade. Jenkins must deal with a painted strumpet, a crime boss named Sinester, a double-crossing male secretary, and a clever typist who doesn't take thirty seconds to discover who Ed Jenkins really is.

In "The Weapons of a Crook" (May 1933), corrupt detective Harden knows that Sabin is really Ed Jenkins. Harden has sold out to the crime boss and demands that Jenkins set Ngat T'oy up to be killed. He should know better. Jenkins manipulates matters so that the crime boss suspects a double cross and Harden dies, along with virtually all of the cast.

A brilliant athlete loses his legs and becomes the Legless One, a murderous cripple, mounted on a wheeled platform, who plots through "A Guest of the House" (January 1934) and "Cop Killers" (March 1934). Both stories end in a brutal hail of gunfire, the first chopping up a millionaire's mansion, the second chopping down the Legless One in an ending of raw-meat violence.

The Bob Sabin disguise reappears in "Hot Cash" (November 1934), a story brimming with double and triple crosses as a crook passes as a banker, a gambling cashier faces blackmail, and $150,000 hides behind a fake wall.

Eventually all things end. Eventually, even the police discover that Bob Sabin is none other than Ed Jenkins. As the hue and cry shakes the city, Ngat T'oy asks Ed to help a dear college friend. Seems that her brother is being blackmailed. Turns out to be more than that, and the body count rises as the volume of lies increase.

The final two Ed Jenkins stories written for *Black Mask* were loosely linked novelettes: "The Incredible Mister Smith" (March 1943) and "The Gong of Vengeance" (September 1943). Jenkins has had his face changed by plastic surgery. He is called by Soo Hoo Duck to meet a mysterious man from India, and the abyss of violence opens again. Promptly a jealous man ends up dead in a girl's apartment, and Ed must open an impregnable safe while a gun points at his head. Without much difficulty, he outwits the gunman. Well concealed behind all these merry goings-on is a Japanese scheme to debase United States' currency. Ngat T'oy spends most of the story locked up in the trunk of Ed's car—to her infinite disgust.

The final story takes care of the Japanese threat. Ed Jenkins left *Black Mask* and was heard from no more. Or not until the short novel, "The Blond in Lower Six" (*Argosy*, September 1961), eighteen years later. This wildly complicated adventure begins with a young woman's death in a Pullman car, moves to grand larceny, switched identities between two women, a frantic search for a missing diary, the drugging of Ngat T'oy, and an elaborate code revealing where the Japanese are constructing major naval vessels. Jenkins is in top form, not having aged at all. And so the series closes in mid-stride. For all we know, Jenkins still glides San Francisco streets, dazzling police and crooks alike, and watching Ngat T'oy with discreet, admiring eyes.

Gardner had begun his impressive group of series characters with Bob Larkin (the juggler armed with a billiard cue, who first appeared in the September 1924 *Black Mask*). The following year introduced Ed Jenkins, also in *Black Mask*, and Speed Dash, the human fly with a photographic memory, in *Top Notch*, February 1, 1925.

His fourth series character was Black Barr, as idiosyncratic as any of the others. Barr's adventures, all appearing in *Black Mask*, extended over a seven-story series, beginning November 1925 ("The Girl Goes with Me"), and ending in 1928.

If brief, the series glowed white with violence. It included rousing gun fights in western barrooms and desert shanties, desperate rides through the sagebrush, and a choice collection of two-gun killers, plotting rancher owners, tough Mexicans and Chinese, and distressed women. All elements would have been suitable for a Hopalong Cassidy, Hashknife Hartley, or White Wolf adventure.

For the Black Barr stories are wild west cowboy adventures with all cliches intact. Except that they occur not in 1880 but during Prohibition.

Automobiles are driven instead of stagecoaches. Airplanes and typewriters are commonplace. All else is western kitsch.

Admittedly it is hard to remember this. Once into the story, the familiar western fable surrounds us with its usual timeless embrace. Barr, as might be supposed, is the familiar outlaw hero, drifting from place to place, correcting evil with .45 caliber enthusiasm. Although he is a man killer with a price on his head, peace shines silver in his heart. Even happiness might be his, if only people would let him alone and stop oppressing the decent, honest, and helpless.

*Barr:* "I have the reputation of being a killer. That is a curse. But I also have the reputation of going out of my way to help the weak against the strong, and that reputation I prize more dearly than my life...." (Gardner, "Curse of the Killers" 96)

Another of Gardner's highly intelligent, driven heroes, Barr once attended an Eastern college and now travels with books bulging his saddle bags. He dresses in black—hat, coat, and angora chaps—and rides a black horse. By choice, he sleeps outdoors, deep in the desert. Towns are too dangerous. In this hyper-kinetic world, as in the world of Ed Jenkins, danger hides everywhere, fangs slimed with venom.

Barr, himself, is thoroughly dangerous. Rage rises easily in him. "I'm getting tired of someone around here," he remarks, in a crowded barroom. "If it's you, this is your warning." He hardly needs to speak. When the urge to kill grips him, his lips begin to writhe and twitch, contorting his mouth into a horrific smile. This change he feels. Sometimes he attempts to control it, without notable success. It is his mark of Cain.

Along the border, he is known as The Executioner of Fate. A woman tells him, the Mexicans "think that you stand for justice. They think that when some man gets too powerful and wicked, Fate sends you along to adjust matters" (Gardner, "Curse of the Killers" 88).

As the convention dictates, Barr is a man alone. Ed Jenkins denied himself the delights of Ngat T'oy because his presence would be a constant danger to her. Barr denies himself all women, for "I am Black Barr, the killer, and the love of a good woman is not for me."

In spite of this constraint, he meets a number of loving young women who do admire him so, another echo from the Ed Jenkins series. Most of these young woman are having severe problems holding on to their ranches. As in "The Devil's Deputy" (*Black Mask*, September 1928). Wealthy, greedy criminals threaten to gulp down the girl's ranch. The story is violent and absorbing, tainted by no discernible scrap of the law's presence. The villains cheat, smirk, lie, stack the deck. They are the dregs of a poisoned cup. At length Barr, aided by the girl's Chinese cook (the "Deputy" of the piece), slaughters five of them and leaves the world a milder place.

"Curse of the Killers" (November 1928 and the last of the series) offers another girl, another murdered father, another ranch desired by the unprincipled, and a two-gun killer deadly as an asp. A substitute heiress complicates matters. Rather swiftly Barr deduces the plot against the girl. After dodging a murder trap in a saloon, he confronts a vulgar woman who fails to seduce him, with words or anything else. Then off to save the girl. Then away on a mad gallop to save the ranch. The girl turns out to be as good a shot as Barr and the two-gun killer dies at her hands, for a change.

But in spite of her manifest eagerness to have a man about the ranch, and Barr's intense interest in her, he backs away. For him happiness can never be:

Because I am a killer I am forced to keep drifting, ever homeless, ever wandering through the waste spaces of the silent deserts. (Gardner 96)

And so, amid clouds of purple bathos, Barr drifts away, never looking back to the ideal woman mourning behind. As far as is known, he was seen no more. Which is rather a shame. From first to last, except for some oddly elliptical dialogue, it was a high-voltage series.

No more than five months after the last Black Barr story, Gardner published "The Painted Decoy" in the February 25, 1929, *Detective Fiction Weekly.* So began the extended career of Lester Leith, gentleman trickster, part detective, part confidence man, who preyed exclusively upon criminals. In doing so, he caused enormous mental anguish to the police and particularly to Sergeant Ackley, that most confounded of policemen.

Of all the characters Gardner created, Leith is still remembered with the most affection, more warmly even than Perry Mason. Gloriously witty, devious, and with an utterly fantastic imagination, Leith was a triumph then and remains a figure to dazzle today's reader.

Certainly Mason has enjoyed more acclaim and considerably more visibility than Leith. Likely that was inevitable. The Leith series contains a single basic situation, a single joke from which it hardly deviates. It was admittedly a joke so embellished, so varied with fertility of invention, that readers never seemed to weary.

Whether that situation was original, or borrowed, or suggested by the editor of *Detective Fiction Weekly* is not known. The core idea is nearly identical to that of the X. Crook series, although the working out is quite different.

The X. Crook stories, by English author J. Jefferson Farjeon, appeared in *Flynn's* during the mid-1925s.⁴ As the astute reader has already grasped, X. Crook is the pseudonym for a reformed criminal, last name never given, who has set up in the private investigator business. Scotland Yard does not believe that he has reformed. Feeling that he is too dangerous not to be watched, they plant Detective Edgar Jones as Crook's butler. Jones goes by the name of William Thomas, as in Doubting Thomas. Eventually he ceases to doubt and becomes an fervent admirer of Crook.

A fragment of this situation appears in the Lester Leith stories. As "The Painted Decoy" opens, Leith, a wealthy young playboy and man-about-town lounges splendidly in his expensive apartment, listening to his valet, Scuttle, read selected crime reports from the newspaper. A pastoral scene.

But only on the surface.

Startling as it seems, Leith is actually a brilliantly clever rogue. His valet is actually a policeman, Edward H. Beaver, sent to spy on him, entrap him, snare him tight in a police web. Whatever it takes to get Leith—that will be done.

Beaver, or Scuttle, as the series better knows him, is a great hulk of a man, six foot two inches, hot eyes, hooked nose, and a long bony jaw. From his upper lip droops a huge mustache. In the first story, the mustache is a detachable fake. Subsequently it appears to be his own hair. Leith fancies that the mustache gives the valet the appearance of a reincarnated pirate and has named him Scuttle, pretending that his actual name is too difficult to remember.

Beaver detests the name Scuttle. He doesn't care for Leith either, considering him arrogant, condescending, and supercilious. Beaver can hardly wait to get Leith into a cell downtown and show him some real hard-knuckled police interrogation methods.

Meanwhile, it is his job to entrap Leith. He proceeds with a will, selecting newspaper stories of crimes involving large sums of money, wheedling Leith to look into these. He is as obvious as a cow in the bathtub.

Whenever Leith shows the slightest interest in a crime, Scuttle glides from the room, heading toward a telephone. For a huge man, he moves curiously. He never opens a door wide, but invariably cracks it partially open, then edges through, pausing to inspect the room he just left, secrecy in every movement. Once on the telephone, his report to Headquarters proceeds with all the rigmarole of a dime novel excitement: "This is Four-Five-Six-Four speaking!"

Just how the police got on Lester's track is never told. How Beaver was planted as Lester's valet is never explained. These matters, we are not meant to know. Enough that the surveillance has been underway for nearly two years. Sixty-four stories and fourteen years later, it will have continued for about three years.

Leith, of course, recognized the police plan the instant Beaver slipped through the apartment door. He finds the whole situation a colossal joke, a challenge, a stimulation, and (although the police don't recognize this) a help. For whenever Scuttle attempts to interest Leith in a crime, he passes along inside details from the police investigation. These—he explains to Leith—were told to him by a woman who dates a Headquarters detective.

These ponderous explanations, inept dodges, clumsy artifices delight Leith, who has a keen sense of the ridiculous. How mischievously he teases Scuttle. How blandly he mocks. Ever so deftly he creates mirages to buncombe the police. Surely this time they will trap him. But no. Somehow he and the loot vanish in a swirl of witty misdirection.

That is the situation. The series begins squarely in the middle of the action and, with no explanation or apology, rollicks away.

"The Painted Decoy" tells how bandits grabbed nearly twenty-thousand dollars from a bank and simply vanished. On the sidewalk outside the bank, they dropped a canvas duck decoy. Leith listens, yawns, goes to bed. Only to rise and slip from his apartment. Within an hour, he has visited the robbery site, met a girl in a leopard-skin coat, a singing blind man, and tracked the gang to their hideout. Displaying a gun (he rarely uses a gun), he proceeds to hijack a suitcase packed with ten-thousand dollars. Then the police interrupt—not unexpectedly, since Leith has neatly orchestrated their arrival. In the ensuing melee, one bandit is shot. The others are taken into custody. Leith and the girl glide away. Remarking "I don't make war on women," he gives her a handful of money and slips off to his own quiet bed.

Scuttle is highly suspicious, since Leith returned with a hand bitten during the fracas. ("I bit it during the night," Leith remarks. "Can't a man bite his own hand?")

Almost as a matter of course, the bag of stolen money has evaporated. Whatever the police suspect, nothing can be proven.

It only proves, Leith remarks, that crime "*might* pay if one...were careful to choose victims who couldn't complain of their loss. Just suppose...that some person with imagination worked out the significance of that painted decoy clew ahead of the police and robbed the robbers. Do you think they'd dare complain?"

"No, Scuttle," he adds, "one must avoid generalities. Perhaps crime does not pay in most instances, but one should avoid saying it never pays " (Gardner 494).

"A Tip from Scuttle" (March 2, 1929) involves the theft of a diamond necklace from Mrs. Follingsby, wife of the war profiteer. Her secretary has been thrown into jail for the theft. Lester promptly bails her out and demonstrates, to the irritation of the police and the Follingsbys, how the theft was managed and by whom. The trail leads to a seedy pawnbroker and his trick safe. At this point, matters get a bit cloudy. Eventually, the police work out what probably happened. But by then somebody has tied up the pawnbroker and carried away the diamond treasure.

Any series featuring a good-natured criminal also seems to feature a bad-natured policeman. To justify the hero's criminal activities, the convention is to present the police as malignant savages and the law and courts as masses of corruption. That effectively decriminalizes the hero's milder transgressions.

Since the Leith series is lightly humorous, the constant confrontation between crime and law proceeds at a much frothier level. Gardner quickly decides that Scuttle does not provide enough direct opposition. What Leith requires to set him off, as dark velvet sets off a pearl, is an aggressive, villainous policemen. Thus a new character appeared in the series—Sergeant Arthur Ackley, Beaver's superior, and the caricature of an irascible buffoon, constantly tricked, constantly inflating with purple rage.

Ackley is a thick-bodied, thick-lipped, yellow-toothed sucker of cheap cigars. He has a heavy beard. When deep in thought, his thumb nail rasps the whiskers along the edge of his jaw. Even his most fervent admirer must admit that Ackley is fairly thick-witted. Also treacherous, a grabber of credit, an abuser of subordinates, and Leith's worst enemy. Story after story, he closes in on Leith, only to take a stupendous pratfall.

As in the August 10, 1929, "It's a Pipe." Seventy-thousand dollars, being transported by automobile, has been stolen in a daring daylight robbery. The thief escaped amid a tempest of shots, none of which, Leith notes, hit anything. Then a bank clerk is found, shot dead in a young woman's rented room, a few bundles of the stolen money beside him.

Leith ponders and smokes, jabbing his forefinger through a series of smoke rings. Then he sends Scuttle out for a pipe and a cheap bag. The bag is filled with Leith's less appreciated Christmas presents. Soon, he has frightened the thief, located the bag filled with money, and substituted his own bag by cozening the clerk at the bag check counter. Thereafter he leads Ackley around by the nose. The sergeant fumbles the case away. He catches no one.

One of Leith's main problems is to locate the property he intends to hijack. A lesser being might fumble blindly and end up working for a living. Leith proceeds otherwise. His method is to raise an unholy uproar—a police raid, a supposed fire, a claim to have already recovered the hidden loot. Alarmed, the real thief darts off to check the safety of his booty. Right behind him glides Leith. No sooner is the hiding place revealed, than it is pillaged. And there go the fruits of crime.

This particular scene happens often during the Leith series. Although differently orchestrated each time, it is the same process: Lester flushes the bird, follows its flight, robs the nest. It is one of the running conventions of the stories, as much a permanent feature as Ackley's consistent defeats.

By May 3, 1930, "Both Ends Against the Middle," the explosive sergeant, now fully in charge of the Leith problem, has installed a dictophone in our hero's apartment and brought in a battery of secretaries to copy down everything said. It does him no good. Lester starts a collection agency. Aided by a mahogany desk, a brass cuspidor, a blonde secretary, and a large bottle of cheap perfume, he manages to make sense out of an arson fire and settle an outstanding fire insurance case for fifteen thousand dollars. Ackley gets profoundly humiliated before the press.

The subject of the stories, Lester Leith, is a tall young man, lean and well built, with slate-gray eyes the color of tarnished silver. His forehead is wide, his intelligence acute. His mind moves at about the speed of light. A member of the Colonial Club, the Hudson Heights Golf Club, and other places where the wealthy dally, he is well known in monied society. A bachelor, he is an asset to every dance. His taste in clothing is as superb as his taste in valets is peculiar.

After some years in the apartment, he moves to a pent house. There he lives in placid luxury, incessantly smoking, planning ever new astonishments for Scuttle and Ackley and new punishment for the criminals of the world.

Part of the punishment is to strip them of their loot. You best deter crime, according to Leith's rather oblique reasoning, by removing the profit. Precisely what the mysterious hijacker does—the hijacker that Sergeant Ackley, for some loutish reason, thinks is Leith.

Not that Lester disagrees with the work of that unknown hijacker:

*Leith*: "As I understand it, the criminals who have been victimized by this hijacker are men who have flaunted their crimes in the faces of the police and got away with it.... Then along comes this mysterious hijacker, solves the crime where the police have failed, locates the criminals, and levies a hundred-per-cent fine by relieving him of his ill-gotten gains. That, Scuttle, I claim is a distinct service to society." (Gardner, "It's A Pipe" 464)

Once the criminal has been adequately punished, Lester withholds ten to twenty percent of the take for collection expenses and donates the rest to charities—among them the home for the aged and the fund for widows and orphans of policemen and firemen killed in line of duty.

These charities are known to the police. But after an unbroken string of failures to catch the hijacker and an equally unbroken string of humiliations at Leith's hands, Ackley is in no mood to be philosophical about service to society. In a contemptuous gesture, Ackley sends a burlesque dancer to confer with Leith. Her brother has been arrested for stealing a diamond necklace. The police are certain he's the thief. But he didn't do it. ("Cold Clews," January 24, 1931.)

Lester hears her story, leans back, and begins to think, abstractedly puffing one smoke ring through another. Occasionally he nods, "little brief nods as though he were checking off a complicated campaign in his mind."

Finally he sends Scuttle off to buy a fantastic mixture of stuff: an iron stove, twenty-eight dice, a vise, drill, emery wheel, a bulldog, and some silk cord. He is also to buy a car that the owner believes to be hoodooed. As a final distraction, Lester announces that he is becoming an automobile salesman.

He makes an exceptional salesman, charging the customer less than the car is worth, then making up the difference to the dealer. The dealer thinks Leith is crazy. Not only does he wreck the car that he was trying to sell, but now he wanders all over town, trying to peddle that car's shattered gasoline tank.

Scuttle and Ackley think he's finally tumbled over the edge.

Soon enough, they learn the hard sense of these arrangements. The burlesque dancer's brother is innocent. The real thief is identified. The stolen diamond necklace has been hidden in an automobile gas tank. Or is it a necklace made of dice? And if so, where on earth did the diamond necklace get to? Lester claims to know. For seven thousand dollars, he will tell the owner exactly where to find the necklace. And to the fury of Sergeant Ackley, he does so, blithely extracting himself from arrest as if nothing in the world were easier.

(To clarify a little: the bulldog guarded the car while the necklace was in the gasoline tank. The stove, stored in the rear of the car, was used to smash the gas tank so that it had to be replaced. And the rest of the stuff was used to make a necklace of dice to slip into the new gasoline tank and trick the real criminal.... It all makes lunatic sense, after it's explained.)

By this time, the stories have developed openings as charming, in their way, as those more celebrated first scenes of the Sherlock Holmes stories.

Scuttle pesters Leith to read about a new crime. Leith demurs: his interest in crime is only a hobby and he has lost interest, what with Ackley's constant accusations and suspicions.

But eventually Lester agrees to listen as Scuttle reads a newspaper account of the crime.

Concentrated thinking follows, one smoke ring tumbling after another.

Finally, Lester announces that he has decided to go into business— unexpected, frivolous business. Rarely does he suggest that he plans to look into that interesting crime Scuttle seems so taken with.

Instead he asks Scuttle to rush out and buy—things. Odd, strange things of no possible application to the problem at hand:

—boxes of chocolates, a blowtorch, powdered alum, quick-drying cement, firecrackers, a few fine pearls, and a police siren. ("The Candy Kid," March 14, 1931)

—$20,000 in gold coin, a silk bag, a nugget of pure gold, a magnet, a dozen of so lunch boxes, a pint of whiskey. And also hire a blonde. ("The Gold Magnet," (September 26, 1931)

—every fireman's costume in town, a red-headed woman with a bad temper who is a trained boxer, and a gasoline-soaked hundred dollar bill. ("False Alarm," November 5, 1932)

—a speed boat, two bird cages, fourteen canaries, a powder puff, some lamp black, passkeys, a magnifying glass, a new automobile, and six suitcases. Also a tape measure and one-hundred feet of rope ("Crooks' Vacation," July 8, 1933).

Somehow these madly assorted items find use. You marvel that Gardner could possibly string them to coherent purpose. Once or twice, he does not quite manage, as in "Crooks' Vacation," when Leith finds no real use for all those canaries. More usually, the miracle happens. Suitcases, gum-chewing blonds, cabbages, mice, and unabridged dictionaries glide effortlessly together and a wonderful shining fills the prose.

Wonderful scenes fill the prose, too, as the story leaps joyously to comedy and outright farce:

—Leith checks into a hospital, a private nurse at his side, and proceeds to throw a birthday party that is as lavish as a Roman festival ("Hot Cash," May 23, 1931).

—Leith, Scuttle, and a blond policewoman drive through the night, handing bums lunch buckets packed with gold coins ("The Gold Magnet," September 26, 1931).

—A red-headed woman boxer, of brittle temper, is harassed once too often and pounds the fool out of Scuttle and Ackley ("False Alarm," November 5, 1932).

—Leith hires a dozen out-of-work burlesque strippers and sets them performing their art at unshaded bedroom windows in an apartment house ("Planted Planets," December 1938).

—Six 1936 Fords roar wildly through town. In each Ford sit a costumed hula dancer and a cowboy wearing an colossal sombrero. Behind them race swarms of frenzied police ("The Seven Sinister Sombreros," February 1939).

Through the pages stroll a succession of beautiful women. They are not heroines, not exactly. They are out-of-work burlesque strippers and fan-dancers. Down-on-their-luck secretaries. Hardboiled typists champing wads of chewing gum. All of a pattern, these women are tough, strong-minded, worldly wise, intelligent. They possess all the virtues lacked by nearly every man in the series. Lester hires them at wildly generous wages to play roles in his living comedies. As a result, each woman begins by suspecting his motives. All of them know too much about the strings tied to male generosity. Commonly they regard him as crazy. Until near the end. Then, unlike Sergeant Ackley, they understand how sane Mr. Leith is. Nearly all of them end adoring him. That would argue sequel, but that does not happen. Lester pays them well and they never return. Which is too bad. Some of them deserved a repeat performance.

"The Play's the Thing," February 27, 1932: Machine-gun fire wipes out two car loads of gangsters. That black bag the gangsters carried—the one loaded with jewels—is found to be loaded with washers.

Ackley orders Scuttle to get Leith interested. But Leith, uninterested in black bags, plans a new career as a motion picture producer. His first movie is to feature Lying Lena McGillicudy. By a coincidence, Lying Lena drove one of the gangster automobiles.

With the help of a black box, an automobile crank, a jar of strawberry jam, and a pillow, Leith lifts the gems from under the noses of gangsters and police alike, swarms of them, yelling and shooting and racing crazily about.

By this time, a few changes rippled the gossamer of the series. In the latter part of 1932, Ackley's dictaphone vanished from Leith's apartment. To Scuttle's piratical features were added a pair of dead, black eyes that protruded like the eyes of an enraged rabbit. Leith now claimed that the theoretical solving of crimes was his hobby; personally, he lacked all interest in discovering whether he was right or wrong.

Both Scuttle and Ackley developed strong anti-social tendencies, each being willing to steal small sums not otherwise accounted for. Ackley began toying with ways to frame Leith into prison—and would have, if the pace of events did not prove so furiously unpredictable.

"Screaming Sirens" (November 2, 1935) presents a jewel robbery and the seemingly unrelated murder of a photographer. Over the photographer's fireplace looms a huge photograph of a fan dancer. Proposing to enter the vacuum cleaner sales business, Leith hires a fan-dancer to listen to Scuttle's sales pitch (Scuttle doing the actual door-to-door work). The fan dancer poses for a photograph that closely resembles the one over the photographer's fireplace. In a luminous burst, Ackley concludes that the jewels are concealed in that photograph. And Leith plans to switch the pictures!

Once again, the Sergeant is the victim of mis-direction. While he hacks frantically away at the frame, Lester and the jewels ease from sight. This debacle does nothing for Ackley's reputation at Headquarters.

After the March 21, 1936, "The Bald-Headed Row," Lester Leith abruptly left *Detective Fiction Weekly*. Two and a half years later, he reappeared in Street & Smith's *Detective Story Magazine*, then struggling to become fresh, bright, and contemporary.

Seven stories appeared, from December 1938 to August of the following year. In these, the tone is faintly darker, the devices not quite so lunatic. Mockery tints the comedy. People swear and other people get drunk. The Police Commissioner chews up Ackley for spending so many dollars and man-hours trying to trap Leith. And Ackley's superior, Captain Carmichael, a non-caricatured policeman at last, frequently expresses amusement and near approval of Leith's more audacious expropriations.

The initial stories each refer to the story coming next month, a device for stirring readers to intolerable levels of anticipation. "Planted Planets" (December 1938) goes so far as to have Ackley insist that Scuttle interest Leith in "that monkey murder," rather than the robbery of a crooked politician. "The Monkey Murder" duly appears in the January 1939 issue. And it does turn on the murder of a pet monkey.

To solve the crime, and collect a pair of rare precious stones, Leith assembles the usual wonderful paraphernalia: an inflatable suit, a pair of hollow canes, fake emeralds and two real ones, and a flashy, gum-chewing secretary. All this adds up to Ackley's profound disgrace, as he is mislead still yet again—and gets a nice punch in the jaw from the obliging Scuttle, all in the line of duty.

"The Fourth Musketeer" (March 1939) also ends in a fist fight. Leith is on the track of a jewel thief who strikes at the top cream layer of society. The police have recovered none of the stolen jewels and the thief is still a mystery. What is required to clear up this regrettable situation is a can of tear gas, a ballroom, a few private detectives, a diver's suit, and a secretary whose boy friend is a jealous prizefighter. You could have thought of that.

Lester holds a masked ball, his costume being a diver's suit, bronze helmet and all. But at the last second, a switch. The jealous boy friend gets to wear the diving suit. When tear gas is squirted into the middle of the ball festivities, the police, disguised as musketeers, pounce upon the diver, assuming that he intends to steal every jewel in the hall. Ackley gets thoroughly beaten up by the prize fighter. The real thief is exposed. It need not be said that the hidden cache of jewels gets neatly cleaned out by Mr. Leith. Anonymously.

An equally wonderful riot ends "With Rhyme Or Reason" (April 1939). Lester has started a publishing house for unappreciated poets and ends mopping up a supply of stolen jewels. The scene in which a poetry reading degenerates into a brawl is one of the golden heights of Leith's adventures. Some of the poetry quoted during the course of the story would curdle the Mississippi River.

After the August 1939 "The Ring of Fiery Eyes," Leith left *Detective Story* as abruptly as he had arrived. The following month, with equal abruptness, he once more became a principal figure in *Detective Fiction Weekly*. His return was celebrated by a cover portrait and the words "Lester Leith is Home Again!" blaring across the masthead.

The story was "Lester Leith, Magician" (September 16, 1939, *Detective Fiction Weekly*), during which Lester gives a magic show aboard a liner sailing to Honolulu. Complications, which are considerable, include swapped shotguns, a stolen Chinese necklace, a Japanese with a camera and a prying eye, a highly educated Chinese girl, and Scuttle and Ackley. Nobody, from spies and secret service to the police lay a hand on Leith.

The stories appearing during 1939-1941 in the Detective Fiction Weekly are complex as novels. They brim with substitutions, feints, and tricks layered in stacks, like German cakes. The pace is ferocious. Loose ends and improbable responses fly like the leaves of Autumn. But the narrative pace allows no niggling criticism. Action and the golden shine of humor numb the critical instincts.

Repeatedly Leith is arrested, hauled to the police station. His pockets are searched and the damning evidence revealed. Lester gaps miserably. Ackley radiates joy. The reader's heart fibrillates. Obviously Leith has finally overstepped himself. All is lost.

All is not lost. In a single instant, the prose shimmers. The earth becomes the sky, right becomes left, Ackley triumphant becomes Ackley the fool. It is an astounding spectacle. Through one story after another, Gardner performs this magic. Lightly as a flower opening, Leith drifts through the story. Nothing he does is as it seems. Every movement, every step, every word is calculated misdirection. Every scene conceals a silent purpose.

Every established fact dissolves, like colored light, into an alternate meaning. At last Leith evaporates with the loot, infinitely graceful, his comedy played. You wonder what it cost Gardner to write these delights.

After his temporary residence in *Detective Story Magazine*, Gardner sharply cut back short story production, particularly for the pulp magazine market. His short fiction was appearing in the *Saturday Evening Post*, *This Week*, and *Country Gentleman*. At the same time, he was writing and publishing novels as rapidly as other writers published short stories.

During 1940, Gardner saw five novels published, including two about Perry Mason, two about Donald Lam/Bertha Cool (published under the A.A. Fair pseudonym), and one featuring District Attorney Doug Selby. Over the following five years, he would produce twenty-three additional novels before reducing his pace to three or four novels a year.

Prolific as he was, Gardner's slick magazine work and novel writing left little time for new Leith or Jenkins stories. Although Lester had returned triumphantly to *Detective Fiction Weekly*, he appeared only twice in 1940 and twice in 1941.

By then, a series of violent changes raged through the magazine. With the January 1941 issue, the publication was transformed to a large, flat, saddle-stitched publication of sixty-six pages of double column fiction.[5] Late in the year, the name changed to *Detective Fiction* (the words "Originally Flynn's" superimposed on that title). The issuance reduced to twice-a-month. Simultaneously the fiction content shrank and true crime articles appeared like a malignant fungus. Madness seemed to grip the magazine.

The startled reader was destined for other surprises. At the end of 1941, Popular Publications bought up several magazines published by the Frank A. Munsey Company. These included titles of venerable age and dignity: *All-Story*, *Argosy*, *Munsey*, *Railroad Magazine*, and *Detective Fiction*.[6]

Popular Publications became the official publisher of *Flynn's Detective Fiction* with the January 1943 issue.[7] The flat, over-sized format was abandoned and the magazine again became a conventional pulp. The title, elastic as rubber, altered to *Flynn's Detective Fiction*.

Gardner and Lester Leith returned only briefly to the new magazine. Two stories appeared. "Something Like A Pelican" (January 1943) borrows a few tricks from the earlier "Lester Leith, Magician," as a shotgun stuffed with fifty-dollars bills becomes a shotgun stuffed with cocktail napkins. And there stands Ackley sputtering.

The final Lester Leith story, "The Black Feather," appeared in the July 1943 issue and, with that, the long, sinuous, charming comedy came to an end.

Lester Leith was a typical character of the pulps, and written for the pulps," Gardner wrote in 1950. "The Leith stories were batted out at terrific speed in a white heat of creative imagination, and they were popular....

They are stories of a period, but, by their re-publication readers will be able once more to greet the dapper, ingenious chap who insisted that there was a higher code of ethics than that contained in our stereotyped laws related to personal property." (Gardner, "Introductory Note" 3-4)

How artful Gardner was. How extraordinary the fertility of his imagination as he poured out these stories. Within the self-imposed limitations of the form, he wrote a series of brilliant improvisations, many as fine as those stories recognized in more classical mystery fiction.

Leith and Jenkins are both honorable men, deftly treading the spiky walkways of criminality. In the tangled morality of the world surrounding them, where corruption is the norm and deceit the usual attribute of human relations, they set their own standards of decency. These standards they honor, firm guides in a world demented, where guides of any kind are in short supply.

Most of Gardner's characters impose a kind of limited order on the social and moral chaos surrounding them. By their own intellectual energies, they create an acceptable world for themselves, defining their own values and living up to these. Their situation differs starkly from that of most earlier series characters.

Return to the characters appearing before the First World War and you find them functioning in a relatively stable society, stiffened by rules that all acknowledged, if not all practiced.

Even when the character, himself, adventured in concealed paths—as a spy, for example, or a secret service agent—he shared with his fellows common values, principles to which all deferred and understood, beliefs and rules of behavior which gave structure and direction to their lives.

Even then, surrounded by such social stability as later generations would never know, series characters found themselves living violent lives. As we shall see.

# Chapter Four
# In Secret Service

The spy and the counter-espionage agent pursued their secret ways through popular fiction long before James Bond, Smiley, Matt Helm, and such juniors tasted that first martini—or saw that first dead man fall, this branch of literature being replete with dead men.

Far far back in the sandstone caverns of the past, the words "counter espionage" were unknown. Diplomatic Agent was the term used then. To speak plainly, a diplomatic agent is a secret agent associated with high levels of government. Not a spy, exactly. Not an official of the government. Rather he is a trouble-shooter brought in when matters between nations grew desperate.

In those remote days of early 1900, when the diplomatic agent flourished, the fiction featuring them had a special flavor. The stories moved in majestic leisure, nodding familiarly to social standing, good manners, and wealth. Women were to be honored; if it were necessary to foil them, proper courtesy would be observed.

For all this, sentiment crept in rather infrequently. Violence frequently jarred the narrative. Steel-eyed people drove the action. From the pages floated cynicism, like the breath of an open refrigerator on a hot day.

Under the social artifice, behind the respectable attitudes, you find metal. The surface conceals a view of life that is flatly spare and unsentimental. No idealism here. No one takes time to talk morality, decency, and such splendid abstracts. Here is the unforgiving, unremitting struggle of the sea bottom or the African veldt. The weak die. The indecisive are cut down. The blade strokes the throat; the pistol drives against the ribs. The struggle for advantage is ceaseless.

We are in the presence of power maintaining itself.

This strange blend of social correctness and merciless struggle rings through all diplomatic agent series appearing during these early years.

The series featuring Yorke Norroy is an admirable example.

When Norroy appeared, the pulp magazine was in its infancy. Dime novels and story papers shrilled on all sides. Proper fiction, neatly dressed, passed chastely through the careful pages of *Scribner's Magazine*, *The Saturday Evening Post*, *The Ladies' Home Journal*, and the *Cosmopolitan*.

However, *The Popular Magazine*, while chaste beyond any reasonable doubt, was neither neat, careful, nor tame. *Popular* was Street & Smith's challenge to *The Argosy*. From its first issue, dated November 1903, the biting winds of action adventure swept its pages. Initially boy-oriented, the magazine swiftly adopted a freer, harsher tone, part realistic, part high romance. Nearly at once, its pages reflected the sharply observed world of Felix Boyd, a private investigator in the Nick Carter style; the equally strenuous worlds of O'Rourke, the Irish adventurer; and such curious worlds as inhabited by Chip of the Flying U, Captain Bantam, and H. Rider Haggard's She.

Richard Marsh and E. Phillips Oppenheim wrote for the magazine. So did H.G. Wells and Max Pemberton. At first, the presence of so many English authors tended to mute the hard American accents of B.M. Bower, William Wallace Cook, and Frederick W. Davis. By 1905, however, fresh winds blew and the prose rhythms of the New World belled in *Popular*'s pages.

One of the most popular writers of this brisk, colloquial, action-based fiction was George Bronson-Howard (1884-1922), newspaper reporter, war correspondent, playwright, silent movie director, and for a brief period, observer of the roots of history. Following the Spanish-American War, during 1895-1900, he was employed in the Philippine Civil Government. Later (perhaps 1902-1903) he was in Imperial Chinese service at Canton. During 1918 he served briefly with US Intelligence in London and afterward as an ambulance driver in France.[1]

From these casual exposures to the underside of history, he formed the character of Yorke Norroy, Diplomatic Agent.

Norroy does not, at first, seem particularly original. In appearance, he is, in fact, that familiar figure of fun, the swell, the fop. Target for ridicule for more than a hundred years, the swell is a brainless popinjay, a butterfly of fashion, a boneless dandy, suave, slim, elegant.

His clothes were just a little too much the mode of the day, and one indefinably regretted that a man of his intelligence should spend the thought necessary for such ultra-fashionable attire. They had evidently been cut not a week before, for they embodied a new wrinkle in evening clothes which had originated at the period. (Bronson-Howard, *Norroy, Diplomatic* 71)

*Norroy*: I am never more serious...than when engaged in overcoming imperfections of attire.... Man, at best, is so unlovely a creature that if the eye can be deflected from him to his attire, it is every man's duty to array himself in the most becoming fashion possible." (Bronson-Howard, *The Black Boot* 27)

Norroy's waistcoats dazzle. He is credited with being the foremost amateur actor in the United States and thus shares, with amateur actors the world over, a reputation for inconsequence.

A fashionable lightweight, so society assesses him. No more.

It is a carefully cultivated reputation. For he is the State Department's major counter-espionage agent.

That term is contemporary. Norroy calls himself a "diplomatic agent." His activities are not identified as spying or counter-spying but diplomacy.

*Norroy*: "For something like fifteen years I've followed the devious intricacies of the craft. Men will do anything when big things are at stake. I have done things officially which I would have never done personally.... Diplomacy—pfugh!

"But it's a disease. It gets into the bones; just as crooked gambling does. That's why we are all diplomats—that and because we need the money." (Bronson-Howard, "At the Night of the Charity Ball" 116)

Money. The note rings darkly, a pedal tone through the series. The State Department hires Norroy by the job. He holds no official position. Ahead lies no recognition for his work. No pension. No honors. He is a hireling. Handsomely paid, certainly. But the bulk of the money is spent maintaining his cover.

He was the dean of his profession, feared by kings and emperors and presidents and he had done much to make the history of his day; but for himself he had done nothing except acquire a reputation for waistcoats and amateur acting (Bronson-Howard, *For the Good of the State* 6:6).

In quiet moments, this appalls him. Ahead, in the icy hollow of the future, he sees the end of his secret professional life and the end of his resources.

Inexorably the money flows out. His eyes trouble him. Fears of failing health nip his mind. He determines to be in bed no later than 1 a.m. each night.

Perhaps he can stage an amateur play. If this is a success—and with his abilities there is every hope that it will be a success—then the Washington Theatrical Syndicate might take it up professionally. He might realize a significant amount of money. He might....

From decades ahead sniggers his hollow future.

Through the polished ballroom, bright with mirrors, he leads tonight's wealthy matron. Their shadows flit across shining wood. Jewels burn against her powdered skin. She smiles, her tomorrows impregnable. Deftly he guides her among the dancers. He has never met a woman he truly cares for. Money frets his mind and the cold of hollow tomorrow.

He smiles graciously to his partner and fetches her a cup of punch.

Three separate men converge in Norroy. The apprehensive inner man blends with the amiable social being. Distinct from these stands the third personality, the secret professional. This third personality may co-exist with the others, but it lives apart. Its world is ruled by frigid laws having nothing to do with the ordinary flow of life.

In this world, expediency directs. Familiar behavioral codes have no validity. Here ethics do not exist. Nor does integrity. Nor truthfulness.

In this bleak world, conventional attitudes and virtues had no meaning.

In the world of the professional diplomat—which is to say, the counter-espionage agent—nothing is forbidden. Except failure.

All actions are excused.

Except failure.

The professional agent exists to accomplish his purpose.

What the private man would not do, the professional must perform without hesitation.

For the professional serves the State, that monstrous abstraction. To the needs of the State, human needs are irrelevant.

All things are subordinate to the welfare of the State.

Morality is defined in terms of the State's well being. The basic reality is the safety of the State and achievement of its goals.

But what, precisely, is the State? And who determines what actions further its welfare?

For Yorke Norroy, in 1905, the matter is straightforward: He receives instruction from the Secretary of State, a man in an office in a rather large building in Washington, D.C., who serves the President of the United States.

These instructions, Norroy performs, using his discretion, never allowing his hand to show. How simple it was in 1905, particularly in popular fiction of an active sort.

As Norroy served the United States government, so other agents served Germany or France or Russia, those abstractions from a geographical premise.

Men exist. The state is a construct of their minds. The security, welfare, and well being of the State are as understood by men and directed by men. At the bottom of the grand talk, flares the human mind, busy within its usual atmosphere of idealism and self-interest.

Which, you must understand, is the steel girder underlying the

Yorke Norroy series: service to the State excuses all actions, removes these actions from the moral and ethical, transplants them to some neutral place where no values exist, save expediency.

Yet service to the State is, after all, defined by the interests of the political group holding office.

On that grisly thought, we turn to the Norroy series. This burst into *The Popular Magazine* in two groups of short stories. The initial series ran from April through October 1905; the second from June through October 1906. After a meager scattering of stories in 1907 and 1908, a short novel appeared in 1911, followed by sequences of stories in 1912-1913 and 1918 which Bronson-Howard later lightly reworked into novels. During 1920, a last serial appeared. After the author's death, a final short story was published.

The series, then, extended over eighteen years, with great gaps separating its parts. By 1923, the series had outlived its vitality. The character of Norroy, "that dandified devil," as he was referred to, seemed faintly ludicrous, like the clothing great-grandmother stored in the attic.

In his first appearance, however, Norroy is dapper, taut, and exceedingly dangerous. "How Norroy Created a New Republic" (*The Popular Magazine*, April 1905) is nothing less than an account of how he saved the Panama Canal Zone for the United States.

As you remember, the United States had bought up the canal strip option from France but, like a good neighbor, sought Colombia's agreement that this country would build the canal. Germany (called Saxonia in these stories) intrigued with Colombia to sign an agreement that Germany would build the canal. Revolutionaries urged the United States to step in with Marines, take the strip, and back Panama in breaking free of Colombia.

Remember all that? Or most of it? Some of the details may be a little off, but then fiction takes a relaxed attitude toward history: never let facts get in the way of a story. For instance, did you know that the United States government had sent to Colombia a young man to represent American interests. And did you know that this young fool actually fell in love with a German (Saxonian) spy? Did you realize that she stole the secret policy papers from him?

Fortunately Norroy soon took these away from her, together with the signed agreement that gave Germany the right to build the canal.

At this point, von Ladenburg, the master Saxonian (German) spy, bursts into the room, waving a pistol. A struggle. Von Ladenburg accidentally shoots the woman, not very badly. With a single blow, Norroy knocks him out and escapes with the papers.

When the President of the United States sees the signature of the Colombian/Saxonian agreement, he immediately directs the Marines to move into Panama. And so they do. The Canal Zone has been saved for the United States, and "Panama," that fine jazz tune enters the Dixieland repertoire.

So now you know.

"A Tilt with the Muscovite" (May 1905) tells how Norroy goes to Moscow with three Broadway showgirls. The Russians have imprisoned an inventor who has designed a repeating naval rifle capable of firing twenty-five miles. Once in Moscow, the showgirls sing ragtime so charmingly that they are able to entice and drug a Colonel of the Russian Engineers. This Colonel has access to the prison in which the inventor lies mouldering. Disguised as the Colonel, Norroy goes to the prison and takes the inventor's place. Once inventor, showgirls, and captive Colonel are clear of Russia, Norroy reveals himself. The Russians, humiliated and fearing a fierce United States reprisal, allow him to go free.

Isn't that remarkable. They fear a United States reprisal. You must admit that things have changed on the international scene.

Norroy, hero of these stirring adventures, was recruited by the State Department when he was twenty-five. He was one of the Norroys of Baltimore, his sister married to a social leader of that city. On his first mission, he spent a year in Peking. Subsequent assignments took him times around the world, and he visited "almost every civilized country, some barbarous ones, and some entirely savage." He speaks unaccented French, Spanish, and Russian. He had been wounded several times, once by von Ladenburg.

Of medium height, Norroy is extremely slender, with small hands and feet. His light hair is clipped close to the scalp, exposing small, rather protruding ears. His cheek bones are high, his chin prominent, and his eyes pale, large and of no definite color; "there was a hardness, a steeliness about them that was not altogether pleasant."

No mistake about it. Under that fancy exterior, he is thoroughly hardboiled. In "The Friend of the Chief Executive" (October 1905), he discovers that a dear buddy of the President is betraying US secrets to Saxonia. For money. That dire demon, Von Ladenburg, is deeply involved.

Disguising himself as von L., Norroy lures the President's friend into a confrontation with von Ladenburg, himself. Both are armed. Both shoot each other dead, while from concealment the President watches horrified.

Heartbreaking, murderous. But that is diplomacy—a filthy, exciting business.

The second series of stories opens with an echo of "How Norroy Created a New Republic." In this story, "The Editor and The Diplomat," June 1906, Norroy must stop publication of a story that will cost the

President the election. Seems this newspaper editor has documentary proof that, by Presidential direction, the United States manipulated the internal affairs of a southern country. Can you just imagine that?

Embalmed in this situation are the bones of the Panama Canal affair. In 1903, with the not-very clandestine support of the United States (as we have already seen) and Theodore Roosevelt in particular, Panama declared its independence from Colombia. Ten days later, a treaty recognizing the new republic was completed; the Canal Zone was leased; the United States bought out French rights in the Zone for forty million dollars and paid the new Panamanian government an additional ten million.

It is characteristic of the diplomatic agent story that it thrives on current headlines. Timeliness is as much a part of this fiction as violence. So history is encouraged to boom through the popular story, giving the illusion of secret bones laid bare.

It is Norroy's job to conceal presidential complicity in such intervention as this. He does so easily, using judicious bribery and blackmail. The editor is in the process of getting out of a bad marriage into one made in Heaven. Norroy, as full of special information as an Edgar Wallace hero, has some documents that will ease the editor's way—and will swap these for the documents about the President.

That's the way it is worked out. Diplomacy, you see.

"On the Night of the Charity Ball" (August 1906), Norroy saves an under-secretary of the State Department from disgrace. This young man is being blackmailed by the Saxonia Foreign Office. To foil them, Norroy commits such unprincipled acts as opening private letters and concealing himself under a sofa in the Saxonian office. With the information he has gathered, so unscrupulously, he causes the Saxonia plot to misfire. The young man is vindicated. The Saxonian Minister creeps home to shoot himself.

By the fifth story, "For the Good of the State" (October 1906), Saxonian officials have learned that Norroy is not the trivial fellow he seems:

The man who gave the Panama Canal to the United States, who brought about Ladenburg's death, who released De Legaspe, the Andevian, from Eagle's Eyrie when a woman had him safe...the man who put Dmitas on the throne of Lugaria...
"Harmless, lackadasical dandy! Herr Gott! Harmless!" (Bronson-Howard 6:6)

They decide to have him killed. He is to be lured to New York's East Side where one of the local gangs will do the deed. But at the last minute, as the gang closes in, Norroy throws eye drops into their faces and strolls away, curses ringing around him.

For the next several years, Bronson-Howard managed to appear in most issues of The Popular Magazine. He gave only spare attention to Norroy who appeared in just two 1907 short stories and a short novel (October 1908) titled "The Return of Norroy."

After that he disappeared completely until 1911 and another short novel, "The Code Book" (February 1). From July through September, however, Bronson-Howard did write three novelettes about John Baedeker Bok, a small-town school master who accidentally becomes a secret service agent. WhatBok lacks in experience, he makes up in luck, oceans of luck. His adventures prance merrily along the edge of farce.

Later in 1912, Bronson-Howard once more turned his attention to Norroy, who returned still again in "The Further Adventures of Norroy, Diplomatic Agent." Beginning November 15, 1912, the series proceeded in linked stories and short serials until April 1, 1913. (Later these were collected and published as the 1917 Slaves of the Lamp.) The narrative line concerns the frenzied search for seven jade plates. On these plates is engraved the secret for making Chandoo opium, that most violently addictive of drugs. Eventually Norroy tracks them down, each plate recovered after a world of danger and violence. At the end, a minor character shoots dead the vile drug manufacturer behind so much bloody business.

In a sort of postscript to the final story ("Behind the Green Lamps," two-part serial, March 15-April 1, 1913), we learn that Norroy has dispersed his intelligence team to China, recognizing that a menace even greater than Chandoo opium is brewing in the East.

Some day, not far distant, those...men, watching ever so near at hand the details of the growing shadow of Japan, will send a final report to the languid originator of decorative waistcoats in Washington, and...he will awake from his passivity, and all the little and devious trains he has laid these many years will be ignited by a single match, and Yorke Norroy will stand before the Senate, the House, and the president, and the muffled roll of drums and the roar of cannon will resound throughout the land.

"Some day—let it be said again, not far distant" (Bronson-Howard 218).

Bronson-Howard missed the prediction by about thirty years and a major war, but it did finally come, as announced. Although it's doubtful that Norroy found it necessary to stand before the Senate, the House, and the president and announce "The day that shall live in infamy."

No further Norroy stories appeared until the five-part Black Book series of 1918. Another group of linked stories, these began May 20 with "The Book of the Betrayers" and continued to the July 20 "A Leaf from the Kaiser's book."

The United States had declared war on Germany the previous year and so Norroy temporarily shifted his attention from Japan to German spy activities in this country. The Black Book (four volumes in all) contains the name and address of each German agent in the United States, each entry written in the agent's own hand.

Now head of the Secret Service, Norroy goes after these volumes in a loose-knit story full of movement and coincidence. The stories were collected in The Black Book (1920).

Once more Norroy disappeared from the pages of The Popular Magazine. Two years later, he returned in the four-part serial "The Devil's Chaplain," a rather disappointing search for a criminal mastermind. After Bronson-Howard's death, a final story was published, "The Lady of the Lost Garments" (February 7, 1923).

Thus early was established the figure of the secret agent, striving for his country in spite of the Ten Commandments. Admittedly, Norroy is described as being far more ruthless than is shown by his actions. His attitudes, as stated, are advanced Twentieth Century. In practice, however, his sentiments and activities remain ripe dime novel. Still, few popular fiction series so clearly distinguished between public and private morality. And few fictional figures achieved the heights of Norroy's personal despair, at least as he expressed it in the early stories. (Toward the end, he cheered up considerably.) The problems raised by Bronson-Howard concerning a man's duty to his State are still with us, still molten hot, still burning holes in the heart.

Few such ripples disturb the glossy surface of the next major diplomacy series to appear. This was reputed to be the longest series ever to appear in a magazine. Titled "Free Lances in Diplomacy," it was written by Charles Herbert New, and ran in almost every issue of Blue Book for twenty-five years. In this series, the secret agent story picked up new life and pulp magazine fiction picked up a penchant for foreign violence and gadgets that it never quite outgrew.

Sir George Llangolen Trevor, First Viscount Dartmoor, a "man in the early forties, with the build and carriage of an athlete—or of a swordsman." His face is clean-shaven, a description to be commented on in 1910. He presents to the world the formal mask of purified heredity: "Square chin, patrician nose, and handsome, magnetic eyes." Before the right eye glints a monocle.

We are in the presence of Superior Stock. Viscount Trevor is an advanced copy of homo splendid.[2] For that reason, he gently downplays his superiority. He cultivates a vacant expression and slows his voice to a lazy, good-natured drawl.

Through life he strolls, relishing immense leisure, invariably at ease. No wonder. For not only does he delight in that swordsman's physique, but he also enjoys "a princely fortune which made him one of the wealthiest men in European private life."

That fortune allows him to experiment with chancy modes of transportation. Automobiles traveling at speeds destructive to the senses, twenty kilometers an hour or more. And airplanes! He is one of Europe's most famous aviators. In 1910, the man who flew automatically gathered a reputation for daring, rashness, and indifference to personal pain.

A sportsman, then; a titled gentleman, on easy termswith most European heads of state. The Kaiser is his warmpersonal friend.

This in spite of Trevor's well-known dislike for politics. Manipulations, intrigues, maneuvering for position and power—these matters bore him. Politics are so tedious, he murmurs. Better to board his yacht, the *Ranee Sylvia*, and sail to some warmly gracious coast where noblemen with patrician noses and magnetic eyes are welcomed and well modulated laughter rises among expensive chairs.

Thus Trevor—the aristocrat at the crest of the wave, before that wave foamed and burst across the Western Front.

Ten years before, matters were otherwise.

We begin, ten years before, with that complicated young woman, Violet Tremaine. She loved a noble young Deputy Commissioner, George Trevor, blessed with splendid ancestry. Regrettably, the family estates had been gambled away during George the Fourth's reign. Since Trevor was penniless, he refused to elope with adoring Violet.

Rent by that anguish peculiar to wealthy young girls, she flung into marriage with Old Lord Kenderby, a creaking oldster, nearly fifty. His personal habits were of gaudy originality. He loved opera singers and chronic intoxication. Quite soon Violet found that marriage was not all she had anticipated.

While Violet progressed toward disillusionment, young Trevor, scorched to the marrow, left England for the deeps of India. There, after inconclusive adventures, he died. Of enteric fever.

When he died, he was tended by a new friend, met not two weeks earlier. They were friends for an odd reason. They were exact doubles, close as identical twins. Comparing notes, they could find no point at which their ancestry touched. The double's name was Cyrus K. Grisscome, the only remaining member of a famous Boston family; he had made a fortune from gold mines in Arizona and California.

Grisscome was close to Theodore Roosevelt. When Roosevelt established the first Diplomatic Service (no mention of Norroy in this series), Grisscome was persuaded to participate. Later, under the Taft administration, the Diplomatic service was essentially dismantled. In disgust, Grisscome withdrew, left his mining interests in a partner's hands, and sailed from Taft's America to visit the Orient.[3]

By degrees he drifted to the Khyber Pass area. There he saved Abdool Mohammed from a tiger. The improbably named Abdool is an Afghan prince and a cousin of the Ameer. Meaning royal blood, high connections, and a prime example of a character type which appeared with great frequency in later pulp fiction.

That is to say, he is the hero's good right arm. Almost always he is a combination of savior, servant, and ferocious fighter—a dedicated warrior loving cold steel. In these early fictions, such men shed considerable blood, since you know how Eastern types consider human life. As a class, they are utterly ruthless, utterly dedicated to the hero.

In the fine old tradition, Trevor and Abdool save each other's life with startling frequency. By 1924, Abdool and several cousins have taken up permanent residence in England with Trevor. Oh, sometimes the Afghans drive a limousine or open a door, and so the ill-informed account them servants. But not so. When in English clothing, none of them look like natives—merely like gentlemen with heavy tans.

These narrative refinements do not appear immediately. They are added to the series a trifle at a time, like garlic to a salad. Abdool (and cousins), strongly intelligent, represent a somewhat earlier convention in popular fiction. Perhaps it was first described by Kipling or Conan Doyle, and involved that red-faced Colonel returned from India with Punjab, a faithful servant and first-class fighting man. Similar figures graced such series as those about Jimgrim and Secret Service Smith during the 1920s, and in the 1930s Spider novels. Many other adventure-fiction figures used the same convention.

But to return to our story.

While Grisscome and Abdool are hiking through the back country of Mysore, they come across Trevor, sick unto death, abandoned by his servants. Ten days later, Trevor died, having spoken of himself in wearying detail. And Grisscome had promised to wind up Trevor's affairs.

On returning to Madras, Grisscome discovered that people took him for Trevor. Amused, wondering how long such a deception could be carried out, he returned to England to carry out Trevor's final wishes. Once in England, he found himself universally regarded as Trevor—a Trevor given to amnesiac lapses because of his Indian fevers.

At about this time, Grisscome bought back the Trevor Devonshire estates and proceeded to refurbish them. "This thing got to be something more than a joke; he decided to play the game and see how long he could get away with it, having secret service work in mind." (New, *The Mystery of the Free Lancer* 25)

Grisscome has not only seen secret service work with Roosevelt, but he had appeared in the 1909 *Blue Book* in a series titled "An Agent of the Government" that pre-dated the Diplomatic Free-Lances.

The Free-Lances series began in *Blue Book* with the March 1910 issue. Not until December of that year, "The Love Affair of a Princess," was there a reference to Grisscome's true identity. But it takes time for these matters to mature.[4]

At any rate, no one questions that the extraordinary American is not Trevor. He walks naturally in the dead man's shoes. Smoothly as the image in a mirror, he slips into the other man's life.

With this difference: he brings a new stimulation to the faltering Trevor line. And more—after five years, he has rendered "immensely valuable services" to England.

Sir Edward Wray, then of Downing Street, knew all about those services. Trevor/Grisscome had come to him with some suggestions concerning the violent disruption of German naval maneuvers at Keil. Although England could officially neither authorize or protect Trevor, he proceeded on his own—a free-lance—and pulled off a coup. Got a submarine and torpedoed the German Baltic Fleet is what he did.

It was the first of many. All unauthorized, all unofficial. He and the several friends who joined him became Diplomatic Free-Lances, working on their own. So the title of their series.

This new Trevor had a taste for manipulation. He relished the concealed mechanism clicking beneath the sunlit social surface. He had a sense of timing, a sense of drama. He loved the secret way.

By this time he has become warm friends with Violet. The old love affair stands between them like scar tissue. She is a widow now. Lord Kenderby has died drunk in a spectacular sports car crash. Now thirty-four, Violet finds herself titled, rather strapped for money, and with an opportunity to indulge her "taste for intrigue and the finesse she often displayed attracted [Trevor] as much as her undeniable personal beauty."

Nothing will come of this. If it is a breech of good taste to assume a man's identity and lineage, how much more tacky is it to assume, also, his former sweetheart.

Eventually, Trevor's services become so valuable that England wishes to make him a peer. He refuses, telling Wray his real identity. And then one of these incredible coincidences occur that you sometimes hear about in real life, but which fiction would never dare employ—Wray discovers that Grisscome of Boston is Trevor's second cousin and the only-surviving heir to the title.

Shortly after, he becomes Viscount Trevor of Dartmoor.

The game is now afoot. In the first series of "The Adventures of a Diplomatic Free Lance" (beginning March 1910) Trevor proceeds to foil German political interests time after time. To summarize, in the words of Colonel Pfaff, head of the German secret agents in the field:

I think the mysterious torpedoing of our Baltic Fleet by a submarine at the Kiel maneuvers, some two years ago, was the beginning.... The Carnstadt Alliance was the most amazing twist of circumstances I ever knew—the tables were too completely turned to admit a theory of chance or accident. And to cap the climax—after other mysterious occurrences—we find a decided coolness...on the proposition to revive the Holy Roman Empire. (New, *Further Adventures* 1279-1280)

But is this the work of a group? Or a man? Who or what? The manipulating hands are invisible. The only common denominator is that invisibility—and the failure of German schemes.

Here begins the second series, "Further Adventures of a Diplomatic Free Lance." The first story, "When the Fox Stole the Bait" (April 1911) opens with the frantic discussion quoted above (in much reduced form). In an outer chamber sits Trevor, very much the empty-headed English Lord, come to the Graf von Schimmerling to sell a nice biplane.

Trevor has also come to probe for information. He expects trouble and has laid elaborate plans against it. For he has the habit of analysis and can deduce more from two men meeting that Sherlock Holmes could draw from a basket of clues.

By a remarkable coincidence, best appreciated by those seeking to write short action fiction, Trevor discovers an envelope loaded with secret German papers under a carpet in the waiting room. Immediately he lifts the packets, substituting another envelope; the papers he conceals behind some books.

Wheels, you see, within wheels. It is a German trap. The papers are authentic and were deliberately locked in a desk. The butler, a foreign agent, has broken open the desk but Trevor's arrival interrupted him. So he hid the papers under the rug. Before the butler can retrieve the papers—which have now been switched, as you obviously remember—the Germans rush in, find the robbed desk, and begin to prance and howl.

Trevor is instantly arrested.

*German*: "Have you been in my private study, back there—breaking open my desk and—and raising the devil....

*Trevor*: Fawncy! Why should I do that, if I may awsk? You're ill, man—you're really quite ill! You should phone for a physician or a chemist, at once. (1286)

Fawncy that!
Trevor is bundled off to a secret place where he will be held till the Germans sort things out.

But outside in the wet night lurks Abdool. Before being arrested, Trevor has instructed him to go promptly to Prince Karl, a personal friend, and ask that the Kaiser be advised of this terrible situation. As you know, the Kaiser is a personal friend of Trevor.

Trevor, in the clutch of the Germans, finds himself locked into a room with an opera singer. Now the main reason Trevor came to Germany is to meet this very woman. He is attempting to do Violet a favor. While still alive and drunk, Violet's husband, Lord Kenderly, signed over most of his estate to this singer, likely for reasons having nothing to do with opera. That assignment may not be legal in England, but it would save Violet many expensive problems is the opera singer would sign a quit claim.

To find this woman here, a prisoner, suspected of espionage, is a most extraordinary coincidence which, under the magic of Mr. New's narrative, seems entirely reasonable.

Granted that New now proceeds to strain the belief of the most credulous among us. He tells us that Trevor recently foiled a political abduction in which the opera singer served as bait. However, if she will sign this document returning the English estates to Violet, he will say nothing and use his influence to get her out of the present mess.

No sooner has she signed that enters a gaggle of Germans and the Kaiser. Trevor is released with apologies. That night, suicide stalks the German secret service. Later, Trevor returns to the house of his arrest and sells a biplane. Apparently he also secures the concealed papers, which the entire German secret service was unable to locate behind those books. For the papers reappear in embarrassing places, and as they discuss the French-Belgium attitudes toward Germany's interests in Holland, their release is most painful.

By later standards, "How the Fox Stole the Bait" is rather slow. But it contains most elements that gripped readers for so many decades. Thunderous coincidences crash massively in paragraphs so elegantly written that the eye slides blankly by. The prose is heavily seasoned with international figures, bits of foreign dialogue, showers of secret agents, episodes of confusion and mystery. Here adventure shouts in places with difficult names. The opposition is competent and deadly. And Trevor is the slickest, most sharp-minded, supple, foresighted trickster who strolled across the printed page.

Above all he is action oriented. If violence is required, he will cheerfully descend to violence. In "A Foreign Office Duel" (March 1912), he goes to the rescue of a British secret agent who has not remained quite secret enough.

The Germans have trailed this boy to England, drugged him, and are now carting him back to Germany. Trevor has learned of their plot.

From a few stray details, he reasons out how the Germans will arrange the thing, deduces their schedule, and their method.

And suddenly, in the black of night, terrible anonymous figures rise around the Germans and their drugged victim. After which things end badly for those headquartered in Berlin.

Details of this plot were supplied to Trevor by his ward, the darkly beautiful Miss Nan Tremain. She is twenty years younger than Trevor, with a gigantic gift for languages, and as artistic as Corot or Thomas Lovell. Somehow she seems related to Violet. Her father was the most gifted officer in the Indian Secret Service.

You will notice that all these people are abnormally talented. Genius scalds their blood. Their energies are unconsumed by the need to earn a living. Their social position is so magnificent that they can hardly rise further. Their mental abilities demand exercise.

Thus, the maneuver. They manipulate.

In time, they will become not only the force behind the throne, but the vital energy that determines the direction of Western Civilization.

That is a later development. For now, the narrative proceeds down through the years in a loose, chronological fashion. The main characters meet, marry, have children, grow old as their children become adults and take up the burden. The political upheavals of the times are faithfully recorded in each story. New never let the larger headlines appear without finding the Trevors silently at work behind them.

In a 1954 article, *Blue Book* editor Donald Kennicott commented on the:

"extraordinary series called 'Free Lances in Diplomacy' which was published almost continuously in *Bluebook* from 1909 until after New's death in 1933—constituting over three million words, according to the New York *Times* the longest novel ever written. His hero was an international adventurer who made a career out of foiling plots of enemy alien conspirators, usually Russians or Germans—indeed, I had a hard time keeping him from declaring fictional war on Germany from 1912 on. The stories were somewhat naive by modern standards, but as the years went on New achieved some variety by introducing his hero's wife, son, and a friend or two as alternate protagonists. Moreover, the author had...acquaintances in the British Secret Service who apparently tipped him off to impending situations before they came to public knowledge, through because of the time-lag between writing and publication, we in the office were more conscious of this than the public." (34)

Through the series creeps a slow, constant expansion. Each feat is faintly larger, each menace slightly more powerful. Slowly slowly Trevor's personal power expands. Today he revitalizes shrunken estates. In twenty years, his financial webs dominate half the world's economy. If the series had lasted into the 1940s, he would have owned the moons of Jupiter.

In 1915, the scope was smaller. "The Neutrality of Bulgaria" (March 1915) is an intensely complicated account of a minor Trevor exploit in the Balkans. The story makes sense, providing that it is read slowly several times. Representatives of the German, French, and Italian secret services appear. Trevor, disguised as a German, is apparently carrying dispatches from the Kaiser to the King of Roumania. At first the Germans attempt to stop Trevor; then, convinced that he is acting in German interests, arrange an audience for him with the King.

It is an unfortunate error. Trevor gives the King an unflattering assessment of Germany's war chances, severely denting the Kaiser's hope for an alliance.

On leaving the King, Trevor is kidnapped by thugs hired by the French. He is almost murdered in a filthy basement. Fortunately, he finds a stray bit of 2-inch pipe, kills two of the three thugs, and escapes to have dinner with the man who hired them—who grins and confesses his error.

During the years of the First World War, Germany and its secret service provided fiction with ready-made villains. When Russia collapsed in 1917, the communist menace immediately provided a new collection of black-hearted, sin-dipped fiends, vermin of the vilest sort. Typical of all radicals.

Radicals included both anarchists and socialists. The public mind wadded them all into a familiar image—a wild-eyed unwashed, ragged of clothing, hair and beard bristling. Think of the lead guitar in a rock group. In one hand this stereotype grips a sizzling bomb. In his mouth is sizzling hysteria.

The anarchists puzzled the 1900s as their counterparts, terrorists, puzzle the 1990s. In 1907, Joseph Conrad had impaled the type in his novel, *The Secret Agent*. In 1908, Gilbert K. Chesterton placed a fanciful anarchist into *The Man Who Was Thursday*, and Edgar Wallace revealed how these insidious types gnawed in society's basement in *The Council of Justice*.

As usual, the dime novels leaped on the subject and ripped all manner of excitements from the headlines. Particularly where bomb throwing was involved. That caught the imagination. The anarchist philosophy received no coverage—all radicals were presumed to be insane—but bomb throwing got worked to rags.

In the Nick Carter series, the great detective sporadically battled these fiends, characteristically in the form of lovely anarchist queens, perverse and deadly:

A Beautiful Anarchist; or, Nick Carter's Bravest Act (*New Nick Carter Weekly*, #559, September 14, 1907)

An Anarchist Plot; or, Nick Carter on a Difficult Trail (*New Nick Carter Weekly*, #606, August 8, 1908)

So popular was the theme that even Buffalo Bill found himself battling foreign agitators, bombs in hand, out to stir up the Indians, as in:

Buffalo Bill's Protege; or, Foiling a Nihilist Plot (*Buffalo Bill Stories*, #360, April 4, 1908)

Popular fiction faithfully records political turbulence. After the war there was plenty of turbulence to record. In 1919, the United States was gripped by hysteria—for, according to no less an authority than the Attorney-General, dangerous radicals tensed to strike.[5] The Attorney-General's frenzies were compounded by a police strike in Boston and a general steel strike—this immediately after a series of bombs were sent through the mails.

Six thousand suspected Communists were summarily arrested (without warrants or due process) and penned in compounds until someone figured out what to do with them. The fever raged to seek out, identify, denounce radicals. Do something, do anything. Action, action! No time to think, as usual; blind, as usual; abusive, as usual; full of political frenzy and opportunism, as usual.

It was a hateful, vicious, deadly time that, as usual, slowly ebbed, leaving the country shaken and uneasy with guilt.

There is a reason, after all, why Russian fiends appear so frequently in the early Tarzan novels. And why Bulldog Drummond felt justified in illicitly kidnapping radicals to his island concentration camp.

In the same way, the Diplomatic Free Lances, being a child of its time, and addicted to the story behind the headlines, could not possibly pass by such rich material. In the August 1919, "The Spreading of the Plague," for instance, Trevor plans to blunt the communist-socialist menace by eliminating major leaders. According to Trevor, the basis for the whole movement is greed:

It is generally believed...that Lenine and Trotzky have upwards of twenty million safely banked in neutral countries where they can get the money whenever they decide to abandon the game—or are forced to escape from Russia.

And again:

As a matter of fact, is there a particle of doubt that every bolshevist leader is using his masses of ignorant followers as cat's-paws and expects to get away with millions in a few years at the outside...when every communistic state which they have organized is butchering itself and its people in a despairing struggle to live without work or normal production. (New 149)

Much of the story is spent tracing the rise of a young Englishman, defective morally and intellectually. It is a sustained attack against a type of radical personality. Regrettably, New is attacking a political caricature, rather than a real target. His descriptions make arresting propaganda, if pitiful art.

These matters to the side, Trevor intends to incite the radical leaders to violence among themselves. After this he will break newspaper stories, revealing to the unwashed how their leaders filled secret bank accounts.

To bring the leaders to dissension, Nan is insinuated into the radical high council. Unaware that it is being manipulated, the Council agrees that, as soon as it takes over the government, women are to be nationalized. The leaders will get first choice, of course; and Nan will be the rare high prize.

Promptly they begin squabbling for possession of her fair white body. When the pistol smoke clears, more than half of them are dead. Nan has glided off somewhere. And after the newspapers reveal all about that hidden wealth, the enraged masses wipe out the survivors of the Council.

How simple these matters are.

Around 1920, Trevor and Nan marry. Truth be known, he dragged his feet. He was twenty years older than Nan and felt it intolerable that she be saddled with an aging husband. She disagreed. After all, Trevor, as you may recall, has the body of a swordsman.

Wed they are. As is customary in this series, she is immediately bedecked with resounding titles that clang across the page like golden bells—Countess of Dyvnaint is one of them. Presently she is being referred to as the Marchioness. Since every paragraph seems to bring forth a new title, it is a major problem to keep track of whom is what. The problem does not grow easier through the series.

Other changes have crept imperceptibly across the page. The series title has become "Free Lances in Diplomacy," reflecting the augmented cast. Principals include Trevor and Nan, Abdool, and two regulars who will remain for years:

*Earl Lammerford of St. Ives.* In the 1910 series of stories, Lammerford is the Dean of the King's Messengers. Retiring from that doubtless exacting position in the 1920s, he continues active in the diplomats' secret world.

*Raymond Carter.* A taciturn American with a family history back to the Mayflower. Now retired, he was once the Charge d'Affairs at the American Embassy in Paris.

These miracle workers are aided by a cast of good guys, all wealthy, titled, astute, steeped in politics and intrigue. Prominent among these is Scarpia, the aged Italian painter, who is featured during the first half of the 1920s. Scarpia spends his winters in the Sahara Desert "to renew his youth," and speaks a dreadful dialect, as if selling bananas from a cart. Only slowly is his vaudeville accent abandoned.

Scarpia plays a major role in the April 1921 story, "In an Old Venetian Palace," during which the forces of Hell and Germany are slickly outwitted. He returns in "The Map of the Mediterranean" (March 1924) when a private conference with a pair of kings is arranged under the noses of a batch of spies.

"A Night in the Kremlin" (May 1924) would raise the hair of a dead man. The time is immediately after Lenin's death. Trevor is in Russia, disguised as a German newspaper representative, to observe conditions at first hand.

Conditions are bloody horror. Trevor and companions are detained, taken to the Kremlin for questioning, menaced by the deadly women who manipulates the Soviet leadership. You may have heard that Stalin was the master, but you heard wrong.

Trevor eavesdrops on a conference of the Soviet leaders. This is depicted as equalling the howlings in a lunatic asylum. Finally the Free Lances escape, disguised as soldiers. It is highly improbable melodrama. It is also disquieting. In spite of its purple crudities, the story generates a feeling of blood savagery rampant. That, at least, was not far from the truth.

"A Call for Help" (October 1924) takes place at Trevor Hall, a castle on the English coast. Under the building the rock is honeycombed with rooms, labs, passages. Beyond the castle, concealed in the woods, lurks a complete aircraft factory. Trevor has created a self-contained world within England.

For years, persistent rumors have linked Trevor and his friends to a group of half-mythical "Diplomatic Free-Lances." Disproved a hundred times, the rumors persist. Finally the Russians, thirsting for the truth, devise a vicious little trap. A slick female spy is planted inside Trevor's household, and a faked message from Lammerford is delivered saying that he has been caught and held prisoner in Moscow. Trevor and company nibble but doubt and do not bite.

Early in 1920, Trevor and Nan have a son. For reasons unaccountable, they name him Ivo. He grows so vigorously that, by 1932, he will be twenty-odd years old, a scientific genius with a thirst for intrigue.

As Ivo matures, so does the series.

"A Weakening of Morale" (December 1924) pits Abdool and his

cousins against a nest of agents newly hatched from their Moscow nest. "The One Irresistible Woman" (June 1925) tells how Nan became the real power behind the French government for many years. In "The Resignation of Michael Radayne" (June 1928), the Trevors frame and force from office a politician who threatens to become an English dictator. And during "A Spy in Downing Street" (July 1928), Trevor tricks a beautiful spy into stealing the wrong papers. In this story, the King of England confers several times with Trevor, loading him with responsibility and honors. To this time, the Trevor group has operated for about twenty years. All but Nan are approaching middle age. It's time, the King points out, that they come in from the cold.

In some ways Trevor agrees. His enterprises have expanded with the years. Gradually they have extended themselves into an invisible state, in certain ways more powerful than England, itself. And now the King offers him political power.

Being a modest man, Trevor agrees only to become the power behind the Cabinet, settling for the less conspicuous position as Keeper of the Privy Seal. (This merely involves leadership of the House of Lords.) For the next few years, the original Free-Lances will slowly yield their commanding roles to new blood—the quickly maturing Ivo for one.

Deadly games continue. No longer are they played exclusively in Europe. As Norroy forecast, the action, beginning in 1932, transfers to the Orient.

For obvious reasons. New is again following the headlines. In 1931, the Japanese had swarmed into Manchuria, China's northeastern region. On hearing the news, Nan, Abdool, and Ivo (frequently called the Viscount Salcombe to the deep confusion of the reader) board the *Ranee Sylvia*. They streak across oceans and, by the April 1932 issue, are anchored in Hong Kong harbor. All around rise the fumes of political intrigue. Here scheme Chinese traitors and vicious Russians.

Against these desperate types, Ivo brings super-science.

He has invented this Doc Savage sort of gadget, an electrically-amplified listening device that can be tuned to speech frequencies. At five miles or more, it can pick up a specific voice. Two devices must be used to follow a conversation between two people.

Using his equipment, Ivo eavesdrops on a Russian agent plotting with a Japanese. The Communists plan to reinforce the Japanese with men and munitions and have bribed three Chinese generals to betray their Army.

This information, Ivo and his fiancee (the Honorable Jean Wallington) take to Tuchan Wu-H'sien-Li, one of the half dozen men running China. The Tuchan smiles blandly, serves tea to all, including the Russian. Next morning, the Russian's head is found at a significant distance from his body. The three generals are gracefully poisoned.

Such silken violence staggers old Duchess Ascoynham, a guest aboard the Trevor yacht. She represents all that is substantial, upright, and Victorian in the Empire. She is dazed by the savage activities around her, horrified by the bland lethality of those nice people, the Trevors, her close friends.

The Duchess is, in a word, a figure of conventional morality. She equates secret service activities with a game and is deeply shocked when the game involves bloodshed, murder, double crossing, and tricking men to death.

The May 1932, "When China Fights" carries the story one step further. Japanese and Chinese officials agree to meet aboard the Ranee Sylvia to discuss peace. Learning of this meeting, Col. Roston, a Russian spy, arranges a night bombing attack on the ship—it being in Russia's interests that the war continue.

However....

Ivo discovers the Russian plot. He arranges an awful surprise for the attackers. Out on the borderland of physics, Ivo has discovered a new ray—the n-ray. When played against an internal combustion engine, the ray damps out the electrical system. It is a ray because a ray is easy to describe and can do almost anything—damp out internal combustion systems, for example. In the military arsenal, the ray is a most satisfying weapon. It is convenient, instantaneous, silent. Its only drawback is that it is magic. The reader does not notice this, since the ray is described by words having many syllables.

For soured individuals unimpressed by rays, Ivo's invention further weakens the credibility of a series that is becoming increasingly improbable. What is acceptable for *Thrilling Wonder Stories* is merely childish in *Blue Book*. Granted, of course, that many people relished *Thrilling Wonder Stories*.

Admittedly, acoustic rays and ignition-damping rays lessen the author's difficult task of plot resolution. Ivo readily fends off the Russians. Two bombers get rayed and down the rascals go.

A few paragraphs later, the Chinese decapitate Col. Roston. They employ no rays.

Roston has had no luck at all. Earlier in the story, he fell victim to another of Ivo's secrets—a violent pressure on the back of the neck.

[Ivo's] hand flashed around under Roston's arm, digging a thumb and two fingers deeply into the flesh at the top of his spine—and the officer's arms dropped limply to his sides. He staggered and fell (New, *When China Fights* 97).[5]

The vulnerability of the neck was exploited lavishly by the next generation of pulp magazine heroes. Scores of thugs, gunmen, and killers, unexpectedly seized by the neck, found themselves temporarily unconscious or temporarily paralyzed. This was a favorite assault tactic of Doc Savage, who left, through his novels, long swatches of mute, immobile criminals, glaring frantically ahead.

That such secret pressure points existed was an article of faith. Apparently their presence was suggested in the various do-it-yourself ju-jitsu handbooks of the period. For ten cents, anyone could learn pressure points and bring down that fierce bully.

Numerous small boys experimented upon each other during the 1940s. There is no official record of unconsciousness being produced, although numerous small battles occurred after it was learned that it hurt to have the back of your neck squeezed.

With the June 1932, "The Sinews of War," the Free Lance series returns to England. There seven men meet secretly. They control all the financial interests in Europe and they agree that Japan has gone far enough. Until Japan begins to pull out of Manchuria, all further financial credit will be refused.

Chief among these dignitaries is George Trevor, luminous under a new title, Marquess of Lyonesse. Secretly the German representative advises Sondermann of South Africa about this decision. And Sondermann is displeased. The Japanese owe him twenty million dollars. In a vast South American warehouse complex, he has collected immense quantities of war materiel for them. In doing so, he has toppled into a financial crack. Unless the Japanese pay soon, his economic empire will collapse.

Logically the solution to his dilemma is to kidnap Trevor, as you have already concluded. And so he does. Both Trevor (Marquess of Lyonesse) and Ivo (Lord Salcombe) end up in an evil cellar.

Only for a moment.

Noting that the series leads have disappeared, the Honorable Jean and Prince Abdool apply cold ratiocination to the problem. They reason out who snaffled the Marquess and the Lord, and where, and why. Within an hour, the rescue is complete.

Since one does not kidnap a Trevor with impunity, retaliation is immediate. A flock of bombers appear over those South American warehouses. (Trevor's private military forces are easily equal to this assignment.) Without warning, twenty million dollars in bombs and canned seaweed spray skyward. Sondermann is bankrupted. The Japanese begin a slow withdrawal from Manchuria.

If history is to be believed, it was a slow withdrawal, indeed. First the Japanese established the puppet state of Manchukuo, and they retained a presence in the area until 1945.

In a related story, "An Asiatic Vendetta" (July 1932), the Japanese attempt to kill those financiers who cut off their credit. Yellow killers slink behind every shadow, loaded with knives and machine guns. Trevor fuddles them with ingenious disguises and the vendetta dwindles away in confusion.

But the situation, like a serial gone mad, hurls out new variations. The Russians now prepare to invade Manchuria ("The Cloud in the Orient," August 1932). Worse they have entered into Secret Written Agreements. Could these agreements be placed before the League of Nations, another war might be prevented. And so....

The Trevor Establishment pumps a Russian spy nest full of anesthetic gas, another bit of technological magic. Taking instant effect, the gas leaves no after effects. Extraordinary as it might seem to a layman, no victim ever suspects that he has been gassed.[6]

The sheets of the signed agreement being conveniently at hand, they are copied and placed in the League's hands. For good measure, a ship from Trevor's private navy torpedoes a Russian cargo vessel carrying munitions to Japan.

Not long after this story, Clarence New died. You would suppose that "Diplomatic Free Lances" came to a sudden end. However, Blue Book's files bulged with material and the series continued brightly into 1933, the final story of the series appearing in June of that year.

In this adventure, the narrative continues to follow the headlines, then concerned with trans-Atlantic flights and airmail service. In "The Transatlantic Air Mail" (May 1933), Trevor competes with the Germans to establish the first regularly scheduled airmail/passenger flights from Europe to America.

But the end is upon us. The final Free-Lances story, "Planes Across the Sea," June 1933, continues the struggle to establish an airline against the machinations of those German villains, who fail miserably and die in swarms.

Fiction by New continued to appear in Blue Book. The editor seemed reluctant to terminate the Free Lances and the August 1933 story, "The Strange Case of Lady Anne," while identified as "An adventure of the Famous Free Lances in Diplomacy," was in reality a new series. This featured Dr. Samuel Adams, an American in England, who solved a number of mysteries. Chief Inspector Beresford of Scotland Yard, who often assisted the Free Lances, and Earl Lammerford, a senior member of the firm, are present, and Trevor's shadow passes frequently across the prose, although he never quite appears. That the editor gently grafted these stories onto the Free Lance mainstream is suspected but not known.

With "The Warburton Mystery" in the May 1934 Blue Book, New's by-line disappeared from the contents page. But the spirit of the series continued in other magazines and with other heroes.

Clarence Herbert New, born in Brooklyn in 1862, early saw enough of the world to describe it convincingly for the rest of his life. Twice he traveled around the world. The first trip, in 1880, proved arduous beyond expectation. Free-lancing articles as he went, he traveled by clipper ship to Australia where he was shipwrecked and his arm broken; he floated for hours, clinging to a spar. After riding a thousand miles across Australia, he was attacked and wounded by Bushmen. Later he traveled to the Philippines, hunted tigers, and, at Papua, was rescued from a burning ship.

His second round the world trip in 1891 was far less stimulating. Then a consulting engineer, he visited Africa, the West Indies, South America, and Europe. The look and smell, the shapes and colors of these places, the details of shipboard life, ring through his fiction with complete authenticity. He had been there.[7]

In 1893 New abandoned engineering to become an editor. He served on *Truth* (1895), *New York and London Literary Press* (1897-1910), and *Reel Life* (1913-1914). From 1909 on, he was a professional writer. His work appeard in *Blue Book*, as well as the English *Cassell's New Magazine* and *Premier Magazine*. As a professional, he concentrated on series—both fiction and fact. He originated about eight major series, among them the "Free Lances," (1909-1933); "Deep Water Men" (1920-1921); "Galt, M.D." (1926-1927)—this signed Culpeper Zandtt; and "Buccaneers Limited" (1927-1928), signed Stephen Hopkins Orcutt. Many of these stories were adapted for the moving pictures.

In 1916, a bear at the Brooklyn Park Zoo tore his arm so badly that it had to be amputated. "After loss of his arm, however, our undaunted author rigged a wire from the shift key of his typewriter to his foot, and continued to type his own stories with one hand" (Kennicott).

He continued to write until his death, January 8, 1933. He was just over 70.

In a series twenty-four years long, you may expect variations in style. The "Free Lance" series does not disappoint you. Early stories lumber along, barnacled by titles of nobility, the paragraphs thick with nicely punctuated conversation, the action sluggish. Over a quarter of a century, the fiction slims down, speeds up, and dresses itself in relatively smoother prose. New's transparent infatuation with English titles raged unchecked to his final sentence.

Down through the years, the stories track international headlines and major inventions, including many not yet invented. Over the length of the series, the characters age, marry, have children. They rise high in the nobility. Their fortunes grow lushly, unaffected by depression.

Their personalities alter, too. You note this subtle change only after transversing the series from beginning to end. Perhaps the Trevors have experienced too many plots, too many deaths. Too many struggles in the subterranean silences of the secret service. Whatever the cause, they show a certain character hardening—that casual iciness so shocking to the Duchess in 1932.

In part this is a consequence of Mr. New's particular brand of fiction. He was not writing of psychological subtleties, but of menace, violence, and falling bodies. No action figure who endures in the public heart ponders over each soul he sends across the Styx.

Yet there seems something more. During those twenty-five years, the Trevors' base of authority gradually shifted. At some point, they began doing for fun what previously they did for duty.

They are heroic figures operating from a gradually dwindling moral base. You can't call them justice figures, for the justice figure draws his justification from the laws of his society. Perhaps these laws are defective and inexplicably wide meshed; but they form the platform from which he strikes.

By contrast, the Trevors (and other secret agents) do not defend a code of justice. No such high thing. They are committed to realizing the policies of their government.

Quite a different thing. That is building a bed for the wind. National goals change. Expediency is the only firm guideline. In the confusion of accomplishment, all direction vanishes, except the need for success.

It is hollow enough justification for action.

To conceal this hollowness, it is necessary to deny the opponents' humanity. That is one reason for the succession of vile Germans, Russians, and Japanese, sneering monsters all, politically out of fashion, and, as everyone knows, treacherous and unworthy. By reducing the opponent to the dimensions of a decal, it is easier to manipulate his destruction, no guilt accruing against the side of Justice and Right.

A similar moral vacuum sucks at the heart of much pulp fiction. It is not only the shallow characters and unrelenting violence that darkened the medium's reputation. It is also that the characters swim in expediency. They are not accountable for the results of their violence, nor have they responsibility for their actions, beyond the need for consistent success. Nothing more substantial dominates them than plot requirements.

They do not feel. The plot will not permit it. The character must remain admirable although he kills five hundred times. Each new story wipes the old blood from him. He has no emotional history. He could not bear it if he did.

Over two generations, the Trevors grow increasingly independent of those laws governing human conduct. In 1911, Trevor supports England by exposing or frustrating German political plots. In 1932, he mounts independent military action—not by government direction but because he has become the ultimate authority for determining the appropriate action. He has become independent of the English government and the English law. As long as he violates no laws openly, he is permitted to flaunt them privately. He has stepped outside the web of law, outside the citizen's responsibilities, outside the strictures of conventional social structure.

Trevor maintains a state within a state. In Devon, he has established a vast industrial complex. Here, in underground rooms dug into a cliff face, secret laboratories spread, manned by a dozen brilliant scientists. For knowledge is power.

The Trevor mansion, that marvel of Jacobean architecture, looms luxurious on London's Park Lane. The mansion is fortified. From it extend massive arms of financial and political power. It is more a center of government than most national capitols.

England is weak. The League of Nations is ineffective. The United States reels through the Jazz Age. Europe sways in political confusion. Real power concentrates in the hands of those eight financiers, the real political state of Europe. A state that has evolved beyond mere national interests, just as, in our strange days, we see towering around us supranational corporations. Interests so huge are beyond nationality.

The Trevors only seem to be British nobility. They are, instead, people fundamentally without a country. Only their power base remains.

Granted that "Free Lances in Diplomacy" does not see matters this way. As far as New is concerned, the Trevors perform within the context of the aristocracy. They may be relied to do the right thing because they are aristocracy—wealthy, successful, highly educated, lauded. The message is clear: the aristocrat in the secret service need be forbidden nothing; his noble blood assures against excess—Wodehouse and Edgar Wallace to the contrary.

By the late 1920s and early 1930s, these elements of the Diplomats series exerted considerable influence on several prominent single-character magazines as Doc Savage, and the Spider. The aristocratic elements were greatly softened. But each series, in its own way, accepted as a convention the image of a powerful individual heading a powerful state within a state. All were fixed in contemporary time, folding current events into the narrative flow. All embraced advanced technology. And the Trevor fortified mansion was certainly echoed by Richard Wentworth's redoubt on Sutton Place.

The fictional conventions accepted by these series passed silently to innumerable lesser series. Which would have pleased Trevor. He enjoyed powerful, silent influences. To affect a major branch of popular literature for better than twenty years.

Amazin'! Fawncy that!

# Chapter Five
# The Improbable Cockney

*Representative Sayings of John Solomon:*

It ain't proper to dig up the past, as the old gent said when 'e lead 'is third to the altar.

'umans is 'umans, and nature ain't to be denied, as the parson remarked when 'e smashed the constable in the eye.

I'm werry unselfish, as the old gent said when 'e gives the 'ousemaid three kisses.

It's the things you don't expect what makes it 'ard for you, as the old gent said when 'e found the butler 'ugging of the 'ousemaid.

You stay with me long enough and you'll know a lot, as the old gent said when 'e 'ired the pretty 'ouse-keeper.

It's a lost art, as the 'ousemaid said when the butler asked 'er for a kiss.

It ain't knowing people as counts; it's 'aving them know you.

*The Appearance of John Solomon*:
He is a fat little Cockney, born and raised in Wapping near the sound of the Bow Street bells, which area is, by definition, home of the Cockney. Solomon is old, his hair grayed nearly to white. His face, although lined with age, seems empty, a tablet unwritten upon, and his two large pale blue eyes stare blankly. Shabby clothing drapes him. Whenever possible, he wears carpet slippers and an ancient tarboosh (a fez shaped like an inverted clay pot). He smokes constantly, sucking noisily on an ancient clay pipe, rancid and black. The tobacco he thriftily whittles from a black plug. As he smokes, he talks aimlessly, deferential, easily abashed, guileless, ineffectual, harmless.

*The Business of John Solomon*:
For about thirty years, he has conducted a ship-chandler's business in Port Said. In Chicago, he was a sort of private investigator, more or less. In London, he seemed, once again, to be a ship-chandler, a seller of marine supplies.

*The Skills of John Solomon*:
He speaks and writes four or five languages fluently, including Arabic.

*The Collections of John Solomon:*

He is a connoisseur of fine oriental rugs, and surrounds himself with them, ancient, lovely rugs, some rather dim and badly worn, but masterpieces of the weaver's art, the rich, soft-spoken beauty of the past. These rugs, he does not display; they reside with him, piling his numerous houses.

Less obviously, he collects notebooks bound in red morocco. He possesses quantities of these, file drawers packed with them. Each notebook is filled with Solomon's neat, copperplate handwriting. These are his accounts, he explains. Each notebook deals with the life and crimes of a single individual.

*Rumors Concerning the Life and Activities of John Solomon:*

That he is wealthy beyond dream. That an invisible vast network of Europeans, Africans, Arabs stands eager to serve him, ceaselessly collecting information for his use. That he exercises gigantic political power. That he is known and respected by the men really controlling Europe, the Near East, and the North American continent, and that any government in this vast area will aid him on request. Aid him immediately, without hesitation or question.

Frequently he needs aid. For John Solomon, like Trevor, often goes adventuring.

He adventured for an extended period through several magazines. He was first introduced in *The Argosy*, in 1914, a fifteen-cent magazine nearly an inch thick, issued monthly and containing 240 pages of text and about 20 pages of advertisements that padded the front and back like fat on a bear. Through the trackless inside pages, the fiction marched double column, unbroken by illustration, except for the undistinguished sketch that introduced each story.

Infrequent poems, tacked unillustrated into the space at the end of stories, fended for themselves, not even recognized on the contents page.

At this period, each issue of *The Argosy* offered a complete novel of 60,000 to 75,000 words, a novelette, and eight short stories. For fifteen cents, you purchased an imposing mass of fiction.

In this massive publication, Solomon made his first appearance: a two-part serial titled "The Gate of Farewell" (January and February 1914).

The story tells how John Solomon and a few others destroyed Parrish, that renegade from Christendom, that black-souled genius. Parrish joined the Moslems, became a force in Islam. He built a stronghold named The Gate of Farewell near the Red Sea. From here he planned to conquer the holy cities of Mecca and Medina, net all of

Arabia, and finally to lead the Moslem world against the Christians, restoring Islam to world power.

Parrish's dreams were backed by the guns and riches of the Senussiyeh, a secret order of fighting monks spread like bacteria through North Africa. With ten million members, fortified cities hidden in the desert, and wealth beyond calculation, the terrible society formed the blood and bones of Islam. It stands, one way or the other, as the dreaded opponent in many early Solomon adventures.

Recognizing that the Senassiyeh and Parrish threatened Western civilization, Solomon negotiated the backing of the Sultan at Constantinople. For the Sultan feared the political power of the Brotherhood. After great difficulty and personal danger, Solomon contrived to wreck Parrish's plans and captured the wicked fellow—who promptly took poison and so escaped earthly justice.

Soon after this, in the July 1914, "John Solomon—Supercargo," the scene shifts to the Mombasa Coast of Portuguese East Africa. Somewhere in that area lies buried massive piles of gold and religious ornaments—gifts from a Viceroy of India to the King of Portugal. But never received. Buried instead in a fort now lost in jungle.

Documents establishing the fort's location have been discovered. A beautiful female archaeologist is in charge of the dig. Unfortunately, a hardboiled German has learned of the treasure. Chartering a yacht, staffing it with a fierce crew, he plans to rip the treasure from its rightful finders.

The narrator of the story, the yacht's doctor, is determined to protect the beautiful archaeologist. He is unsure whether he can trust that odd John Solomon, supercargo of the yacht, who knows so much and speaks so mysteriously with evil-seeming Arabs.

Then murder strikes. The evidence is queerly garbled. Soon the doctor has slugged the German squarely in his glowering face and flees through the jungle, captured, escaping, aided by Solomon, recaptured.

Until all is lost, utterly lost. Solomon is checkmated. The doctor, holding the beautiful woman in his arms, balances on a ledge half down a deep shaft. Above him sneers the terrible German. Below coil puff adders. His legs tremble. Agony locks his back. Darkness edges his brain. He falls....

Into a spectacular cheat. Since there was no obvious way out, H. Bedford-Jones merely rendered the puff adders harmless. It was a wicked thing to do, equivalent to that famous line:

"With a single, super-human effort, he leaped from the inescapable pit."

However, it did preserve the hero and heroine, until Solomon and his men wipe out the enemy forces. At some personal cost, the hero guns down the German fiend. The treasure, it is pleasing to report, finds its way to responsible hands.

Prior to the final dead march, however, we enjoy that interesting scene played out in each of the John Solomon stories: the moment when Solomon faces the villain and presents his accounts:

[Solomon] drew out his red, morocco-bound notebook. Then, wetting his thumb, he opened it and shuffled over the leaves until he found the place desired.

"Ah, 'ere it be, all shipshape and proper!" He held it out and Krausz [the villain this time] took it....

"Werry sorry I am, Dr. Krausz, sir" went on the little man apologetically, "for to bring this 'ere account to your notice, but you asked a question, sir, and so I answers according. If a man can't tell 'is business honest like, I says, why 'e ain't got no business 'aving any business, says I. If you'll just turn over the page, sir...."

...[As Kransz] read, his heavy jaw snapped shut and a dark flush rose slowly to his brow....

Deeper and deeper grew the flush, though he forced himself to turn over the page and read to the end; then with a swift movement he dashed the note-book down and sprang up with fists extended and shaking....

"Swine!" he roared, furious almost beyond control. "Swine!" (Bedford-Jones, "John Solomon—Super cargo" 796).

It is never divulged what Solomon writes in these notebooks that so enrages men of otherwise reptilian calm. Always the notebook entry explodes them. Always the book is thrown into the dirt and Solomon, together with his friends and associates, are herded toward violent death. Which never quite arrives. Not for Solomon and his friends and associates. On the other hand, the villain and his cohorts die in exceedingly large numbers, scattered over the final chapters.

And at the end of it all:

"There!" and Solomon clapped his note-book shut with a very complacent air. "I'd been and overlooked that 'ere account wi' Dr. Kransz; but it's all shipshape and proper now to file away and 'ave done with."

*Friend*: "That's the one you presented to him, eh? Do you always keep your accounts, John?"

"Werry good plan, sir. They come in 'andy, like, mortal often, even if they're filed away" (Bedford-Jones, "John Solomon—Super cargo" 817).

"The Seal of John Solomon" (June 1915) is a glowing lost city adventure. Far and away in the African desert rises an ancient volcanic crater. Inside the crumbling cone stands a Norman castle inhabited by the rather demoralized descendents of Crusaders who lost themselves in these forlorn parts. Secret in the belly of this place hides a slick stone slide, this designed to spiral unfortunates down to the fire at the earth's heart. Rising from this devil's toy bulks a huge rock, engraved with a symbol of interlocked triangles. Precisely the same symbol graven on the rings John Solomon provides his agents; it is the mark of Suleiman, otherwise known as Solomon the King.

Aside from these varied distractions, the castle also contains an ancient document attesting that Mohammed, founder of the Moslem faith, had become a Christian and died professing *that* religion.

The Sultan Osmanlis, head of the Islamic faith, has heard rumors of that document. He is consequently warm to destroy it, together with its group of protectors. This is how Solomon, friend of the Moslems, finds himself opposing the Moslem world. The prospect scares him badly. He knows that world too well.

Set down where he was [in Port Said], dealing with Moslems more often than with Christians, much more at home in Arbi than in English, it is not strange that others have asserted that John was a convert to Islam. It must be confessed that he held secrets rigorously guarded from all Christians; that he possessed gifts of regal splendor and letters of friendship from Sultan and emir and sheik; that he had small regard for the law of Christian nations, and that on at least two occasions the head of Islam had decorated and honored him. (Bedford, "The Seal of John Solomon" 465)

But what a man must do, he will do. Risking the rage of all Moslems, Solomon and a few friends, the narrator included, struggle across the desert toward a strange mountain range. There, rumor has it, the document may be found, protected by fearful guardians. After prolonged and graphic suffering, they find the castle. A fanatical army of Moslems rage after them. The castle is besieged, assaulted, overrun. The resulting battle, like much else in this novel, echoes *Allan Quartermain*, and rises nearly to the heights of an H. Rider Haggard combat.

At the end, the remnants of evil face the fragments of good, not much being left of either side. Things look black for John and company. Till the last possible second. Then Solomon's acutely developed foresight provides just barely enough edge for good to survive. This issue's fiend slides the stone spiral to a hot end.

Taking the inflammatory document with him. So the world loses the knowledge of Mohammed's conversion, and Islam remains unshattered.

By the end of this novel, you begin to observe that the stories share a certain common structure. The narrator, a highly competent professional (usually engineer or doctor) meets Solomon amid mysterious happenings. While not quite trusting Solomon, the hero is drawn into the storm. For a beautiful girl is involved. She is menaced by an extremely competent bad man. Before you known it, bodies tumble about, Solomon has disappeared, and hero and heroine race through an exotic scene, hotly chased by the hordes of Hell. After a succession of captures and escapes, the hero faces the villain. Solomon presents his accounts. And the whole adventure winds up in a blast of white-hot violence, the hero slugging away industriously till unconscious. But he wakes triumphant.

Thoroughly interesting; thoroughly exciting; thoroughly satisfactory.

Although the series belongs to Solomon, he appears infrequently. The essential story is about the narrator, and is told from his point of view, usually first person. The narrator favored by H. Bedford-Jones is highly intelligent, alert, and quick witted. A big, well muscled man, he is as competent with his fists as with weapons. His one deficiency is that he is not John Solomon. He does, however, get the girl during the final paragraphs of each novel. This would seem a woeful waste of narrators, but Bedford-Jones thriftily economizes, in later novels, by having the narrator of one become a secondary character in the next.

Although problems, characters, and scenes differ in each work, this underlying structure remains predictably present. It is a product of Bedford-Jones' method of writing. He claimed never to plan out his stories. "In general, he just let them write themselves."[1]

As Jones, himself, wrote (using the third person, as if he were some eye objective in the heavens): "Jones himself was never one for plot. I doubt if he could have lined out a decent three-act drama in merest synopsis. He believed with Poe that a story had a first class plot when none of its component parts could be removed without detriment to the whole and he suited his work to this belief. Perhaps this is why his stories seldom got into the movies; they simply lacked plot. Yet they sold like a shot"(18).

With the publication of "The Seal of John Solomon," that interesting character abruptly disappeared from *The Argosy*. There was a reason and an excellent one: his series had switched to *People's* magazine, the first Solomon adventure appearing in the March 1915 issue. Of necessity, he ended in *The Argosy*. Major series characters did not spread themselves across multiple magazines, since the primary function of a series character was to draw readers back again and again to a specific publication, thus generating a lustrous stream of coins for the publisher.

While no one explained why Jones transferred his character from *The Argosy* to *People's*, it was likely a matter of increased payment. Authors are susceptible to improved earnings. For whatever reason, the adventures of John Solomon continued in *People's* for the next six years.

Published by Street & Smith, this publication had been originally issued as *People's Magazine*, the first issue dated July 1906. At first the magazine attempted to please every reader, offering a rambunctious mixture of brief news stories, quotes from famous people, articles, theatrical news, poetry, painful jokes, biographical sketches, quotations from selected newspapers, and a scattering of serials and short fiction. Most of this dross swiftly vanished in the fierce clawing of the market place.

There followed a series of name changes: *People's Story Magazine, People's Ideal Fiction Magazine, People's,* and (later) *People's Favorite Magazine*. At various times, under various titles, the magazine was a potpourri, then all fiction, then fiction plus illustrated articles. For a time, the pulp paper grew glossy. The page count rose and fell like a fluttering heart. But by mid-1920, the editor abandoned tinkering and *People's* reached its final identity, a thick, all-fiction pulp. Having achieved Nirvana, it was discontinued with the June 15, 1924, issue, only to rise again, a few weeks later, as *Complete Stories*, July 1924, proving that death is but a dream.

Back in 1915, and at that moment titled *People's*, the magazine was a 15-cent monthly, containing 224 pages of fiction. It offered a complete novel, a novelette, three serial stories, and five short stories. As in *The Argosy*, which *People's* closely resembled, only a single sketch appeared at the head of most—not all—stories. Unlike *The Argosy*, the only advertising appeared on the back cover. Format and type closely resembled that of its sister publication, *The Popular Magazine*.

"Solomon's Quest" (March 1915), first of the new series, begins with a situation that would be used to rags over the following years in every pulp magazine published and nearly every B moving picture made: an incongruous object, sought by fierce men, causes a string of murders. Thus, in "Quest," murder follows the trail of blue lacquer beads, marked with an Arabic sign.

One hundred beads exist, making up the Moslem rosary of Mohammed. If the villain collects them all, he will be acknowledged as the head of Islam, will expel the Turks, and raise a new war against Christendom.

This sounds familiar. And so is the villain, none other than Lionel

Parrish, resurrected. (Instead of poison, he drank a hypnotic drug that caused him to look dead.)

Parrish has a few beads; Solomon has more. And the prize is the physical body of Mohammed, buried beneath a Christian cross, in ruined Theopolis, the City of God. This forgotten place is surrounded by a swamp, remote in the parched lands of The Abode of Emptiness. The location was discovered by the beautiful girl's uncle.

Meaning that presently, the hero (a ship's doctor), the girl, Solomon and a few men, gather in the city to discover wonders. Trapped there by Parrish, you'd think nothing whatever could save them.

But perhaps you noticed that camel wandering away across the path over the swamp? Did you remember that a few of Solomon's men lingered on the far side of the swamp?

Don't give up hope. The doctor escapes, initiating an extraordinary series of captures, rescues, and escapes. In a frenzied finale, the swamp reeds are set afire, Solomon's men arrive barely in time, Parrish is thoroughly shot dead. He will never return.

On the negative side, the mummy of Mohammed is blown to flinders by dynamite. And John Solomon is so severely wounded in the final fight that his right leg must be amputated below the knee.

That wound, and the fight with the monastic brotherhood, has exhausted Solomon. His organization has been badly damaged, and, in the next novel, "Gentleman Solomon," June 1915, he travels to the United States to distance himself from the Moslem world.

Peace he is not to have. Within four chapters, he is in the Belgium Congo to investigate atrocities at the King's rubber plantations. (The atrocities—exploitation, torture, and murder of slave labor—were not fiction but fact and an international scandal; as would be expected, the popular fiction magazines, always sensitive to headlines, exploited the situation enthusiastically.)

Not only does Solomon find atrocities in rubber, but such other interesting things as white pygmies, a sacred mountain mined with explosives, and a couple of down-right wicked men attempting to steal an enormous cross of pure gold. Before the action is over, Solomon is trapped in a cave and almost roasted, the heroine threatened with dire consequences, which need not be expanded upon, and the hero is shot nearly to death. At that, they end better than their opposition, which fails to survive the final chapters.

"Solomon's Carpet" (October 1915) is a distinctly minor effort set in Chicago. The problem is the wholesale faking and theft of rare carpets, with murder tossed in to spice up proceedings.

And why, might you ask, has Solomon established himself in

Chicago in a corner office on the upper floor of the Gas Building at the intersection of Adams Street and Michigan Boulevard. According to Bedford-Jones, he is there because the war has flung across the United States a wave of master criminals driven from Europe by the war. These Solomon plans to search out. We may suspect that the presence in Chicago of Vincent Starrett and other friends of Bedford-Jones played some role in Solomon's choice of cities.

Exactly what Solomon does in Chicago is difficult to say. Apparently he is some kind of investigator. It is hard to tell from his office furnishings, which are spare. On the floor is a tattered fifteenth-century Ispahan rug. There is also an easy chair, two straight chairs, a small table, a huge built-in safe filled with boxes containing red morocco notebooks, and locked sectional cabinets solidly lining the walls. Here Solomon smokes and muses in wonderful solitude.

On his door is painted the following brusque legend:

JOHN SOLOMON
Entrance by Appointment Only
KEEP OUT!

To enter, you must have a special key. This is how the favored know that they have become Solomon clients: he mails them the key. All this seems wonderfully eccentric. As does his habit of seeking no pay and allowing the police all the credit.

Why does he do it? How does he live?

It does you no good to ask questions:

Solomon: "Them as asks questions get less 'n they asks, says I."

The following story, "Solomon's Submarine" (February 1916), leaves Chicago to hare around islands off the California coast. Plans for an advanced submarine have been stolen. So has an operating model of the sub, so advanced that it can replace its periscope, if shot off, up to twenty times. And if the conning tower is shot away, that can be automatically replaced two or three times. These rather freaky design innovations are accompanied by special gasoline engines and batteries that will not react with sea water. The whole suggests that neither the inventor nor H. Bedford-Jones enjoyed much familiarity with submarines. But the Japanese want this invention most extremely.

They nearly get it. The hero, beautiful girl, and the inventor are cast away on a lonely island. Escape, recapture, violence. Solomon attempts a trick. It fails. Captured, he faces the grinning villains, alone, helpless, absolutely whipped:

*Villain*: "Let us first remove our friend Solomon...."

...Solomon lifted a weary, aged face.

"...you ain't a-goin' to 'ave me killed?"

*Villain*: "Too brutal a word. You are to become a martyr, let us say to the cause of...science."

Solomon dropped his head again, in hopeless despondency. Brune [newspaper man and hero] felt a thrill of pity for the little man, whose carefully planned scheme had proven so futile, so puerile, against the infernal cunning of [the villain]....

Solomon seemed dazed, stupid....

"...Would you mind lettin' me 'ave a whiff o' baccy afore Mr. Carlisle jabs that 'ere [poisoned] needle into me?"[2]

He gets his smoke. And just like that, amazing to anyone who hasn't read one of these novels before, the tables turn. Concealed guns blaze. The spies and neer-do-wells are cut down. The hero and villain meet in a murderous hand-to-hand battle. And it's over. By misdirection and craft, Solomon rises from defeat to victory resplendent.

*Hero* (to Solomon): John, you're a wonderful man, but I'm through with you. Why, you infernal scoundrel, up to the last minute I was pitying you and figuring on making a jump for Carlisle!... I have every respect for you—I like you up to the hilt—I'd do anything on earth for you; except to work with you again! I'd not go through another half hour like that for a million dollars, flat. You worked the same trick when we handled those rug thieves, and it nearly gave me heart failure then. This time I'm done. (71)

As we have noted, this scene, The Defeated Hero Helpless, is played repeatedly through the Solomon series. Twenty years later, similar scenes, with equally strong effect, ended many of the Doc Savage novels. Except in one feature. Doc, rigorously emotionless, never showed that artful dismay and regret expressed by John Solomon, just before the jaws of his trap whacked shut.

*People's* magazine presented Solomon in about ten novels and a serial between 1915 and 1921. His final adventure was "John Solomon—Incognito" (four-part serial, October 25 through December 10, 1921).

Then fell a nine-year silence, during which Bedford-Jones occupied himself with other projects. Solomon was not forgotten, however. One fine day at the beginning of 1930, he sprang to life once more, as baffling and eccentric as ever. He returned to his origins—*Argosy*, *People's* having been cancelled and, thus transformed to a collectible, fluttered away on luminous wings.

*Argosy* had also transformed itself. In the late 1920s, *The Argosy* had merged with All-Story Weekly to become the admirable *Argosy-Allstory Weekly*.[3] With the October 5, 1929, issue, the title slimmed down to *Argosy*, a ten-cent magazine of 144 pages, padded front and back with advertising pages, and filled with "Action Stories of Every Variety."

Action stories have a regrettable tendency to substitute caricature for character drawing and to abstract human emotions to simple grimaces, some plaintive, some stirring. Argosy had streamlined its fiction wonderfully since those casual days of 1915, and was in the process of concentrating its stories still further, rendering to bouillon what had been soup.

What *Argosy* wanted, H(enry) Bedford-Jones could provide, for he worked at the business of writing without pose or sentimentality, as a business. A thorough professional, Jones had been born in Canada in 1887. In Ireland, the family name had been simply Jones, but his grandfather, when emigrating from Dublin to Canada, had added the hyphenation.

Jones attended a year of college, decided that it was a waste of money and dropped out (a decision he would later bitterly regret). Leaving Canada, he worked for a Michigan country newspaper. He learned typesetting and stenography, became an extraordinarily rapid typist, and labored through early attempts to write. Eventually he took a job as stenographer in Chicago "for a railroad superintendent whose dictation was too fast for anyone to take. Jones merely forgot it and wrote letters in the general gist required. The super began to get so many compliments on his literary letters that he investigated, and offered Jones the job for life..." (Bedford-Jones, *Post Mortem* 9).

Instead Jones quit the job. For he had begun selling his writing. First, verse to Sunday-school magazines. Then boy's books (titles unidentified) which he wrote for $100 apiece, each book taking about two days. At the same time he ghosted fiction for a friend, William Wallace Cook, whenever that gentleman got over-committed. When Cook's wife died, Jones attended the funeral and learned that Cook had a deadline, that night, for a Merriwell novel. The novel had not been started. So Jones turned to the typewriter and wrote the complete manuscript, 25,000 words, that day.

When he was twenty-five, he sold a Foreign Legion story to Argosy under his own name. Thereafter, his career flamed. A facile, quick writer with a strong narrative sense, and the will to work brutal hours, he became one of the most successful writers of the period. By the late 1920s he was earning more than $60,000 a year. Largely self-educated, he became an authority on history, particularly military history. His work appeared in a staggering number of magazines. The list includes *Argosy, Blue Book, Black Mask, Adventure, Magic Carpet, Golden Fleece, Thrill Book, Clues, Detective Story, Nickel Detective, People's, Mystery, Star Magazine, Far East Adventure Stories, Clues, Detective Fiction Weekly, Doc Savage, Air Adventures, Tales of Magic and Mystery, Weird Tales.* He also published extensively in the slick magazines, among them *Collier's* and *Liberty.* And he published perhaps one hundred novels in the United States and England—he was, himself, unsure how many.

He was a prominent member of that unstructured group which made 1920s Chicago a literary center and included such well-known people as Vincent Starrett, Don Marquis, and Carl Sandburg. Early in his career, Bedford-Jones become interested in the collection of books, letters, and historical documents, and in book binding and the printing of monographs. He became a naturalized American citizen, developed heart trouble, lived in France many years with his collections, returned to the United States on the outbreak of World War II, and died in Beverly Hills, California, 1949. He had enjoyed a complex life, crowded with work.

Bedford-Jones adjusted the Solomon series to *Argosy's* more stringent requirements with no noticeable strain. Again he provided a tale of danger, menace, and violence as experienced by a competent hero, while John Solomon floated at the edges of the action like some peculiar moth.

In deference to the readers' interest in technological marvels, Solomon now followed in the path of the Diplomatic Free Lances. His secluded headquarters in Paris brimmed with wonders: a wall-sized, flat-screen television, for example; this created for him by dedicated scientists in his employment. They have also provided John with quartz violet rays to keep him from getting old (he sits bathed in them). Apparently the rays have also cured his wooden leg, which is not mentioned in the *Argosy* stories. The scientists have worked up a telephone so advanced that all Solomon need do is speak into the air and, behold, the air answers him ba This in the days of stiffly upright desk telephones with separate receivers.

These wonders appear in "The Mysterious John Solomon," a novelette in the January 25, 1930, *Argosy.* The hero, a discredited American engineer adrift in Paris, meets a pudgy little man whittling plug tobacco into a clay pipe. Off we go through shifting mists of intrigue, the action savage.

Although a naturalized American citizen, Solomon seems to have regained his interest in Europe. He has set up a new headquarters in Paris, at 13 *bis* Rue Montorgeuil, staffed by the usual faithful Arabs and brave with advanced technology. The story concerns a gigantic stock swindle that turns upon an irrigation project at the Algerian border. The hero is captured, drugged, recovers to disrupt the plans of a villain and villainness. Presently Solomon appears to present his accounts. Graphic violence. There the story ends, loose plot threads fluttering in the breeze: matters of an unexplained death ray and a grim mystery figure named Dominetti who did not appear....

All this is prelude to "John Solomon's Biggest Game" (six-part serial, February 15 to March 22, 1930). Solomon faces the brilliant master criminal, Prince Dominetti, head of a gigantic criminal ring in Europe, and a financier of world-wide power. With each serial part, the scope of the story expands.

It begins with the beautiful girl being decoyed to London; she is bringing Solomon reports of her father's experiments with the disintegrating ray. But sudden war has opened against Solomon's organization; an unseen hand murders his men wholesale. All over Europe, his headquarters explode and blaze; his Paris laboratories are blasted to gravel. As you might expect, police of all nationalities cannot cope.

Confusion reigns as Solomon reels helpless from the pages and most of the novel proceeds without him. Instead, the story focuses on the private vendetta between Warden, hero of this serial, and Dominetti's people.

Dominetti, you see, plans to conquer Russia and place a corrupt Grand Duke on the throne. These plans are opposed by Solomon, who has persuaded Benito Mussolini to support a Romanoff for the throne. No one appears to have asked Stalin's opinion.

These plans proceed against a frenzied storm of murder, druggings, abductions, rescues, fights, and burglaries. A corrupt Inspector of the *Surete* plans and tricks. Solomon's chief chemist is captured and tortured. Warden steals a secret treaty, signed by the United States, which would throw Europe into chaos if published. Then Warden is captured and must struggle for survival by matching wits with Dominetti, himself.

As for Solomon, it appears that his collapse is total. "Dang it!" he cries. "Dang it! Dang it!" It is as close as he ever gets to swearing. At the end of Chapter XVII, completely whipped, he capitulates. Prince Dominetti stands in Solomon's laboratory examining the disintegrating machine. He has succeeded in everything. The world is his.

That's Chapter XVII. Before the end of Chapter XVIII, Dominetti and his henchmen are dead, melted to atoms. Abruptly the world menace is not even a memory. But even Solomon, who can watch men die without any response at all, is shaken by the efficiency of the beam, the ultra-sonic wave, if you wish a more technical description.

*Solomon*: I'm done with it! I'm done with all this 'ere scientific deviltry, that's what. I'm a goin' back to simple things, just like that—I'm a goin' to Egypt, and I'm a goin' to stay there the rest o' me days! (Bedford-Jones, "John Solomon's Biggest Game" 139).

But Heavens above, there's no peace for a successful series character. Not only did Solomon continue in *Argosy*, but he burst out in a six-part serial, "Gold of Ishmael," which appeared in *Far East Adventure Stories*, February through November 1931. (Mid-way into the serial, the magazine's issuance changed to every-other-month.)

The main thrust of Solomon's adventures continued in *Argosy*. First came that expedition to the south of Tunis where caves concealed Moorish treasure—treasure protected by invisible angels serving an Emir who lived for hundreds of years. Other tangible opposition included the leader of an international hashish syndicate, who badly wanted that treasure, too ("Solomon's Caves," four-part serial, August 15 to September 5, 1931).

Then another fight developed with the Senussi brotherhood. The final fight, as it turned out. Aided by several Italian destroyers, Solomon intercepts the crucial arms shipment and the brotherhood withers into history ("Solomon Settles Accounts," February 13, 1932.)

The pace of the stories accelerates and the prose glows eerily as chapters are compressed to scenes and scenes to paragraphs. Solomon appears ever more frequently, working beside the hero, rather than manipulating the action from a distance.

Those fine villains of the past, all brains and muscles, have split into two parts, like some malignant cell. Solomon now faces not only a big, tough criminal, ruthless and cold, but his female accomplice, her painted lips frigidly twisted, her intelligence as swift as electron flow.

In the rather loosely knit "Solomon in the Catacombs" (May 20, 1933), Beauty and her kill-crazy brother have burrowed into Rome's catacombs. Down among the stacked skulls, they plan to assassinate Mussolini, an idea Bedford-Jones opposes. (At this time the era of the dictators was just beginning: Hitler had barely seized power; Mussolini would not confer with him till 1934. And not until the following year would Italy invade Abyssina and disgrace itself in the face of the world. In 1933, Italy's dictator and his black-shirt hordes were seen as benign, bringing order to an archaic and feckless country.)

Thus, at the beginning of "Catacombs," Solomon, the man of international contacts, has a personal interview with Mussolini, who seems more reasonable in fiction than in life. For the rest of the story, Solomon seems hopelessly outclassed. Physically he is not well, and suffers a mild heart attack during the story. Even so, he triumphs at the end, aided by a pipe loaded with gas and hundreds of black shirted troopers surrounding the catacombs.

The four-part serial, "The Terror of Algiers" (December 2 to 23, 1933), describes the battle against a gigantic blackmail and extortion ring. Told in first-person by a hardboiled American, it begins with a string of suicides somehow associated with an envelope containing a single negative. Such a fuss to grab a negative, you never saw. The beautiful bad girl is very beautiful and very bad; the villain is exceedingly tough; the American hero is both tough and intelligent; and the hand-to-hand fight at the end is admirable. Solomon lives through another heart attack, which doesn't slow him up much. As is usual, the ending switches from black despair to triumph in a matter of paragraphs.

"The Terror of Algiers" is the final John Solomon novel. From this point, the stories shrink to novelettes, meaning moderately long short stories. The scene shifts to London, where Solomon has unaccountably set himself up, once more, as a ship-chandler in a frowzy shop by the docks. John Carson, an American, becomes Solomon's able right hand.

Three stories appeared in this revised setting, lesser adventures all. The first, "John Solomon of Limehouse" (June 9, 1934), is concerned with US gangsters in London and the theft of entire trunk-loads of gold.

"The Case of the Kidnapped Duchess" (January 5, 1935), begins with Solomon stealing a gentleman's wallet and ends with Solomon and Carson spending a night in jail. In between, a duchess is drugged into a hateful marriage, and Solomon stage manages a murder, foils an attempt to steal a huge collection of emeralds, and shatters a savage gang of killers and thieves.

The final story, "The Case of the Deadly Barque" (February 9, 1935), is a Sherlock Holmes association piece. Working with Scotland Yard, Solomon investigates a string of ghastly murders which accompany an ancient sailing vessel: wherever it docks, corpses are found with throats torn out. Eventually Solomon finds the solution in a dark old London mansion. There Sir Ronald, the brain specialist, lies with his throat ripped away, victim of his own experiments with the Giant Rats of Sumatra.

So the series ends in the satisfying shadow of Sherlock Holmes, which had begun, twenty years earlier, in the shadow of H. Rider Haggard. The earlier adventure novels are of a texture and solidity superior to the later Argosy serials. The heart of the series lies in the early novels; the rest is repetition.

John Solomon began as an eccentric variation of the concealed mastermind, manipulator of history, his organization huge, his power immense. Many prominent fictional names have played that role, from Dr. Fu Manchu and the original Gray Phantom, to Trevor, Moriarty, and Clark Savage, Jr. In this role, Solomon manipulates, deals, and power brokers to great effect.

To the reader, that huge international organization has no more substance than a chorus girl's stockings. But as a character, Solomon is sufficiently outrageous to numb all criticism. We can forgive him much. We can forgive even the formula which gripped the series as a starfish grips an oyster. It does no harm to read how defeated good rose unexpectedly to crush triumphant evil.

It encourages us to hope in the face of overwhelming experience otherwise.

# Chapter Six
## Adventures of the Two Americans

Between operas, Richard Wagner was treacherous about money and inclined to seduce your wife. Between explosions of literary merit, Goethe tangled himself with a succession of young women, all much surprised when he finally fled into the night. Ernest Hemingway smoldered for years if criticized, and it was unkindly said that he got a new wife every time he published a novel. On a possibly less exalted level, Talbot Mundy married five times and divorced four, while concealing from wives and world alike the lurid wonder of his past.

His past impelled discretion. Born in London, 1879, as William Lancaster Gribbon, he was the oldest of three children. His brother would have a distinguished military career, his sister a less happy life. But their accomplishments and problems seem trivial beside the raging thunderstorm of William's personal history. In hindsight, that history divides into two strongly contrasting parts, the epiphanies of which must have bitterly puzzled him. How could matters have tangled so? He was a man of intelligence and considerable sensitivity.

At sixteen, his world disintegrated. His school career fell apart; his father died. Rather than study for ministry or law, he ran away from home. Ran to Germany to self-destructive freedom. For the next fifteen years, he would lead a scandalous life, at various times a swindler, con-man, drunkard, bankrupt, poacher, convicted felon, thoroughly unscrupulous with money, women, and the truth. Barely ducking the police, he skipped across the globe. To India and Cape Town, to Zanzibar and East Africa. He married and deserted one wife, took up an adulterous relationship with the wife of another man. Repeatedly he changed his name, inventing aristocratic histories for himself. After serving a brief prison term in Africa, he married for the second time. Served another short prison term and, under the name of Talbot Chetwynd Miller Mundy, sailed with his wife for New York, September 1909.[1]

The day after he arrived in that city, he lay penniless in Bellevue Hospital with a fractured skull, having got into a card game on the East Side, followed by blackjacking and robbery.

At this low point, that evil cloud enveloping fifteen years of his life began to dissipate. Recovering in the hospital, cruelly pressed for money, he began to write. Accidentally he had stumbled upon his golden key. He was a natural writer, creating a scene in two sentences, a breathing character at a stroke. He had the gift of authenticity, of taking places and things briefly seen, or only heard about, and converting them to solid presences on the page. Under the name Talbot Mundy, he sold fiction to *The Scrap Book*—his first published story being "A Transaction in Diamonds" (February 1911). In April of that year, he began his long career in *Adventure* with an article titled "Pig Sticking in India."

For the next twenty-nine years, Talbot Mundy was one of the most important names in popular fiction. His work appeared in *Argosy, All-Story, McClure's, The Cavalier, Everybody's,* in *The American Weekly* and *This Week,* in *Liberty and the Saturday Evening Post.* In England, he contributed to most of the major magazines of the period, including *The Strand, Cassell's, The Grand, The Storyteller, London Magazine, and The Thriller.*

In 1914, his novel, *Rung Ho,* was published, the first of about fifty books. He became an American citizen, became a member of the Theosophist Movement in California. He visited Palestine, saw a motion picture made of his most famous novel, *King of the Khyber Rifles.* Certain instabilities continued to haunt him. He was frequently married and as frequently sought Mexican divorces. Traveled widely. Established homes in Massachusetts and Florida with his fifth wife. From 1935 to 1940, he wrote scripts for the popular radio program, *Jack Armstrong, the All-American Boy.* And died in 1940 of complications resulting from diabetes, a disease which had ravaged his family.

He left behind a number of fascinating novels, packed with fascinating characters. But no character was more bizarre and unusual than the character he had fashioned for himself, through God knows what anguish, resentment, and pride. Undeniably he had a talent for fiction. Even the less credible moments of his life reveal that.

Of the several groups of series stories Mundy wrote for *Adventure,* two stand out, peaks against the sky. Tros of Samothrace and his struggles against Julius Caesar will be considered in the next chapter. Here we turn to the adventures of Jim Grim, formally known as James Schuyler Grim and referred to by the Arabs as Jimgrim.

Grim is an American who has made himself indispensable to the British secret service. The scene is the Near East soon after World War I. Initially the series tightly focuses on the regions around Jerusalem and the social/political problems swarming there. Thus, in the first story, Grim prevents war in Palestine. Subsequently he prevents Islamic war against the British. Then, after outmaneuvering a succession of murderous sheiks, he alters the destiny of the Near East.

Since the exploits of heroes necessarily expand as their series balloon through time, Grim eventually finds himself battling world-wide conspiracies in India and Tibet, and concludes his adventures by destroying a would-be world emperor armed with ancient science and occult powers.

The series, then, strides bravely from realistic action into high fantasy. Yet every step is described in such specific, concrete, circumstantial detail that the reader is barely aware of the improbabilities buoying up the story. The action boils. The characters of the story seem entirely real: they cast shadows; they think; they hold opinions and speak with hard-won wisdom. Danger permanently surrounds them. Through taut pages, they fear and laugh, struggle, travel with huge effort, suffer, and die by battle or by accident. Each character seems to have stepped briefly from real life into fiction, soon to step back again. It is extraordinary character drawing, marred by a single omission: these people do not love. When that sentiment intrudes, it is invariably couched in such terms that it must be refused. In compensation there is a wealth of male bonding. Perhaps this emotional artificiality reflects stress in the much-married author; more simply, it may only reflect the convention of male-oriented adventure magazine.

"In real life," Mundy wrote,:

"Grim was an American officer attached to British Intelligence in Palestine, where I met him in 1920. He very kindly introduced me to the lewder fellows of the baser sort with whom it was his business to deal. They were excellent company, as he was also, although he was a difficult man to understand." (Mundy, *Jimgrim* v)

The preceding may be true, although only the rash accept uncritically anything Mundy wrote about himself. But apparently he was in Palestine in 1920. There his brother had served British Intelligence for some years. However it came about, a flash point was reached in the writer's imagination. The true artist does not require an encyclopedia to describe a man or a locale. Given an image, the tone of a voice, the way a man carries his body, the angle of light against a wall, the artist can construct a world. It may be a true world or a very silly one, but, as long as it holds the reader, it will seem the only possible world. So Jim Grim materialized, distinctive from his first appearance. And the world in which he lived was as sharply defined as a steel engraving.

Behind us, the sky-line was a panorama of the Holy City, domes, minarets, and curved stone roofs rising irregularly above gray battlemented walls. Down on the right was the ghastly valley of Jehoshaphat, treeless, dry, and crowded with white tombs—"dry bones in the valley of death." To the left were everlasting limestone hills, one of them topped by the reputed tomb of Samuel—all trenched, cross-trenched, and wear-scarred, but covered now in a Joseph's coat of flowers, blue, blood-red, yellow and white.

...And as we topped the hill the Dead Sea lay below us like a polished turquoise set in the yellow gold of the barren Moab Mountains. That view made you gasp. (Mundy, *Jimgrim and Allah's Peace* 21)

"The Adventure at El-Kerak" (*Adventure*, November 10, 1921) introduces Grim and the ferocious turbulence of the Jerusalem area. There would appear to have been small change in that area since 1920, homicidal fanaticism being nearly impervious either to reason or time.

A wide-eyed, panic-stricken poor devil with slobber on his jaws came tearing down-street with a mob at his heels. We stepped into an alley to let the race go by, but he doubled down the alley opposite. Before he had run twenty yards along it some one hit the back of his head with a piece of rock. A second later they pounced on him, and in less than a minute after that he was kicking in the noose of a hide rope slung over a house-beam. I don't know what they hanged him for. No one apparently knew. But they used his carcase [*sic*] for a target and shot it almost to pieces. (Mundy, *Jimgrim and Allah's Peace* 69)

All eleven Grim adventures from 1921-1922 are short novels containing about 35,000-40,000 words. Like "The Adventure," they are usually told in first-person, apparently by Mundy, himself. (Not until "The King in Check" (July 10, 1922) will the narrator be identified as Jeff Ramsden and provided with a personal background.) Grim persuades the narrator to assist British Intelligence by traveling to the hamlet of El-Kerak, there to express an interest in establishing an American school. Grim accompanies him, disguised as an Arab.

El-Kerak merits this devious attention. A group of sheiks have gathered to debate the invasion of Palestine. That action, defying the British peace, would explode insurrection through the region. Chief instigator is Sheikh Abdul Ali of Damascus. Grim's mission is to capture Ali and spirit him from El-Kerak, knowing that the sheiks will regard the Sheikh's sudden disappearance as planned treachery and promptly discontinue their plotting.

The novel, reeking of intrigue and accumulating danger, is exciting enough to melt a steel door. After elaborate machinations in an atmosphere of choking menace, Ali is trapped, tied, and lowered head first from the parapet of a ruined castle. The narrator, unlike hosts of similar narrators before and after, positively contributes to the success of the mission. Then follows a nightmare flight from El-Kerak, hunted by the hordes of Islam, blundering, shooting, howling behind. Grim seems impervious to excitement; the reader is rendered limp.

At this time, James Schuyler Grim is thirty-four years old. He is an American commissioned a major in the British army and attached to Intelligence. It is an unusual arrangement but Grim is an unusual man. During World War I, he served Lawrence of Arabia, "doing the unseen, unsung spade-work." Fluently speaking more than a dozen languages, he understands the Arabs, is sympathetic to them, but is without illusions about this volatile people:

He looks as if he were half-Cherokee, although I believe there is only a trace of red man in his ancestry. He has a smile that begins faintly at the corners of his eyes, hesitates there as if to make sure none will be offended by it, and then spreads until his whole face lights with humor, making you realize that he has understood your weakness and compared it with his own. (Mundy, *The Devil's Guard* 10)

His eyes are blue, dark blue, iron gray, different colors at different times. His eyebrows are bushy, his hands large, and he is of medium height, his skin rather dark. He wears an upper plate. When this is removed, his entire face changes. It is a useful phenomena, for he is often in disguise and wears Arabian dress as if born in the desert.

Physical descriptions are interesting in their way. But choices define a man's personality, what he thinks and what he does. In these aspects, Grim is well documented. Highly sensitive to character, he knows whom to trust and when and for how long. He has a genius for manipulating others:

*Grim*: "Do you mind if I use you?"
*Ramsden*: "That's a hell of a silly question. Any use my minding? You've already used me. You will do it again without consulting me. I like it, as it happens. But a fat lot you care whether I like it or not."
*Grim*: "Oh, well. You know the hangmen always used to beg the victim's pardon." (Mundy, *Jimgrim and Allah's Peace* 73-74)

Ramsden has got it right. Under his air of civility, Grim is ruthless. But he does know how to use men. He exploits no one. He will endanger no man without his agreement. All who work with him understand the hazards. Some men he binds by orders; others he allows vast latitude, trusting their judgment. It depends on the man. Grim excels in the art of selecting men.

The similarities between Grim and John Solomon are obvious. During most of his career, Solomon selected a new assistant on every adventure, chosing each by some arcane intuitive process that Bedford-Jones never quite explained. Grim made do with a few select friends who stayed by him throughout the series. The relationships between these characters, their thought processes, opinions, and beliefs, are detailed in Mundy's stories in a way that the Solomon series only superficially suggests.

Neither Solomon nor Grim is particularly communicative. Their friends find themselves moving blindly into perfectly dreadful situations that would raise the hair of a dead man. Solomon seems constitutionally unable to explain what his plans are, if he has plans at all. Grim has plans but prefers not to tell them, claiming that they are subject to sudden change.

*Ramsden*: [Grim's] one annoying quality is that of keeping his thoughts to himself, hardly ever discussing a plan until it is perfect in his own mind and then telling you, perhaps, not more than half of it; after which he springs the rest on you as a surprise. But if you want to be friends with any man on earth you'll find there's something or other to put up with. (Mundy, *The Hundred Day's* 173)

During the 1930s, the convention of the close-mouthed leader was common as fictional gunfire. Doc Savage was as uncommunicative as a stone wall. The Shadow, while constantly maneuvering his agents, explained nothing to any one. Typical. Only Mundy bothered to justify the leader's silence. Other writers merely accepted the convention and swept grandly onward, not wasting time with psychological subtleties when somebody could be getting shot.

"Under the Dome of the Rock" (December 10, 1921) takes place in Jerusalem. Two tons of explosive have been stolen. Grim hears whispered plans that the Mosque of Omar, the Rock of Abraham—the most sacred spot of the Mahommedan world—is to be blown up. The Jews will be blamed and there, instantly, will come holy war against the British. Under the turmoil, the French will quietly, gratefully, annex Syria.

Leads to the stolen explosive are sparse. Grim, however, has his ways. One of them is named Suliman, an eight-year old street boy. Grim found him starving one night and took him in—but not to adopt him; Suliman has a mother. It's just that the man she's living with doesn't like the boy.

Suliman and one or two others are Grim's Baker Street Irregulars.

They move invisibly through Jerusalem's streets, collecting all manner of information. The street boy recruited by the detective is an old familiar device. You find him in Holmes as in Cleek, Nick Carter, and Sexton Blake, to mention a few early sources. Nowhere is the boy treated as honestly and realistically as in Mundy's work. Suliman is a gambler, thief, and profound smoker and has the vocabulary of a sewer. Impulsive, full of angers, he is tied to Grim by delicate cords of respect and admiration. The boy appears in several stories, then is dropped as the series grows beyond Palestine.

Aided by Suliman and the narrator, Grim slowly pieces together the plot to blow up the mosque. Beneath that building lies a concealed room, cut deep into the underlying stone. In this room the piles of stolen TNT. At the climax of the story, Grim, the unnamed narrator, and a detachment of Sikhs crawl along a dead-black passage toward that hidden room. Ahead whisper a gang of conspirators. At any moment the fuse may be lighted. Silence must be kept. Yet they must hurry. The suspense is barely endurable.

"The Rock" introduces two other characters. Col. Goodenough, commander of a Sikh regiment assigned to Jerusalem, is plump, neatly dressed, monocled, and appears briefly in several stories. The most important new character, however, is Narayan Singh, one of the soldiers, "a six-foot, black-bearded stalwart...with a long row of campaign ribbons, and the true, truculent Sikh way of carrying his head. He looked strong enough to carry an ox away" (Mundy, *Jimgrim and Allah's Peace* 238).

Narayan Singh is that familiar figure from Haggard and Kipling, the wonderful native fighter. Turbaned, bearded, ferocious, we met his like in the Diplomatic Freelance series. We will meet the same figure again, wonderfully lethal, striding through the unrelenting violence of the 1930s Spider magazine (Samspon, *Spider* ).[2] Narayan Singh's appearance in "The Rock" is minor; Mundy has yet to explore the man's possibilities. But that will come.

"The Iblis at Ludd" (January 10, 1922) is linked to the events of "The Rock." That stolen TNT came from British stores. Now a corrupt Brigadier General has shifted blame for the theft to a subordinate and presses the man's court martial. The story, told in third person, relates how Grim comes to the military camp to investigate the theft of supplies. Soon he finds himself, with Narayan Singh and Suliman, wandering the desert by night in search of an "Iblis"—a whirling ghost. Immediately they plunge into a storm of hidden plotting and a racket in arms and munitions stolen from the camp. A torn banknote carries incriminating evidence in a rather obvious way; and the Iblis—a hypnotizing devil— seems too ready to believe that he has dominated Grim. Aside from these minor blemishes, the novel races furiously to the final court martial scene, when you have the pleasure of seeing impregnable evil thoroughly punished.

"The Seventeen Thieves of El-Kalil" (February 20, 1922) introduces Ali Baba and his sixteen sons and grand-sons, thieves to a man. Worse, they have become fire-breathing thieves. It is the Fire Gift—a signal to Allah's faithful to rise up in the petty town of Hebron and kill and kill and kill. To begin with, they will kill the Jews, then the British governor and his ten policemen. Also Grim and Ramsden, who have come to help keep the peace. No help is forthcoming from Jerusalem where rioting and uprisings proceed as usual, claiming the full attention of the Sikh troops stationed there.

Action begins with the theft of a gold watch and inflates madly. Grim has ten hours to divert 15,000 loot-hungry, blood-raging Arabs, using tricks, disguise, blackmail, psychological manipulation, and sheer violence. All his efforts collapse as a double-crossing Sheikh of the local mosque flings a furious mob toward the tiny British enclave. Doom seems certain.

You need not be concerned. In the final pages, the Marines, or rather Sikhs, arrive, and their machine gun makes all problems simple.

The following two novels are closely linked. In the first, "The Lion of Petra" (March 10, 1922), Grim and friends seek out the inaccessible city of Petra, so defended by nature that even Alexander the Great could not conquer it. Here lurks Ali Higg, the Lion, who plans raids into Palestine. These, as usual, would tip the whole area into war.

Within the story, wheels spin within wheels. Ali Higg rules, but his first wife, Jael, (an American born in Bulgaria) does all his thinking. She has her eye on the conquest of Mesopotamia. Higg's second wife, Ayisha, who covets the position of first wife, is a self-possessed beauty with a habit of murder. Grim wishes to discourage Higg from adventures into Palestine but wants to establish him as a strong chief who will keep the peace in that area.

All these interacting wheels are revealed during the story. Which tells of a strenuous trip across the desert toward Petra. Their caravan is riddled with intrigue and double-dealing. Grim rather closely resembles Ali Higg and plays this resemblance for all it's worth. Ayisha woos Grim. Narayan Singh woos Ayisha (only to sniff out her plots; he despises her). In the course of the action, they pick up and discard a succession of tricksters, traitors, and general cutthroats. It is an uncomfortable trip. And a bloody one.

During the final chapters, they finally confront Ali Higg. He is suffering boils and is very fierce, if not all that bright. In a tight, tricky ending, Grim cons Higg into promising not to invade Palestine for three years. In turn, Grim must deal with Ben Saoud, The Avenger, a southern sheik who prepares to obliterate Ali Higg.

That is the subject of the following story, "The Woman Ayisha" (April 20, 1922), a direct continuation of "The Lion." Once more Grim and his friends set off on an intrigue-ridden struggle across the desert. First they must enlist the aid of a fraction of Ali Higg's tiny army. Both Ayisha (who has been divorced by Higg for attempting to poison him) and Jael, the Number One wife, do their treacherous worst. Grim must evade their malice, while he gets uneasy control of the army fragment. His maneuvering occupies most of the book. As a result we meet the Avenger only in the final two chapters of the book. Just as in "The Lion of Petra," Grim requires only those chapters to confront Higg and resolve most problems.

By an elaborate deception once used by Stonewall Jackson, Grim bluffs the Avenger into signing a peace agreement with Higg. Thereafter Ayisha marries the Avenger; Jael rides off in a killing snit; Grim and company return to civilization. If the murderous instability of the Arabs can be honored by that word.

In "Ayisha," Mundy rather reluctantly begins to flesh out the background of the narrator. He uses bits of his own more presentable background, all shined up by what looks suspiciously like wish fulfillment. Thus the narrator (as yet unnamed), is an American who has prospected and professionally hunted big game in Africa. Middle-aged, quietly conservative, he has carefully saved and invested his money and is reasonably well off. He is a massive man, weighing about 230 pounds, heavily muscled, powerful. He is uneasily aware that his mind operates slowly. Only recently has he learned Arabic and the art of riding a camel. All learning interests him, particularly ancient history and men's faces. Unfettered by wife or family, he finds that Grim and Narayan Singh are men he likes and respects. Granted that their adventures are dangerous enough and uncomfortable enough for a dozen lifetimes. But the narrator plods stolidly along. Now and then he makes mistakes. (All of them make mistakes. Even Grim.) More often, he does the exact, right thing, regardless of the emergency, being a lot less slow-witted than he claims.

While the narrator's personality steadily complicates, so does that of Narayan Singh. His intelligence and ferocity increases with each novel. A skilled hunter across World War I battlefields, the Sikh has won a chestfull of medals. He loves combat. Dozens of men have fallen at his hands, many of them by his sword. He fusses over that weapon, sharpening, polishing.

As brilliant soldier as he is, he can never be promoted. For this valiant killer has a character defect. About every six months, he gets raging drunk, insubordinate, savage. So we are told; the reader sees none of this behavior. When sober, he is the most valued soldier in Col. Goodenough's Sikhs. Profoundly admiring Narayan Singh's abilities,

Grim frequently borrows him for the more deadly missions. Behind the lacquer of his professional skills, the Sikh is a highly intelligent man with towering standards of honor and friendship.

Another man now joins this small group. During the events of "The Lost Trooper" (May 30, 1922), we are introduced to Jeremy Ross, an Australian. Eventually he will change Grim's history. A merry trickster, impulsive, disrespectful, Ross is joyous, swift of mind and fleet of tongue. A Boer War veteran, he makes an unorthodox soldier. When captured by Arabs, as explained in "The Lost Trooper," he kept himself alive by a series of sleight-of-hand tricks and his own quick tongue. By the end of the novel, he has acquired a rich gold mine. His indifference to wealth is amazing. With lavish hand, he offers shares to his friends and, in "The King in Check" (July 10) turns the whole thing over to the Emir Feisul— the only man who can possibly unite the Arabs to a common state.

The fortunes of Feisul, an actual historical figure, drive the story line of "The King." A direct descendent of Mohammed, Feisul was supported by the Allies at the end of World War I. He was to be King of the Arab nation. But power politics intervened. British support weakened. At this point, Mundy inoculates history with an invigorating dose of fiction. He does so as deftly as Somerset Maugham would do five years later in Ashenden, his own memoirs as a British secret agent. In Mundy's version, the French, seeking a way to grab Syria, forged an inflammatory letter and signed it with Feisul's name, hoping to stir up insurrection and so bring in their troops.

By accident the letter ends up in the hands of Grim and company. During a long ride on a ramshackle train through Syria, they play a slippery game of cross identities with a murderous little adventurer and his fifty-knife gang of killers. A decoy letter slips back and forth. Murderous violence explodes in a cramped train compartment. To strengthen his position, Grim introduces a spurious Lawrence of Arabia. There follows an interview with Feisul, a man entirely too gallant for his own good. The ending, a rousing piece of action, describes the Battle of Damascus (French against Arabs), as vividly as if Mundy had occupied a box seat at the front line. The French win. But Grim spoils an assassination attempt on Feisul and leads the French Army a merry chase until the Emir gets safely away.

Although the story's fictional content is immense, the battle actually occurred and Feisul did escape into history.

In the course of "The King in Check," Grim delivers a succinct lecture on the conduct of secret service operations. His remarks have application to fields other than clandestine games:

*Grim*: No play to the gallery! That's where secret service differs from other business. Applause means failure. The better the work you do, the less you can afford to admit you did it. You mustn't even smile at a man you've scored off. Half the game is to leave him guessing who it was that tripped him up. The safest course is to see that some one else gets credit for everything you do.

...You've got to work like ____ for what'll do you no good, because the moment it brings you recognition it destroys your usefulness. You mayn't even amuse yourself; ...most of the humor comes in anyhow, from knowing more than the other fellow thinks you do. The more a man lies the less you want to contradict him, because if you do he'll know that you know he's lying and that's giving away information, which is the unforgivable sin. (41)

Of this speech, Ramsden later remarks, "I think he told Jeremy and me the secret of power that morning."

At this point, violent change shakes the series.

Ross has been teasing Grim to leave British service and set up as a professional adventurer. In "A Secret Society" (August 10, 1922) he does so, going into business with Ross and Ramsden. They are joined by Narayan Singh. Their operation is bankrolled by one of the world's wealthiest men, Meldrum Strange. He wants the group to sniff out international criminals—a transparent pretext for Mr. Mundy to move the series from Jerusalem and Palestine, those abscesses of fanaticism. Now he can change the scene at will, allowing Grim and friends to frisk about the globe, risking their necks under strange new skies. Their opponents remain aggressively lethal.

Almost the first place Mundy takes Grim is to Egypt, not far from Palestine, after all. "Khufu's Real Tomb" (October 10) begins in the United States, where Ramsden meets the effervescent Miss Joan Angela Leich. He has known her since she was a teeny. Now about twenty-three and nearly the richest girl in the world (oil on her property), she prances unattached through life. She is not superficial and not mindless. Her intelligence is acute, calm, detached. So here we have a beautiful, intelligent, wealthy woman, who is also agog with the desire for adventure. Delights in places interesting and remote. Elated by exciting events. Eager for thrilling activities.

Which guarantees that any story in which Joan Angela appears will be rigid with suspense. Nothing so enhances narrative heat as a (beautiful intelligent wealthy) young woman in danger. She finds plenty of that.

The date is late 1922. Ahead, in the misted plains of the future, stand Susan O'Gilvie (Peter the Brazen series), Patricia Savage (Doc Savage series), Nita Van Sloan (Spider series), and various other adventuring sweethearts from such representative 1930s cluster novels as Secret Agent X, Operator 5.... The list grows long.

We have met the adventurous woman in stories appearing much earlier than Joan Angela. Back near the edge of memory lurk Arietta Murdock (Young Wild West series), Stella Fosdick (Young Rough Riders series), Marie LaSalle (Jimmie Dale series), Betty Calwood (Avenging Twins series), Lucy Shannon (Lone Wolf series), so many, so many. (Sampson, Vol. 1)[3] To these names we wouldn't go far wrong in adding Pearl White and other of those self-sufficient ladies of the silent dream screen. All contributed to the convention of the adventuring lady during the 1920s and 1930s. Fictional figures need not have all their roots in fiction, and the pulps never blushed to borrow a strong image, wherever it might be found.

Whatever her literary origins, Joan Angela is a living presence on the page. Routinely, she operates at levels rather different from the rest of us. Thus: on a one-lane road high the side of a mountain, she stands with Ramsden observing his car. Joan has just driven headlong into that machine, knocking it half off the road. The front end of his car hangs over an abyss. The back end angles across the road, blocking it.

Sizing up the situation in an instant, Joan remarks: "Your car's in the way. Push it right over, and I'll buy you a new one"(Mundy, *The Mystery of Khufu's Tomb* 14).

As Scott Fitzgerald remarked, the rich are different from the rest of us.

Ramsden discovers that a swindler and a shyster lawyer plan to strip Joan of her oil properties. Complications flare with a treacherous secretary and her deceitful boy friend. By the time Ramsden straightens out these problems, it's evident that someone bad is eyeing Joan's Egyptian properties. Immediately the narrative leaps to Egypt. In that scalding country, Grim and Narayan Singh rescue a singularly odd Chinese mathematician who can prove that every proportion and measurement in the Great Pyramid has symbolic meaning (Wilson, *The Accult* 332).[4]

Leading to a trap inside the Great Pyramid, itself. And, shortly afterward, the discovery of Khufu's real tomb, not in the Great Pyramid, at all, but close by, concealed underground. And stuffed with treasure of staggering proportions, protected in booby-trapped darkness surrounded by blind white crocodiles wiggling in a secret channel from the Nile—all this on Joan Angela's property.

The story is gripping, if episodic. You feel that Mundy forcibly rammed together miscellaneous story chunks to create a kind of literary Jugoslavia. Even with this disadvantage, his narrative magic does not fail.

In "Khufu's Real Tomb," we get a strong hint of those "hidden knowledge" themes which will increasingly find their way into Mundy's fiction. Early in the 1920s, he joined a California theosophical group, contributing to its journal, listening hard to its revelations.

Theosophy is a simply extraordinary stew of Eastern and Western mysticism, liberally anointed with the waters of occultism and teaching secrets of the earth's past that would astound scientists, were they not so enslaved by niggling attention to fact.

One of the major facts so far ignored by Science is that previous Races, strange beings of great power, once ruled the earth. All perished. Humanity is the Fifth Race to rise up, but the Sixth and Seventh, which are to come, shall be greater than mankind. Still Humanity tends toward godliness, and, by study and struggle, might someday attain what the unenlightened call supernatural powers.

After all, similar powers, including technological miracles that look exactly like magic, were routinely enjoyed by the people of Atlantis (the Fourth Race). Unfortunately they all died from black magic. Atlantis, itself, collapsed into what is now the Gobi desert. Fragments of their knowledge live on, secret, accessible only to a few. It's powerful knowledge. Oh, my, goodness, yes. Explains nearly everything, including womankind, which may be why it's all kept so secret (Wilson, *The Occult* 333).[5]

Some of these ideas leak into "The Nine Unknown" (five-part serial, March 20 through April 30, 1923). Meldrum Strange starts Grim and friends on a quest to see where all the money that has been coined through the ages has got to. (As is apparent, little of it is left.) The trail leads to India. There they meet, and eventually admit to their inner circle, the sly, fat Chullunder Ghose, hen-pecked husband, father of fourteen children. Ghose is a crafty and conniving rascal, cowardly, cynical, and enormously, immensely intelligent. He appears in a number of other pieces not directly connected with the Jim Grim series.

Soon after Grim and friends arrive in India, odd things begin to happen. As the confusion slowly clears, evidence suggests that human destiny is manipulated by forces supernaturally powerful and malignant. These lurk unseen out there somewhere in the world, the Nine Unknown.

Unknown they might be. But Grim *et al.* keep meeting their emissaries who paralyze at a glance, appear, disappear, hypnotize, and act spooky.

Matter of fact there seem to be two emissaries. Before you can cry out in amazement, the struggle between Evil and Good flashes to focus. To be entirely correct about the matter, Good doesn't struggle. It doesn't have to. That's because it is good. While Evil, on the other hand, being bad.... But you get the gist of the matter.

The novel is wildly exciting, as narratives with a touch of paranoia tend to be. (Paranoia, of course. Invisible conspiracy driven by unseen, malignant minds! Of course paranoia.) Grim and his friends are indifferently aided by the forces of Goodness, Light, and Spiritual

Illumination. By the end of the novel, they have battered Evil, all envious and bloody, to a temporary stand off.

The disappearing coinage, whose absence initiated this adventure, is eventually explained, providing you have reasonable toleration for improbable explanations. Seems that part of it is converted (by Atlantean technology) into radiation that is used to cleanse the Ganges River. Explaining why those who use the river water don't tumble over green and stiff.

All this is intense, fantastic stuff. Equally intense is the following short novel, "Mohammad's Tooth," published in December 10, 1923. No fantasy elements swirl mistily here. This is harsh, brutal adventure, full of guns and violence among the rocks of India's north-western frontier.

When collected in book form, the novel was retitled "The Hundred Days." That refers to the length of time it would take to send a ransom demand from the Indian frontier to the United States and get back a freight car of gold. The kidnapper is Kangra Khan, a border thug, leader of fetid hordes. The kidnapped is Miss Joan Angela Leich.

Joan came wandering over to India to observe the English Prince visiting the Raj. Originally, Kangra Khan targeted the Prince for kidnapping but then assumed there would be more profit and less uproar by snatching Joan.

There he made a mistake. For Joan is under the special protection of Ramsden and Grim.

Immediately matters grow ferocious. Joan is saved and recaptured till the mind grows giddy. Ramsden is captured. Troops led by Grim, King (the same King of the Khyber Rifles), and Narayan Singh ambush Kangra Khan. The battle flows and ebbs, until Ramsden faces the Khan in a vicious hand-to-hand fight. Even after he wins, matters hang in the balance until Grim hands over to Kahn a religious relic—a tooth of Mohammed. Not a particularly authentic relic, since it came from Grim's upper plate; but after all, it's what people believe that moves their hearts.

Nearly all this combat occurs over three days and nights. Days and nights of death, blood, anguish, sniping, screaming assaults across slopes of raw stone. Hot rifles. Bloody steel. Concentrated killing, relentless, continuing. Ramsden, himself, is hurt so badly that he nearly dies. All this because Joan Angela went sight-seeing near the border.

That was only one of her mistakes. The other was to lose her head and slap Ramsden when he was trying to remove her from a dark deep pit. For one lunatic moment, she thought rape.

Ramsden is entirely outraged and snarls through most of the novel, eyes slitted, muscles white around his mouth. Until the final pages, he snubs Joan brutally. At the end she apologizes—and more than apologizes: she proposes marriage to him.

Ramsden loves her. But he is a man of solid sense, who knows the difference between gratitude and love. "God knows," he says to her, "I'll wear your offer in my hat until I die, and will try to live up to it. But I'm a middle-aged man, of middle-class means. You're a young girl, with millions, and all your life in front of you. There's the right man somewhere. I won't wrong him—or you" (163).

Warm, adult, succinct, generous. Ramsden doesn't add that marriage would likely mean the end of banging around the world with his friends, being nearly butchered once a week. He doesn't have to. People who read series fiction know that, just as they know that no author is going to discard a major character by marrying him off.

Authors are, however, likely to fly off on tangents. For about two-and-a-half years after "Mohammed's Tooth," Mundy wrote no more Jimgrim adventures. Instead he involved himself with Indian-Tibetan mysticism in the six-part serial, "Om." Then he began the Tros of Samothrace sequence. That continued until mid-1926. Not until June 1926 did he publish more about the Jimgrim group in the five-part serial "Ramsden." (The United States book edition was titled *The Devil's Guard.*)

The scene is Tibet. That being the case, you might assume that you're in for a stiff dose of mysticism. And you're right.

Ramsden receives a frantic note from Rait, an old acquaintance. Come and rescue him from Tibet, the land no one is permitted to enter and only the dead leave. Ramsden doesn't recall much in Rait's favor but is willing to try. Grim and Narayan Singh are willing to come along. Chullunder Ghose comes reluctantly. The Sikh smells fighting and Grim is probing for clues to Sham-bha-la, a secret city filled with secret seers simply boiling with secret ancient wisdom.

They leave for Tibet, appropriately disguised. Winter is commencing in the mountain passes. Their struggles to force through are atrociously painful, the descriptions guaranteed to ice the reader to his chair.

Worse they find themselves at odds with the Black Lodge (a group assiduously cultivating evil). Or perhaps they are opposed by the White Lodge (which abstractly studies life). Hard to tell which is which. The representatives of both have inordinately odd powers. They paralyze at a glance, turn into other people, disappear from under your nose, have supernormal strength, stun with mind waves. They are astonishing.

During this trip, Ramsden has even worse luck than in the episode of Mohammed's Tooth. This time he gets stabbed during a simple scuffle. His life is waning fast. They flee a snow-choked village, take refuge in a freezing monastery. There a smiling stranger emerges from the blizzard to pull Ramsden back from death. But he remains deadly weak. In the novel that bears his name, he is constantly the victim, nearly always too weak to help himself. Chullunder Ghose is in even worse shape. Considering the climate of Tibet, it's a wonder either of them lasted through the book.

In a deep cavern full of beauty and strangeness, representatives of the White Lodge recognize that Grim might benefit from instruction in higher matters. Unfortunately no other member of the party qualifies. Well, maybe Ramsden might be marginal. Before anything is settled, the Black Lodge attacks Grim through Ramsden. They barely escape in a climax of savagery and heroism.

Narayan Singh does not escape.

It is unbelievable. This vivid man, this colossus, dies fighting along a narrow stone causeway crossing an abyss. In that final fight, he slaughters six monks of the Black Lodge and settles the treacherous Rait, no friend of Ramsden's, after all.

Rait fired again. I think he hit [Narayan Singh] a second time, but up—through his forearm—through his throat—and out behind his head the saber went with one of those long lunging thrusts for which Narayan Singh was famous.

...Narayan Singh clutched air, fell forward on to Rait writhed—slid—and the two went over, separating as they plunged into the abyss. (302)

Juicy, rich melodrama, satisfying as a two-inch thick Kansas City strip. Narayan Singh's startling death echoes that more celebrated death, in H. Rider Haggard's *Allan Quatermain*, of the splendid Zulu giant, Umslopogaas. In both cases, death of the resident warrior appeared to end the series. Alan Quatermain died in the book bearing his name; and, in Ramsden, Jim Grim (and Ramsden) vanished into the deeps of Tibet to study occult teachings, which would be nearly as effective as death.

As Mundy later remarked, "...even supposing that [Sham-bha-la] is mythical—no man who had been there and received the said-to-be imaginary teaching ever could behave like any ordinary person..." (*Jimgrim V*).

Even authors make errors. In Haggard's case, the adventures of Alan Quatermain continued for years through a series of flashbacks. And, in spite of the occult training, Grim's adventures did not end, either. Not quite.

Slightly more than four years after "Ramsden," the final Jim Grim serial began in *Adventure*. Titled "King of the World," it ran in seven parts, November 15, 1930, through February 15, 1931, It was later published in book form under the title *Jimgrim* or, as in one of its paperback reincarnations, *Jimgrim Sahib*.

The story is not only odd but downright peculiar. Cast in the form of a hard-action adventure story, it is packed to bursting with science-fictional devices, fantastic events, and occult lore. The whole seething mass is presented in prose sharp with realistic detail, showing every shadow and line, and crowded with those incisive character portrayals that Mundy did so brilliantly.

The story begins in France, leaps to Egypt and India, and ends in Tibet, a frantic search all the way. Grim and Ramsden, returned from Tibet after partially completing their studies, attempt to track down Dorje. Whoever Dorje is. Wherever he is. Whatever Dorje is. They know only that Dorje is out to become king of the world. And perhaps he will.

This unknown, Dorje, discovered a city buried in the Gobi. The place was packed with the science of Atlantis. Including weapons able to suck up electricity until transforming to pure vibration that detonates any explosive within range—pistol bullets, bombs, gasoline tanks.... Turn on your flashlight and blow up your automobile. Other weapons include a liquid that vaporizes to a lethal gas. And a bell-shaped weapon that smites victims instantly dead, leaving behind no wound, no burn, no trace. Only a corpse.

Atlantis also developed less murderous toys. From these, Dorje selected a flying machine that silently propels itself along lines of magnetic force. He has learned the Atlantean technique of communicating by thought waves over distances incredible. Less positively, he has become addicted to soma, a drug that magnifies the intelligence for short intervals.[6]

With all these technical advantages, Dorje has set out to conquer the world. What eventually brings him down is organizational failure—a matter never before addressed by sensational literature and rarely enough by sober, main line fiction. The question, simply enough, is how to control a world-wide operation, working through lieutenants. Even using thought waves, an elaborate code, rich rewards, and instant punishment, Dorje's system breaks down. It is a problem faced by no Emperor of Crime before or after him. Never once did Fu Manchu or Black Star suffer such difficulties. It is an interesting, if oblique, commentary on the level of reality offered by most magazine series.

Dorje's communications fail. His lieutenants ramble beyond control, governed by impulse and self interest, rather than their leader's marvelous plans, which they only imperfectly realize. Operations become impossible. Management becomes impossible. Even the leader's iron facade begins to crack.

Similar failures commonly occur today at corporate level, within projects major and minor, in the administration of governments. How could they not occur during an attempt to seize the world? And so they do.

The story is narrated in first-person by Major Robert Crosby, a nice, competent young man who is out of his class with Grim and Ramsden. In Chapter I, the three of them observe a suicide, are nearly knifed, see a French cruiser explode in the bay, and learn the name Dorje. After this relatively sluggish beginning, the pace increases.

Grim manage to trace Dorje through his associates. Among them, an Arabic sea-captain, a woman who claims to be the reincarnation of the Queen of Sheba, her deadly twin, and a murderous blind man.

The trail leads to Cairo. There law and order collapse as everything that can explode explodes. In the Great Pyramid of Gizeh, Grim corners some of Dorje's men and impersonates Dorje. Well, why not? Who knows what the King of the World looks like.

Eventually, after savage fighting in, above, around, and under, Grim and his friends destroy Dorje's supply of weapons and break his code.

From Egypt, the trail leads to India. They are joined by Chullunder Ghose, fat and cynical as ever. Once more Grim impersonates Dorje to draw out the enemy. It is once too often. Dorje appears, snatches Grim away in the flying science-fictional device. Grim's friends are left to die in a flaming house of joy.

But they don't. Chartering an airplane, they head toward Tibet, where Dorje seeks to enlist Grim as a lieutenant. For good lieutenants are few and Dorje is in dire administrative trouble. His organization is dissolving. No longer can he control his men. The plan of world conquest shimmers and melts. Rebellion seethes around him. Seeking to isolate the rebels, he compromises with Grim. He promises and punishes. Nothing works. As his organization rumbles toward the cliff, Dorje fuels himself with soma. Even that is no longer enough. The grandiose hope of world mastery reduces at last to a hand-to-hand struggle between the drug-raddled Dorje and Grim, followed by an explosion like the detonation of the earth.

Ramsden, Chullunder Ghose, and Roberts escape. But Grim remains at the center of the blast.

...Dorje's monastery and all its suburbs blew up in an incandescent splendour. It was shot with spears of flame that resembled lightning. Clouds of the stored up poison gas rolled upward and shone like opal and mother o' pearl as they were rent away by hundreds of explosions underneath them. Then the thunder of it reached us, and a blast of hot wind drove us to take cover behind the shoulder of a dune.... [There] was only a crimson furnace, shot with green and indigo, where Dorje's citadel had been, and where Grim went...to [his] chosen death." (Mundy, *Jimgrim Sahib* 318)

According to Mundy's wife, Dawn, it was not intended that "King of the World" be the final Jimgrim novel. Somehow Grim would escape;

Mundy would work it out later. But time passed. Mundy did not get around to writing that further adventure. One day he died (D. Grant 165).

So here the series stops, the adventures of Grim and Ramsden. It was not, however, the end of novels about tight-knit groups of friends adventuring around the world.

The form was not original with Mundy. It seems a primary narrative type. You find stories of men (and the occasional woman) traveling and adventuring together at least as far back as the voyage of the Argonauts. Some few years later (skipping over such major contributions as Indian wonder tales and Norse epics), H. Rider Haggard polished the form to a hard glitter in She and King Solomon's Mines. The Diplomatic Free Lances presented the adventuring friends in the context of secret service operations. And the Tom Swift series kept them busy through libraries of shallow, busy prose. Only a month before the Jim Grim series opened, Arthur Friel introduced his own group of adventurers treading the "Pathless Trail" across South America.

Two years after Grim's final appearance, the Doc Savage Magazine began. From its first novel, "The Man of Bronze" (March 1933), five close friends and their extraordinary leader flung themselves into peril around the world. Using some science and considerable physical mayhem, they fought criminals flaunting machine-guns, geniuses flaunting science-fictional devices, and assorted villains flaunting assorted kinks. After Doc Savage rushed additional series, each employing a variation on the adventuring friends theme, each with a shining leader and a few close associates: the Spider, Operator 5, Captain Satan, Captain Fury, tough men jointly facing hazardous worlds.

These groups remained small. As Lester Dent (author of the Doc Savage series) quickly discovered, it was difficult to manipulate six lead characters, two pets, a hardboiled woman (such as Doc's cousin, Patricia), a villain or so, three or more subordinate characters, a lost race, and a truckload of snarling gangsters all within a novel of 65,000-75,000 words.

Whether the adventurers were many or few, the general form of the fiction remained the same: a group of well-identified personalities embark on an extended expedition into danger. The format and subject matter vary. The form remains the same. Although the Star Trek adventures seem unique, they are connected, as by a transparent thread, with the Argo and its crew, as they rowed together toward high adventure, so many centuries ago. The adventuring friends are a persistent fictional form.

*The Popular Magazine,* October 7, 1925. The boisterous, powerful Bulldog Drummond, here turning the tables, continued World War I combat practices against post-war criminals and other social rabble.

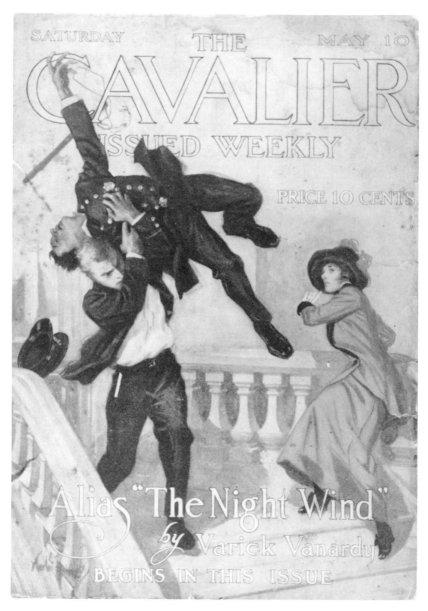

*The Cavalier*, May 10, 1913. Framed by a crooked detective, the Night Wind, who possessed superhuman strength and agility, was frequently short-tempered with policemen.

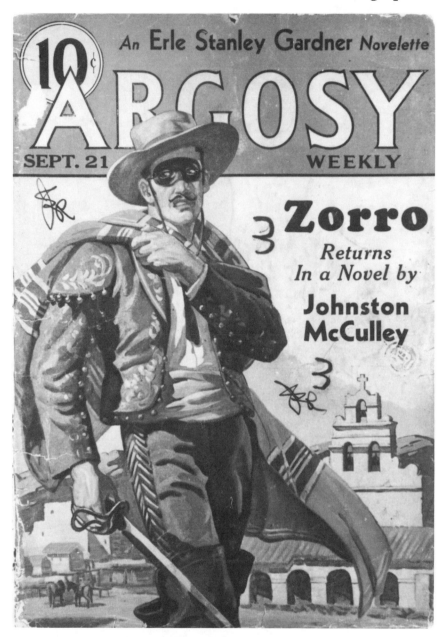

*Argosy*, September 21, 1935. Hero of dozens of adventures, all strikingly similar, Zorro made famous the joys of being an unknown, masked avenger.

*Complete Stories*, Second February 1931. Offering world-wide adventure, the magazine was home to the extended White Wolf series (1927-1934), afterward continued in *Wild West Weekly*.

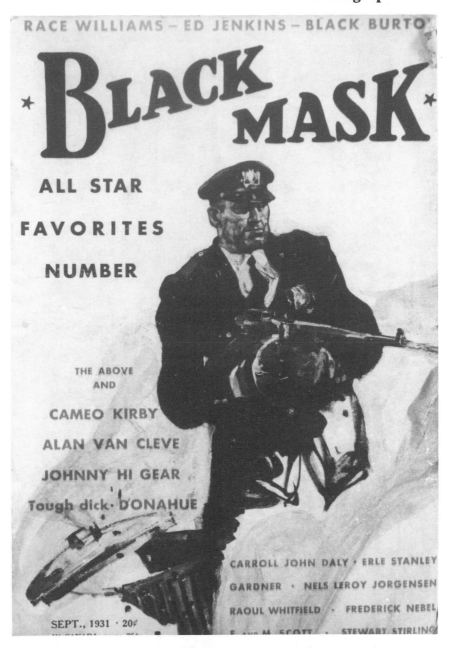

*Black Mask*, September 1931. Not only hardboiled detectives and police prowled these terse pages, but also Erle Stanley Gardner's western gunslinger, Black Barr, and tough Ed Jenkins, The Phantom Crook.

*Detective Fiction Weekly*, November 23, 1929. The self-possessed Lester Leith observes Sergeant Ackley about to make a fool of himself, once again.

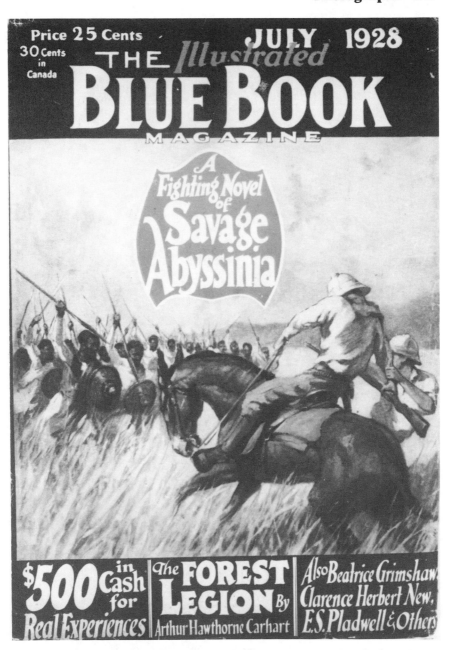

*Blue Book*, July 1928. For twenty-five years the magazine featured Clarence New's "Freelances in Diplomacy," sometimes called the longest serial ever published.

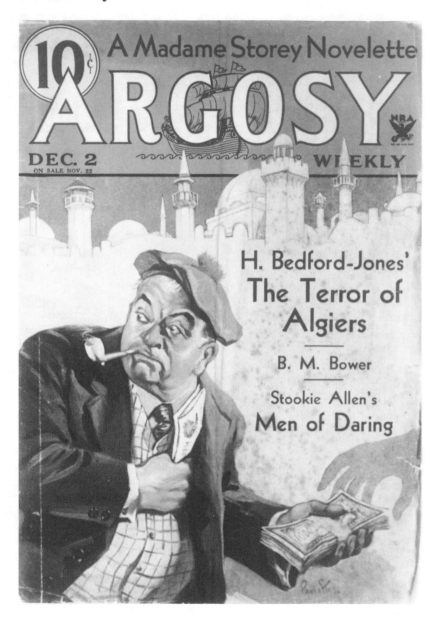

*Argosy*, December 2, 1933. The eccentric Cockney, John Solomon, manipulated international politics in his own secret ways, always winning, if by terrifyingly close margins.

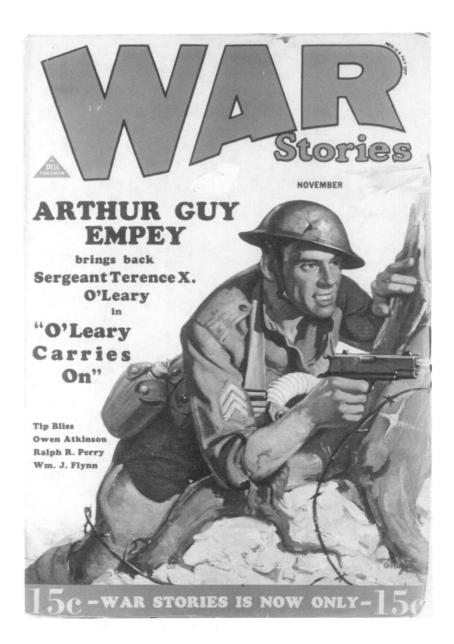

*War Stories*, November 1931. T.X. O'Leary, that Irish whirlwind, enjoyed a lunatic career in war and air war magazines and in his own science-fiction adventure series.

*Triple X*, March 1929. Adventure stories featuring airplanes and aviators appeared in all general magazines during the 1920s. Only late in the decade was the first specialized aviation fiction magazine published.

# TAM O' THE SCOOTS

## By Edgar Wallace

### ILLUSTRATED BY L. A. SHAFER

*T*HESE stories are a faithful study of a little Scotchman fighting under unique conditions. Not all air-pilots on the Great Front are officers. Some are men of the people. In these stories Mr. Wallace describes a rare character, a Glasgow mechanic, who becomes a Royal Flying Corps pilot. "Tam" is a real person, and all the adventures set forth have actually happened, though names and places are necessarily fictitious.—THE EDITOR.

*Everybody's*, November 1917. Heading of the first story in the "Tam O' The Scoots" series; here begins World War I air combat fiction.

(Left) *Wings*, July 1934; (Right) *Battle Aces*, September 1931. Magazines of air adventure stories appeared before air war magazines, but air war soon ruled the field. *Battle Aces*, suspended late in 1932, was reincarnated the following year as *G-8 and His Battle Aces*.

# Chapter Seven
## Riders and Swordsmen

How exquisite the joys of war!

Not perhaps, modern war. The joys of being bombed, gassed, and sprayed with machine-gun bullets or neutrons are seriously overrated. Nor, to be honest, was war much fun during the flintlock rifle and tomahawk era, since it is not particularly amusing to be struck by a .60 caliber hunk of lead. Neither was it edifying to have some Indian hacking around in your hair, when you had never even been introduced to him.

The joys of war, like a lot of other joys, are proportional to your distance away from them. Thus the Medieval period radiates delight, for it is all aglitter with armor, brave words, and crusades to free the Holy Land. That enthralls some. Others feel their hearts lift to the clash of armies near Italian city states, or the rhythmic tramp of Roman legionnaires, pressing deep into Gaul, or the shout and fury of Ghengis Khan's hordes pounding toward Europe. Those battles are far away in time, quite far enough that only the pageantry remains after all the less glamorous stuff has been forgotten.

What pleasure, then, to feel the power of your horse, the exultation of your heart as the enemy wheels into view. The heady wind of war gushes over you. Your great sword swings free. To test yourself against an armed man. To strike him down. To hew your way valorously to the center of the milling uproar.

To triumph. To acclamation. To be admired, honored. To become a legend, your name written beside that of Vercingetorix, Anthony, Custer, and Haig. To collect bags of gold and jewels as booty. Lordy, me!

So the joys of war. Quite ignoring that people get hurt. That wounds bleed and afterward pound with infection. That death has an evil stench and a field of corpses is rarely, in any sense, artistic. Ignoring that wars are a stupid way of conducting history, whether necessary or not. Who thinks of such matters when the blood runs hot, hurrah, hurrah.

Certainly readers of the more active pulp magazines enjoyed stories of combat. Ancient combat. The more recent slaughters on the Western Front were less amusing; people remembered too much about those orgies of murder. Stories set in earlier times resonated at a different pitch. They did not concern themselves with futile dying in French mud but with heroics. Through the fiction swarmed exotic names and places. The action was hot. Evil was cut down. And at the end of the adventure, all the suffering and violence made sense, in a way that modern battle did not. For in these stories, a single man made all the difference. A single man. Such a romantic notion. Such a far cry from four hundred thousand corpses anonymous in the muck of the Somme.

Toward the end of the 1920s, the pulps began addressing the First World War. By then, memory of that conflict had softened and the myth-making had begun, particularly concerning the war in the air. We will consider this in the following chapter. At the beginning of the 1920s, however, World War I was too close. The blood still pooled; the smoke still drifted. Authors wrote about war because that subject had consumed readers' attention since 1913. But they wrote about different war, war subject to fiction's silent order, in which one man could make a difference. Above all, they wrote about war distant in time.

Say the end of the Sixteenth Century, on the western border of Russia on an island in the Dnieper River. The bank on the west is Russian; the bank on the east, Tatar. Spreading across the island is the Cossack war encampment, called Zaporogian Siech. There, polishing his saber, sits Khlit, about to begin years of crafty battle in the *Adventure Magazine*.

Khlit is known as The Wolf or Khlit of the Curved Saber. He is tall, heavy-boned, shaggy-haired, with chunks of blue ice for eyes. In the Cossack custom, his head is bald, except for a scalp lock trailing over his shoulders. His mustaches are long and gray and a small pipe rides in his mouth. His clothing is rough and simple: a round sheepskin hat, a gray sheepskin coat clenched by a broad leather belt, and brilliant red pants tucked into massive boots. The pants have been smeared with tar to show that he disdains ostentation. He is a Christian (Greek Orthodox) and wears a gold cross chained around his neck. He can neither read nor write. Small matter. First and always he is a horseman, a rider, a warrior, living for war. He has worn away his life at war. He has fought in Poland and across the Volga against the Tatars (called the Tartars in this decadent time).

The saber, which travels with him through the adventures, is a lightly curved Turkish blade, forged in Damascus. It rides in a leather scabbard "stamped with strange lettering and strengthened with bronze. From it projected a hilt...[of] ivory inlaid with gold.... The blade was... an arc of blue steel, unstained and sharpened to a razor edge. [Along its length ran] a line of writing, worked in gold. This writing was not Turkish, nor was it any Christian tongue" (Lamb, *The Curved Saber* 531).

Constantly Khlit polishes this weapon, touching up the edge with a fine sandstone. The two are one, warrior and mistress. It is the only real marriage he will know.

Khlit is aging. Already he has lived longer than any Cossack can expect. The strength of his arm wanes. Soon it will be difficult to fight for extended periods. Yet he is not entirely dependent on the curved saber. For Khlit was born filled with guile. An untutored strategist, an audacious tactician, he will soon become one of the great war leaders of the period. He has the kind of ability that you would have had, if your mother hadn't smothered your talents by forbidding you to play with swords and horses.

Little of Khlit's genius is shown in the first story of the series, "Khlit" (First November 1917).[1] (All stories appeared in *Adventure*.) His initial appearance is in a brief, minor piece, no more than a ranging shot.

War impends and the Cossacks wait for news. Challenged by a gambler, Khlit wagers a fortune that his foster son, Menelitza, will arrive in camp in a display of unrivaled daring. To make sure the boy cannot cross the raging Dnieper River, the gambler gets the only ferryman dead drunk. But absence of the boat means only that Menelitza swims the river to bring news of war to the camp, thus performing that astonishing feat Khlit promised.

At story's end, we learn that Khlit had concealed the oars, making sure the boat was out of action so that Menelitza would be forced to make his dramatic swim. While the point of the narrative is confused by that double chicanery, matters will soon get better. And Harold Lamb has served notice, if you were paying attention, that the Khlit stories will have plots and end in unexpected twists.

Khlit was the first series character created by Harold A. Lamb, born in Alpine, New Jersey, 1892. Lamb was the author of an imposing library of historical novels and studies. His work was known for its accuracy and precisely recreated cultural details. He had a passion for history and the peoples swarming within that enormous block of the world curving from the Near East to the Far East, from Persia and Russia to India and China, and countries in between, all ferocious and bloody of history.

Passion for remote times and far cultures blazed in Lamb from the beginning. In 1914, he left Columbia University, disliking the required studies. He worked briefly as a make-up man for trade magazine and a financial writer for the *New York Times*. At the same time, he plunged deeply into private study, while trying his hand at fiction.

Returning to Columbia, he received a B.A., married, began selling fiction to the *Adventure Magazine*, and served briefly in the infantry. After the war, he continued to write for *Adventure*. (He would do so through 1936.) He traveled extensively through Russia and the Near East. Wrote travel and historical articles for *The National Geographic* and *Asia* Learned Arabic and Persian. Went into the field to trace the campaigns of Ghengis Khan and Alexander the Great across the actual terrain. In 1929 he received a Guggenheim fellowship, and, in 1932, was decorated by the Persian government for his book, The Crusades (two volumes, 1930 and 1931).

Lamb left the pulp magazines at about the time *The Crusades* was adapted to a moving picture, the first of several of his books to become film spectacles. He continued to write deeply researched adventure fiction and to publish "Biographical and Historical Narratives" based on such celebrated figures as Ghengis Khan, Suleiman, Omar Khayyam, Alexander, and Hannibal. Several of these were rewritten to boys' books. From his home in Beverly Hills, California, he produced a steady stream of historical fiction until his death in 1962. Two collections of short fiction featuring Khlit the Cossack were published posthumously: *The Curved Saber* (1964) and *The Mighty Manslayer* (1969). *The White Falcon*, a novel featuring Khlit, had been published generations earlier in 1926. Other magazine novels and short stories about the old Cossack remain uncollected.

*Adventure* published the Khlit stories in two groups. The first, from 1917 to 1920, tell of his experiences among Cossacks, Tatars, Chinese, Afghans, and peoples of India, each culture being a hook upon which adventures were hung. The second group, 1925-1926, takes place when he is very old, wandering on the Russian frontier and in places less hospitable.

"Khlit," "Wolf's War, " and a portion of "Tal Taulai Khan" display the Cossack scene. At this point, we pause for a delightful nugget of history:

In the 13th Century, Mongolian Tatars overran what would become Russia. They stayed 300 years, hacking around, ripping out tribute. Finally Ivan the Great (Ivan II) drove them out and proclaimed himself Czar (or Caesar). After the death of Ivan the Terrible (Ivan IV) in 1584, all authority fell to pieces. Anarchy shrieked along the borders. Although the Cossacks guarded the Ukraine and Russian lands, Russia endured nearly constant attack from Poland and Sweden in the West and Tatar tribes in the East. That period is called "The Time of Troubles," from the late 1500s into the 1600s. In that period, the Khlit series is placed.

In "Wolf's War" (First January 1918), Khlit must find a way of rescuing the pepper-tongued woman that Menelitza adores. She has been taken by riders of the Khan Mirai, a Tatar chieftain and Khlit's deadly foe.

Khlit has little use for women. He regards them as "the baggage of Poles and Turks, useful otherwise in making and serving wine and cooking food." They chatter and their words are as smoke. At their best they are decorative; at their worst, they distract a man's attention from war.

This iconoclastic view he holds to the end, in spite of considerable experience to the contrary. For in nearly every adventure he meets clever, dangerous, forcible women, who shape the action to their private agendas.

At any rate, Menelitza's beloved has been carried off. Since he is away fighting the Poles, Khlit undertakes to rescue her—by sending word to Khan Mirai that if he releases the woman, Khlit will ride into his camp. Knowing that Khlit will keep his word—honor is honor—the Khan releases the woman and prepares red-hot pinchers for his enemy. Khlit does ride into the Tatar camp, but unexpectedly, amid a stampede of horses. And out again he flies through quite satisfactory devastation.

The Khan burns for revenge. In "Tal Taulai Khan" (Mid-February 1918), he nearly gets it.

With this story, Khlit begins his wanderings through the pages of *Adventure*. He begins by cutting ties with the Cossacks. They consider him too old for war, suitable only for rotting in a monastery—the old age home of the 1590s. Seething Khlit rides across Tatar lands, past his immediate enemies, toward the realm of the great Tal Taulai Khan, Wonderful and Mighty, descendent of Genghis Khan, leader of 300,000 horsemen.

Being bored, Tal Taulai has arranged a winter hunt in the mountains. To his court has come Mirai Khan, seeking alliance against the Russians. When Khlit arrives, all unsuspecting, he soon finds himself prisoner in a tent filled with riches—furs and gems and gold that Tal Taulai is sending as a casual gift to the chieftains of Mirai's tribe. Shows he doesn't plan to obliterate them anytime soon.

Khlit is well trapped. But, as always, he has a plan. He has offered himself as living quarry for Tal Taulai's huntsmen. Mirai Khan comes sneering to the tent of wealth. A mistake. The old enemies duel:

> Whirling his saber down, Khlit slashed savagely at the other's side. Under the cloak of Mirai Khan the blade passed.... Writhing back, the blade of the Cossack fell full upon the neck of Mirai Khan, and the latter's head dropped, held to the body only by the flesh muscles of one side of his neck. The curved sword of his enemy had nearly severed head from shoulders. (Lamb, *The Mighty Manslayer* 75)

Beheading is a casual pastime in these adventures. Lamb blithely embraces the drama and ignores the consequent blood geyser. Reality tends to be messier than fiction.

Mildly cheered by victory, Khlit rides forth to be hunted. The participants find it hard to catch a Cossack, born in the saddle. Narrowly evading them, Khlit watches as the hunt collapses into a bloody fight between Mirai Khan's tribe and the hordes of Tal Taulai.

Seems that when Mirai Khan's people opened the first basket of treasure, their leader's head rolled out. Naturally they took offense. Naturally Khlit had tucked the head in there.

By the third adventure, certain characteristics of the series are already clear. Early in the story, the terminal action will be predicted by a dream or prophecy. A device for resolving the action will be planted in the middle chapters. To intensify suspense, a spy will betray the heroes. Khlit will always be less helpless than he seems. And the story will end with a surprising revelation.

"Alamut" (First August 1918) uses all these devices. Khlit comes to the Persian stronghold of The Old Man of the Mountain, filled with drug-dazed assassins, and containing, as a jewel, a secret Moslem paradise of beautiful women, wine, and perfumed enchantment. Through an intense, frightening narrative, the Cossack plans the destruction of this place. He manages to do so with a trifle of help from the author.

As a matter of police, Khlit walks boldly into these nests of human bushmasters:

...when dealing with enemies more powerful than himself [he would] enter their ranks, whatever the danger might be. A single man, he reasoned, was useless fighting against an overpowering force. But in the stronghold of his enemies that man might accomplish much. To learn the plans of his foe and to defeat them from within by a stroke of the coldest daring was possible only to one of Khlit's craft.... (Lamb, *The Curved Saber* 220)

Which explains some of the hair-whitening situations he gets into during the series.

As, for instance, in "The Mighty Manslayer" (Mid-October 1918), one of the triumphs of the series. This is the first of five stories dealing with his adventures among the Tatars. The beginning is reasonably mild: Khlit buys free a girl slave, Kerula, and accompanies a conniving merchant on a long trip to Karakorum near the Gobi Desert. The expedition is to find the tomb and treasure of Genghis Khan, The Mighty Manslayer. At last they find the tomb. It is concealed deep in a cavern, accessible by a rock bridge stretching over an abyss fuming with strangling vapors. All the Great Khan's gold has been cast into the form of two immense elephants guarding the pathway.

Before looting the tomb, they are betrayed into the hands of the Chinese army. Some two hundred thousand soldiers are besieging a fortified city in which the last Khans of Tatary are trapped. Khlit and the merchant are hauled before the Chinese general.

And the merchant reveals wonders.

As he points out, Khlit's curved saber has been handed down, father to son, for generations. Along the blade are inscribed golden words. These prove that the weapon is the sword of Kaidu, great Khan of the Kallmark Tatars, descended directly from Genghis Khan. "Khlit, although he does not know it, is one of the few who are of the royal blood of the grand khans of Tatary." And traditional enemies of China.

Khlit knew nothing of this. So much for the disadvantages of illiteracy.

These revelations merely mean that the merchant is tortured to reveal the location of the tomb. Thereafter, the action boils: Khlit punished by heavy labor. Return of his saber by the girl slave, who has been impressed into the Chinese General's woman collection. Death of the merchant. Death of a Chinese detachment in the tomb of Genghis Khan. Khlit's dramatic entry into the Tatar's besieged fortress—he carries the yak-tail standard of Genghis Khan, borrowed from the tomb. Destruction of the Chinese by 65,000 Tatar horsemen. Flames livid in the Hall of Judgment around the defeated Chinese general. It is quite some story.

"The White Khan" (Mid-December 1918): Khlit comes among the Jun-gar Tatars but, in spite of his descent from Genghis Khan, is eyed with jealousy and dislike. When a Chinese ambassador demands that he be brought to the court of Emperor Wan Li, the Cossack rides to China. With him goes Chagan, a giant of a man, immensely powerful. He is the hereditary bearer of the Khan's sword.

They head toward Shankiang. So does General Li Jusong, head of a Chinese army, out to punish the Tatars. Since internal feuds tear the Chinese, the general attacks Shankiang just after Khlit and Chagan arrive. His troops pour into the city, giving Harold Lamb opportunity to describe enough hand-to-hand combat to satisfy the most ferocious reader. The first Chinese troops our heroes meet have just murdered a young girl:

...Khlit's curved sword flashed up. It whirled swiftly against the throat of the pikeman. The soldier dropped beside the girl, his head hanging from his shoulders by a strip of flesh.

The spears of the others were lifted at Khlit, who had slashed the face of a second man with the same stroke that slew the murderer of the girl. He sprang back, only to see three of the menacing pikes knocked to the ground by a stroke of Chagan's huge sword, with its foot-wide blade. He warded off the stroke of the fourth man, drawing a pistol at the same time.

Khlit discharged his pistol at the waist of the man who had struck at him.... Chagan's blade, falling again, had dashed two of the men to earth with split heads. The survivor had dropped his pike and taken to his heels....

"The hunting has begun, Chagan," cried Khlit... (107)

It has, indeed. In short order, Khlit meets the General, Li Jusong, refuses service to the Emperor, ends up tied in a temple, swarming with corpse-eating rats. Freed from this bothersome situation, he regains his sword by plot complications too elaborate to detail and escapes to a defense tower.

That tower is defended by Chagan and Arslan—Arslan being a merry minstrel type, who is also one of history's great archers. After sending Chagan for the Tatar army, Khlit and Arslan defend the tower, driving home arrows and chopping off heads.

The bloodshed climaxes when the Jun-gar arrive and kill everyone standing erect. For his exploits, Khlit is elevated to the status of the Kha Khan, The White Khan, a rank extended only to descendents of The Great Genghis.

As the Kha Khan, Khlit has one violent adventure after another. In "Changa Nor" (First February 1919), he saves a descendent of Prester John's ministry and the Christian treasures protected in a remote stone tower. In "Roof of the World" (Mid-April 1919), he faces a plot by the Dalai Lama to set Khlit's Tatars and those of Iskander Khan at each other's throats. The danger is resolved during a Love Chase—pursuit of a beautiful woman on a horse by an army of men who haven't bathed in five years. However, she catches the man she wants; a lot of yellow-hatted priests catch death; Khlit catches the villain and flicks off his head. Which he presents to Iskander Khan, thus cementing their eternal friendship.

You can't have fun forever. One day, the Jun-gar Tatars learn that Khlit is a Christian. That distresses their Mohammedan souls. In "The Star of Evil Omen" (Mid-July 1919), he gives up his rank as Kha Khan and leaves the Tatars, vowing to send them a gift. He finds service with the Chinese Emperor Wan Li. Once again he meets the archer Arslan and learns of the murderous intrigue webbing the Emperor—for his Chief Eunuch and his Royal Favorite plot to place the Favorite's child on the throne. The plot fails. But not before Khlit and Arslan are hunted by the millions of China for murder of the Emperor. Who is not dead. Treason has secretly imprisoned him in the tomb of his ancestors. Khlit rescues him. With the help of nearby Tatars, he also rescues all the treasure from that tomb. So the Jun-gar receive their rich gift after all.

Arslan is killed in this story, a regrettable waste.

Of new characters there is no lack. Two join the series as the narrative moves to India. "The Rider of the Gray Horse" (Mid-September 1919) begins on the fringes of the Gobi Desert. There Khlit meets Nur-jahan, another hard-minded, flame-tempered beauty, immensely clever, with character enough for ten men. Sentenced to death by the Mogul of India, she is fleeing to Jahangir, the man she

loves. Quite swiftly, Khlit finds himself crossways with the priests of
Bon, the Destroyer. (Whenever priests appear in this series, they are
overripe plotters, treacherous as a campaign promise. Khlit loathes them
all, excepting only the Prester John successor in "Changa Nor.")

After the usual string of betrayals, menaces, and physical anguish,
they are trapped in a temple. Toward them slobber a mob of religious
fanatics. However a faithful, if equivocal, Sikh keeps a promise and Nur-
jahan's beloved arrives in time, terrible with horses and swords.

For the next half dozen stories, Lamb left Khlit to write about the
fortunes of Abdul Dost, a deadly Afghan swordsman, tall and agile, his
face scarred, his blood royal, and his luck good enough to keep him alive
through savage exploits. Soon he would join forces with Khlit.

Who returned, after a six-month absence, in "The Lion Cub" (First
June 1920), a coming-of-age story about a headstrong young nobleman,
a murderous Persian, and an even more deadly Tatar hill chieftain.
Ultimately the young nobleman gets some sense. A small army of men,
including the Persian, get no older.

Abdul Dost meets Khlit in the taut story, "Law of Fire" (Mid-July
1920). Khlit is hired to escort a caravan through high passes. It is a
caravan of thieves and liars, lugging along stolen women. One of those,
Yasmi Khanih, is of interest to Abdul Dost, who comes like the Drums
of Fate after the slavers, and ends up battling Khlit.

It is nearly Khlit's final fight. He enters it with an arrow through
his leg, fights till exhausted, then crumples. Before Abdul Dost chops
him, Yasmi explains that Khlit has already killed three of the slavers and
is her protector.

Khlit, more practical, tells Abdul Dost: "I shall not wield sword
again, warrior. The strength that once was mine is gone. My arm is
weak. Something that was here—is sped." (Touching his chest.)
"You—overmastered me. It is my last fight" (173).

Not quite his last. But isn't that dramatic?

The pair ride together into the Punjab, where they meet the original
Juggernaut ("The Bride of Jagannath," First August 1920.) "The
Masterpiece of Death" (Mid-September 1920) is a twisting, tricky
narrative, with a surprise villain. Those famous hereditary murderers, the
thags (or thugs), play a prominent role.

The Indian stories end with the novel-length "The Curved Sword"
(First November 1920). This remarkable piece is a *tour de force*
summation of the series, bringing back past characters, past situations
(brightly refurbished), and bits of guile Khlit has used before, always to
our great satisfaction and delight. The narrative, a prose opera, is packed
with big scenes and dramatic confrontations, and celebrates war, fame,

love, gallantry, sacrifice, regret, disaster, triumph, melancholy, joy, and a long sequence in which she is nearly raped.

She is Nur-jahan, now referred to as The Light of the World. She is engaged to Jahangir, become the Mogul or, as he modestly puts it, Lord of the World and Master of Ind.

He rules by proxy, rather like a President to whom state governors report directly. And to whom they pay pre-set taxes. Like state governors, the proxies are corrupt. Alacha, who oversees Afghanistan, is not only corrupt but ambitious, a terrible combination.

Khlit and Abdul Dost ride into the center of the trouble. Immediately, Dost becomes the focus of an incipient Afghan rebellion.

To spy out the situation, Khlit obeys a summons to come to Jahangir's court. After learning much, he departs to enlist the Jun-gar Tatars in Abdul Dost's cause. And of course they are willing, what with loot at the end of the trail, and a chance to fight and howl and watch the blood spurt and heads bounce around.

After a harrowing ride from the southern Mongolian plain across high mountain passes into northern Afghanistan, they arrive, barely in time. To chaos. Abdul Dost's forces, unwilling to wait all those weeks for Khlit to return with the Tatars, have attacked the Mogul's army.

Plot complications: Nur-jahan, the Light of the World, being three hundred and twelve times smarter than the Mogul, has entered Afghanistan in disguise. She intends to seek out Abdul Dost and reconcile him with the Mogul. Unfortunately, she runs afoul of Alacha and gets kidnapped. His ambition has outreached itself.

So has his luck. Berang, the Tatar Kha Khan, slices open Alacha as if carving a watermelon. Then on to the great fight, chapters of it, hacking, slashing, bashing. Khlit leads the Tatars in the *tulughma*, the Mongol sweep of Genghis Khan—howling clouds of horsemen striking the enemy flank, the rear, then breaking off, only to strike elsewhere, minutes later. Mobilized warfare, relentless, brutal, effective. Through it all, horses dying, elephants dying, men dying. Even Chagan gets killed, that near immortal, destroyed in a casual sentence from which all emotion has been omitted, accidentally, we may suppose.

Despairing of defeating the Tatars, with Mr. Lamb as their ally, the Mogul's army flees.

Darkness falls across the prose. Above miles of dead men, the birds circle. The surviving Tatars, loaded with loot, fade north toward the high passes. Khlit remains behind, broken sword in hand, kneeling exhausted beside Abdul Dost. Severely wounded, the Afghan will henceforth be a cripple. But the two of them have caused the wreck of the Mogul's army. Henceforth Afghanistan remains free.

On this somber note, Lamb may have intended to end the Khlit series. Months passed. Other sword-proud heroes moved through Lamb's fiction—Aruk and Kam, Prince Mign, Ivak, Borasun, and Ayub, the big solid powerful Cossack.

Years passed. Then in 1925, Ayub stumbled into a tavern on the Russian eastern border. By the fire lounged a smiling, black-eyed adolescent, strumming a three-stringed guitar. The story is "Bogatyr" (September 30, 1925). "Bogatyr" means hero, and within a few pages, the old hero, Khlit, steps gauntly from the darkness. Now he is an old man, tall, thin, white-mustached. Age has not diminished his cleverness. Only he sleeps more. And he no longer wears the curved saber.

That swings at the side of Kirdy, the young man with the guitar. He is Khlit's grandson.

In the casual way these writers have, Lamb drops a few pages of information, not particularly consistent, to bridge the years between "The Curved Sword" and "Bogatyr." Of Khlit's wife, nothing. Of Kirdy, that he was born on the Gobi, son of a Mogul chieftain and a princess of Kublai Khan's line. Both parents were killed in a raid by tribesmen. Kirdy escaped and somehow his grandfather discovered him. Somehow they both served Jahangir, the Mogul the one who was Lord of the World. Abdul Dost, himself, taught Kirdy how to rob caravans and steal horses. Khlit taught him swordsmanship.

Finally tiring of the Court, Khlit and Kirdy traveled to Persia and into Turkey. Thoughts of death bit the old man. Before he died, he wanted to introduce Kirdy "to his old companions of the Zaporogian Siech, who were the chosen warriors of the Cossacks." So they returned to Russia. There they meet Ayub. In "Bogatyr," they also meet a Russian Prince who has angered the Czar and been banished to the sticks. Prince Vladimir's job is to protect the settlers. He doesn't. Nor does he keep his promises when Khlit negotiates an exchange of prisoners with a Tartar raider. Resulting in Khlit and Kirdy riding with the Tatars to attack upon Vladimir's fortress. Which is defended by two cannon.

At the critical moment, both cannon refuse to fire. Khlit cleverly spiked them when you weren't watching, several pages past. And Harold Lamb had allowed the discipline to be so slack that no one checked the touchholes of the weapons. Anyhow, Vladimir gets his death, the girl is saved, and Kirdy has taken another step toward manhood.

That is one of the internal structures of the Khlit-Kirdy adventures. In each, Khlit sees his grandson take another step toward maturity and pre-eminence.

As in "White Falcon" (three-part serial, November 30 through December 20, 1925.) This tells the story of a 500-man Cossack raid on Urgench, a city 2000 miles away. They take the city, loot Muhammad Khan's treasure of jewels, and ride back toward Russia. The Khan, blue with fury, pounds after them. The Cossacks are massively outnumbered. Tactics, evasion, open flight. Kirdy, captured, faces the cheerless prospect of torture by people who love their work. Before that happens, Khlit, alone and disguised, stampedes a horse herd through the camp. They escape. After finding Ayub, wounded, at the Black Sea, they return to Moscow, a 3000-mile trip, little of it pleasure.

For his deeds during the campaign, Kirdy is feted by the Cossacks and given the name White Falcon. Khlit presents the Czar, Boris Godunov, with the Khan's jewels. But Boris is more interested in the news that the Khan's city was burned removing an obstruction to Russia's trade routes with the Far East. For this dubious achievement, five hundred Cossacks died. Ayub, Kirdy, and Khlit are the only survivors.

Kirdy must be further tested. Khlit fears that he "has not learned to see what lies in another man's soul—treachery or good faith." In "The Winged Rider" (January 10, 1926), the boy tests this ability against river pirates, a dwarf, who seems to be a shape-shifter, and a spooky woman who may have both wings and immortality. Khlit seems fairly satisfied with the progress of his protege.

There followed "The Wolf Master" (December 8, 1926), a long novel in which Khlit takes command of the Cossacks. They have been defeated by the Poles after betrayal by a false Czar. Kirdy is assigned to kill that wretch and does so, after tracking him across most of the Asian land mass.

With that novel, the series ended. It had extended over about ten years, peaking in 1920 with "The Curved Sword." While the later stories, with Kirdy and Ayub, are interesting and always suspenseful, their intensity has faded, like an opal untouched for years, only occasionally flaring to green or blue or scalding red to remind you of what had been.

Other writers, other characters carried on the burden of war fiction. One of the best, the most vivid, and the most popular, was Tros of Samothrace, who appeared in a succession of novels by Talbot Mundy.

First published was a string of seven short novels in the 1925-1926 *Adventure*. (These were later collected in the book *Tros of Samothrace*, 1934.) In 1929, Tros appeared as a major character in the novel, *Queen Cleopatra*, a work that did not see magazine publication. Finally, Tros was the subject of four short novels, continuing seamlessly from the conclusion of *Queen Cleopatra*; these were published in *Adventure* during 1935 and collected as *Purple Pirate* that same year.

Twelve novels, then—formal historical novels, hardened by recorded events and richly seasoned by a slew of other events not documented at all. Through the novels swarm figures from the past, great and small, known and otherwise: King Caswallon of Britain, Commius of Britain and Gaul, General Ganymedes, Prince Herod of Jerusalem, Roman notables such as Brutus and Anthony and Cassius, Queen Arsinoe of Crete, King Ptolemy of Egypt, the eunuch Potheinas, the powerful and deadly Charmian. And Cleopatra of Egypt, Queen Cleopatra, the Serpent of the Nile. And Julius Caesar, that dominating figure, who drives the series, like a great engine pounding behind the paragraphs.

Characters and events alike stand in hard-edged detail, drawn as if from photographs, specific as the back of your hand. The prose is as close to reality as ink on paper can get. Gripped by the coherence and force of the narrative, you forget that it represents neither reality nor that slightly different thing, history.

What you are reading is fiction disguised as history, fiction so cleverly wound around fact's bones, so adroit at explaining history's web, that your critical sense melts away. Warmly acquiescent, you accept Mundy's version of characters' motives, how they thought, what purposes their actions served. The links he forges between historical events are so impellingly right that you accept them as facts. Perhaps some are. Who knows?

But remember, as you turn the pages hot-eyed with admiration, you are reading fiction, not history.

The story opens, 55 B.C., in Britain, immediately before Julius Caesar's first invasion, and continues through battle, intrigue, death, love, and excitement to conclude in Alexandria, Egypt, some thirteen years and seventeen hundred pages later.

Tros, that extraordinary seaman and battle captain, is from the island Samothrace, a collection of rocks surrounded by the north Aegean Sea. Desolate, sun-scoured, of no economic value, Samothrace is, at this time, the heart of religious mysticism in the ancient world. Secret wisdom, secret communications, secret aspirations and secret, difficult disciplines link the initiates of the island with the Druids of Gaul and Britain. (According to Mundy.) Their purposes and beliefs, being secret, are left as shadowy as a crypt.

Tros finds it so. His father, Prince Perseus of Samothrace, is an initiate of the Mysteries. Tros, himself, is not. He found them rather more vapory than his brisk practicality could accept. Still, his father trained him from youth to examine himself, to define and perform his duty. And, particularly, to be "mistrustful and even scornful of all women," never allowing love to interfere with duty.

He didn't. But such training left him vaguely uneasy in the presence of the intelligent and compelling women met during his adventures. Tros is not the first hero to find large gaps between theories about women and the real thing.

In person, the man blazes like the sun. He is an amber-eyed giant, muscled like a marble statue, bearded, his black hair restrained by a golden circlet. Confidence glows from him in a nearly visible aura. He is a seaman and a leader. He commands.

[Tros] wore his purple cloak..., and his sword in its vermilion scabbard hung from a belt set with jewels. His eyes glowed beneath the gold band that encircled his forehead. The crushing obstinacy of his jaw and chin, the oak-strength of his neck and the masterful lines of mouth and nostril were exposed for whoso would to read. One would oppose him at one's own risk. (Mundy, *Tros of Samothrace* 641)

Unlike most fighting captains in pulp magazines, he is also articulate and piercingly intelligent. Honor rides his shoulders. He will not betray his word. He will perform his duty, as he sees it, to the last crumb.

Which doesn't mean that he is inflexible or lacks guile. Quite otherwise. He is quick to devise new strategy as the story line froths and bubbles. Like Jim Grim, he meets problems with what seems to be intuition, but is actually a formidable mix of training, skill, technical knowledge, and superb understanding of his opponent. You never catch Tros praying for help. He makes his own help: the gods "have no use for men who pray to them and waste good time and energy on whining..." (Mundy, *Tros of Samothrace* 914).

Of the many fictional figures examined by the *Yesterday's Faces* series, Tros is the most sensitive to human motive and political complexity. His assessment of those around him is swiftly accurate; he gets their nature nearly at a glance. His assessment of a situation is rapid as a knife stroke. Granted that he is a master seaman, a prodigious fighter, and fascinates the girls. Beyond these things, he understands men and how to deal with them. That makes him a great Captain.

Such a paragon must have at least a few faults. And, indeed, Tros has some minor flecking. From time to time he makes errors, wrongly judging a situation or a person. He is, perhaps, a bit humorless; somewhat apt to magnify the importance of the people and events of his past. His sense of honor is both a strength and a weakness, since it leaves him vulnerable to the unsubtle blackmail of hostage taking—and once his men are hostage, Tros is as good as chained by the leg.

Call those faults, if you will. Or keys to his character. There are other keys: he wishes to build a ship according to his own design. And he wishes to sail around the world.

For the world is round. The secret wisdom of Samothrace proclaims so. Tros believes so. He intends to sail forth to prove it.

One day. One day he will sail.

After seventeen hundred pages, he has not sailed. But one day....

*From the Log of Tros of Samothrace*: ...I will strike such a blow on the anvil of life as shall use to the utmost all I am. Thus, though I know not whither I go nor what I shall be, I shall go to no home of idleness. I shall be no gray ghost lamenting what I might have done, but did not. (Mundy 501)

Those are words to lift and shake. The eloquence shouts with power. You are not negligible; you shall make a difference. Likely enough you will even quit smoking.

(Similar inspirational passages appear at the head of each chapter throughout the Tros series. Some are credited to the Druid Taliesan, some to Olympus, Cleopatra's astrologer; most are from the Log of Tros. Each comments obliquely upon the action to come and each has the sound of a man musing on the unpublished laws of human conduct and the art of reading life.)

We first meet Tros, that commanding presence, in "Tros of Samothrace" (February 10, 1925). The shadowy, secret figures of Samothrace have sent Tros and his father, Perseus, to Gaul to offer encouragement to the Druids there. Who need encouragement, since they are being slaughtered wholesale by Julius Caesar and his clanging legions.

Immediately the men from Samothrace are taken prisoner by Caesar. Their ship is burned, Perseus made hostage, and Tros sent to Britain to scout landing places for the Roman legions. (Rome knows land war but has only feeble seamen, and Tros is obviously a master seaman.)

With him goes Conops, the reliable and unfailing Conops. He is "a short man, of about the same age as Tros, possibly five-and-twenty, and of the same swarthy complexion.... One bright-blue eye peered out from an impudent face, crowned with a knotted red kerchief. His nose was up-turned, as if it had been smashed in childhood.... His thin, strong, bare legs looked as active as a cat's" (Mundy 3).

Under the red kerchief is red hair. You see only one eye because Caesar ordered the other burned out after Conops smart-mouthed him. "Master," he calls Tros, since they live in a time when the middle-class and its intelligent values were hardly evident.

Not to make a thing about it, but Conops is a roistering, wine-swilling, harlot-hunting, knife-quick seaman, enjoying his many personal flaws to the utmost. He is also completely competent and absolutely dependable. Tros relies on him totally. Conops is a luminous example of that fictional convention, the secondary lead who is first mate, chief confidant, lieutenant, friend—as Ramsden, for instance. This figure does all the detail work and most of the impossible assignments, thus keeping the narrative rushing brightly along.

The discerning reader may notice that Tros lacks bad habits. He neither belches, overeats, or gazes meaningfully at the dancing girls. Conops does all that for him. As is usual in action fiction, the hero gets most of the virtues and the associate gets most of the faults. In spite of that lopsided distribution, both characters are richly developed, Tros in particular. His abilities not only compel the action but are enhanced by fine battle set-pieces. His mind, thoughts, and motives are explored in detail. As a living, if somewhat idealized, character, he would make the reputation of any contemporary novelist willing to forego descriptions of sexual activity. To which, in these 1920s fictions, you note oblique references only.

Conops lasts through the series, eventually earning the rank of Captain. It doesn't change him. To the end he is a hardboiled first mate, knowing how to extract the utmost from his men:

*Conops* (on entering a small boat immediately after having been appointed Captain): "You tow-haired druids, toss oars. You lubbers!... By Pluto's teeth, I'll teach you Caesar's leavings decent manners or kill you trying. Ready! Give way! Hold your chin up, Seven! Bow, you're deep—get your hands down! you're not fishing—Three, are you afraid to bend that stretcher? Legs to work, and row your weight, you lump o' dunnage—Now then, swing to it, my hearties—yeo—ho! yeo—ho!" (Mundy, *The Purple Pirate* 311)

It's not cruelty or pride, but driving force and attention to detail. Makes you ache to go to sea.

After landing in Britain, Tros and Conops are captured and taken to Caswallon, one of the more powerful local chiefs. (Britain was ruled by hundreds of petty chieftains, each claiming a few miles of territory, bitterly suspicious of their neighbors—and rightfully so.) Caswallon and his wife, Fflur, will become Tros' fast friends. Fflur has second sight and later predicts correctly, if in broad generalities, the course of Tros' adventures.

Over two or three chapters, Tros wins the Britons' confidence. He meets with Druids, unsnarls plots by Commius, Caesar's spy, and spins a few plots, himself. Finally he returns to Caesar's camp, only to discover that great men do not always keep their word. Tros' father is not freed and Tros is required to pilot the Roman fleet to Britain.

After an abortive attempt to wreck that fleet on the British coast, Tros witnesses the initial battle of the invasion. Later escaping, he returns during a furious storm to cut the cables of forty Roman ships and wreck them on the beach. (The wrecking, at least, is historical fact.)

That disaster causes Caesar to withdraw. The first Roman invasion of Britain ends, as does the first novel of the series. The fate of Tros' father remains to be decided.

Bringing us to "Enemy of Rome" (April 10, 1925). Through a hot-paced narrative, apparently written by an eyewitness, considering the wealth of precise detail, Tros attempts to save his father. He does, too late. The father, tortured, dies. In turn, Tros evades a trap and captures Caesar, himself, only to allow him to escape for excellent, if intricate, reasons.

By this point in the series, the dullest wit will have noticed that Julius Caesar is a major character. Caesar's personality draws Mundy like an enchantment, transfixing him, drawing forth elaborate miracles of description and interpretation:

Caesar...was hardly forty-five, but he looked very bald and very old.... His cheeks looked hollow, as if all the molars were missing, and the wrinkles at the corners of his mouth twitched slightly, as if he were not perfectly at ease.

Nevertheless, he was alert and handsome from self-consciousness of power and intelligence. He sat bolt upright like a soldier; his pale smile was suave, and his eyes were bold and calculating as a Forum money-lender's. Handsome, very handsome in a cold and studied way—he seemed to know exactly how he looked—dishonest, intellectual, extravagant, a liar, capable of any cruelty and almost any generosity at other men's expense; above all, mischievous and vicious, pouched below the eyes and lecherously lipped, but handsome—not a doubt of it.  (Mundy, *Tros of Samothrace* 81)

This ruthlessly unfavorable portrait will be amended over many pages. Eventually, it will include wit, enormous military talent, audacity, ironic humor, and calculated lechery. Coolly remote, a master manipulator and orator of genius, Caesar dominates any gathering—he simply understands any situation better than any man there. Toward the end of his career, he shows a curious eagerness to consider himself a god on earth. That hubris, and a contempt for petty affairs, temporarily blurs the clarity of his intelligence. Assassination follows.

Caesar is brilliantly drawn. Mundy loathes him. He reiterated his dislike in *Adventure's* February 10, 1925, letters department, "The Camp-Fire":

I have followed Caesar's Commentaries as closely as possible in writing this story, but as Caesar, by his own showing, was a liar, a brute, a treacherous humbug and conceited ass, as well as the ablest military expert in the world at that time...I have not been to much trouble to make him out a hero. (Mundy, *Messenger of Destiny* 151-152)[2]

These remarks resulted in bellows of wrath, or agreement, from the readership of *Adventure*. "The Camp-Fire" took on the appearance of a sack containing a cat fight. Every month or so, Mundy would publish another segment of the Tros story. Immediately the brawl would explode again as the letter writers howled forth to praise or batter Mundy and each other with fine impartiality. It was wonderful. They disagreed about Caesar, the Roman Empire, the state of civilization in Britain, the authenticity of historical records, the culture of Gaul.... For example:

> I think that Mundy is a Grade A certified fiction writer but as an historical philosopher I think he is punk.... Mundy is in good company, of course, in knocking the Roman Empire. Lots of people disapprove of it. H.G. Wells disapproves of it because it wasn't Socialist and I take it Mundy disapproves because it wasn't Theosophist....
>
> ...Mundy has some color for his argument in that Rome was at its worst, politically and morally and from the standpoint of administrative efficiency, in Caesar's day. All the big politicians were pretty tough just then; they had to be to get anywhere. Caesar was the best of the lot; the only one who could see ahead, could try and reform the terrible mess that the Roman Republic had become... His private morals, no doubt, were not those of a deacon in the church; but Suetonius, whom Mundy seems to follow, is a far less reliable authority in such matters than the *Illustrated Daily News*. (Davis, *The Camp-Fire 176-177*)[3]

Those remarks caused a new round of detonations. And so it went.

That was long ago. Today, Mundy's ambivalence toward Caesar is much more apparent. His fiction displays that attitude more clearly than his inflammatory letters to "The Camp-Fire." While Mundy flailed away at Caesar's failings, he consistently emphasized Caesar's superiority. Depicting Caesar as heartlessly corrupt, he also showed the man as a clear-headed realist, conscious of minute shadings of behavior, a genius whose mind, civilized and agile, never failed to distinguish between appearance and reality.

Decidedly, Mundy's portrait of Caesar is ambiguous. So intensely does Mundy blast Caesar's crimes, moral and ethical, so exactly does he weigh out praise for this man nearly two thousand years dead, that the wary reader hears alarms. You notice at once that the faults ascribed to Caesar are remarkably similar to the faults of Talbot Mundy during that fifteen-year period of dark and shameful behavior, mentioned earlier.

On his deathbed, Tros' father addressed this point: "All is warfare with self. All that you know of Caesar is your own image, cast in the reflection of your own unconscious thought" (Mundy, *Tros of Samothrace* 228).

Julius Caesar triggers powerful emotions in Mundy. It suggests personal implications beyond our ability to examine. We may only surmise. Sparingly.

We have the sense of a great pool whose surface, opaque and black with shadow, trembles occasionally. Not much, not often. Some deeply submerged thing has stirred. What it is, we do not know. But there is no safety here. In this place, something dangerous hunts.

"Prisoners of War" (June 10, 1925), introduces Olaf Sigurdson and his hardboiled Northmen—Vikings to you. Tros fights Sigurdson, wins, eventually marries his sister, Helma, a gifted, capable woman. While he is about it, he helps Caswallon defeat a group of Britons stirred up by one of Caesar's ex-mistresses and Skell, a congenital liar, who reappears in the next several novels. Skell's like will reappear later in the series, for Tros encounters liars, greed-heads, and back-stabbers on nearly every page.

"Hostages to Luck" (August 20, 1925), tells how Tros finally builds his dream ship. Helped by the Britons and the Northmen, he creates a classic anachronism, a gigantic, three-tiered galley with three masts, built on the general lines of a Norse dragon ship, enormously magnified. Below the great serpent head, with flexible tongue, projects a figurehead resembling Helma. The hull is sheathed in tin. Above the decks rise heights of sail as purple as Tros' cloak. The ship is armed with catapults of unique design, firing whole banks of arrows or chunks of cliff. Its armament includes Greek Fire and a special preparation that fumes out an incredible stink, sprays molten blobs, and frequently explodes. [4]

As Tros completes building the Liafail, the enigmatic name of his vessel, Roman agents kidnap Helma and Fflur, Caswallon's wife. (The kidnapping of Fflur is an historical event.) Tros mounts an expedition to Caesar's camp, even through his ship is only partially manned, and his seamen untrained.

Again Tros arrives too late for rescue. Wounded by a Roman arrow, Helma dies in his arms. Once more he captures Caesar, only to exchange him for Fflur. At the same time he squeezes from Caesar a written commission as Caesar's Admiral. Caesar grants the request casually, knowing that, since the commission is not stamped with Caesar's seal, it is not official. Several novels earlier, however, Tros captured Caesar's flagship, Caesar's payroll, and a box of Caesar's documents, including that precious seal.

All these he uses wisely in "Admiral of Caesar's Fleet" (October 10, 1925). After assisting Caswallon to crush a conspiracy that would have betrayed Lunden (London) to the Romans, Tros captures three of Caesar's ships and gets enough Spanish seamen to operate Liafail.

Then he takes leave of his British friends. He plans to sail to Rome, there to plea the Britons' case, and, somehow, draw Caesar back to Italy.

Along the way, he stops at Gades, Spain, where simmers a plot to murder the Roman governor—and assassinate Caesar ("The Dancing Girl of Gades," December 10, 1925). To Tros' intense disgust, he finds, once more, that to aid himself, he must assist Caesar out of difficulties.

Once in Rome, Tros visits people you read about in textbooks, Cato and Pompey among them, as he seeks some way of forcing Caesar to abandon his invasion of Britain. The story, an intense three-part serial, was published in *Adventure* as "The Messenger of Destiny" (February 10, 20, and 28, 1926). Through a mist of lies and treachery, aided by Helene (a spy for Caesar in Rome), Tros finally finds a lever. In an eerie interview with the head of the Vestal Virgins, Tros hands over pearls supplied by the British Druids. In turn, the Virgin gives him a message for Caesar: Leave Gaul pacified, return to Rome. And make Rome yours.

Carrying this message to Caesar isn't all that simple. Tros, and his Northmen, end up in the Circus Maximus, fighting lions, African tribesmen, and a gang of professional gladiators. They escape with their lives—certainly better off than the lions, tribesmen, and gladiators.

After that blood-letting, Tros leaves Rome to seek out Caesar on the beaches of Britain. During the final chapter, the two sit and talk, Tros often grim, beating his hand into his palm; Caesar urban, pleasant, eerily quick to understand. They speak of war and politics, how matters ripen in time, of Tros' wish to sail around the world, and a select, few words about their differing goals.

The conversation is quiet. It echoes softly with all that has gone before. And at last:

*Tros*: "Caesar, I hope for both our sakes not to meet you again until after death. Eternity—"
*Caesar*: "Oh, do you believe in that?" (Mundy, *Tros of Samothrace* 949)

On that wonderful line, the first group of stories concludes. For an action-adventure series there have been an extraordinary number of scenes like this, conversations between two or three people. Nothing physical happens. But the talk grips like an octopus. Men discuss others, take stands, expose their minds. Deception meets counter-deception, and self-interest exposes itself among polished lies. Gusts of emotion rush between the speakers, shaking them like poplars in hard wind.

This is writing commanding attention and respect. You have the impression that Mundy stood silently by, watching the scene happen, for the narrative is constantly cued by brief descriptions of business:

*While in conversation with Druids*: "[Tros leaned] back against the table, squeezing the edge of it in both hands until knuckles and muscles stood out in knots" (Mundy, *Tros of Samotrace* 641).

*Tros besides his father's body*: "And for a while he stood steadying himself with one hand on an overhead beam, watching the old man's face.... It was dark in there and easy to imagine things. The body moved a trifle in time to the ship's swaying (Mundy, *Tros of Samotrace* 243).

*During an interview in Rome*: Cato, spreading out his knees with both hands resting on them, leaned back; he had done with arguing (Mundy, *Tros of Samothrace* 822).

Some scenes evoke multiple layers of sound:

In the outer hall [Orwic's] voice kept rising sharply. There were hot answers in almost incomprehensible Gaulish, and every once in a while a Roman centurion added his staccato warning to the noise. (Mundy, *Tros of Samothrace* 777)

At other times, the scene is set by a paragraph or two of description vivid as spilled blood. As in this picture of the Circus Maximus in early morning:

Dawn heard the roaring begin, as the populace poured into the seats to make sure none should forestall them by bribing the attendants.... The Circus was a sea of clean sand glittering in sunlight. Colored awnings, stretched over the seats on decorated masts threw one half of the spectators into shade, except where hot rays shone through gaps where the awnings were roped together. There was a constant thunder from the canvas shaking in the morning wind. Roaring and baying of starved animals provided grim accompaniment. The blended tumult resembled thunder of surf on a rock-bound beach. (Mundy, *Tros of Samothrace* 921)

Each novel features battle, usually on water. For those unresponsive to the thrust and parry in conversational scenes, Mundy provides descriptions of several minor clashes at arms and at least one major engagement. It is war hand-to-hand, savage and without pity, with men dead and men hurt after each encounter:

There was no discipline. No order, no command could have been heard above the shouting and the crash of breaking ships....

Blood and spray churned into scum. A dozen Britons, cornered in the bow, loosed flight after flight of arrows humming through the darkness, so that both sides struggled for the shelter... And it was there that Tros's long sword began to turn the tide of battle, for he caught the stoutest Roman of them all and skewered him through the throat against the bulkhead.... (Mundy, *Tros of Samothrace* 233-234)

The battles, impressive as they are, become more violent and even more graphic as the story switches locale from Britain to Egypt. In real time that took three years. Until 1929 Tros simply disappeared. Which should not have been and was not intended. But the unexpected keeps happening so unexpectedly, doesn't it.

What happened was this: In 1924, Mundy had planned a novel about Cleopatra. One of the characters would have been a Sait of Samothrace (Mundy, *Messenger of Destiny* 151). Tros seems to have evolved from Sait and promptly charged headlong into his own 1925-1926 series, as we have seen. Several years passed. The Cleopatra novel was finally completed. It sold to *Adventure* and, in due course, should have appeared there as a serial, generating more pugnacious howls in "The Camp-Fire" columns.

At this particular time, however, Editor Arthur Sullivant Hoffman, profoundly irritated by the Butterick Publishing Company's policies on handling *Adventure*, abruptly hurled up both hands and left the magazine. (His farewell was printed in the June 15, 1927 issue.) The editorship devolved upon Joseph Cox, who left after eight issues. Cox was succeeded by mystery writer Anthony Rud, who would stay until the early 1930s (Bleiler, *A History of the Adventure Magazine* 23-24). One of these editors felt that Mundy's Cleopatra manuscript did not meet new editorial slants. Mundy withdrew the manuscript. It would never appear in a magazine but, in 1929, was published as *Queen Cleopatra* (Mundy, *Messenger of Destiny* 80).

The novel begins in Alexandria, 48 B.C., as the twenty-one year old Cleopatra watches a great purple-sailed war ship glide into the harbor. From this point to the end of the series, Tros' fortunes will be tangled with the power politics of the ancient world. Particularly with the fury of events wheeling about the tiny figure of Cleopatra VII Philadelphus Philopator Philopatris.

Stunning beauty is ascribed to Cleopatra. Her true appearance, however, is debatable. One of the courtesies of history is that any woman whose smile would not actually crack a stone wall is celebrated as a beauty. She was of mixed Greek, Macedonian, and Syrian blood. She was small, probably hook-nosed, probably dark complexioned (Grant, *Cleopatra* 5).[4] In a recent biography of Caesar, she is described as no beauty:

...Cleopatra embellished nature with art. Antimony and lamp black on eyebrows and eyelids magnified her eyes and drew attention from a nose too long and aquiline; ochre on lips softened a pouting mouth, and seaweed and mulberry juice brightened full cheeks and a blunt chin; henna on her nails accentuated the delicacy of her hands and feet.... She moved with grace and spoke in a low music. Ready with a saucy wit or a pretense at helplessness, she also knew the seduction of gorgeous attire and feline guile." (Kahn, *The Education of Julius Caesar* 171)

Not much of this appears in Mundy.[6] He focuses upon her high intelligence, quickness of mind, manipulative skill, and her ruthless determination to establish Egypt as an equal partner with Rome, rather than a territory to be plundered.

That spring drives these stories. Cleopatra's every action is directed to preserving Egypt. It is harder than threading a needle in an earthquake. Civil war rips Rome. Egypt foams with plots, intrigues, and insurrections. On every side, neighboring states, eyes blazing with greed, probe for weakness. Within Cleopatra's palace, murderous dissension flares: her sister, Arsinoe IV, sets up, savagely defiant, as a competing queen. Her younger brother Ptolmey, manipulated like so much dough by advisors, squeals for her life. Queening in Egypt is violent, unsafe business.

So in history. So in Mundy's work.

As usual, Mundy uses history's bones to spread fiction's silken tents. History explains that Julius Caesar came to Alexandria, the jewel at the mouth of the Nile, while fighting a Roman civil war. There he met Cleopatra, settled the problem of succession to the Egyptian throne, had a son by Cleopatra. She followed him to Rome. While there, Caesar was assassinated by conspirators who claimed that they wished to restore the Roman Republic. They did not. Civil War erupted again, the conspirators intriguing against each other, each clutching for power, all opposing Anthony. To Anthony, Cleopatra would turn, estimating his side as best able to preserve Egypt. She was wrong by a fraction of a hair. By mischance, Anthony was defeated. Soon after, Cleopatra was dead, likely by means less dramatic than an asp.

So much for history, that incoherent area.

The novel, *Queen Cleopatra*, includes events from Caesar's arrival in Egypt to his assassination in Rome. During the first part of the novel, Tros plays a major role. But Cleopatra is the principal, the hinge upon which the action turns. However admirable, Tros is secondary. With a fine flair, he performs missions for the Queen. Later he even assists Caesar. Tros is valuable to the novel but not indispensable. During the later chapters, he disappears altogether, reappearing at last to convey Cleopatra from Rome.

They sail secretly by night. Behind, the sky shivers orange with Caesar's funeral pyre. Emotionally broken at last, Cleopatra sobs in the bow. Tros bends over her, groping for words of comfort, as the Liafail hisses across the dark sea toward Egypt.

Not until 1935 did Tros reappear in fiction. That year, four novels were published in *Adventure*. These were immediately issued as *Purple Pirate*.

The tone of these stories is firm, dark, and with a harder edge than in *Queen Cleopatra*. Cleopatra, herself, has taken on many of Caesar's characteristics. She is far more crafty, conniving, and treacherous than in the previous novel. She drives Tros unmercifully, taking the Northmen and Basques of his crew hostage, requiring heart-straining service in return. Once they were friends. Now she suspects his every action—which is a splendid way to establish conflict and suspense, although it makes for character inconsistency. Tros holds his own against her. Barely.

In "Battle Stations" (May 1, 1935), he must unravel the problem presented by a fleet of fifty corn ships harbored at Crete. ("Corn" meaning barley or wheat; corn was native to the Americas and, at this time, was unknown to the Mediterranean world.) He must also fight pirates, Romans, and evade the intrigues of Queen Arsinoe of Crete, Cleopatra's sister and dangerous rival.

Now matters complicate. In "Cleopatra's Promise" (June 15, 1935), Tros is in deep disfavor with the Cleopatra, who suspects him of plotting with Arsinoe. Because of his recent sea battle with the Romans, he has been declared a pirate. Glum with problems, Tros travels to Memphis to crush a rebellion threatening to topple Cleopatra's throne.

Matters now get as tangled as five hundred pounds of boiled spaghetti. Arsinoe is in Egypt, together with her power-hungry half sister, Boidion. (They look exactly alike.) Cassius (Caesar-assassinator and plotter) has cooked up a scheme where Boidion pretends to be Arsinoe and heads up a small army of invasion in Egypt. Arsinoe escaped assassination in Crete and came secretly to Egypt, where she slipped up the Nile, heading toward Memphis. Along the way, she finds Tros' Northmen and joins them.

All these wondrous complications are soon simplified. Tros arrives. The rebels are thoroughly whipped. Arsinoe unofficially abdicates as Queen of Crete, allowing Boidion to take her place. Boidion still calls herself Arsinoe. (The point of this substitution is that, in history, Anthony would soon remove Arsinoe from the throne of Crete and execute her.)

Tros changes the real Arsinoe's name to Hero. And marries her. Why not? She is intelligent, brave, valiant, beautiful, wears armor well, is handy with sword and bow, commands fighting men well, and can take orders. Thoroughly qualified to be his wife. He finds her fairly irresistible.

The marriage causes violent reactions in the following story.

Cleopatra is livid ("The Purple Pirate," August 15, 1935). Her spies have brought news of Tros' treachery and ingratitude, as she terms it. In punishment, she has the Liafail burned. Still holding his Basque seaman hostage, she demands additional service—capture Pelusius, on an East mouth of the Nile, before Cassius foments rebellion. During the course of a violent novel, he does so, capturing Cassius, and narrowly evading Cleopatra's army.

"Fleets of Fire" (October 1, 1935) more or less resolves these interlaced predicaments. After blackmailing a small fleet out of Cassius and whipping pirates, Tros sails to Rome. There, by breaking the grain blockade imposed by Brutus and Cassius, he makes it possible for Anthony to move his army against the two conspirators. So that's why history turned out the way it did.

In appreciation, Anthony pulls strings elevating Tros from a pirate to a Roman admiral. Returning to Alexandria, he massively defeats Cassius' fleet and is reconciled with Cleopatra (to the great disgust of his new wife, who would be just as happy to knife her sister).

"Tros—you fool," Cleopatra says, giving her sister the cold, calm eye, "you could have been King of Egypt" (Mundy, *The Purple Pirate* 384).

That sort of glory never interested Tros. Sailing around the world did. And that is what Mundy meant him to do ("Messenger of Destiny" 88). But he died before the book got written. Regrettable. In one portion, Tros would have visited the land of the Mayas.

The Tros series had ended, although not even the author recognized that. Other series continued to explore battle and the glory associated with chopping large numbers of people into cutlets and roasts. Which is as good a method as any for dealing with the the Roman, the Tatar, the Saxon, that fellow next door with the funny expression.

By all means, cut them down. As we have already seen, a curved saber does the business with a minimum of fuss. So does this blade, a thin gray sword, long, light, eagerly responsive to the hand.

This blade loves blood. It cries to be used. The gray metal thirsts. The blade surface is "marked by convoluted lines and whorls, and graven in the metal [are] a series of letters and symbols," a few Egyptian hieroglyphics, Greek inscriptions, lines of English doggerel:

Gray Maide men hail Mee
Death doth Notte fail Mee. (Smith, *Grey Maiden* 92)[7]

You hold in your hand the lethal Gray Maiden, heroine of a brief story series by Arthur D(ouglas) Howden Smith (1887-1945), who had contributed to Adventure since 1913. That series, subtitled "The Story of a Sword Through the Ages," followed Gray Maiden from its forging through selected major battles and historical crisis points. All were intensely researched, peopled with rather flat characters having a tendency to emote, and all featured a grand blood-letting at least once during the action.

"The Forging" (June 23, 1926) tells how Pharaoh Thutmose III (around 1500 B.C.) orders a sword forged for himself. The smith is perhaps a wizard, and certainly a worshiper of Baal. He requires that the metal of the blade be tempered in the blood of one the Pharaoh hates and one he loves. Both blood sources the Pharaoh provides without much trouble. (The one he loved had just betrayed him).

So to the ceremony:

*The Smith* (*Using the Blood of the Hated One*): "Make the blade keen and terrible, O hate that was relentless unto death.

Let the edge be without mercy, and the point as cruel as your purpose. Gift this sword with a rage which shall never know fear. Be ever hungry of life, O gray strength...." (*The Forging* 75)

(*Using the Blood of the Loved One*): "Pour your vigor into this metal, O blood of the loved one!.... Let no weapon resist it. Let no brain outwit it. Be a staunch guard for him who holds the sword. Resistless is Baal, O love, and in Baal's name I conjure you, fight always for the sword's master...." ("The Forging" 76)

All this undoubtedly accounts for Gray Maiden's pretty ways, as the sword travels through the ages. In "The Slave of Marathon" (July 23), she passes into the hands of a Greek slave during the Battle of Marathon. "A Trooper of the Thessalians" (August 23) tells how the Maiden kills its coward owner during a crucial battle between Alexander the Great and King Darius.

The events of "Hanno's Sword" (November 8) occur during the retreat of fragments of Hannibal's army through Italy. Gray Maiden works its way through four owners, each one dying violently—but not by steel weapons. The sword seems to protect against that kind of death. It offers no protection against being walked on by an elephant, being hung, being stamped upon by soldiers. Once the owner dies, the sword passes to another hand. Hanno of Carthage says:

There is no luck in the sword unless it comes to you of its own accord. So my father said and he had it of a Roman in the sea-fight of the Aegates Isles;

and the Roman had it of a Cretan pirate, and the pirate had it of a drowned man.... It has a long history, old as human life, I think. Men have slain each other with it for ages." (Smith, *Grey Maiden* 38-39)

Gray Maiden continues to slay so for the rest of the series. It sees the decline and decay of the Roman Empire ("The Last Legion," December 31), then falls into Islamic hands in "The Rider from the Desert," (February 15, 1927), as the hordes of Mohammed gather for the first time.

A final story, "Thord's Wooing," appeared April 15, 1927, and after that Smith moved to other subjects, although, Heaven knows, he hadn't exhausted all possible situations in which the sword chopped somebody up.[8] The Gray Maiden stories extend across two thousand years of battle in half a dozen countries. The Luigi Caradosso series, less expansive, takes place in Italy from about 1520 to 1580. If the Gray Maiden stories are grim to downright somber, those featuring Caradosso are smiling pleasantries, each containing enough plot for a novel, blithely relating battle, intrigue, maiming, treachery, and sudden death.

The stories are in the form of letters written by Luigi Caradosso, once a professional free-lance soldier, a captain, now an old man over eighty years old. For more than thirty years, he served the Dukes of Rometia before being pensioned off to a little vine-covered cottage. Here, in the golden glow of his elder years, he writes letters that have theguileless charm of a conversation with Long John Silver.

Each letter responds to a request or an accusation. Each is cast in the form of a story to illustrate a point. And, in an off-hand manner, to mention to the Duke (that glorious, condescending, and altogether splendid personage) certain matters demanding his attention:

The floor of this cottage hath become so uneven, from the roof leaks, that my table joggleth whenever I dot an i; moreover there is no bedroom for the maid-servant, which entraineth regrettable results; but until the floodwaters rise to my neck or the parish priest excommunicate me, I continue; as becomes a recipient of Your Lordship's hospitality. (Buckley, "Deadly Weapons" 60)

One does not ask Lord Duke Pietro IV of Rometia for benefits, but no law says you can't prod his pride of generosity. At this delicate technique, Luigi is a world expert.

At eighty plus, he is still a big, tough, resilient rascal, able to empty the wine skin. He is as sudden as a youth, touchy about infringement of his rights, and wonderfully quick to retaliate. Not that he seeks out trouble:

Much as enemies have belied me—and I had to break a man's nose for it only last week—I am not a man of violence. Save when acting under orders, or when I apprehend danger to myself or my master, or when I am personally affronted, I am as mild as any lamb; always have been. I should think that my face, bearing no fewer than twelve of my thirty-seven wound scars, would convince any reasonable person that during my sixty years of soldiering, I was more sinned against than sinning. (Buckley, "Of Glamour and Gunpower" 50-51)

I am [he continues elsewhere] essentially a man of frank and open nature, abhorring duplicity, stratagem and concealment—except, of course, in cases where these are necessary to confound the wicked. If everyone were as I am...this world would be a better place, an earthly paradise. (55)

In his prime, this paragon of mildness was a bold-eyed soldier, tall and full-bearded, with a huge capacity for wine. He is tough as fried moose. And quick, with the powerful wrists necessary to a sword fighter. (He is the originator of the *colpo di Caradosso*, a thrust with the blade that seems aimed at the stomach but ends slicing the artery just under the right ear.) He lacks a little finger (lost at Mantua in 1528) and the top half of his right ear. He has collected plenty of scars.

What a fine, hard-fisted scoundrel he is, a ferocious disciplinarian, and, on the field of battle, a cold-eyed realist...

Understand that the soldier's trade, back then, was rather different from the way it is practiced today. At that time, Italy was a collection of independent cities, each with its own army. Between the cities scattered hundreds of small dukedoms, each containing a handful of fields and hills, a rabble of small towns. These aspirin-sized kingdoms were maintained by force of arms, and Heaven help the Duke whose strength softened.

When it became necessary to strengthen themselves, dukedoms could hire small professional armies. These offered one or two hundred men, some mounted, with perhaps a cannon or two. These armies contracted to supplement and stiffen the raw forces of the dukedom. As professionals, the leaders of these hired armies were well acquainted with each other. With glorious impartiality, they fought side by side or beat each other over the head. Since they were in the same business, certain professional courtesies were extended:

...war [was] conducted on reasonable and proper principles: hand-to-hand, so that one could see with whom he had to deal, and with a very pleasant, brotherly give-and-take attitude between the officers. It was understood that we were professional men, paid to direct any killing that might be necessary, but no more expected to be killed ourselves than great artists are expected to clean their own brushes. We would make our dispositions, placing and moving our infantry and cavalry according to the rules of the game. We might, while the battle was in progress, foregather in some corner of the field and hammer each others' hauberks a little, just to give our lordships their money's worth; but it was all very friendly and harmless....[The] drudgery of knocking out each others' brains was left to the common soldiers. (Buckley, "Of Glamour and Gunpowder" 42-43)

Commanders were not eager to die for their slender pay. Most of them had home obligations, assumed very casually. At one period, Luigi, himself, had four wives. Household expenses kept him poor. Like most other professional soldiers, he had quantities of children, numbers of them not by his wives. These irregular offspring, he did not find it necessary to support, to the great relief of his purse.

Infamous behavior today, but not in 1540.

So, Luigi Caradosso, born 1500 (once he says 1511), serving the Rometia Dukes for most of his professional life except when the Dukes hired him to other princes as a military expert. Pensioned off in 1553, he continued to answer Pietro IV's questions and to volunteer a large number of opinions not requested.

Caradosso first appeared in "Cartel to William Shakespeare" (*Adventure*, November 30, 1924), fiercely raging against that errant author for messing up the true story of "The Taming of the Shrew." Luigi tells what really happened. It is fully as remarkable as Shakespeare's version.

By the end of the story, Luigi has softened a little against the villainous playwright:

There stands Wm. Shakespeare refuted; but after seven months of working at this his trade, God forbid I should gloat upon this poor wretch, much less slit his ears, as was formerly my intention.... [None] who has not essayed the business can know how an author's fingers ache, how lightnings pass before his eyes, how his back breaks in the middle, how the band is tied around his temples, how the ink runs up his arms even as far as the elbow-joints, how his appetite deserts him, to be replaced by a burning thirst—which having spent his money upon writing materials, he can not satisfy.

I had sooner work as a mason with blocks of stone, than ever again as writer... (Buckley, "Cartel to William Shakespeare" 79).

He did, however. About a year later, "State Paper" (February 10, 1926) was published. Slowly other stories began trickling into *Adventure*.

"Concerning a Musician" (December 15, 1927) tells how a young fiddler, with pretensions to art, saved the Duchy of Rometia from annexation. In spite of the humor that flashes like sun between leaves, the ending is grim personal sacrifice. Few of the thirty-odd stories of the series conclude with such dark overtones.

F(rederic) R(obert) Buckley (1896 to 196?) was the real author of Luigi Caradosso's letters. Born in England, he came to the United States as part of a British military mission during World War I (McSherry, *Captain of Adventure* 15). Journalist, screenwriter, and foreign correspondent Buckley contributed to *Adventure* from 1921 to the early 1950s. He also contributed largely to the western pulps, among them *Western Story Magazine*. For *Adventure*, Buckley wrote many brief historical fact articles, several stories about the sea and seamen, and much fiction set during the Italian Renaissance. Of these, Luigi Caradosso's adventures were the most popular.

The series appeared in two general groups, excepting that single story published in 1924. The first group ran from 1926 through 1934; the second, including a break for Buckley's military service, from 1940 to 1949.

The initial stories are longer, darker, rather more intricate, than those written later. Luigi's character is sketched in early. His humor and understatement are present almost from the beginning, his sardonic asides glinting like a dagger. Through this period he is rather more the hardboiled, straightforward, uncomplex fighting captain, and less the subtle trickster who appears toward series' end.

Most stories are titled "Of....," the first of these being "Of Gallantry" (January 1, 1928). This tells how an arrogant count, besieging a city, captures the city's champion and tortures him to death in sight of the walls. Terrible error. The city has captured the count's beloved brother and administers the same tortures to him. Mad with grief, the Count charges the city all by himself and ends his life bristling with arrows.

A similar dark narrative is "Of Moonsickness" (December 1, 1928; reprinted in *World Wide Adventure #4*, Fall 1968). A young Duke and Countess wish to marry. That sets off an explosion of intrigues, fierce raids, and small wars, for obviously—so neighboring Duchies believe—these marriage plans conceal dark motives of terrible menace. In consequence, one Duchy is wrecked, another bankrupted, and Luigi ends up in prison, nursing eighteen wounds. All this hyperactivity for nothing. The proposed marriage concealed no devil's plot; the couple was merely in love.

"Of Animal Musick" (May 15, 1930) tells of the sly and hateful Arturo Sacco. Once two fine captains treated him disrespectfully. Then they fell to fighting each other for the favors of the Black Countess and finally wasted both their armies against each other, carelessly getting killed themselves. After all that blood, we learn that the Countess was secretly married to Arturo Sacco, who had just demonstrated that you don't have to strike a blow to avenge a slight.

Like Caradosso's memories, these stories bound randomly among the years. The dates are not always consistent, nor are the names of Luigi's many employers. But these are trifling complaints. The strength of the series is its recreation of remote times. Mediaeval Italy opens around you, full of stinks and violence, shabby and gaudy, completely engrossing.

Through the action Luigi strides, masterfully flicking off an ear here, there cutting down three or four opponents, or gracefully whisking off an astonished head. He is tender of his honor and quick to strike: his day is a succession of trivial fights. The adventures customarily end in major fights. During these Luigi collects wounds sufficient to drift him out of consciousness. By the time he wakes up, the story has done a flip. He is as amazed by the outcome as his readers.

"Of Education" (November 1, 1931): The Lord employing Luigi orders our hero to take an impregnable castle—and the Lord knows it to be impregnable. After losing half his force, Luigi creeps into the castle alone and touches off the powder room, demolishing castle and doing himself no good. Awaking, swaddled in miles of bandage, he discovers that the attack was a diversion. The Lord planned to strike elsewhere, setting in motion incredibly complex plans that would result in his acquiring a vast estate without spending a cent.

Unfortunately for all this Machiavellian pitty-pat, one of the nobles being manipulated, brains the Lord with a chair. So much for excessive subtlety.

Caradosso relates these violent deeds in a voice of bland innocence. The Grand Duke Pietro II gave, as his considered opinion, that Caradosso was "All beard and breastplate." But the man has more wit than that. His observations prance merrily along, and they glow with wit:

Old age and idleness breed advice (Buckley, "Of Vanity" 21).

[He] was a hard man and of violent temper; subtle of mind, moreover, and singularly free from those scruples which, by holding lesser men to observance of their given word, or the Ten Commandments, keep them back from the attainment of wealth and honor. (Buckley, "Of A Vanishment" 41)

...[these] were symptoms only of that fell malady called Age; for which there is but one remedy—earth upon the chest. (Buckley, "Of Vanity" 21)

I have oft noted it as a strange phenomena that those whose lives have left least sins on their consciences have the most time for deathbed repentances. (Buckley, "Concerning A Musician" III)

...a red uniform it was, that I had made by a tailor named Strappi, in the Via Nuova at Florence. It was a vile fit, but on the other hand Strappi had a wife that suited me, exactly. (Buckley, "Of Education" 43)

I have oft wondered why those who'd tell folk how to live in one country should usually come from some other. 'Tis strange; though not as strange as the faculty folks have for believing manifest lies if shouted. (Buckley, "Of Penitence" 40)

In the sparkling story, "Of High Command" (August 1934), a dirt-poor young nobleman manipulates his way to command of an army. The Captain of that army has just married the woman he thinks the young nobleman loves. But it's all a set-up to work on that Captain's conscience. In penitence, he allows the young nobleman, that direly slick fellow, to assume command. You feel that the Captain will live to regret it.

No more Caradosso stories appeared for nearly six years. When he returned ("Captain of the Guard," May 1940, reprinted February 1951), the Germans were eating up Europe. France was ready to collapse, and World War II was about to become intercontinental. Scraps of this great fight showed up in the Caradosso stories—to author Buckley's apparent surprise. He said that he merely wrote them and only later discovered that the fiction contained such unexpected correspondences with contemporary history as the Fifth Column (secret traitors boring from within: "Single Combat," September 1941), war profiteers ("Of Treachery," June 1944), and popular uprisings against tyranny ("Captain of the Guards").

During this second series of stories, Buckley begins to organize Luigi's biography into more coherent form. The events of "Red Is the Blade" (July 1940, reprinted May 1951) begin at the beginning—his first combat and slaying.

Luigi, we learn, was of humble origins. As an infant, he was left in a basket at the door of the convent of San Luca. "Convent" is the word used, although this one is filled with monks of a rather peculiar type, not much given to praying, and only ill-associated with the church.

One day young Luigi went to market with a wagonload of vegetables, saw a young nobleman defending himself against four attackers. Luigi hits one of these on the head with a turnip. Promptly a swordsman charges him. A few moments later, in blind fright, he has killed the attacker and launched his own distinguished career.

The story, itself, follows the fortunes of that young nobleman, who soon gets ensnared by a really bad murderous mercenary, thinks his reputation is destroyed forever, but is saved by the intriguing of an old hag—and, of course, his own skill with the blade. In the ripe tradition of "B" moving pictures, the bad mercenary dies in a bloody duel to the orchestration of a thunderstorm.

"Of Penitence" (June 1941) is somewhat grimmer than usual for these later stories. A young Duke, not very bright, runs afoul of a preaching friar who is against all entertainment but praying. For a while the Duke reforms. But then he backslides and it is all due to the silent, malevolent, intelligent maneuvering, far off-stage, of the Red Duke, Pietro II. The young Duke dies of his foolishness. Luigi takes service with the Red Duke, who is busying himself with establishing the Duchy of Rometia.

The Red Duke is one scary fellow. For pleasure he lounges in a tower room, listening to screams from his torture room below. His eyes are red rimmed, his thin whiskers are red touched with gray, he nibbles ceaselessly at the nails of his bony fingers, and he laughs without making a sound.

Luigi has such a respect for the Duke that when they have a trifling misunderstanding ("Of Chain Mail and Green Cheese," September 1944), Captain Caradosso gets three hundred miles between them. He takes service with a Duke who believes that mankind is not really evil. He learns otherwise.

Luigi gets a large part of his scalp shot loose, serves temporarily under a woman commander, saves the Duke but is charged with treason, and finally goes, fairly gratefully, back into the service of the Red Duke and the Pietros of Rometia for the rest of his life.

Many charming fights are described in this story. It fizzes with them. One of the more pleasing erupts when Luigi and another captain try to go through the same doorway at once and fall to squabbling. The captain draws his sword and yells for his men. Luigi knocks him down with a chair, and....

...flinging away the chair (it chanced to knock three or four fellows down in its flight), I put my foot gently on this captain's face and took [his sword] from him....

[Four or five guardsmen] came foining and pointing as if they desired to fence with me. I was sorry for them; I was indeed; my intention was merely to disarm them and I would have done so without a wound save to their vanities, had not the men I had knocked down with the chair arisen and gone yelling into the inn for firearms. There was no time for fancy-work; I chopped one fellow across the wrist, ran another through the shoulder, cut two more on the inside of their knees [hamstringing them], and had no time to do more than kick the fifth in the stomach with my foot when out came a rascal with an arquebus.... I know he fired at me; but whether it is true that I beheaded him...or if so how I managed to do it when his friends were practising at me with their pistolets and halberds and what not, I have never been able to discover. (Buckley, "Of Chain Mail" 85-86)

As mentioned, the Red Duke does not consider Luigi very bright. (Understand that compared to the Red Duke, a searchlight isn't very bright.) Luigi has his moments, however. As in "Of Glamour and Gunpowder" (April 1944), when he sees through a plot to get rid of a love-sick Duke by use of astrology and love potions. Or "Of Treachery" (June 1944), when he artfully arranges the death of a rascal selling defective cannon.

Luigi says: "Unlike most of my trade, I have always been of a reflective turn of mind, which is one reason why imprisonment has never palled upon me as it hath upon others. I can be left alone, and contented with my own thoughts, for almost any period up to fifteen minutes, at the end of which time I have usually drifted off to sleep. (Buckley, *O Chain Mail* 89)

After 1944, the series again paused for three years. It resumed after Buckley's war service, the stories being lighter, less complex, and rather more obvious. In "Of Treachery and Tradesmen" (December 1947), Luigi is hired by a trade guild to attack a town. Whereupon everyone begins to betray each other for more money, Luigi included.

The series wound quietly down, or quietly as these adventures got. "Red Runs My Blade" (May 1952) and "Gateway To Treason" (March 1953) are Captain Caradosso's final appearances.

What a wonder he was. Granted that it would be safer for your ears and general health to know him only through his writings. But how he shines and flashes. How sensible and witty. A sword edge could not be more brilliant.

To this point, we have glanced at some of the war fiction set in ancient times, long before central plumbing and weekly baths. Then as now, great armies moved and it was possible to die for glory with no difficulty. It was no harder then than now.

But after all, the pulps contained more contemporary than historical fiction. If their pages welcomed swordsmen and riders, they offered even more space to warriors handling modern weapons. Halberds and pistolets are all very well, but what the modern reader wanted was a Colt .45 automatic pistol, a machine-gun, and a Spad. Or so you would assume from the fiction published.

As we will see in the following chapter.

# Chapter Eight
# Rather Irregular Warriors

Back around 1898, during the Spanish-American War, the word "filibuster" rushed into the popular vocabulary. Time has changed the meaning. Now it refers to a prolonged gale of oratory, intended to immobilize the ship of state; then it meant a military adventurer of an irregular sort, a kind of land pirate.

Were you a filibuster, back then, you smuggled arms to Central America and Cuba. You trained and fought with guerilla bands. Could you bring the filibusters forward in time, they would joyously support the Nicaraguan Contras.

The activities of these gentlemen immediately attracted the attention of the pulps. Even so early in the history of these magazines, they were never inclined to moon about peace. Action sold copies. So, immediately, magazine fiction began celebrating the mercenary, the soldier of fortune.

Early adventures appeared in *The Popular Magazine*, *Adventure*, and *All-Story Weekly* from 1905 to about 1914. After that date, for the next decade, big war absorbed readers and filibusters gradually drifted out of style.

In previous volumes, we have followed the fortunes of Geoff, Commander McTurk, and Captain Bantam, all filibusters of a sort, military or otherwise, their eyes firmly set on the pot of gold at the end of the story.

In the case of the Lost Legion series, written by Francis Whitlock, filibusters pranced all over the place. The Lost Legion, itself, was not so much an formal organization as a device to unify disparate tales, the way a rack unifies pool balls. Stories of the Legion were spotted all over the world, each featuring a different hero.

The series began in *The Popular Magazine* as seven short stories and a two-part serial (1907-1908). Thereafter it returned irregularly, usually as a serial, to 1914.

Mr. Jabez Cooper pulled these uncoordinated pieces together.

Mr. Cooper is very tough. He has the same sentimentality quotient as a fire brick and he is suspicious as a wounded fox. His stock in trade is an office, a commanding manner, and a list of names. When your need is desperate, you seek out Mr. Cooper.

[At Cooper's] beck and call there were a number of adventurous men who were eager to undertake any enterprise from the exploration of an unknown wilderness to the direction of a revolution...so long as adventure promised and the pay was good there was always an available supply [of these men]. Owing to the peculiar nature of the employment of these members of the Lost Legion, vacancies in the ranks were of frequent occurrence, but recruits were always clamoring for admission. (Whitlock, "Tales of the Lost Legion" 172)

For a substantial slice of your worldly wealth, Cooper will find a man to handle your problem—whether that problem is to remove a ballet dancer from a sheikh's harem ("A Diplomat of the Desert," July 1907), or to extract you from the clutches of anarchists ("Anthony Atwater, Amateur Anarchist," February 1908). Cooper will even set you up as the king of a tiny country where you have slim, if legitimate, claims ("The Time That Was," three-part serial, December 1, 1913, through January 1, 1914).

These are thoroughly entertaining stories, although only barely classifying as a series. The heroes are not supermen, certainly not angels. Their exploits involve a lot of stress, and they face dangers not slurred over or presented as negligible difficulties to be resolved in the final paragraph.

These men sweat. They feel fear. Fortunately for them, Mr. Whitlock is there manipulating matters so that the stories end without unusual volumes of blood. It is quite easy to picture yourself in the midst of these adventures. You, too, can feel fear and sweat off your skin, if you enjoy that sort of thing.

A somewhat later variation on this idea was The Gringo Legion, another sub rosa crowd also packed with adventurers. It was more formal than the Lost Legion, being a quasi-military group. As such, it was a good deal less oriented toward good deeds.

To be exact, the Gringo Legion was filled with uncaught crooks and unhung murderers. The ranks bulged with bad men, tough men, men with a past, men with no future. They operated in Mexico, just south of the California line in Tia Juana and Mexicali. They did a little scouting, a little chasing of bandits, a little muscle work:

*Legion Chief* saids: "We're very much misunderstood on the subject of plunder; a good many believe that it goes on openly and enlist for that purpose only. But don't make any such mistake. All men caught in the act of looting are either disarmed and put across the border or they're tried and shot. Bear that in mind."

[The new recruit] thought, but was by no means certain, that the Chief's right eyelid lowered for an instant. (Graham, "US Gold" 189)

The Chief is General Crosby, described as young, fearless, strong, and gray-eyed. He is also a first-class gun swift, a necessary art considering the toughs he commanded. Administrative work is handled by Captain Curtain. Crosby has enough on his hands without paperwork.

The Legion accepted any man who wished to become a member. "The only requirement was that he be able to handle firearms with more or less dexterity, and the greater his proficiency in this grim art, the more cordial was his welcome" (Graham, *US Gold* 189).

Written by Sidney M. Graham, the series ran in *People's* during 1916-1917. It was harsh, often brutal. Little romance of the sagebrush and Old Mexico seeped in. Instead, cold violence, treachery, and self interest drove the stories. Each ended with a sardonic twist.

As in "The Lizard's Revenge" (November 1916). The Lizard, a wonderfully skilled Mexican outlaw, has been betrayed by his cousin, Gonzales. Captured by the Legion, the Lizard waits execution.

Crosby sends Gonzales north. He has no use for a traitor. Unfortunately, the Lizard promptly escapes and also heads north. After him pounds the Legion behind a screen of Yaqui Indian scouts.

Near the border, the fugitive is cornered in a hut. After two men are killed trying to reach him, Crosby goes in alone. As he does so, the gunman in the hut is killed by a shot from a distant hill. The dead man is discovered to be Gonzales.

At this point, the story gets as murky as a pool full of elephants. The need for a surprise ending has taken precedence over narrative clarity and coherence. Explanations are few. We may guess that the marksman in the hills was the Lizard, patiently keeping Gonzales bottled up until the Legion arrived, so that he, Gonzales, would fire on them, the Legion, and they would kill him, and....

"U.S. Gold and Treachery" (December 1916) introduces bad man Collins. He has shot up a U.S. Post Office and a U.S. Postmaster and slid over the border to join the Legion. Where he immediately learns that one of the men, Steffens, has a $5,000 reward on his head. Collins gets to negotiating with a government agent—standing just across the border—for that reward. He plans to lure Steffens to the border and shove him across into the arms of the law.

The plan works, more or less. Collins gets Steffens to the border and shoves. Somehow both tumble over. As handcuffs click on Collins' wrists, he learns that Steffens is really the Sheriff of California's Imperial County.

"Consequences" (May 1917) tells how that mean Mexican, Sore-Toe Mayol of the Legion, discovers that he is a gunfighter born. He kills three legionnaires and wounds another. One of those killed was the brother of The Lad, an inexperienced gun-fighter but strong on family ties.

The Lad prepares to kill or be killed. But Crosby orders the boy not to fight. Mayol has been eyeing Crosby's job, in intervals between raising hell, and the General is mildly annoyed. He orders Mayol to leave by the next morning. Or fight him.

That night, Mayol gets falling-down drunk, an unlikely way to prepare for a morning gun battle. Comes first sunlight. Crosby strides forth. He finds Mayol still in bed. But the Mexican will never gun fight again.

The preceding night, The Lad found Mayol helplessly drunk. Since the boy was under orders not to kill the man, he did not. Instead, he cut off both the killer's thumbs.

Frivolously amusing as these tales may be, neither the Lost Legion nor the Gringo Legion forms a tight-woven series. Their primary continuity is through each group's hardboiled leader. He always appears, either as a walk-on or in a supporting role, whipping along the action. The Legions serve as framing devices, conveniences, like plastic clothes hangers, upon which various stories are draped.

When stories about the French Foreign Legion became popular, about ten years later, the same lack of continuity made itself felt.

The fad for Foreign Legion stories seems to have been ignited when Christopher Wren's *Beau Geste* became a best seller in 1925. The following year, J(ohn) D(immock) Newsom (1893?-1954) began an intermittent series of Legion stories for Adventure.

Newsom had begun contributing to the magazine in 1922 and would continue to do so until 1935. Born in Shanghai of American parents, he would become an expert on the French Foreign Legion, an anthropologist, and eventually the Director of the Federal Writers Project during the heart of the Depression (Bleiler 261).[1]

His Foreign Legion series continued deep into the 1930s, each novelette different, each the same, long tales of brutality, privation, combat, stupid commanders, and rough men enduring the unendurable. The plotting was involved and the overall effect left the reader with a sun-burned tongue.

The Foreign Legion of these stories held together better than either of the fighting legions mentioned earlier. Fairly soon, Newsom introduced a strong continuing character, the formidable Grellon, who arrived in "The Gorilla of No. 4" (*Adventure*, January 1, 1927). Grellon was the gorilla. He was a sergeant, a ferocious, fighting hulk, looking like an ape, lacking an ear and a half. Sloppily dressed, smoking a stinking pipe on all occasions, violently direct in discipline, he spent twenty years in the service, rising slowly to Captain's rank. He continued into the 1930s, as often a secondary character as a lead.

Newsom's Legion was an exceedingly tough organization. You could get killed in it almost any day for any reason. Somehow this discouraging prospect spoke to readers' hearts. At one time or another, each major magazine offered at least one Legion series, among them *Top Notch* (series by R.E. Dupuy), *Argosy* (series by F.V.M. Mason, Theodore Roscoe, Newsom, and Georges Surdez), *Blue Book* (by H. Bedford-Jones), and *Adventure* (by Newsom and, again, Georges Surdez).

Surdez was an honorary sergeant in the French Foreign Legion. Born in Switzerland around 1900, he came to the United States at 17 with the French High Commission, serving until the Armistice of World War I. Afterward he "went to the Ivory Coast for a timber firm; dabbled in general trading in North Africa and French Soudan, then started to write" (Surdez, *The Men Who Make the Argosy* 142). In his early twenties, he began selling fiction to *Argosy* and *Adventure*. In the later magazine, he had, over the course of 37 years, around 120 stories and serials published. His fiction appeared in Adventure into 1959, long after the magazine had lost contact with its own golden past.

Like Newsom, Surdez did not immediately begin to write Legion stories. He had traveled widely through Europe and the Near East and, during the mid-1920s, his first fiction was of the French Colonial Infantry in the bitter lands of North Africa.

At the end of the 1920s he began publishing stories of the French Foreign Legion—highly authentic stories, since he had seen Legion operations at close hand and had a number of correspondents within that organization.

"The French Foreign Legion," Surdez wrote, "is something more to me than mere subject matter. I heard Legion yarns before I could walk or talk, have studied about the unit always, have visited garrison towns and outposts on various fronts in many colonies. I have intimate friends and dozens of acquaintances in the Corps.... Legionnaires told me: `The Legion is what you make it. Be good and you'll be treated well. Get tough, and it will be tougher than you can hope to be'." (Surdez, "The Men Who Make the Argosy" 142)

Eventually the Second World War opened new vistas of combat. The Foreign Legion story lost much of its popularity. But not all. In August 1940, the Munsey Company published at least one issue of *Foreign Legion Adventures*. To the end of the pulps, a Legion story was always available, somewhere. Like a good cup of coffee, you just had to hunt for it.

For some time after the First World War, battle fiction was set either centuries in the past or limited to small actions in which a single man could make a large difference. After the regrettable events of 1914-1918, public enthusiasm for modern war had diminished.

Then the success of the 1924 stage play, "What Price Glory?"

reignited the war fiction market. Rather soon appeared that highly specialized form, the war stories pulp magazine. *War Stories* (1926) was followed by *Battle Stories* (1927). In 1928 came *War Novels, Over the Top*, and *Under Fire*. Simultaneously, aviation and air war pulps arrived in all their ecstatic romanticism, beginning with *Aviation Stories and Mechanics, Air Stories, Wings,* and *War Birds*, Followed, in turn, by a storm of similar magazines whose fiction, like a painted butterfly, floated high above dull reality. In the following chapter, we will glance at a few of the early air war series characters. For now, let us turn to the ground war in France, and a series hero whose destiny was one of the oddest in the pulp magazines.

Into hell itself! Ear drums bursting, eyes aching, each breath an agony, the men climbed mechanically under their heavy burdens. Brain and body had lost their coordination. The command was forward drummed on dull brains. Cries of terror! Shrieks of pain! Curses! Hysterical laughter! Mad shoutings! All lost in the terrific din of exploding steel and the staggering red flashes. God, for just one breath of pure air. Why was Private Miller writhing in the underbrush there, red, clawing hands digging into the ground? *Blood!* He was dying. *Pow!* The earth split asunder. *Crash!* The heavens were falling! But the command was *forward* and must be obeyed. *Brammp!* A dull, sickening pain, then blackness, and *peace*. And so it went until the crest was finally gained. (Empey, *Battle Stories* 45)

Through the untidy fuss of World War I storms a red-headed Irishman, Private Terrence X. O'Leary. "Storms" is, perhaps, too grand a word. More accurately, he stumbles, crawls, tumbles, shoots, plots, brags, trembles, rolls his blue-gray eyes. He has a world-shattering hangover and a thirst quenchable only by cognac—pronounced "cone-yack" in these parts.

He is the most peculiar series hero you ever met.

O'Leary's series is pretty peculiar, too. Beginning in the 1926 *War Stories*, it shifted to *Battle Stories* in 1928, then back to *War Stories*. During 1932 O'Leary appeared in both magazines, quite impartially. Then he dropped them both and, for the next two years, was featured only in *War Birds*. That magazine, apparently afflicted by the general nuttiness of the series, suddenly transformed to an lunatic science-fictional magazine titled *Terence X. O'Leary's War Birds*. After that magazine flopped, individual O'Leary stories cropped up once more in *War Birds* and *Battle Stories*, still rehashing World War I.

Until 1936.

At that time, with a ghastly grinding of gears, the series chronology abruptly lunged ahead seventeen years. O'Leary became a soldier of fortune in Ethiopia, his adventures recorded in one issue each of *War Stories* and *Battle Stories*. The two stories are sequential; the publishers are Dell and Fawcett, respectively. How sequential stories got printed by rival publishers requires more mystic intuition than is available here. But you have already noticed that the series has a strange history.

Its history is no stranger than the remarkable T.X. O'Leary, himself.

He begins as the traditional comic Irishman of dime novel and stage. He is a thick-headed blunderer, an inspired liar and braggart, his cheek swollen with chewing tobacco, his brain swollen by fancies and frights. His every action leads to trouble, mockery, and disgrace. He loves to fight. He would rather get drunk than breath. Hunger for honor, fame, recognition lures him into deadly danger; his fabulous luck swirls him out. He hates the Infantry, the English, and all those dirty scuts from North Ireland, bad cess to 'em. His character omits no known Irish cliche.

His formal career begins with a series of six stories published in War Stories, December 1926 through May 1927[2] For all practical purposes, the stories are a crazy serial, continuous in time.

To call them stories is to be generous. Most are strings of ancient jokes, narrated in a military setting, with a big dumb Irishman as the patsy. Thus:

—Dying for a drink, O'Leary pretends cramps. The Colonel gives him a dose of castor oil.

—Tricked by friends into seeing Germans everywhere, he challenges an in-coming scout. Orders were to keep silent, and he is disgraced.

—Led to believe that cloth hats hung on barbed wire are lurking Germans, he reports the enemy's presence to the Colonel. More disgrace.

—Challenged to prove his courage by hanging empty jam tins on German wire, he does so. And then can't prove it. Is regarded as a bragging liar and scorned.

—During a violent hand-to-hand fight in No Man's land, he accidentally blacks the Colonel's eye.

—After capturing a German and leading him back through to British trenches, he loses his prisoner, is disbelieved, is mocked.

So much for the events of "O'Leary Proves His Courage" (*War Stories*, February 1927). Through later adventures, he finally blunders to success, saves his friends, dismays the enemy, and nearly wins the war single-handed.

The background for all this foolishness is that O'Leary has been detailed as orderly to Colonel Tiernan of the US Infantry. The Colonel has been assigned to the English sector to learn trench warfare at first-hand. Major Thwaites and Lieutenant Babcock are assigned as the Colonel's instructors.

O'Leary isn't so fortunate. His instructors are disdainful and ham-handed jokers: Sergeant Angus MacQuarrie (of the Black Watch) and Sergeant Elkins (of the Cold Stream Guards). There is no further need to describe the sergeants since they arc, like O'Leary, walking stereotypes, representing, in their case, the Scotsman and the Englishman.

These characters remain with the series for years. A few others will be introduced later. But most of the supporting cast is established early. Eventually the sergeants become O'Leary's bosom pals and regard him as a walking god. But that doesn't happen yet, nor for some years.

The series was written by Arthur Guy Empey (December 11, 1883—February 22, 1963). Born in Ogden, Utah, Empey graduated from high school in Brooklyn, New York. For some years, he bummed around the world, served in the New York and New Jersey National Guard, and spent six years in the US Cavalry.

Enlisting as a private in the British army in 1915, he served 18 months in France. Receiving severe facial wounds during the battle of the Somme (1916), he was discharged after convalescence, and returned to the United States. While recovering he wrote up his experiences in the book *Over the Top*. This was published in 1917 and became a national best seller.

Skeptics abound in this cruel world. Some were heard to whisper that *Over The Top* contained more fiction than personal experience. That Empey remained snug in England, no closer to the trenches than Picadilly.

Horrors! That war heroes should be so maligned, suffering all those slings and arrows.

Whatever grains of truth are buried in these shocking accusations, so undoubtedly unfounded, I mean the man published a book and it's all right there in it, big as day, it is known that Empey joined the US Army in 1917. He served in the tank corps, earning a captain's commission in 1918. As a national celebrity, he was sent on a recruiting tour of the US, an event which keeps cropping out in the O'Leary stories.

During 1918 Empey published four books of war stories and later in the 1920s some sentimental novels. He organized the Guy Empey Pictures company, (Arthur Guy Empey, President) which produced several silent movies, including Over the Top. In this he quite naturally starred. The company produced four or five other films, then vanished.

Empey, however, went on to other things—including the war pulps. To these he was a frequent and celebrated contributor for some ten years. In 1935 he headed one of several paramilitary groups that sprang up in California around that time. Naming his group the "Hollywood Hussars," naturally serving as Colonel, Empey reportedly recruited several movie stars (Ellis, *A Nation in Torment*). Apparently the purpose of the "Hollywood Hussars" was to fight un-American activities, that exquisitely vague battle in which the foe is everywhere and nowhere, and only a military man in gorgeous uniform can protect the national interest. Eventually the movie stars dropped out, the Hussars disbanded, and Empey turned to American Legion and VFW functions, and shooting at various gun clubs across the country. He died in Kansas, 1963.

As for T. X. O'Leary—nothing could kill him. He sampled all the services: the infantry, the tanks, the field artillery. Was assigned to all of these for special duty, just as he was later assigned to the Flying Corps and Secret Service. Wherever Empey's flaring imagination carried him, there swaggered O'Leary.

The reader, being wonderfully astute, recognizes at once that Empey had not much experience with Flying Corps and Secret Service and his stories were going to lack that hard edge of observed detail found in his infantry fiction. And that's so.

Not that the infantry fiction published between 1926 and 1932 is excessively realistic. The characters are no more than paper cutouts. The stories are at first rudimentary, and later incredibly convoluted. Even for action fiction in an action magazine there seems a gassy unreality about O'Leary's adventures, which are frenzied, frightening, ridiculous, all at once. The writing is crude as a red-neck joke. Every situation is a cliche. Every emotion is a fake. Every paragraph grabs for the easy effect—the sentimental death, the hackneyed joke, the incredible coincidence, the unbelievable escape.

But the narrative force, the flow of event, the intensity of suspense sweep away these trivial cavils. Paragraphs of vivid description burst suddenly out. These have the sound of truth in them, as if a curtain, cheap and gaudy and vulgar, were swept aside to expose a clear pale light in a simple room.

Somewhere in the town a one-pounder started ping-ponging away, its diminutive, but deadly, shells creating havoc in a large clump of bushes where a trench mortar battery was preparing to go into action....

...It seemed that from every house top, from every window, from every place large enough to shelter a gun, death spurted; wicked, jumping darts of flame that spat destruction. Even from the slopes on each side of the town could be heard the dreadful tac-tac-tac of hidden machine guns and the air sang and cracked with steel.... (Empey, "O'Leary of the Rainbow Division" 151)

The truck rumbled along a shell-pitted road through an area ravaged and devastated by nearly four years of war. Splintered tree trunks and shattered houses, mere piles of brick and stone, dotted the tossed up landscape all about them. It was a drab, desolate scene....

A shell whined over, singing its death song in a rapidly rising scale.... Not fifty yards ahead a mighty geyser of earth and flame shot skyward from the roadside with a terrific detonation, then a rain of heavy clods and the thudding of steel fragments. (Empey, "O'Leary Carries On" 29-30)

This peculiar mixture of over-writing, cliche, and exact detail has cumulative effect. You may suspend belief while immersed in one of O'Leary's extravagant adventures, but the descriptions of battle impel belief. Within the feeble fiction, they shine like lights in a mist.

Dell Publishing Company first issued War Stories in November 1926. The magazine would continue until the early-1930s. For a short time, it was discontinued, then began all over again as a Second Series, Vol. 1., No. 1, dated February 1936; that was likely the only issue.

Henry Steeger edited the magazine in its early days:

*Steeger*: "I was with Dell Publishing Company between two and three years, during 1927, 1928 and 1929. My duties there began as co-editor with Ernest V. Heyn of Famous *Story Magazine*. I was then shifted to the post of assistant editor to Gene Clancy on War Stories Magazine and *War Birds*...and after Gene Clancy's departure, took on the editorship of *War Birds*...." ("An Interview with Henry Steeger" 3)

*War Stories* featured covers by William Reussing and the Rozen brothers, George and Jerome. At first an unillustrated, 126-page magazine issued monthly and costing 20 cents, it expanded to a remarkable 192-page magazine in 1930; by then it cost 25 cents. Stories were illustrated by line drawings and photographs. The Depression soon slapped the publication back to 128 monthly pages with less enthusiastic illustration and a 15 cent price. After returning in 1936, as Vol. 1, No. 1, the cost reduced to 10 cents, the pages shrank to 112. Issuance became quarterly.

A number of well-known writers appeared in War Stories. Among them you found Ted Tinsley and Victor Rousseau, Raoul Whitfield (who seemed to have a combat aviation story in every issue), Harold F. Cruickshank, George F. Eliot, and, of course, Empey.

After six stories in *War Stories*, Empey moved O'Leary to *Battle Stories*. There he appeared in two serials and a novelette—or so it seems. The pieces are loosely constructed and the narrative chronological line is more or less continuous.

"Hinky, Dinky, Parle Vous" (February through June 1928) is a five-part story, if a series of unrelated events strung on no particular narrative line can be called a story. At one time or another, O'Leary is imprisoned as a German, thought to be insane, foils a spy plot, saves Colonel Tiernan's life, and escapes from Germans and a burning building.

The British Fifth Army is being overwhelmed by fierce Germans. Colonel Mercer, defending the town, asks for a rear guard holding action so that the battalion can pull back to rejoin the brigade. Col. Tiernan volunteers to organize the rear guard, requesting that O'Leary remain with him. Hearing this, O'Leary strides forward to give his enthusiastic agreement, whether the colonel asked for it or not:

*O'Leary*: "Glory be, sir! 'Tis th' first time meefficiency and ramifications has been publicly declaimed, sir, and I was growin' hot over th' delay. With me and ye together, Colonel Mercer, it's a lead pipe cinch. Not only does I volunteer. but I agrees to go. E pluribus union, which when difinitioned from th' Greek means, there is strength in our union. But how th' lousy Greeks ever came to form a labor union is beyond me. There's somethin' I'd like to remind ye of, sir. 'Tis not only good luck that an O'Leary brings, but with him comes th' art of knockin' 'em horizontal and prone." (Empey, "Hinky, Dinky" 109)

Whether you have noticed it or not, this is rather a different T. X. O'Leary than starred in *War Stories*. No longer is he a comic buffoon, a blunderer and a butt of jokes. Suddenly blazing with self confidence, fearless, brilliantly able, he brags, interrupts officers, dominates enlisted men with serene assurance.

Empey has found O'Leary, and O'Leary has found his voice.

Off O'Leary goes with Elkins and MacQuarrie to resist the Germans. They are accompanied by a cowardly boy, who redeems himself wonderfully by falling on a German grenade and getting dramatically killed. His sacrifice saves all three men.

Par for Empey's world. Whenever a soldier appears wearing a large placard marked COWARD, you can bet your bottle of cognac that he will redeem himself by dying for his pals. It is an honored fictional convention, here worked a few inches past the point of nausea.

Barely escaping from the German hordes, they meet Col. Tiernan. The Colonel has disobeyed orders and, instead of retreating, is holding a trench until Col. Mercer's men can escape. That pleases O'Leary inordinately:

*O'Leary*: "Glory be, sir! I'd a done th' same thing meself! To hell with orders, is me sintiminits ixactly. Th' army would be a helluva sight better off without 'em. Ain't it th' truth, colonel!" (Empey, "Hinky, Dinky" 122)

Somewhere around this time, *Battle Stories* seems to have accepted a story from Empey that did not get published for seven years. One suspects that it may have been the concluding part of "Hinky, Dinky,

Parle Vous," since the story ends with those words. But who can tell, "Hinky, Dinky, etc." being nothing but a rag-bag. Whatever the story or piece was intended for and whenever it was written, it was published as "O'Leary Tames the Boche" in the October 1935 *Battle Stories*. We will deal with this fragment later on.

The *Battle Stories* magazine began September 1927. It was Fawcett Publications' restatement of the *War Stories* theme—for Fawcett adroitly exploited the success of other people's magazines by bringing out titles almost, but not quite, similar. At the beginning, *Battle Stories* was a massive magazine, 25 cents, 186 pages, a novelette, a serial part, several short articles, six or seven short stories, and a variety of departments. Not surprisingly, many of the writers also contributed to *War Stories*. Covers were by the Rozen brothers, F.R. Glass, Remington Schuyler, and were fairly predictable.

"Terrance X. O'Leary of the Rainbow Division" (*Battle Stories*, four-part serial, September-December 1930) concerns O'Leary's adventures when on detail to the Rainbow Division. The lean thread of plot through the story is that O'Leary attempts to:

1) wise up the Rainbows that he is the top fighting man in the sector.
2) get out of an assignment as MP, so that he can get back to the fighting (he does so by fouling up the traffic he is supposed to be directing).
3) to protect two young infantrymen: he promised their mothers that he would.

Each of these events is more or less the subject of a serial part, if you would call this slovenly narrative a serial, rather than typewritten bead-stringing.

Event, event, event. Part III (November 1930):

—Trapped in a German trench, O'Leary captures a flock of Germans, rescues the two young infantrymen, and idles in a dugout until the Rainbows retake the trench. For this he wins the Congressional Medal of Honor and gets recommended for the Distinguished Service Cross.

Since he has become so famous, O'Leary is detailed to go back to the United States and make speeches for the Liberty Loan, a recurring theme. (Promise not to get tired of this theme, because it shows up over and over, like a flea in the sheets.) Instead he gets a YMCA man drunk, puts him on ship as O'Leary, and returns to the front.

—He goes out on patrol and captures an arrogant, loud-mouthed "boloney," O'Leary's term for "German," who tells the location of all the concealed machine nests.

—During house-to-house fighting, O'Leary is almost killed by a wounded young German. Instead of killing the boy, T. X. O'L dresses his wounds and makes him as comfortable as possible. "Shure, and he's jest out o' school. Look around, and you'll find his pencil and slate."

—After being trapped in a smashed house by shelling, O'Leary and friends are spotted on the roof by a German patrol.

End of Part III; reserve December's copy now.

After that December issue, O'Leary was absent from *Battle Stories* for a year. When next seen, he had switched to *War Stories*, beginning a group of loose-linked novelettes.

These began in November 1931 with "O'Leary Carries On." The more cynical among you might expect that some of the facts about O'Leary might have changed during the transition to another magazine.

The cynics are correct.

In *War Stories*, O'Leary is now a sergeant of the Military Police. He has had four enlistments in the cavalry, is expert with pistol and rifle, has won five decorations and been cited for the Congressional Medal of Honor. And speaks German perfectly, "having been adopted by a German couple in his youth."

The story is the usual chaos, amusing, violent, episodic. The faint plot line keeps getting lost in the activity. The general idea is that O'Leary will get deliberately captured by the Germans so that he can rescue a pilot who has valuable information about enemy gun emplacements.

O'Leary wants out of the MPs. (You will get pretty tired of this bit of business, too.) So he and Jones cook up a plan to send the army up a wrong road, get it tangled up, and get themselves sent to the front. They do and get jailed. But the Germans shell the wrong road, so both O'Leary and Jones are heroes.

They don't know that. To punish them, they are told the Germans shelled the other road, and they, O'Leary and Jones, are responsible for immense loss of life.

Bitterly remorseful, they break out of jail, escape to the front, and get themselves captured by the Germans, with the idea of rescuing the aviator. Before the end of the story, the Germans have seen through O'Leary, and O'Leary has tricked the Germans, shot down two double agents, arranged the destruction of the prison camp, and escapes, with Jones and information, to Switzerland and the US consul. It is very exciting. Not particularly realistic, but exciting.

By January 1932, *Battle Stories* had shrunk to 146 pages. In mid-year, it sweated off another 20 pages, reducing its price to 20 cents. In October and November, it experimented briefly with a larger format (8-

1/4 x 11 inches, 82 pages), and strongly emphasized non-fiction. The following issue, (Number 62), contracted to standard magazine size. At this point, the date vanished from the cover and title page. That was a ploy resorted to by publishers who would shift unsold magazines from the east to the west coast (and points between) and didn't want them carrying a tell-tale date. Beginning with issue #62, the volume number somehow became the whole number. By 1933 (#63), the price reduced to 10 cents, the page count to 98. The magazine had become a disguised annual, appearing once a year through 1936 (#66).

The impending collapse of *Battle Stories* isn't reflected in its 1932 fiction. In April, "O'Leary, Wagon Soldier," our hero eliminates German spies nested in an artillery battalion, beginning with the obvious clue that when a Frenchman buys a soldier a drink, something is very wrong.

"O'Leary, Secret Service" (June 1932) introduces a device which will be used until it becomes intolerable, after which it is used again. To put it as gently as possible, O'Leary has a double. In this story, the double is a German spy. Looks just like O'Leary without the red hair.

Now the Secret Service feels they can exploit this similarity. So they ship O'Leary off to the sector of a tough colonel. O'L. has been drunk in Paris for two weeks and is not up to his usual brilliance. In short order, he has arrested the tough colonel, kicked him in the pants, tied him up, hauled to Headquarters him under a stinking tarpaulin in the back of a truck.

This is farce, pure and simple; what follows is melodrama, also pure and very very simple.

O'Leary impersonates the spy at German Headquarters. After various panics and frights, he doodles the Germans completely. While they celebrate the presumed destruction of the US artillery by getting drunk, the artillery is zeroing in on them. O'Leary's pal is knifed while radioing the proper coordinates to the US forces. But he isn't killed, which is more than you can say for the Germans.

To this point, we have moved half through 1932 in *War Stories*. Now we return to the beginning of 1932 to skim a group of five stories published in *Battle Stories*.

In "The Curse of the Iron Cross" (*Battle Stories*, January 1932), O'Leary undertakes to transform a bunch of tough military convicts into soldiers. Not only does he weld them into the O'Leary Brigade, but they capture that impregnable hill the Germans had fortified as if they had been Japs. "O'Leary's Rough Riders" (April 1932) concerns the fortunes of a troop of cowboys who have enlisted to fight the Germans. They drink a lot, disobey orders, practice the quick draw, and charge their broncs heroically at German lines. Get chopped up but win the day. Naturally.

Of the remaining three stories, "The Y.M.C.A. Goes Over the Top" (June 1932) and "That Fightin' Irish Son-of-a-Gun" (July 1932), O'Leary and two pals have been ordered to return to the United States and support Liberty Loan campaigns. Instead, they end up dressed as a chaplain and two Y.M.C.A. men. Pursued by Corporal Halligan, who wants to bring them all before the general, they flee to the front lines. In their disguises, they go over the top and confront the Germans. Later, O'Leary cleans out machine gun nests and gets trapped by the Germans in a bunker, only to be saved by Halligan.

Who was only trying to get them to the general, so he could pin Congressional Medals of Honor on them all.

Ah, and true it is that O'Leary is of medal fame. He becomes the most decorated soldier in the army, winning the Congressional Medal at least four times. And naturally enough, when you think about it. 'Tis because of Terrence's name. T.X. O'Leary—the X, he continually points out, "stands for ixellint."

*O'Leary*: "That's what the 'X' stands for. It's a Latin word meaning trouble.... If I git into trouble, I'll enjoy getting out o' it ag'in. It's me natchur. An' never let it be said that Sargint Terrence X. O'Leary, of medal fame, ever blowed his own horn...." (Empey, *Sgt. O'Leary's Tank Buster* 41-42)

"Sgt. O'Leary's Tank Busters," (*Battle Stories*, #62, 1933), has all the earmarks of a story previously written about valiant tankers which was later spiced up by adding O'Leary. Four tankers, jailed for stealing the General's gasoline, break prison to lead the infantry on a suicide mission against a fortified hill, studded with pill boxes. On entering the pill boxes, all webbed together by concealed corridors, they discover O'Leary inside the labyrinth, massacring Germans single handed. Desperate, the enemy floods those corridors under the hill with phosgene. Is it doom for O'Leary and the tankers? Is it fearful strangling death for all?

Of course not. One tanker sacrifices his life to give O'Leary an undamaged gas mask. This is the usual sacrificial set-up and is guaranteed to draw tears from a steel girder.

Cheap theatricals? Good gracious, what can you mean? Just because Empey invariably reaches for bathos and obvious melodrama? That's only because he realizes that he can't write prose that's real and touching and true. So he does the next best thing and offers the deep purple scene. What's wrong with squeezing your heart?

But let's tear ourselves, if reluctantly, from this critical discussion, and glance once more at "Tank Busters."

This story is distinctly unusual in that it ends darkly, in silence and grief, in stark contrast to the contrived heroics and upbeat endings of other stories. For one moment the facade of facile fiction breaks open. Just for an instant, you smell death. Just for an instant, the shallow prose is touched by sorrow. Genuine sorrow. For an instant, we hear that war is, after all, something more than accumulating medals and foxing Fritz. Even in an O'Leary story.

Empey may have served with the British Army and caught himself a nasty wound, but his writing is nearly devoid of reference to the mutilation, dismemberment, filth, boredom, pain, fear, infestation, and horror beyond assimilation which were part of the daily combat experience.

Curious that the war fiction of an ex-soldier, published in a war fiction magazine, so carefully evades the face of battle.

Neither *War Stories* nor *Battle Stories* were in the habit of depicting World War I as the soldiers found it. They were pulp magazines, published to sell issues. Iron-faced realism had no place here. What was wanted was fiction of heroic daring-do, of villains to be hated, and admirable heroes, plus nostalgic glimpses of World War I with the vileness and horror quietly rubbed out.

During mid-1933, O'Leary simply up and left the faltering markets of *War Stories* and *Battle Stories* and took himself to the vivid fantasies of the air war pulps. He was as improbable as a pilot as he had been an infantryman. His spectacular career will be reviewed in the next chapter.

But first, let's finish with O'Leary as a combat soldier.

In 1935, *Battle Stories* #65 published "O'Leary Tames the Boche," that throw-back to and probable final installment of the 1928 "Hinky, Dinky, Parle Vous." Thus, in 1935, the British Fifth Army is still in retreat. General Stephens is still in command. Colonel Mercer is still acting as rear guard. Col. Tiernan is still present, as are Elkins, MacQuarrie, and Flannagan of the Irish Guard.

During the story, the battalion ends up in a shell-bashed French hamlet. The only house left is a former tavern.

Afflicted by raging thirst, O'Leary organizes a midnight raid on the tavern. While he and friends are swilling their heads off in a cellar under the tavern, they discover the corpse of Nannette, killed by a shell. She ran the tavern with the help of her grandfather.

Apparently, all of them are about to die by shell fire, for they are trapped in the cellar and nearly suffocate. Following a current of air, O'Leary finds a secret passage—behind which sits the Grandfather, signalling to the Germans.

Ah, they're in a spy nest. From this point, it's a stream of heroics, as O'Leary and the boys capture a German machine gun nest and battle the German army to a standstill.

For all his wonderful doings, O'Leary is commissioned First Lieutenant. He is to be awarded the Congressional Medal of Honor, the Victoria Cross, "and a few French and Belgium decorations." And he is to be returned to the United States to assist in the Liberty Loan drives.

That echo from the past whispers away to silence. It was possibly the last O'Leary story in *Battle Stories's* inventory. But we have not yet done with T.X. No no no.

Open your copy of *War Stories*, Vol. I, No. 1, February 1936, now published quarterly. Before your delighted eyes shimmers a brand new O'Leary adventure—"Soldiers of Death."

And here he is once again: O'Leary, the Famous Fighting Mick of Medal Fame, "tall, well knit, lithe as a panther and slightly bowlegged" with steel-blue eyes and tousled red hair. He is, this very instant, a Major in the Ethiopian army, commanding a cavalry squadron which is performing scouting and liaison duty. His adoring troops call him "The Green Lion of Judah," since he wears a bright green uniform, designed by himself. For six years, he has been training these men in American battle tactics.

He is accompanied by his close companion, Captain Peter Maher McGuffy. And they have a problem. The Italians are preparing to attack. Since the United States is a neutral, O'Leary doesn't figure that he can personally fight against the black-shirted hordes. It isn't much plot motivation for a soldier of fortune, you'd think.

At this moment of dramatic conflixt, an Italian bomber attacks the troops. Leaping into an ancient biplane, O'Leary and McGuffy take after the bomber. Naturally they fly brilliantly but their ship is too old. It crashes.

When the bomber lands to investigate, O'Leary gets a gun in the ribs of the young pilot:

*O'Leary*: "War is war and orders is orders, Kid, (but) let a guy old in the game steer ye straight. There's somethin' bigger an' higher than orders in any old war. It's plain, ordinary homespun humanity. In other words, mercy for the underdog." (Empey, "Soldier of Death" 91)

These are the same sentiments that once got him sentenced to a firing squad, many years before. But no matter.

With another gesture from the past, O'Leary allows the young pilot to fly his bomber the hell out of there. For other, more serious business demands O'Leary's attention. It seems that his command is part of a larger war group commanded by that dark villain, Chief Vesta Baneh. The Chief is enthusiastically betraying Ethiopia to the Italians. Even now, 5,000 Italian soldiers and 10,000 tribesmen approach the pass.

Once through, they will shatter the forces of Ethiopia's Emperor, Haile Selassie, The King of Kings, The Lion of Judah, Defender of the Christian Faith, The Chosen of God. With such titles, you know positively which side to cheer for.

With his scanty forces, O'Leary defends the pass. After beating off one attack, he captures that wretch, Vesta Baneh. And not a second too soon, for the tribesmen, aided by the Italian bomber, come roaring at the pass....

Howling and shouting like fiends the savage horde reached the mouth of the pass, those in front actually fighting among themselves to be the first to enter.

Volley upon volley [O'Leary's men] poured into the seething mass of blacks, but there was no stopping the tide because the places of those who fell were instantly filled by the warriors from behind.

The carnage was sickening. A bullet couldn't miss.... O'Leary and McGuffy pumped steel slugs into the feathered warriors as fast as they could pull trigger. Sweat rolled down their dirty faces and the choked in the clouds of acrid dust rising up and engulfing them. (Empey, "Soldier of Death" 107)

Just as they are about to be swept away, in the final seconds, as doom arrives, as the grinning skull of death extends its bloody talons, as hope is lost, as the front collapses and hordes of screaming natives pound forward, in the final seconds of O'Leary's adventures—

—the Italian bomber pilot, disdaining such turncoats as those natives, and at the same time mindful of O'Leary's little lecture, drops a few bombs smack into the pass. That temporarily discourages the attack.

In the next instant, reinforcements arrive. The day is won and on that jubilant note ends both O'Leary's career in *War Stories*, and the magazine, itself. February 1936 is the final issue.

*War Stories* was gone. But O'Leary lingered a moment longer.

Only four issues of *Battle Stories* had been published from December 1932 (Whole #62) to October 1935 (Whole #65). When Issue #66 edged timorously onto the newsstand in 1936, it contained what would be the final O'Leary story, "Terrence O'Leary in Ethiopia." (Note the spelling of "Terrence"; it was "Terence" in *War Stories*.)

This adventure continues the story begun in "Soldiers of Death." Once again O'Leary and McGuffy ponder leaving Ethiopia. Their contract to train troops has expired. And they have been offered a fat bribe by Joseph Werner, special agent to German munitions seller, Karl Schlossen. That renegade is selling tons of defective arms and ammunition to Haile Selassie.

To earn the bribe, all O'Leary and McGuffy have to do is return to their troops at the pass and make sure they are unprepared for attack.

That's because native troops from an Italian African colony are about to grab for the pass.

Our heroes accept the bribe and proceed to doublecross Schlossen and company. Which has prepared a double cross of their own. And so the story proceeds through flight in a death-trapped Spad, a terrible crash, a dramatic return—just in time to foil the tricky Germans.

O'Leary forces Schlossen to help battle the attacking natives. To encourage the man's interest in the work, T.X. makes sure Schlossen gets the defective ammunition to fight with. After withstanding murderous attacks and enduring a shelling by Italian batteries, Schlossen has a complete change in heart.

And to prove his sincerity, he offers O'Leary and McGuffy directorships on the Board of his Syndicate. Since all of them live through the final attack and the hand-to-hand combat that followed, it could be that our heroes accepted the offer. But honestly it's hard to guess what might have happened later.

Schlossen, after all, had been introduced as a renegade selling exhausted war equipment; he ends the story as a businessman whose enterprises manufacture, among other things, modern bombers. Lord knows what the Schlossen Syndicate actually does. The idea behind the story is the familiar one of making the villain experience a situation he has created, after which he has a change of heart. Any inconsistencies that cropped up between the beginning of the story and the end were simply ignored.

As far as is known, this was the final appearance of Terrance X. O'Leary in the pulps. He had enjoyed a remarkable series. It was spread across three pulp magazines over a ten-year period, with an internal chronology of more than twenty years. Like all war fiction, it professed accuracy and realism, drawing upon Empey's reputation as a WWI author and wounded veteran. In reality, O'Leary's adventures were melodramatic fantasy, strongly influenced by moving pictures, stage plays, and comic strips. Although the series touched almost every aspect of war as it was known to the mid-1930s, it got few of them right. Now and then from the insincere pages blaze a few realistic lines about infantry in World War I combat. These moments are infrequently met. The bulk of the series offers the usual action narrative, featuring ethnic stereotypes blasting away at each other. The tone is vigorous. The action hot. The pages fly beneath your fingers. And the content is the literary equivalent of a dinner of air.

Not always. In two cases, perhaps three, a sympathetic enemy character appears. The Germans are not always caricatured. At least once, a story ends with somber regret for the dead. For the most part, however, the Germans are cruel maniacs; the dead of the battlefield are dramatic devices. Devices. Nothing more. Ten thousand fall in two paragraphs and that is the end of it. The narrative hies itself brightly along, leaving the dead behind, without horror, without regret, without sorrow, with hardly a single human emotion expressed at what has been experienced.

And no wonder. To express human emotion is to slow the narrative. Possibly it would allow the reader to slip the thrilling grip of the melodrama to realize that he is enjoying an account of how large numbers of men got transformed to corpses, in all the gay ways that war accomplishes that doleful change.

This moral numbness is a constant in most of the action pulps. The pages of the Spider and Operator 5 writhe with social catastrophe. Against a background of human horror and human agony, the busy story flicks along, unreeling its stimulating account of mass murder. For all practical purposes, only the Spider is permitted to feel emotion about the immense disasters surrounding him. Other series heroes rarely react emotionally to equal events. They enter, perform brilliantly against their ghastly backdrops, and then leave the stage, smiling fixed, empty smiles.

That same anesthesia of soul is apparent in the Jimmie Cordie adventures, first published at the end of the 1920s. This series approached the World War I experience more obliquely than the boisterous O'Leary saga. The Cordie story line reverts to the more familiar tale of the fighting legion, a small group of mercenaries continuing that good work begun on the Western Front.

The series, itself, is hard-edged as a razor. It brims with violent gun action, male bonding, combat in exceedingly foreign climes. Through the adventures echoes of the Great War ring like the aftertones of some huge bell.

There were six of them, the Jimmie Cordie crowd:

They were all dead shots with either rifle or revolver, and Jimmie Cordie could make a machine gun sing a death song for anything within range. All of chilled steel nerve, any of them would have gone singing to his death for the others, collectively or individually (Wirt, "I'm Shootin' Velly Good" 31).

From 1928 to 1935, these men shot slugged bled through *Short Stories, Frontier, Argosy,* and perhaps other magazines. Much of their fighting took place in China, although their appetite for action carried them to such other distant places as Central America and Turkestan—anywhere you could get killed messily by natives who loathed white men.

What were they doing out there? Having fun, of course. Earning a living. All six were soldiers of fortune. Mercenaries, to use the "m" word. Adventurers who sold their weapons skill to this war lord or that, and, after the immortal example of Luigi Caradosso, shot down that lord's opposition for a fee.

It was not that soulless. Cordie and company aligned themselves with the side of right. They were men of honor. Yes, they might sell their services for gold. But when they bent over the sights and hosed streams of copper-tipped slugs across the charging masses, they knew that the charging masses deserved to be mowed down. No doubt of it. The more rabble of that kind you blasted, the quicker the world became gentler and kind.

Not ten years earlier, the Allies had battered down the Kaiser and his hordes. Now Cordie and friends applied their talents to eliminating other blots of evil from this world. A humanitarian service. And it also offered the adventure that their war-stimulated nerves required. After years of fighting the Boche, peace seemed so boneless.

It was a complaint common to the majority of series heroes appearing during the 1920s and 1930s.

Great numbers of these heroes developed specialties in World War I combat techniques and applied these usefully in the Post-war period. Bulldog Drummond learned to prowl the battlefields by night, cutting throats and bashing in heads. Kent Allard, later to become The Shadow, did something in the Intelligence and was an ace who flew by night. Jimmie Cordie became a specialist on the placement and use of heavy machine guns.

Considerable information on that arcane subject had accumulated during the war. Most of that wisdom came too late. Throughout the war, battle plans of the high commands, were drawn as if no such thing as a machine gun existed. That is because European generals were guileless souls, filled with sentiments concerning bravery, honor, valor, and courage. They learned nothing from the American Civil War. Particularly they learned nothing about the folly of frontal attacks against entrenched men armed with repeating weapons.

Thus, the introduction of the machine gun meant nothing to the generals. They pursued Honor and Glory, those luminous visions. Their armies surged in frontal attack against massed machine guns. The British did it. The French did it repeatedly. As did the Germans, who certainly should have known better, since they themselves had developed the tactic of massed machine guns and interlocking fields of automatic fire. Only the American General Pershing refused to so squander his troops.

Generals learn slowly, slowly. Men, however, are fragile and, when shot to pieces, tend to die. Before the general learns, you can shoot a generation of men to rags.

Which happened.

After each battle—a term in common use for massed slaughter—grateful governments loaded the generals with medals. Later, nations eulogized the generals, and the pulp magazines breathlessly recounted how valiant men leaped laughing into battle. As for the dead, you never heard a word of complaint from them.

When Jimmie Cordie appeared, he was the latest bud on a venerable vine. The war pulps had demonstrated that American males would spend fifteen or twenty cents to buy magazines dedicated to war fiction. That being so, *Short Stories* and *Argosy All-Story Weekly* were delighted to offer such fiction. Not necessarily fiction about the Western Front. Already that was becoming tedious, as the *Battle Stories* magazine was in the process of discovering.

The new battle fiction was set, instead, in the Far East, where war lords hacked each other and life was cheap and only action was certain.

The characters of this fiction were of the proper age to have served in Europe. No slackers here. Splendid military credentials encrust Cordie and associates. Most had been officers in the American Expeditionary Forces. Many had also served in the French Foreign Legion. One, an Englishman, had been a combat flier for the RAF. Three were experts in the handling of the heavy machine gun, that weapon playing such an important role in the series:

...Chan-king's men came from the hills — more than had ever come in any two charges. He was attacking with every  man he had. Behind the regiments there came a swarm of swordsmen, and the men of some hill tribes who fought for him....

[Then] the snarling voices of six perfectly handled Browning machine guns, and the roar of rapid-fire one- and two-pounders, operated by Manchus trained by Jimmie Cordie. It was a searing, destroying fire, and Chan-king's troops melted away under it. They were approaching in more or less close formation, so as to have as many as possible hit the wall at the same time....

....Within fifty feet of the wall it ceased to be acharge and became but a writhing, wailing mass of dying men. (Wirt, "The Devil's Tattoo" 31)

The Browning machine guns mentioned were the standard US Army infantry support weapons. Not the somewhat lighter air-cooled guns that were mounted on vehicles, but massive Browning M1917A1s—a .30 caliber, water-cooled weapon, firing 500 rounds per minute. Swiveling on a substantial tripod, the weapon could cook off its coolant in two minutes. If you were fool enough to fire continuously for two minutes. Then more coolant had to be added—water, coffee, wine, or, in extreme urgency, urine.

By then, however, such undisciplined firing would have burnt out the barrel. Which meant that not even the Holy Saints could guess where the next rounds would go. Until the searing barrel was unscrewed and a new one attached, the weapon was out of commission.

The Browning gobbled ammunition, ate barrels, and demanded continuous maintenance. But any weapon imposes its own special demands. This machine gun was standard military equipment well into the Second World War.

This is the gun that Jimmie Cordie hauled all over the Oriental landscape. Unlike other series stories, Cordie's adventures invariably ended in full dress combat, 1918 vintage—with trenches, shells blasting away, machine guns and rifles yammering, corpses all over the place. A mess.

Thus machine guns are an essential element of the series. But such weapons presented certain problems. One man could lift the gun, minus its tripod; he could then trudge along, bent and dismal, gasping under the weight. To carry any substantial quantity of ammunition—canvas belts of cartridges neatly folded in a steel box—transport was required. Meaning automotive power. Or mule power. Or man power.

Few of these logistical realities make their way into the series. Occasionally the Cordie bunch run out of ammunition. They seemed untroubled by other problems that gave people fits on the Western Front.

The initial Cordie story appeared in *Short Stories*. Soon the series switched to *Frontier*, and then, in mid-1929, to *Argosy All-Story*, where it ran intermittently until late 1934. As a coda, a few additional exploits were published in the 1935 *Short Stories*.

"Private Property," the first of the series (*Short Stories*, October 10, 1928) is brief, brutal, and has a sentimental ending, thus resembling a panther whose tail dangles into a honey jar. In summary:

Four soldiers of fortune have accepted an assignment to secure a bronze Ming vase from a Chinese temple. Sailing their yacht upriver, they arrive at the temple, only to be opposed by hordes and swarms and armies of Chinese.

Now the Chinese have every right to resist this piracy. That's what this vase assignment is, although the pirates are white and presented by that substantial icon, Short Stories. However, back in 1928, the moral and ethical content of action fiction was not particularly important in a 25-cent magazine of manly fiction. What was important was the quality of personal performance under stress.

You must admit that Cordie and friends perform brilliantly.

The Chinese attack [using watercraft] was swift and deadly but it met a defense equally so. The Browning, operated by Jimmie Cordie and Red Dolan, swept the rafts clear of men, the sampan oarsmen and helmsmen going down under the thirty-thirties of Grigsby and Putney.

[Cordie's] trim little launch lay in the center as deadly as a diamond-backed rattler and as poisonous. For a space of two hundred yards in a circle the water was clear, beyond that, it was a welter of rafts and sampans with bodies lying in grotesque positions on them and men trying to swim ashore....

They came on again—to meet a sheet of steel-jacketed bullets sent to greet them by men who were all entitled to wear the distinguished marksman cross.

There was no mercy shown. It was cold, deliberate, accurate shooting by veterans and the Chinese melted away... (Wirt, "Private Property" 83).

Having chopped the defenders to confetti, the adventurers land and three of them head toward the temple. Cordie remains behind. A young girl, daughter of the Chinese leader, seeks to lure him from the boat. She fails. Instead, he takes her prisoner.

Moments later, the three return. They have been ambushed. While they fought free, they were unable to secure the vase. They did, however, capture the Chinese leader.

Out of respect for the girl's bravery and her father's courage, Cordie gives them their freedom—without ransom. That generosity so touches the leader that he delivers the Ming vase into the adventurers' hands.

The story reads well. Except that when you think about it later, you want to tear off your Distinguished Marksman Cross and fling it away.

Writer of this immoral adventure, William Wirt, was born in Boston, Massachusetts, in 1876. "My father," he remarked, "represented English interests and was one of the few Americans ever in the English secret service." When not on active duty he went to the places 'over back of beyond' for English and American syndicates, getting the inside dope on what's what—why—and how come."

In 1892, Wirt's father made the boy his assistant. Thereafter William lived a strenuous, adventurous, and tingling life. Or so Wirt reports in various biographical sketches published in *Argosy* and *Detective Fiction Weekly*.

It is perilous to rely on such information. Witness the solid glass diamonds dished up by Talbot Mundy for *Adventure*, or the fantasies that Dr. Poate and A.E. Apple(baum) wove for *Detective Story Magazine*. Nevertheless Wirt's account of his life seems reasonably coherent, if couched in slang so self-consciously hearty that it cracks the enamel of your teeth.

The tissue of truth is often stranger than you can imagine. Wirt's biography is strange. To compress many words into a necessarily juiceless skeleton: he served in the Navy, volunteering around 1899. Thereafter he traveled with his father in the Orient, later in South America, Mexico, and the United States. Married about 1908, Wirt served during World War I in some sort of intelligence capacity. (His comments are ambiguous but the service seems connected with the British Admiralty.) After his father's death, following the war, Wirt became, first, a deputy sheriff, then a US Federal Agent. He worked with the "US District Attorney" and as a "special agent"—for whom and doing what are not explained. Retiring from the Federal Government in 1927, he began publishing fiction the following year. Initially appearing in *Short Stories*, he would regularly contribute to *Argosy* and *Frontier*, as well as *Top Notch*, *Blue Book*, and *Ace G-Man*, using his own name, as well as the pseudonyms Robert Winchester and Wilson Cobb.

Most of his magazine work was signed "W. Wirt." Faintly disguised by the initial, he wrote serials featuring John Norcross and his hardboiled regiment of negro troopers, and many series featuring Secret Service agents, a bunch of gun hots, if you believe what you read. But any W. Wirt fiction is crammed with guns and men who do not hesitate to use them:

(*Argosy All-Story Weekly*, July 13, 1929, "I'm Shootin' Velly Good": (On a Hong Kong wharf, Jimmie Cordie and Red Dolan are saving a Manchu princess from pirates...)

...two beachcombers within ten feet [of them] and on three sides forming half a circle that ran from junk to junk were the Chinese, swords and daggers out.

The Chinese surged forward....

Red Dolan shot the nearest through the heart. When guns began to do the talking, Red's only idea was to kill. He fired three times more directly into the faces of the Chinese.

Jimmie shot the other [beachcomber] through the shoulder and, as the man reeled back against the Chinese, shot twice more. This time Jimmie also shot to kill....

Here was no easy prey; these were not men who drew guns but did not use them.... (Wirt, "I'm Shootin' Velly Good" 26-27)

Casualties pile up. New enemies swarm toward them. At that moment, a war junk sweeps toward the wharf. It flies the flag of that dreaded secret society, the T'aip'ing. This is simply bursting with Manchu swordsmen, ready to hack and carve.

Not on Jimmie and Red. Commander of the junk is Shih-kai, one of Cordie's dearest friends. He is a young man, scarred of face and tough as a cast iron steak. His father, Yen Yuan, heads the T'aip'ing and is a man to whom you speak softly and infrequently as possible. To four million Chinese, his word was law.

Seems improbable, but Jimmie's friendship with Shih-kai began at a New England university. The young man was sick and miserable in that sinister New England world. Jimmie nursed him back to health and attempted to explain the queer ways of the exotic Americans. Yen Yuan firmly believed that Cordie saved Shih-kai's life.

With the pleasant side effect that, when Jimmie came to the Orient after World War I, he found the most powerful secret society of the region solidly behind him. Never be ashamed of influential friends.

*Jimmie Cordie* is the unofficial leader of the group. A slim, dark-haired man of medium height, he has black hair and vivid blue eyes. He moves with quick precision, "graceful as a panther," according to Mr. Wirt, always swift with an original description. Cordie has served in the French Foreign Legion, together with several members of the group. During World War I, he had been a captain of an AEF machine gun company. The Chinese call him The Smiling Black-Eyed One.

We return to the wharf in Hong-Kong. Consider the princess who caused all this fuss to begin with. Poor thing is a pawn in a private war between the T'aip'ing and the White Lily society. To return the princess to her father, Cordie must sail up river past the White Lily stronghold at Chi-nen.

A battle plan is called for. They must strike the White Lilies unexpectedly, reducing them to embers. Then the princess may be escorted home.

Which is the reason a perfectly nice yacht, belonging to John Cabot Winthrop, gets converted to a floating fort, snarling with machine guns, field guns, and swarms of Manchu soldiers hunched sweating in the scuppers.

*John Cabot Winthrop*, nicknamed The Boston Bean, the Codfish Duke, and similar hilarious nicknames, is of the Boston Winthrops. You've heard of them. His name glints from the social register; he is worth millions. But he prefers to spend his life hunched behind a machine gun. Tall, lanky, thin face drawn by a sorrowful expression, he has a casual "You Be Damned" attitude. Once he had been Cordie's lieutenant in that Western Front machine gun outfit. Later he became a Captain in G-2-B American Intelligence. After the war, Winthrop joined John Norcross, adventurer, military man, secret service agent, for a campaign in Turkestan, as related in the Argosy All-Story Weekly serial, "War Lord of Many Swordsmen" (December 8 and 15, 1928).

Up river the yacht sails. To strike a mine at Chi-nan. Winthrop is barely able to beach the wreck.

Now begins howling war. After the attackers are temporarily beaten off, the princess and Red Dolan slip away, attempting to reach her father, some fifty miles off.

*Red Dolan*, six feet, three inches, and 230 pounds of red-haired violence. Tough, a master of weapons, his method of fighting is to "slap 'em out of the way." As you surmise, he speaks with a pronounced Irish brogue. He met Cordie in the Foreign Legion and, during World War I, was a lieutenant in the Military Police. (The Norcross serials present a character exactly like Red Dolan except 1) his name is Red McGee, 2) he is one inch shorter.)

Back at the wreck of the yacht, ammunition is running low. Toward them swarm junks filled with fierce Chinese. Leaving the yacht stuffed with explosives, Cordie and company establish a defensive perimeter. The junks close in, howling with demoniac pleasure, until the explosives are touched off.

Ignoring losses, the White Lily society continues to attack. Its field guns flame and blast. Waves of soldiers, horrid with bayonets, fling themselves at the perimeter. The Western Front lives again:

> The 'wh-e-e-e-e' of a shell coming to say howdy met their ears, and with one movement, like well trained weasels, they dived into the trench, and rolled into the nearest holes....
>
> [The bombardment] kept up, steadily getting worse. Shell after shell hit along the trench, one or two landing squarely. But the trenches had been laid out by men who had built trenches before, and no man was hit. (Wirt, "I'm Shootin' Velly Good" 41)

When all hope seems lost, the crash of new battle rings from the distance. The Princess' father has arrived. In a column and a half of type, the enemy is shattered.

This is a recurring pattern in Wirt's violent little amusements. Cordie or friends get pinned down by the enemy. A brave soul or two slip through enemy lines to secure help. And do so. Time after time. It is wonderful.

It is also wonderful the number of wounds that our heroes receive. Routinely they are shot, stabbed, hit on the head, tied up, blown up, ravaged by fever, starved. Still, they survive to the end of the story. That is more than you can say for their opposition.

"What Kept You?" (September 28, 1929, *Argosy All-Story Weekly*) introduces that lovely blond English orphan girl, Katherine Neville. Her uncle, a mining engineer and her guardian, brought her to the border mountains of China. Heaven knows why. The story pace is too furious to permit explanations.

As the story opens, Uncle lies dying. A minute later, he is dead. Two minutes later, Katherine meets the Boston Bean and Abraham Cohen, the Fighting Yid. Promptly the story boils.

Seems that the Bean and the Yid are searching for a shrine packed with ancient jade. After them snorts the local war lord.

Who corners our heros on the bare mountain top. Katherine's

Chinese boy is sent off to fetch Cordie. The two men and the woman prepare for siege.

*Abraham Cohen*, the Fighting Yid, is short, hulking, seemingly fat. Only it is all muscle. He has a good-natured face, although his blue eyes constantly seem to pop from his head with surprise. But he is never, *never* surprised by anything. A child of New York City, he effects a dense Yiddish accent, except in moments of intense stress. Then his English flows pure and exact. During WWI he was Cordie's sergeant. Later he campaigned with Norcross. Remarks Wirt, "The Yid had no morals, no ethics, and absolutely no fear of anything."

While cornered on the mountain top, the three drink from a drugged canteen. Captured, they are taken to the fortified city of the war lord, Chow-yang. The Yid and the Bean are hung in punishment cages outside Chow-yang's window, fifteen feet above the ground. Katherine is to become the war lord's love slave, subject to his fiendish lusts, as you may well expect.

Meanwhile! Cordie has received the message for help and chartered a beat-up old bomber. Loaded with machine guns and ammunition, the airplane flies to the mountain top where this silliness started. With Cordie are Red, George Grigsby, and Arthur Putney:

*George Kenneth Grigsby* is from Kentucky, a big, metal-hard man, with a dark, tight-lipped face, and a profile like a hawk. Formerly of the French Foreign Legion, a major in the AEF, he is an expert machine gunner and a first-class leader of men.

*Arthur Putney*, from Vermont, is tall, solid, taciturn, the way fictional New Englanders are. He is very fast to action. Has the usual Foreign Legion/AEF experience. A few months from now, he will be killed during a rear guard action that saves the lives of his friends.

The Yid came down on [Chow-yang], arms outstretched, fingers bent, great shoulders hunched. The Yid's face in repose was a handsome one, but now he looked very much like some prehistoric ape....

Katherine Neville, her back to the wall by the window, saw Chow-yang, War Lord of the city of Yunh-ning, bend slowly back, one of the Yid's great arms around the small of his back, one hand at his face, covering it. The Yid's body seemed to sway forward and then she heard a snap, as if a tree limb had broken (Wirt, "What Kept You?" 763).

Takes care of the War Lord. Just as he dies, machine guns open up. The rescue party has arrived.

From that point to the end, it is shoot, pull back, shoot again. The War Lord's minions attack, are cut down, reform to attack, are cut down, pull back to charge shrieking crazily....

Repetitious, predictable, exciting. The Cordie crowd, variously wounded, collect the prisoners and depart, ever slaying. The machine guns run out of ammunition. Still the assaults come. Handguns and rifles hammer. As the final cartridge is expended, the final enemy dies.

That's the end of it. Except that the Boston Bean has proposed to Katherine and she has accepted him. It was an intense, if short, engagement.

Change comes slowly to this series. But it comes. Over the following months, Putney meets a hero's death. Katherine becomes Mrs. John Cabot Winthrop. And the whole bunch of them seem fated to die.

"He's My Meat!" (three-part serial, December 20, 1930, through January 3, 1931):

All the series regulars are on a yacht in the middle of the South China Sea. Whenever a magazine character gets near the South China Sea, a typhoon strikes. This story is no exception, danger being a necessity in action pages. The typhoon also generates a tidal wave. The yacht is swept far inland on an island off Indo-China.

Evil luck fetches more evil luck. The island is ruled by that renegade Englishman, Henry Warrenne, who works for Soviet interests. At his command are a thousand pirates.

Naturally he wishes to obliterate the Cordie bunch. All but Katherine. He has plans for Katherine. All the wicked men shambling through this series have plans for Katherine.

The yacht is undamaged, if grounded. But they are cut off from the ocean by a stone ridge. As is immediately obvious, to escape, they must manufacture gun cotton from raw materials, then blow out the ridge, letting in the water.

At the same time, they must fight off armies of pirates armed like the Kaiser's hordes, swarming in to kill:

The Chinese regiment was flowing around the house on both sides, and when [Cordie's] machine guns opened up, there must have been two or three hundred of them. Two machine guns, manned by men who had operated them in France, opened up on the Chinese at almost point-blank range, shooting into the 'brown.' They blew wide swaths through the Chinese on both sides. (Wirt, "He's My Meat" 652)

After pages of this, Jimmie and his friends escape. That Soviet-loving renegade gets his, and another adventure ends amid the mounded dead.

The action proceeds with maniac energy. So furious is the narrative sped that you hardly notice the peculiar blankness of the prose. Almost every possible sensory description has been omitted. There is no smell of gunpowder, sweating men, death. No color intrudes, no warmth or cold or insect sting or bird call. The wholesale slaughters, the remorseless, unending battles, are conducted without sensory or emotional content.

We are told that Jimmie sings tuneless little songs as he handles his gun. That Winthrop shoots with a fixed, icy smile. That the Yid constantly talks to the enemy:

"Vell, now, vhy don't you hurry and come. Vere are you. Vhy don't you hurry. Now, dot's nize. Dun't esk vhy. Just come, now."

Other than these shadows of stress, nothing. Before the killing, they have no fear. After the killing, they have no regrets. Wonderful. The slaughter goes on and on, narrated in a prose tone as dry as a voice reading tonnage statistics.

As a further peculiarity, the stories are illustrated by John McNeill. For decades, McNeill had illustrated the Oz books, the work for which he is remembered today. How strange to see his characteristic drawings in *Argosy*. Nearly familiar faces peer from the artwork: Speedy, perhaps, or Ojo, or some scheming magician. Essentially they are nice faces. You find few hopelessly bad faces in the Land of Oz.

What a strange mixture this series is: brutal accounts of battle and massacre, narrated in the thin voice of an elderly professor, and illustrated by faces from Ozma's wonderland.

A new character has now replaced Putney. He is:

*John Cecil Carew*, a slender Englishman, ex-commander of the Royal Essex Flight Squadron. A born flier, lean, quick, aggressive, he is a first-rate fighting man. His features are of that sharply drawn type called "aristocratic."

"Aztec Treasure" (*Argosy*, December 5, 1931) drops the usual series props of war lords, machine guns, and 1918 tactics. The story is about treasure hunting, which is familiar. The locale—Guatemala—is not. Hidden in the jungle is an Aztec temple stuffed with gold. Priests guard it, as do murderous jaguar men. For additional protection, there is a mechanism that can flood the whole temple area. Before the adventure ends, that mechanism has worked, trapping our friends inside the temple.

Floating on the flood outside writhe a mixture of snakes and ferocious animals. Cordie is forced to boat among these in a hollow idol, as he desperately attempts to halt the flooding.

It may occur to you, in placid moments as the organ drones near the close of day, that Cordie and friends were in that jungle to loot somebody else's temple and steal somebody else's valuables. Fortunately for the reader's moral and ethical fibers, the adventurers find little more than excitement. Except the Yid. He always prospers. True to form, he escapes with a bag of jewels.

This adventure reflects, if very dimly, real experiences and real characters. As Wirt remarked:

I first met Red Dolan and the boys in this wise. In 1901 or 1902 I was in the federated state of Kelanton, Malay peninsula. Along came three husky looking gents who had just finished a hitch for Uncle in the regulars. They had been discharged in Manila and were en route to some temple back of the old ruined city of Angkor Thom. Did I want to go or not? There was a big bag of diamonds and everything that a guy in Manila had told them about....

I regret to report that we found a temple, but nothing more....

While we were looking over the old ruin we were jumped. Whether by Malay, Semang or Sekia, I don't know to this day. All I know is that they had these curved swords....

We drove them to cover and decided to postpone any further hunt for the jewels, as we had a feeling they were going back for the rest of the gang. We got back to the boat and they ran us ragged down various rivers.... Then they drew off, and we came back, as Red said, "widout a damned thing but wan million bites." (Wirt, "The Story Tellers" 176)

The August 6, 1932, "War Dragons" returns to the familiar story form which has begun to harden around Cordie and friends like old toast. In this variation, Jimmie and Red are captured by still another war lord. They escape in the improbable disguise of a small dragon. There follows the usual slaughterous climax. The point of it all was an attempt to enlist a war lord on the side of the Manchus against invading Japanese.

That Japanese presence will soon permanently mark the series. Before that, several impelling stories appear, offering interesting variations on the theme of World War I in China.

"The Devil's Tattoo" (November 12, 1932) is laid within a Manchu city shattered by airplane bombs and siege guns of an attacking war lord. Ammunition is running low. A deadly traitor creeps about unsuspected. Red Dolan lies in a pool of blood. Things look perfectly terrible. For a few pages.

"The Face in the Rock" (April 29, 1933) is a lost race story. Hotly chased by Japanese troops, Cordie and company find their way into a hollow mountain. Inside they discover a tiny colony of Jews who fled oppression centuries before, only to fall victim to oppression by their own priests. Our heroes fare poorly. When they finally escape, they are naked as eggs, and only sheer, pure, undiluted coincidence saves them. The Yid, foresighted as always, comes away with a statue carved from a single emerald.

After this less than glorious experience, the series faces away from the past and the 1914-1918 war. Now the subject becomes war as of

1933. The villains are Japanese. The particular villain is Colonel Nagayo of Japanese Intelligence, cruel, hateful, imperious.

The scene is Manchuria, where the Big Swords, those slashing, dreaded fighters, charge tremendously across the page.

But first, we pause for a delightful glimpse into the past.

In mid-1931, the Japanese army took over Manchuria, renaming it Manchukuo. So much is history. From here we descend into fiction. The Japanese could not pacify the country. It swarmed with tribesmen, fierce, unorganized, undisciplined. According to Wirt's scenario, the Japanese troops killed the family of a Manchu noble. Swearing eternal war, he organized tribesmen, the Big Swords, into a military outfit equipped with modern weapons. Those great, razor-edged swords they retained for close-in fighting.

Most of the combat actions described by Wirt have a quaint, dated quality, like woodcuts of a cavalry charge. The sabers wave and no machine gun lurks under a bush. Most picturesque.

One group of Big Swords, led by Cordie, have made themselves perfect nuisances to the Japs. These irregulars have just swooped down upon a military prison, freed a prisoner, stolen an armored train in which they escaped. That raid cost Japanese Intelligence and Military Police endless shame, disgrace, loss of face. They have moved Jimmie Cordie to the top of their Eliminate List.

Cordie's most dedicated foe is the treacherous Colonel Nagayo. At least once a story, it seems he has Jimmie at last. As in "Ammunition Up" (September 16, 1933):

Four of Cordie's bunch are fighting Japs on an island in the Fengning River. Jimmie plans to join them with a shipload of ammunition. Before he arrives, Nagayo traps the four and prepares to ambush the ship.

To everyone's immense surprise, except, perhaps, inveterate pulp magazine readers, the ship is spiny with concealed guns and ambushes the Japanese. A great killing follows. Nagayo gets his face smashed in by a sword hilt. Jimmie doesn't bother to kill him, an oversight he lives to regret. However a gentleman and former AEF officer doesn't kill helpless, unarmed men, no matter how obnoxious they are. Certainly not in the pages of a 1933 magazine.

"The Mad Monks" (July 7, 1934) tells of wonderful adventure in a secret city off in the Kara Kara Desert. At stake are the survey plans for a railroad between Siberia and Chinese Turkestan. A lovely adventuress has the survey; the mad monks have the adventuress; and Cordie must enter the sacred city to save map and woman.

By this date, Colonel Nagayo has failed so many times that you would assume he had been demoted to Private and sent to guard the chopsticks. So you would assume. Every now and then, however, realism flickers through the series. And so, just as in real life, after all his failures, Nagayo is promoted to Lieutenant-General.

In "The Assassin" (three-part serial, September 15 through 29, 1934), one of Lt.-Gen. Nagayo's underlings has hatched a plot to set off war with the United States. He has hired an American gunman to kill the Emperor of Manchukuo.

Learning of the plot, Cordie attempts to locate the gunman. Who is in Japanese hands, being fed drugs that float him out of the Solar System and leave him malleable as boiled socks. To get near the gunman, Cordie and friends pretend to be the captives of a nearby hill tribe.

Hearing this, Nagayo flames with hope. He attempts to capture Cordie. Cordie captures him. But not for long. Immediately after the assassination is prevented, Nagayo is accidentally killed by Japanese troops.

Ever so put out, those troops assault, and, as things happen in this series, get themselves obliterated. It is the usual end to the story and, in this case, the conclusion of the series, which ends as it began, in a chatter of automatic weapons.

Beneath the simple narrative surface of Cordie's adventures, which so resemble a simple little transparent stream about one inch deep, tangle social attitudes and fictional conventions from another time. That includes a great deal of he-man posturing in the panting tones of 1920s popular fiction.

Wirt was fond of such posturing. When he writes that Grigsby and Putney were "just about as dangerous to cross as a wounded grizzly," he feels that he has paid a compliment. When his male characters insult each other with crude jests and ethnic references, he feels that he has demonstrated warm male bonding.

In spite of Wirt, the stories do brim with recognizable male bonding, and that limited sort of manliness identified as aggressive hard competence. Like the cowboys of Clarence Mulford and the detectives of Carrol John Daly, Wirt's characters stoically endure hardship, danger, and pain. The real possibility of death never changes their expressions of inflexible determination.

Needless to say, love, sex, or tender emotion never disturbs their iron minds. Only the Boston Bean yields to feminine charms. Only briefly. Only for a few years. After which he returned to his place behind the machine gun. If the rest of the cast thought about women, the reader never knew it. Such socially sensitive material never reached the page.

All this is familiar territory, most of it stuff of the hardboiled tradition. The Cordie series imitates that tradition without ever convincing us that it is, after all, truly tough. For the hardboiled story contains a core of resilient romanticism wrapped in a personal code, whereas the Cordie stories, like drugstore greeting cards, have sentimental hearts. And they are wrapped in inconceivable callousness. Thus we have the anomaly of characters chattering of honor and fair play, even as they massacre thousands.

In the Jimmie Cordie series, the moral field is split and cannot be healed. Cordie's standards include appreciation for bravery under fire, steadiness under stress, technical gun work performed skillfully and professionally. Those same standards include no response to the dead created as a consequence of that professionalism, except to admire the orderly way the dead men fell.

We speak here of professionals engaged in literary battle. Wirt does not seem to have had direct battle experience. Probably for that reason, the blood and stink and horror of a field of bullet-shattered corpses never disturbs the ceramic surface of his prose. Like the battles of Khlit and O'Leary, and the later actions of The Shadow and the Spider, the fight is the subject, not the aftermath.

That is convenient and perhaps necessary. Too much reality is not welcome in popular action fiction. Wounds from .303 or .45 caliber projectiles are hideous. A field littered with dead is a vile place, offensive to the fastidious taste. As Hemingway pointed out in "A Natural History of the Dead," the consequences of death are rarely pleasant.

What interests us, as readers, is not realistic depiction but the menace and the fight. The war lord howls behind. Just beyond the next hill crouches incredible danger. Ammunition is low and the Boche poses to attack. Or the Japanese. Only the most optimistic dare think of living until night.

We can deal with these matters, the customary suspense materials of action fiction.

What we don't care for are all the tedious plodding details that fill up time between these points of high excitement. Such as loading the ammunition carrier or selecting a shovel for the burial detail.

We have a tacit agreement with the author. We will allow our sense of reality to sleep; he will allow his imagination to play.

So Wirt plays at war. The reader absorbs vicarious excitement. Each, in his own way, is happy. Fictional war ends with the final period. Only in real war are there consequences.

By 1936, the World War I-based story was seriously obsolete. Grisly doom had devoured the few magazines devoted to that conflict, although *Battle Stories*, flaunting O'Leary in contemporary war, still lingered. Although not for long.

The war story, itself, did not die. Through the years of world battle, from 1939 to 1945, war fiction filled *Argosy, Blue Book, Short Stories, Adventure*, as well as most other magazines from *Love Stories* to seed catalogs. These stories appeared about fifteen years from the time that the Jimmie Cordie series had begun. Yet they sprang from a different world. As so it was.

The war stories magazine had exploited a brief fad, found its audience too narrow, and melted away. On the other hand, the air war magazine prospered marvelously. In the following chapters, we will note the background of this phenomena and glimpse a few of its early characters.

# Chapter Nine
# War Birds, Sky Hawks, and Red-Hot Aces

During 1926 the *Liberty Magazine*, a weekly found in many American homes and innumerable barber shops, ran a rather grim memoir about World War I combat flying. No author's name was given, then or later that year, when the work received book publication as *War Birds, The Diary of An Unknown Aviator*. The author—or more correctly, editor—was Elliott Springs, himself a combat pilot, who had edited, and perhaps fluffed up, in the manner of plumping a pillow, the diary of a friend killed during the air war.[1]

*War Birds* served as a preamble to 1927, a year of aviation wonders. For a decade, airplanes and pilots had drifted across public consciousness, part entertainment, part prophecy. Flying, it was suspected, was an activity pursued by the unstable.

Then, in the manner of a summer squash plant, aviation burst forth, prodigiously. Elliott Springs published another book about World War I combat flying, *Nocturne Militaire*, this under his own name. The moving picture, "Wings," was released, filled with heart-gripping visuals of biplanes whirling. Most important of all was Charles Lindbergh's non-stop flight from New York to Paris. His 3,600 mile flight took thirty-three and a half hours and, among its unexpected side effects, exploded a wave of adulation that utterly astonished the shy young pilot. Quite suddenly, aviation became a national passion.

The pulp magazines never neglected major public passions, particularly when expressed in such material form as moving pictures and newspaper headlines. Lindbergh touched down in Paris on May 21, 1927. By June (dated July) appeared *Aviation Stories and Mechanics*, the first magazine concentrating on aviation fiction. A month later (dated August) followed Fiction House's *Air Stories*, "Thrilling Stories of the Sky Trails," and, at the end of the year, its companion magazine, *Wings*, dated January 1928.

Fiction House published both magazines on a staggered schedule, *Air Stories* on the first of the month, *Wings* on the 15th. That assured devotees of aerial adventure that they need not endure an empty, aching month between issues. The title pages of both magazines were "Dedicated To American Flying Men Who Have Carried The Stars and Stripes To The Skies." They didn't say Lindbergh and they didn't have to; readers knew who was meant.

Issues were 20 cents each; subscriptions $2.50 a year. For these enormous sums, readers received a novel, thirty pages long, and a novelette, plus a serial, and perhaps half a dozen short stories.

Which were, exactly as stated, air adventure:

"Horizon Hoppers" by Jack Smalley. ("Treacherous seas below—raging winds above—and two skyhawks dice with Doom.")

"Kiting Emeralds" by Nels Leroy Jorgensen. ("A flyer answers the call of adventure and gets rapid-fire action!")

"Wings of the Law" by Thomson Burtis. ("The day of the six-gun is over—and winged motors carry the law to the Border country.")

"Flying Twins" by Frederick C. Davis. ("It's the code of the game! And it sent the flyers of the reel to battle for a scoop.")

The air adventure magazines used only an occasional article or short story recalling World War I flying. The first magazine to concentrate on air war, *War Birds*, was not issued until February 1928 (dated March). After a few months' delay to test the vigor of public acceptance, other publishers offered *Flying Aces* (August 1928) and *Aces* (December 1928).

By that time, air adventure magazines were boiling out as if a pipe had ruptured. *Air Adventures, Air Trails, Sky Riders, and Flying Stories* were issued during 1928. Now, in 1929, nearly a dozen new magazines were offered: *Sky Birds, Airplane Stories, Eagles of the Air, Flyers....* The list included Hugo Gernsback's *Air Wonder Stories*, science fiction involving flight using science so advanced it seemed pure imagination; and Harold Hersey's *Sky Birds*, one of the first titles of Hersey Magazines.

In the aviation magazine, the machine is the hero. True, there is a helmeted, goggled, leather-coated individual at the controls, but he isn't a he-man *per se*; he is a superman. He is similar to the Galahad of the Plains in one respect; he is only himself when he's in the saddle of his mechanical steed.... Everything in an aviation yarn leads up to and away from the tarmac. The wise writer keeps his hero up in the air...as much as possible. Why? Because the hero loses some of his God-like quality when he walks the earth. He belongs somewhere up in the sky, zooming about the crags of Mount Olympus. (Hersey, *Pulpwood Editor* 184)

But here Hersey is speaking of air war fiction. Between 1927 and 1930, nearly twenty-five flying magazines leaped from the presses. Perhaps five of these concerned themselves with high violence in World War I skies. The others offered the more usual pulp adventure story, adapted by adding aircraft and fliers in the manner of a doctor giving an injection. The airplane (or Zeppelin, balloon, or other flying amazement) was simply a device to carry the hero into trouble, someplace where men were bad and guns quick. Matters had hardly changed from dime novel days, when Frank Reade Jr. invented those extraordinary contraptions that flew or floated his characters off to wonderful experiences in the far elsewhere.

Now the contraptions were called airplanes. As, in a different context, they were called submarines (*Submarine Stories*, 1929), steam locomotives (*Railroad Man's Magazine*, 1906), and Zeppelins (*Zeppelin Stories*, 1929). Had the public enthusiasm been directed to camels, you could confidently have predicted publication of *Ship-of-the-Desert Action Adventures*. The device, whatever its nature, carried you to adventure. The device was frequently wonderful, making the jaw drop and the eyes shine. But the whole point of the story was the adventure after the device got you there.

In contrast, the air war magazine, focused upon a needle's point of time, offered adventures above Western Front skies during 1917 and 1918. It would seem incredible that so much fiction could be written about such a sliver of history. But it was done. Out poured the magazines, their covers of exquisite beauty, the bright aircraft of 1918, rendered in minute detail, caught in moments to catch the heart. The fiction was as white hot, improbable, and limited in time, as the usual pulp fiction. But in this meager area, what variations were played.

Obviously the fiction had to sustain itself on something more than descriptions of combat. Those seasoned the narrative. Still, the most optimistic editor knew that constant focus on Spads shooting Fokkers, or Fokkers shooting Spads, wearies the reader, who might then keep his twenty cents pocketed when the next issue arrived.

So the air war story developed as an alternate form of the adventure story, focused on a character and his tribulations. Intermittent bursts of aerial combat flecked the narrative and during the final battle, all problems got resolved to the sinister snittering of machine guns.

Thus heroes were glorious eccentrics. Or lone wolves. Or inspiring leaders. Perhaps they were thought cowards, or they were hated for imaginary faults. They were suspected traitors, or were driven by circumstance to battle the German Air Arm alone, or flew in disguise, or faced some fearful German weapon threatening the Allied air fleet, or were menaced by fleets of new German aircraft, or a new German ace of superhuman ability. They were cowboys riding biplanes like a bronc, men of gloomy destiny and bad reputations with hearts glowing for the Allied cause. Some had bad luck. Some had all the luck. A few were comical cusses who fell down a lot but always landed with hands full of roses, admired by the Colonel.

Thus aerial combat fiction, from 1927 for perhaps a decade, pinned to the skies over the Western Front, 1917- 1918, issue after issue.

When the Second World War reared hugely up, smoking and stinking, the air war magazine modernized its cover and more slowly updated its content. Spitfires gradually replaced Spads. Nazis, Italians, and Japanese slowly replaced the Boche. Otherwise the magazines continued through the 1940s, blasting Messerschmitts and Zeros from the skies as obsessively as once they had blasted the Fokker and the Pfalz.

That would be the future of air war fiction. From those coming wonders, we turn to scenes less sensational. To origins. To that remote time when the air war story was new and World War I a terrible presence crouched just outside the window, scratching on the glass.

Ten years before the first issue of *War Birds*, March 1928, a startling new fiction series began in *Everybody's Magazine*. Written by Edgar Wallace, the first installments were considered so compelling and timely that two were published in the November 1917 issue and two the following month. Titled "Tam O' The Scoots," the series skipped the January 1918 issue, then continued monthly through June 1919.

These stories are a faithful study of a little Scotchman fighting under unique conditions. Not all air-pilots on the Great Front are officers. Some are men of the people. In these stories, Mr. Wallace describes a rare character, a Glasgow mechanic, who becomes a Royal Flying Corps pilot. According to the introduction to the article. "Tam" is a real person, and all the adventures set forth actually happened, through names and places are necessarily fictitious.— THE EDITOR.(*Tam O' The Scoots, I*)

How distressed the editor would have been to learn that the adventures and the character of Tam were also fictitious. Perhaps an analytical chemist of more than normal skill might have precipitated out the molecule of fact concealed in these stories. But he would need to be immensely skilled. Wallace had been a reporter, skillfully grasping an attitude or an emotional context, and was already adept at molding a narrative from a few pallid facts.

Tam was supposedly based on a South African youngster who rushed to join the British Army in 1914, was assigned to the Royal Flying Corps, and got shot down on his first combat flight (Morland 5). The character of Tam MacTavish varied largely from these doleful facts.

Tam being a brown-faced Scotsman, redheaded, small, and built like a bundle of sticks. Before the war, he performed small repairs at a local garage. Strongly against war in all forms, he refused military service, dodging from job to job. By chance, he became a mechanic at an air field—aerodrome, as 1917 had it—and the glamor struck. Within a few months, he qualified as a pilot. But refused a commission: "A'm no' a society mon ye ken." He remained a sergeant, and you will just have to get used to Scotch dialect of the vaudeville variety, for that's all Tam speaks.

Not only did this small Scottish pacifist prove to be a natural flier but a genius with the machine gun. In the illustration introducing the series, he is shown attacking a German bomber. Tam flies a thoroughly improbable single-wing aircraft, drawn with gay disregard for authenticity, and he manipulates an enormous weapon dimly resembling a Lewis machine gun.

Immediately this Scotch pacifist begins slaughtering Boche wholesale. Where he passes, clusters of Albatros and Fokker tumble from the skies. Like white light, his fame bursts through the Allied air arm. At age twenty-seven, he holds the French Medille Militaire, the Russian medal of St. George, and the French Croix de Guerre. Even the Germans know his name and admire his skill. "Ach, dot man vot down Ich geshotten, Tam he vos, yah?"

On the ground he is somewhat less a hero. He is the J. Wellington Wimpy of smokers, a constant, relentless, formidable moocher of cigars. He is also a passionate dime novel reader. Has a staggering library of these, receives more in every mail. In his bare little room, containing only a bunk, a chair, and stuffed bookshelves, he spends his nights with Seven-Gun Don, Terror of the Hutchison Wilderness; or Deadwood Helen, the Spectral Heiress; or Fearless Van Der Linde, the Golden Avenger.

To the delight of his friends, his oral reports of combat are in the language of the dime novel:

*Tam*: "Did ye no look thoughtfully at yeer obsairvor when, wi' a hooricane roar, the Terror of the Airr [Tam] hurtled across the sky. 'Saved!' ye said to yersel'; saved an' by Tam!" (Wallace, *The Case of Lasky II*)

Most of the initial story, "The Case of Lasky" (November 1917) is devoted to introducing Tam. It is a story by courtesy. It begins nicely, as a story should, then veers off into Tam's history and personality, and ends with the report of Lasky's death. This is unfortunate but not unendurable, since Lasky has not appeared since page 3. All he did then was listen to Tam chatter. The piece is more a character sketch than anything else, and the bits of incident it contains are no more related than the contents of a waste basket.

"Puppies of The Pack," the second of the series and also published in the November 1917 issue of *Everybody's*, is marginally better. Tam composes doggerel, for which he is regarded with awe. Off camera, he shoots down two of the more violent German aces, and tra-las about the sky with an American (who flies with the French). Finally he drives the fierce Captain Muller off the American's tail. Still it isn't a story. More like the introduction to one.

In the December 1917 issue, which again contains two stories, Muller becomes a menace (in the first story) and Tam shoots him dead (in the second).

Tam swung around and stared fiercely as Muller's machine fell. He saw it strike the earth, crumple and smoke.

"Almichty God," said the lips of Tam, "look after that yin! He wis' a bonnie fichter an' had a gay hairt, an' he knaws richt weel A' had no malice agin him—Amen!" (Wallace, *Tam O' The Scoots* 75).

The initial stories are rich in character, over rich in dialect, and weakly imagined. Too much action is as boring as too little, but there is no feel here for either the exhilarations or the terrors of combat. Often the action is only referred to, or Tam does a dime novel take-out on it. When aircraft do whirl and the machine guns hammer, it is in sentences stripped bare. No color, no smell, no sound, no emotion. The plain declarative sentences are thin as a ghost by daylight.

[Tam] came at the leading German and for a second the two machines streamed nickel at one another. Tam felt the wind of the bullets and knew his machine was struck. Then his enemy crumpled and fell. He did not wait to investigate....

He swung around and saw the [American bomber] diving straight for the earth with the German scout on his tail. Tam followed in a dizzy drop....

He banked over to follow the pursuing German and in the brief space of time which intervened before his enemy could adjust his direction to cover pilot and gunner, Tam had both in line. His two guns trembled and flamed for four seconds and then the German dropped straight for earth and crashed in a flurry of smoke and flying debris. (Wallace, "A Question of Rank" 186-187)

It is as easy as a day dream. All the problems and fears are pared away, leaving only the juiceless rind of action described in juiceless words. As future air war fiction would show, it was a problem endemic to the type. So many of the writers did not fly. Many of those who flew never experienced combat. Imagination compensated for these lacks, not quite adequately.

Apparently Wallace felt that the series required more than whizzing machines, sputtering guns, and trick endings to narratives that were probable by only the most generous standards. Human involvement made the story, however fancy the other trappings.

So, presently, we are introduced to Vera Laramore, a rather wealthy American darling, come to the Western Front to drive an ambulance. Tam's motorcycle and Vera's ambulance bump heavily on a muddy road and thus, in "A Question of Rank" (May 1918), romance is born.

Romance thin and constrained. For Tam is but an humble sergeant, feeling, for the first time, the social gap existing between the enlisted ranks and officers. Vera invites our hero to lunch, wartime conditions making girls forward. Unknown to her, the cafe where she has reserved a table is officer's territory. Crushed and despondent, Tam flings skyward and blasts Huns right and left. In the process he saves the life of Vera's brother. Then discovers that he has been promoted to Second Lieutenant, just in time to keep that luncheon date.

During "A Reprisal Raid" (June 1918), the Germans become increasingly sinful and bomb quite a few hospitals, that being their way. (By 1918, it was an article of faith among writers of the more casual fictions that the Germans methodically cut off children's hands, bombed hospitals, and wiped their boots with the Union Jack.)

In "Reprisal," Boche bombs kill a hospital mascot, a chimpanzee. Somewhat later, a faulty engine forces Tam down inside Germany. The engine he can fix; a lack of gasoline he cannot. You must not be concerned. Soon he encounters a German who exactly resembles the murdered chimp and captures him, then captures a staff car carrying gasoline. Presently he flies away, carrying with him the strange-looking German. Who will, from this time on, understudy for the chimp at the hospital.

"The Last Load" (July 1918) is Vera's final appearance. As you have surmised from her shining eyes, she loves Tam. And he loves her. But how can he tell her, when she has all that wealth, education, and social position?

Besides which, her brother has been retired to England after a near fatal crash.

Besides which, her application for leave has been approved.

She will drive just one more load of wounded to the hospital. And then, and then, with so many things unsaid, with her heart spurting white fire, with burning eyes, and choking throat, and so on and so on, she will leave the Front. To see Tam no more. Perhaps, even, forever.

The resolution of "The Last Load," in case you haven't read any fiction for the past eighty-five years, is this: Tam is shot during a dog fight and ends up, bloody and pale and full of Spandau slugs, in Vera's ambulance. Whereupon she kisses him:

*Vera* (to the attending physician): "Tam is going to live...because he knows I want him to—don't you, dear?"

*Tam* (faintly): "Aye—lassie."

*Vera*: "Because—because we are going to be married, aren't we, Tam?"

Tam (whispering): "Say it —in — Scotch." (Wallace, *Tam O' The Scoots* 245)

After this extraordinary outpouring of emotion, they get married, settling down in Devonshire, of all places. Or so we learn in "The Gentlemen from Indiana" (August 1918). In this story, Tam does not make a formal entrance until the final page. By then he has destroyed three German aircraft in as many seconds. Then, mysterious in helmet and goggles, he descends from his little fighter:

*Tam*: [I'm back from] "ma honeymoon, an' just as I were getting used to it—mon, war's hell—have ye a segair in ye'r pouch?—ah'm travellin' wi'oot ma baggage!" (Wallace, *The Fighting Scouts* 12)

To trace the publication history of the usual Edgar Wallace short story is to hurl yourself into a thorned tangle of forgotten publications, unknown issue dates, and generations of reprints, with the same story repeatedly changing title as it ricochets from newspaper to pamphlet to magazine to book. In this respect, the Tam series is tame. The stories appeared in England slightly before their publication in *Everybody's*. Immediately, the initial ten stories were collected into *Tam Of the Scouts* (1918) — the American edition titled *Tam O' The Scoots* (1919). The rest of the series, minus two stories, was issued as *The Fighting Scouts* (1919); no American edition is known. A final Tam story, "Christmas Eve At the China Dog," has the more usual involved history, but may be found in *The Stretelli Case* (1930), a collection of crime stories.

After marriage and return to combat, Tam enjoyed a stirring series of adventures, all rather remote from the life of the usual combat pilot. In "The Duke's Museum" (September 1918), Tam wings off to capture the Grand Duke of Friesruhe, a clever inventor of experimental aircraft. These the Duke tests in combat, his "museum," you see. In Germany, Tam pounces upon the Duke's hanger, burns the Duke's deadly new aircraft, and kidnaps the Duke back to Allied lines. He performs these miracles as easily as would G-8, The Flying Spy, some fourteen years later, who flew to Germany each month, landing to investigate some Hell's broth or other.

"The Man Called McGinnice" (October 1918) was not reprinted in *The Fighting Scouts*, possibly because it suggests that an Irishman might hate the English enough to shoot down their airplanes. McGinnice does. He fights his own private war against the British until Tam shoots him down. The fierce Irishman is captured and imprisoned. Only to escape. Tam must fly after him, shoot him down once again, and haul him back to justice, tied to the airplane's landing gear.

"Billy Best" (January 1919) introduces Cadet William Best of the United States Army. He become Tam's roommate, and his flying skills are to be burnished bright under Tam's instruction.

Best promptly snatches up the series, folds it under his arm, and attempts to carry it out the door. He is gray eyed, all fresh and pink and young and lucky, a glutton for candy, dime novels, and cigars.

"Ah dinna buy segairs," said Tam. "They're donated by ma friends, admirers — and pupils.
"I get you," nodded [Billy], puffing luxuriously.
"A'm a prood an' tetchy feller," said Tam; "ye must no' hairt ma feelings by handin' 'em to me in a coorse an' brutal manner. Ye must just leave 'em around careless an' ah'll find 'em.... (Wallace, "Billy Best" 56)

So much of the story is occupied with pleasant back chat that little space remains for a formal story. Which involves a multi-millionaire German ace who is mentioned on the first couple of pages and shot down by Billy on the last couple.

"A Day with Von Tirpitz" (March 1919), another story not reprinted, is all galloping action. Tam and Billy bomb a meeting of the German naval staff—have engine trouble—land in Germany—meet an escaped English seaman—escape from the Germans—bomb a submarine—crash 50 miles out to sea—are rescued by an American troop transport. All this crammed into a single breathless day.

"The Infant Samuel" (June 1919) contains a double story line, the series having grown complex since its earlier simplicities. The Infant Samuel, a German flier of incredible skill, is slaughtering Allied pilots. Faced with this menace, Tam is, at the same time, torn by doubts that his wife still loves him. Her letters are restrained. He has not seen her for six months. Perhaps she is ashamed of his low origins. Perhaps she is tired of him.

All dismal in mind, he encounters The Infant and is shot down. Billy Best instantly shoots down the German. At the crash site, Tam and Billy discover The Infant to be a girlish-looking seventeen-year old, soft-spoken, charming of manner, pleasant even while dying. Tam regards the German ace so highly that he names his new son Samuel. ("After Uncle Sam," he adds cautiously.) That son, by the way, was the cause for Vera's remoteness; she didn't want Tam to worry while she was having the baby.

Some years later, "Christmas Eve At the China Dog," brought Tam back in a contrived story about a faithless wife, her more faithless lover, and a husband with a homicidal plan. Tam is called from his labors at inventing a nonflammable dope for airplane canvas to fly various people to Paris and back. All very secret. The smirking seducer gets his, the wife reforms, and Tam guesses the identity of the murderer from the evidence of the stained hand. But call the police? No, indeed; in Tam's opinion, justice has already been served.

The "China Dog" is one of those nearly transparent trifles Wallace fabricated so effortlessly. But the Tam series, as a whole, is rather more substantial. The series is a concentrated sample of what the air combat story would become in less than ten years. Already Wallace had anticipated major elements of the form:

—the unusual hero, a caricature, vividly sketched and engagingly eccentric....

—who is a brilliant combat flyer, successful on nearly every flight, whose metallic nerve and gunnery skills....

—make him legend at his fellows, venerated by the Allied air arm, respected by the enemy....

—although the hero repeatedly flies "suicide missions," landing deep in Germany, only to emerge glowing with glory, having enjoyed an exciting, if not particularly dangerous, adventure....

—during which several air combats appear, rather scrappily described. You might think the air combat to be the primary purpose of the story, but it is only incidental, like pepper on a steak....

—and while there is a great deal of action, it is described in only general terms, using fragments of slang and a few enchanted words, such as Spandau, Fokker, Lewis gun, Spad, Albatros, Baron von, aerodrome, to resonate through the story and create a living presence....

—although, admittedly, the minor characters exist only to die, for their mortality rate is exceptionally high, particularly among German pilots....

—who are shot down in vast numbers. Not that they mind. Most of them are gentlemen, skilled and gallant, knights of the sky, who give death gracefully, or receive it with a smile and a shrug, never lowering themselves to unsportsmanlike conduct, at least during early years of the war; although it is noticed by the Allied fliers that this knightly quality in the German replacements slowly deteriorates—to the point where gallantry between opposing aviators disappears, and the Sportsmanlike German aviator is replaced by the Atrocity-Committing Hun, bestial face distorted, as he machine-guns little birds and flowers.

As Wallace wrote in his autobiographical book, *People*, the Tam series was written with an axe to grind:

My idea was to convey to America a picture of English soldiers and English [war] effort which would create an atmosphere of sympathy, if not for our cause, for the men who were fighting our battles. I never worked so hard in all my life to bring my stories to perfection....

I confess that I did not know that there was such a thing as a Propaganda Department fostered by the British Government, and even if I had known, it is doubtful whether I should have approached the bigwigs of Whitehall, for what help could they possibly have given me? It was sufficient satisfaction to me to know that my independent efforts were going into 500,000 American homes each month. When I was in New York fours years later, an American editor told me that Tam was the inspirer of the American Flying Corps spirit, and although I would not endorse this extravagant estimate, I feel that I did something to put a branch of the British fighting service "on the Map" in the United States (Wallace, *People* 233-234).

A benign enough motive, certainly. It does not explain Wallace's far more ferocious series, "The Companions of the Ace High," but that requires little explaining. Not when you read the stories.

The Ace High, a most peculiar air group, flew against the Germans, and they flew for hatred and revenge.

*Commander of the Ace High*: "...these boys of mine are the original suicide club. We are men with scores to settle—general and individual." (Wallace, *The Companions of Ace High* 62)

Elsewhere he remarks, more poetically:

Some of them have died twice—their hearts have gone all shrivelly and their hopes have dried up like raindrops dry on a hot stove. They've all died once..., carried by their despair to a hell of their own and come back to the world looking at things from a new angle. (Wallace, *V. Hooky Patterson Die Once* 185)

So they flew to combat, their wings marked by a circle around a star enclosing a black ace of spades. They killed in the high clean clarity of the air. They were killed. If forced down, they continued the battle on the ground. For the point of their battle was not survival but death. Death at the greatest cost of the enemy—who was the German, the unspeakable German.

Suddenly we are in a fictional world far from that of Tam. Suddenly we are in a world that is not benign fiction but fiction adulterated with propaganda.

The series was originally published in *The Post Sunday Special,* an English newspaper. Five parts appeared, titled "The Sign of the Black

Ace" (November 24 through December 22, 1918). The author was anonymous. The series immediately skipped across the Atlantic and, under Edgar Wallace's byline, was published, in six parts, in *The Popular Magazine* (March 7 through May 20, 1919), as "The Companions of the Ace High."

March 1919 was an odd time for an anti-German propaganda series to begin. About four months before, the Armistice had been declared, November 11, 1918. Again the world was safe for democracy. They boys were returning home to a brief ecstasy of parades and speeches and public gratitude, as well as to the more enduring agonies of national depression, unemployment, and Prohibition.

The War To End War had ended. Its celebration in the pulp magazines had barely begun.

As Wallace had previously remarked, Tam glorified the British war effort. In this, his series succeeds, and in this, his series differs from that of the Ace High. Try as you will, you can hardly find anything in the Ace High series that is glorified — other than the need to kill the vile low despicable Hun.

But let's begin with the incident that sparks the series:

After the torpedoed ocean liner sank, the German submarine surfaced near the life boats. It began shelling them, quite methodically, until an approaching war ship drove it away. The first shell killed the mother of Sanford Seyers. The wife of a man named Dexter stared at what the shell had done and went loudly mad. She stayed that way. Both Dexter and Seyers were in the United States at that time.

Dexter was a millionaire cattleman who had made a fortune in the Argentine. After the incident with the submarine, he dedicated that fortune to the destruction of the German cause.

He reached an agreement with the republic of San Romino, a tiny free state on Italy's north border. San Romino declared war on Germany. Dexter was appointed Chief of Air Operations and all the country's aircraft production was placed in his hands.

It was a gesture of grand insignificance, San Romino being the size of a stadium parking lot. Its primary industry seemed to be looking at mountain peaks.

No difference. Dexter gathered together pilots of many nationalities, all with this in common: their lives had been wrecked by the Germans. All simmered with steady black rage. All panted to slaughter the Boche.

Each man was to provide his own aircraft and pay a hefty $10,000 deposit toward incidental expenses. As a result, the Ace High collected a weird mixture of aircraft — SE-5s, Nieuports, Curtiss scouts, Spads, Camels.

In the interest of narrative flow, Wallace slides over the problems keeping this flying menagerie operational. Granted that someone, somehow, had to procure spares and replacement parts. Someone had to order fuel, ammunition, bombs, flares, machine tools, picture frames, chairs, potatoes, and bar supplies.

On how this was done, Wallace is loudly silent. Writing fiction is more fun than operating a logistical supply system.

Let us agree with Mr. Wallace to ignore these niggling details. Around us spreads the Ace High base, closely ringed by mountains. A neatly clipped hedge borders the tarmac and hangers. A lawn leads smoothly to a luxurious building, fancy as the Paris Hilton, where the pilots room and lounge and brood. Inside, Dexter chain smokes cigars and studies intelligence reports. He plans new strikes against the Hun.

Occasionally, Dexter will cooperate with the French or British arm arms. More usually, the Ace High sails out on its own, hot for vengeance.

Pictures of those who found death are displayed on the panels of the lounge room.

Having neatly constructed this elaborate background, Wallace proceeds to ignore it for most of the series.

The first story, "The Woman of the Lorelei" (*The Popular Magazine*, March 7, 1919), sets up the background. But then it leaps sideways into a sort of vendetta adventure. It tells how an Ace High pilot, his military career compromised by a lovely female German spy, tracked her down, deep inside Germany, and took his deadly revenge.

To an even greater extent than in the Tam series, the Ace High stories feature the flight into Germany, the landing, and the adventure thereafter. Happens constantly. Wallace was inspired, no doubt, by the exploits of the few spy planes which did perform such feats, although not so regularly as did the Ace High. These people enter and leave Germany as routinely as if they were taking a bus.

The second story of the series bears the extraordinary title, "Loving Heart and The Man With A Charmed Life" (March 20). This introduces the hero of the series, Hooky Patterson. Originally Dexter may have been intended as hero. But he fades to mere continuity before Hooky's brash glare.

Patterson belongs to a top cream New England family and has all the money in the world. He acts insufficiently New England, being flippant and intensely undisciplined. He has been bounced from all other military flying services because he can't obey orders, can't hold formation, neglects to go where he's sent, and constantly goes where he shouldn't. That is why he is called Hooky.

He is a handsome boy with the gray eyes of a Wallace character, tall and remarkably strong. He flies with brilliance, shoots like Dan'l Boone, is merry, light-hearted, and babbles painfully:

Hooky: "...here I am, commander of the faithful. A Bristol or a Curtiss scout is my passion and hobby; Spads I adore, the British B.6 I abominate. Give me something with a stagger, something with short wings and a quick rise, something that loops if you breath on the control, and I will darken the sky with falling Huns." (Wallace, "Loving Heart" 63)

Dexter is doubtful. The boy seems too scatty even for the irregular Ace High operation. Taking the youngster into the panelled room hung with dead mens' pictures, Dexter talks tough: "You are not bound by any promises or oath save to the republic in whose service we are. If you fail us, I shall ask you to go, for you will have broken faith with the living who will die and the dead who everlasting live in our hearts" (Wallace, "Loving Heart" 63).

Dexter is inclined to ponderous sentiments. Although these are exceedingly rich for our present taste, they seem to have been just right for 1919 popular fiction, where sentimental intensity was much appreciated. Whenever Dexter grows serious, he begins talking like that. Either put up with it or skip forward to the action.

Now arrive plot complications.

Dexter tells Hooky the doleful story of Oliver G. Weatherby. (That's his picture up there on the wall.)

Oliver enjoyed a charmed life. Germans couldn't lay a sight on him. Through crowds of flying circuses he darted, evading the Fokker, the Albatros, the ravenous Pfalz, and such renowned terrors. In and out of Germany he flicked on secret missions, elusive, evasive, incomparable.

One day he vanished. Later a German plane dropped a note announcing his death. His picture joined the company on the panelled wall.

Rumor had it that he died under the guns of Loving Heart. That was Hooky's pet name for a German ace named Lowenhardt, whose reputation was so sour he might have stepped from a 1917 editorial cartoon. Loving Heart skulks about the sky at the edge of action, a flying jackal who pounce on crippled aircraft, machine-guns downed airmen. He does not expose his precious self to the hazards of air battle. Word is that he is a spy and a transporter of spies.

By that system of wonderfully accurate information customarily available to the hero of an Edgar Wallace story, Hooky learns that Loving Heart is operating close by. Since this is a short story, he immediately goes Lowenhardt hunting, locates the sneak within a few paragraphs, deftly shoots him down.

As he does so, Hooky recognizes the German's face.

For wasn't his picture prominently displayed on the squadron wall? Loving Heart, that slinking coward, used to be Oliver B. Weatherby, a German mole in the Ace High operation.

A better class of German pilot is presented in "The Kurt of Honor" (April 7). Kurt, an honorable German of ancient family, and his mother, are the only decent Germans to appear in the series. All others are monsters, slobbered in the blood of babies, their souls, tiny and black, resembling desiccated raisins.

Kurt learns that his cousin had once kidnapped an American girl, hauling her away to his castle, there to work his will upon her. She escaped but, according to the cousin, was accidentally drowned. That she was engaged to Lane of the Ace High is of no particular surprise to the sophisticated reader, who is hardened against improbability.

With no great effort, Wallace joins all these flopping ends. Kurt shoots down Lane, which is too bad. But Kurt also punishes his cousin's behavior by killing him in a duel. The deaths nicely balance.

"Hooky Who Played With the Germans" (April 20) is another goofy story about flying into Germany and landing and messing around. Hooky does this. Promptly he discovers a double murder in a deserted village. Also a terrified girl locked in a room, a helpful Fokker pilot, and a landscape savage with army renegades. To a man, and woman, the Germans prove treacherous. Hooky barely escapes, downing two Fokkers as he whizzes away.

The moral is clear. But if, for any reason, the message eludes you, Dexter emits many wise saws in the manner of a exploding volcano — Huns are Huns, Germany is peopled by the spawn of Hell, and similar measured assessments of the enemy.

"Hooky Patterson Dies Once" (May 7) restates this idea by introducing that ever-popular character, the fiendish German professor. The story is another affirmation that Germans are inhuman monsters.

We begin with a taste of combat. Although the series is about combat fliers, little air fighting has been described. The stories are mainly intricate plots about this vendetta or that. When air combat does occur, it proceeds like the day dream of a twelve-year old who has just absorbed the works of Robert Hogan. The action is romanticized and inexact, high-hearted, wonderful, glowing bosh.

Up shot the nose of the scout as though to climb. Before it reached a stall, Hooky rammed over the rudder sharp and the head of the machine fell leftward. It was a lightning turn which brought his nose to where his tail had been.

The attacker rolled to avoid the shower of nickel that was coming his way,

"Of the dead speak nothing but good," said Hooky, and threw two quick bursts at the assailant.

The intrepid leader of [the] chasing squadron fell, emitting smoke and flame to advertise his uneasiness.... (Wallace, "Hooky Patterson" 185).

Wrapped in glory, Hooky returns to base. There he discovers another vendetta at full boil. This time it is between pilot Bertram and that German scientific lunatic, Herr Professor Zonnendorph. The Professor, a specialist in poison gas, has invented a new searchlight. This travels on an armored train. Hooky and Bertram fly forth to blast this equipment With sad results. Bertram is shot down. After various adventures and delays, Hooky dives on the searchlight, only to discover that Bertram has been tied to the thing.

Too late. Too late. By then, Hooky's machine gun fire has killed Bertram.

In a few more paragraphs, bombs destroy the train. The mad Professor gets thoroughly machine gunned.

So the evil meet doom. But Hooky feels just terrible about the whole thing.

The final story, "The Man Who Shelled Open Boats" (May 20) flashes back to that incident which set Dexter against the German nation: how Submarine Captain Casselmann shelled those life boats, killing Seyers' mother, driving Mrs. Dexter insane.

Now Dexter has received intelligence reports revealing Casselmann's whereabouts. Dexter plans a trap.

To begin the action, Hooky flies into Germany, lands, and taps a military telephone line leading to the castle where Casselmann struts and smirks. Faked orders draw the vile Captain to an isolated crossroads where Hooky greets him with drawn pistol. Overhead, Seyers and Dexter circle in a two-man bomber. Casselmann is given a choice: Die now. Or attempt to escape across miles of bare fields, pursued by the airplane.

He chooses to escape—and is hunted down with bombs blasting all around him.

At the end, he is not killed. Only left a nerve- shattered wreck, writhing and blubbering in the dirt. The ending is curiously weak. As you know, however, popular magazine heroes are not allowed to murder anyone except in self defense.

At which point the series concludes, all problems unresolved. Likely it was the fault of the Armistice. Had the war continued, there would surely have been additions to the series. As it stands, it is a fragment in six parts.

The series holds together by charm. Wallace brightens his iron-gray subject matter with wisps of humor, like flowers on a metal wall. He seduces you with comic touches. His primary characters are so agreeable that you willing overlook their lack of substance. Not one of them casts a shadow.

The stories, themselves, are imperfectly coordinated improvisations. At their heart lies a complex situation, tangled enough to drive a novel. But these are short stories. They require that a situation be revealed, groups of isolated and hostile characters interact, and an adventure be told. All in a few pages. All mixed with elements of war and propaganda. No wonder Wallace uses coincidence with lavish hand. It could hardly be otherwise.

The overall effect of the series is of a bright heap of fragments— rags and photographs and bits of colored glass and fruit and flowers, all tumbled upon a tightly-wound clockwork that ticks crisply down under it all.

Wallace continued to works better known. The excesses of the First World War were swallowed by the excesses of the Twenties. The Companions of the Ace High, like Tam, dissolved slowly into the past, artifacts of an earlier time when fiction toyed with that dangerous female, Propaganda, and the air war adventure first flapped infant wings.

While 1927 saw the birth of the aviation fiction magazine, you could already find stories of fliers and airplanes in the general magazines — *Argosy, Blue Book, Triple X, Short Stories*—and in such specialized titles as *Black Mask* and *Battle Stories*. A small cadre of writers produced a large library of aviation fiction, among them Nels Leroy Jorgensen, Arch Whitehouse, Joe Archibald, Thomson Burtis, Herman Petersen, George Bruce, and Raoul F. Whitfield.

Early in the 1930s, with the sudden popularity of publications devoted to the adventures of a single character, aviation fiction was prominently represented by the gaudy figures of *G-8 and His Battle Aces, The Lone Eagle* (1933), *Dusty Ayres and His Battle Birds, and Bill Barnes* (1934). Before and after these spun up a swarm of lesser characters, bright as camp fire sparks and often as fleeting.

The Red Eagle, *Battle Birds*
The Three Mosquitoes, *Dare-Devil Aces, Battle Birds*
Bill Dawe, the American Sky Devil, *Dare-Devil Aces*
Smoke Wade, *Air Trails, Battle Birds*
Buzz Benson, *Sky Birds*
Buck Kent, *Air Trails*
T.X. O'Leary, *War Birds, Terence X. O'Leary's War Birds*
Philip Strange, *Flying Aces*
Most of these fascinating figures stand slightly beyond the scope of

this work, which seeks to examine the origins of the 1930s characters, rather than histories of their series. A few might be briefly noted upon to suggest the flavor and variety of this fictional type.

Raoul Whitfield, for example, gave *Black Mask* the hard-fighting Bill Scott and his mechanic; they flew the US/Mexican border country in a frazzled J.H.6, having violent adventures. For *Adventure*, Whitfield devised Captain MacLeod, US Army pilot, who flew initially in the Philippines, in stories strong on character drawing; later MacLeod transferred to *Black Mask*, where he fought air-borne gangsters through the six-part "Border Brand" series.

Or consider Barbe Pivet, heroine of a short series written by Herman Petersen.

Barbe was that unique being, a female lead in a hard-action series. Her adventures began in the October 1927 *Air Stories*, appeared twice, then shifted to *Wings* (April 1928) for seven more appearances, the final story—after an eighteen18month delay—being dated March 1930. Barbe shared the series with Roy Burnett, who wanted to marry her just as soon as he located sunken treasure. The scene was the South Seas and the quest for treasure was severely complicated by pirates, thieves, and moral reprehensibles. In the course of the series, Barbe learned how to fly and became a competent combat pilot, saving Roy's life rather more often than he saved hers (Drew, "A Pulp Heroin" 23-25).

(Herman Petersen [1893-1973] worked, at different times, in the composing room of an Utica, newspaper; as a casual farmer and postmaster in Poolville, New York; and, from the early 1920s, as a writer for the aviation pulps, *Black Mask, Detective Fiction Weekly, Dime Detective, Adventure,* and *Blue Book*, among the more prominent titles. Later he published many mystery, western, and historical novels, stopping writing only after his eyesight began to fail.) (Drew, "Herman Petersen" 17-19).

The Barbe Pivet stories are adventure with airplanes, seasoned with much personal danger, and a few casual air combats, experienced and passed swiftly by like a relative with bad personal hygiene. On the other hand, Robert J. Hogan's series, featuring that flying cowboy, Smoke Wade, was unashamed World War I air war fiction, complete with eccentric hero and plenty of death-dealing Fokkers.

Wade's series began in *Air Trails*, August 1931, soon transferred to *Battle Birds*, and continued briskly through the 1930s.

Lieutenant Wade, born in Arizona, was a drawling, ironic cowboy, complete with six-shooter, steel wire muscles, and a penchant for betting. On occasion, he talks painful western jargon:

*Wade*: "Lead this hoss to a good box stall and watch out she don't kick you." Meaning pull the Spad into a hanger and service it.

His Spad, painted brown and white, you may consider a pinto.

For all this foolishness, he is an astounding marksman and, as usual in these stories, can outfly and outfight skies stiff with German aircraft. In "Wager Flight," his first appearance, he competes with a loud-mouthed flight leader for the honor of blowing up the evil ammunition dump. Having placed heavy bets that he will do so, Wade sails forth, shoots the fool out of those Fokkers, blows up the dump after the flight leader fails, and cleans up wads of francs on his bets.

Hogan's descriptions of combat are faintly more realistic than those of Wallace:

[Wade's] keen gray eyes peered anxiously through the sights. He needed only a glance across those rims. Old practice had coordinated his finger and eye to the highest degree. He hunched low over the stick—waited.

The first Fokker opened fire. Tracers flashed just past his cockpit—close; but not close enough.

Then he had the cockpit of the first Fokker in the ring. His finger flexed for an instant. A burst of a dozen rounds blasted from the muzzles of each gun. He did not have to watch the tracers. He knew where they were going the instant that he pressed. He kicked over and tore down at the next Fokker.

...Again the Spad vibrated slightly from the Vickers recoil and tracers fluffed out once more in that death haze.

Another Fokker wheeled over on one side like a sick pup and began to fall.... (Hogan, "Wager Flight" 96)

These realistic touches—tracers fluffing, practice had coordinated finger and eye, Spad vibrated—are in place because Robert Jasper Hogan, 1897-1963, had received flight training in the United States during 1918. After a severe bout with the Spanish Influenza, and the ending of the war, he became a sales manager for Curtiss-Wright. Laid off at the onset of the Depression, he began writing for the pulp magazines. While specializing in aviation adventure, he also wrote western and sports fiction, such single-character magazine series as *G-8 and His Battle Aces, Wu Fang*, and the *Secret Six*. Later he published many western novels, contributed to the *Saturday Evening Post* and *Collier's*, and saw several of his works become moving picture or television programs. His pulp magazine fiction is characterized by high-tension, rapid-action adventure, filled with gaudy characters, science-fictional devices, improbable events, and a general atmosphere of hurtling down an icy chute from the top of a mountain (Bradd, "Flying Spy of the Pulp").[2]

Hogan's best known air war fiction is from the 1930s, more than a decade after the First World War had rumbled to silence. The intense passions generated by that war had cooled. But they had not guttered out. Their heat fueled innumerable popular fictions which demanded a villain to struggle against, the flint to the hero's steel. It was relatively easy to assign the Germans to this role. The propaganda of 1917 had already done so, denying humanity to the people who had given Goethe, Beethoven, Schopenhauer, Mozart, Wagner, and Schiller to the world, and would presently contribute Einstein, Strauss, and Mann, the Germans having genius for nearly everything but politics.

Most air war writers accepted the convention of the German fiend. Although Wallace's Tam series had, at first, showed the Germans as courtly opponents, few of the later writers adopted this point of view; as we have seen, Wallace, himself, swiftly discarded it, preferring the brighter colors of a propaganda poster. That the enemy was as sensitive, honorable, and worthy of life as a series hero disturbed few writers. That was not the point.

The point was that action fiction required intense conflict, soul-freezing escapes, and a triumphant hero with whom the reader could identify.

And, after all, in these stories, only Fokkers died. Those bright machines, all multiple wings and gaudy paint, got shot apart in vast numbers. It was quite impersonal. Who cares whether a machine dies.

It was a falsification that usually ignored the exceedingly unpleasant ways death came to the pilots of the losing machine. But that, too, was a convention, just as the German butcher was a convention, accepted without thought and used as convenient. The story was the thing. Action was the final criteria. Who listens for the voice screaming from that blazing Fokker?

Of all air war series, the one featuring Terence X. O'Leary stands solitary and alone, a sublime monument to meretriciousness. With engaging grin, it embraces all fictional conventions, parades every cliche exhausted by other writers, and prances joyous through improbability into fantasy, unconstrained by reality's gravity. In its own lunatic way, the series is wonderful.

When last noted, O'Leary was appearing in *Battle Stories* (Fawcett Publications) and *War Stories* (Dell Publications), two magazines in the sear and yellow leaf. However, Dell's *War Birds* still maintained a monthly schedule. So it is notsurprising that T.X. O'Leary, of medal fame, would bloom bloom forth, unexpectedly, as the Sky Hawk, a fighting aviator.

*War Birds* advertised itself as "The Oldest Air War Magazine." Its first issue was dated March 1928 and, with one aberrant excursion, continued to

October 1937—although, for an extended period in the first half of 1936, the magazine did not appear. Henry Steeger was editor for a short period before he formed Popular Publications. In mid- 1933, as O'Leary joined up, *War Birds* was a 10 cent publication of 96 pages. (It would increase to 128 pages almost at once.) It contained five or six short stories, a novelette, a true fact article, and a scattering of single page features.

Covers were painted by illuminaries such as George Rozen, Sidney Riesenberg, Rudolph Belarski, and Eugene Frandzen. Belarski specialized in groups of colorful aircraft whirling at each other; Frandzen tended to limit his canvas to oddly-shaped airplanes, decorated by weirdly painted designs.

Many of the writers filling the pages of *War Birds* would later revel through the magazines of Popular Publications: Arthur J. Burks, Robert J. Hogan, Robert Sydney Bowen, William E. Barrett, Frederick C. Painton. Lester Dent also published a few stories in the magazine. And Empey, of course. Lots of Empey in *War Birds*.

The last time we saw O'Leary was in "Tank Busters" (*Battle Stories*, 1933). Six months lapsed between that story and O'Leary's maiden appearance in *War Birds*. In that time, his personal history grew a new set of facts. It happened whenever Empey changed magazines. O'Leary's biography got reworked as the tide reworks the beach.

This time, we learn that O'Leary had not only served four hitches in the US Cavalry but had been in the Foreign Legion and in both the Escadrille and Royal "Flyin' Corpse." His prior activities in Battle Stories and War Stories are not mentioned. Oversight, probably. His recent exploits have earned his recommendation for a third Congressional Medal of Honor, so some things remain unchanged.

Observe our hero, of medal fame, transferred to the Black Wings Pursuit Squadron, sometimes identified as the 411th, sometimes as the 417th. Whatever the number, it is one of those weird organizations common to pulp war fiction. All men in the squadron are civil and military outlaws; every one has a long prison sentence hanging over his head, unless he fights fiercely. Men don't get relieved from the 411th (or maybe the 417th); they get buried from it. Captain Wilkey is in charge.

Enter Terence. X. O'Leary, with his bosom pal, Mike Rafferty: "O'Leary, Sky Hawk," July 1933.

As in *Battle Stories* and *War Stories*, the O'Leary adventures came in clusters. Each was focused by a single villain who menaced and scowled and strutted and got the reader all worked up.

In the first story group, he was named Baron von Stilzer, the Green Falcon. Flying a Fokker all decorated with green falcons, he headed the Green Circus. In the great Empey tradition, von Stilzer was pure stereotype—the lean, mean German stereotype. He lasted four issues.

Action blazes up at once. Baron von Stilzer attacks, and they organize a bombing raid on the Green Circus' base. Spies jam Terence's guns. Skillfully he dodges the Falcon, lands at the German base, escapes with a captured US pilot and the Green Falcon, himself.

For the most of the series, you will be hammered flat with wonderful escapes from German air bases. And with spies. O'Leary moves through a haze of spies; they fester and plot, whisper significantly, hone their plans to murder.

Every time, their dirty work fails. Before they know it, O'Leary lands at the German air base, disguised as someone else, creaming their plans and spreading confusion.

Have you already noticed that he now spells his name "Terence" rather than "Terrence"? All part of the new, trim O'Leary.

In "O'Leary Flies A Ghost" (August 1933), he is surprised by spies at his base and kidnapped to Germany. The spies have also rescued the Green Falcon, who accompanies them, sneering "schwein" und "sauerkraut" und gesmacking peoples in der faces till you vunder vhy they him bothered to gerescue.

Once in Kaiserland, helpless among human demons, O'Leary meets a distinguished representative of the German Secret Service. This rare gentleman is Captain Karl von Essen, astute, honorable, and a magnificant example of European culture. For a few stories he's like that. Then Empey, whose grip on character was none too stable, forgets that von Essen was a distinguished, honorable, cultured gentleman, and changes him to another arrogant Prussian blood-drinker. But more of this later.

Von Essen, by one of those coincidences that makes this series so refreshing, looks exactly like Terence X. O'Leary, except for the red hair. Astounding, isn't it? Even more astounding when you consider that in "O'Leary, Secret Service" (*War Stories*, June 1932), another German spy looked exactly like O'Leary, who pretended to be the spy at German Headquarters, and was able to smash all their plans, and....

Well, anyway, in "O'Leary Flies a Ghost," O'Leary manages to capture von Essen. (This is after the Green Falcon murders Mike Rafferty in a scene that achieves heights of inadvertent comedy.) Stealing a two-seater, O'Leary flies to Allied territory. Then, because von Essen is such a grand fellow, our hero permits the German to fly the airplane back to his airdrome.

Returning to the Black Wings base, O'Leary promptly slaughters one spy, captures two others. While he is being celebrated as a hero, he learns that von Essen was shot down over Allied lines. But he has been captured alive.

Our dazzling hero returns in the November 1933, "O'Leary, Falconeer." In this he is condemned to death for shooting his

Commanding Officer and murdering a Black Wings ace. (It's all a trick to fuddle the Boche.)

The ace was a spy, and the whole affair is a clever plot of Thomas Richards, US Intelligence. The idea is to have O'Leary pretend to be dead so that he can impersonate von Essen and trick the Commandant of St. Pierre into giving information on German troop concentrations.

*Richards*: "O'Leary, you are daring to the point of foolhardiness, but withal possess a brilliant brain."
*O'Leary*: "Brilliant is a weak adjictive, sir."
*Richards*: "Besides, you are intensely patriotic."
*O'Leary*: "George Washin'ton had nothin' on me, sir. I admit he beat me to the crossin' o' the Delaware, but this is another war."
*Richards*: "Would you give your life for your country, *O'Leary?*"
*O'Leary*: "I'm thinkin' I'd be a damn sight more valuable alive."
(Richards explains the plot to the incredulous O'Leary, finally persuading him, after much difficulty.)

Richards: "You are a true patriot."
O'Leary: "Me only regrit is that I ain't a cat, sir. Shure, if I was, I'd give eight o' me lives to me country an' keep one fer me personal use." (Empey, "O'Leary, Falconeer" 9)

The scene is set for the usual frenzied action. As follows:
—The German Secret Service learns that O'Leary is masquerading as von Essen. They set a trap. He is to be murdered by Apaches.
—He is not murdered by Apaches.
—The Green Falcon shoots down his plane—but only because O'Leary was planning on landing in Germany anyway.
—Suspecting that O'Leary is not von Essen, the Falcon sets a trap.
—But O'Leary escapes by luring Germans into a cellar and conking them on the head as they enter, one at a time, just as in a Three Stooges feature.
—O'Leary gets the troop information and escapes in a Fokker. After him rages the Green Falcon amd a skyfull of Fokkers.
—Cleverly faking a crash and his own death, O'Leary throws off pursuit and escapes to Allied lines.
—He is shot by his own infantry but not permanently.
—As a result, the German attack is crushed.

All this in eighteen pages, a "complete novelette," novelettes being shorter in those days. Throughout the novelette, O'Leary addresses Mike, invokes Mike, celebrates Mike, just as if Mike weren't dead since the last issue.

Tough sleddin', Mike, but we got to deliver for Uncle Sam.
If that don't fool 'em, I'm a cockeyed Swede. Thanks Mike.
I could bump 'em both off, Mike.

The dialogue is continuous, if one-sided. Presently it will become less so, when the phantom of Mike, flying a vaporous airplane, will appear to warn O'Leary of danger. It's his mystic Irish blood, no doubt. You just have to put up with such wonders.

The saga of the Green Falcon concludes with "Suicide Wings" (December 1933). That arrogant martinet, Captain Thurston Galloway Grantland, is placed in temporary command of the Black Wings. Immediately O'Leary is jailed for insubordination.

Not that he stays in the clink, or even goes there. Instead he picks up Lulu Belle and leaves for a fight with the Green Falcon. Lulu Belle is not a bar maid but the generic name for all O'Leary's Spads. He goes through Spads in amazing quantities, crash landing them behind the lines, getting them shot to fragments when he dog-fights 2000 Fokkers, having them destroyed by spy traps.... Rarely does he keep the same Spad through one story.

All Spads, by the way, are decorated with the picture of a large flying hawk. This carries the Kaiser in its beak; the Kaiser is wearing a diaper.

To return to our thrilling narrative....

Up flies O'Leary, straight into one of those sensational dog-fights which punctuate these pages. Like the aerial combat in the pages of Edgar Wallace, that described by Empey is about as realistic as glass hair. But it certainly is exciting:

Forward went the stick. Like a meteor, down dived the Spad, a gray wraith on destruction bent.... Into his gun sights flashed the Fokker. Simultaneously (O'Leary) tripped his black-barreled Vickers. Two bursts of fire....

It all took but a fleeting space. Upward and backward he glanced. A Fokker diving on his tail. Zooming, he half-looped into an Immelmann and reversed the situation, but not before the diving Fokker had cut loose its guns. The withering death-blast had riddled his fuselage, but miraculously he escaped. A darting shadow in his ring-sights. His Vickers pounded. Up he zoomed.

A look below. He had made his kill. Out of control, the pilot's limp form hanging over a side of the cockpit, the Fokker was crashing. The odds now were four to one....

Like the crack of doom a menacing shadow whizzed over him, vomiting steel. A wire snapped and a jagged line of holes shot along the fabric of his left wing. His shoulder burned like fire. Blood ran down his wrist and dripped from his fingers. Gritting teeth, he dived just in time to escape another whizzing shadow lusting for his life. Strangely his goggles had misted over.

An abrupt turn. Up again. Dimly a Fokker in front of him. He tripped his guns. Tac-tac-tac! Missed!....

Two of the green hornets winging at him. He threw his ship into a series of twists, turns, rolls and dives that would have put to shame a Fourth of July devil- chaser. Cracking steel lashed the air.

Too eager to destroy the famous Yank ace, a Fokker over-reached itself in a dive and paid the penalty. Fore and aft O'Leary raked it with his guns. Like a wounded duck it shot down, wing over wing, slipped into a flat spin and cracked up in a burst of smoke and flame. (Empey, "O'Leary, Falconeer" 55-56)

In every fight, O'Leary manages to shoot down quantities of Germans. And why haven't you heard of him, instead of that amateur, Rickerbacker? Because O'Leary doesn't bother to file reports on his kills, of course.

To continue. Finally shot down, O'Leary battles the German infantry on the ground, is rescued when his tough CO, Captain Grantland, lands in No Man's Land and fetches him out. The CO then throws O'Leary back in jail.

But soon, Grantland, himself, has crashed in the German mountains. To save him, O'Leary must land a two-seater in a rock-strewn canyon, in the middle of a lightning storm, under a swarm of Fokkers.

They swarm too close. Using the two-seater's flexible guns, O'Leary shoots down two of them, including the Green Falcon. Who lives to battle O'Leary hand to hand at the lip of a cliff. The Green Falcon loses. O'Leary takes off from the canyon, returning safely to base with Grantland. The CO has a change of personality and becomes a new man. And so to a merry ending.

If the Green Falcon was terrible evil, his brother, Baron Heinrich von Stilzer, the Black Eagle, is even worse. O'Leary threatens to paint him green — and does so after some extraordinary adventures in and out of Germany.

This story, "O'Leary Paints the Eagle" (January 1934), introduces Rags, a starveling, flea-bitten mutt whose ominous howls prompted O'Leary to carry the beast off to Germany with him. And why, you ask, your handsome face distorted by scarcely suppressed anger, does O'Leary carry a dog—particularly a dog that can't keep its mouth shut—on a secret mission to a German airfield?

The reason, dear friend, is that there is no coherent reason. We must assume that Empey was improvising the story as he hunched over the typewriter and happened to think that a dog would be appealing.

What happens to the Black Eagle is never disclosed. O'Leary smacks him in the jaw and leaves him in the dirt, all green and sticky. Who needs him? The next story, "Ghost of the Black Wings" (March 1934) features another German menace even more ferocious than the von Stilzer brothers.

Count Joseph von Krassner, the Black Roc, is straight out of the silent movies, a cliche crossed with a stereotype, a cartoon of the mean German:

Advanced a tall, gaunt man with slow, catlike tread. Dressed in black, a cape of the same color thrown over his stooping shoulders, he stopped a few feet from the cockpit. On his sunken chest was embroidered a white skull and crossbones. From a pinched, cadaverous face, devoid of all hair, including eyebrows and eyelids [sic], stared unblinking eyes, sure sign of the killer. His long nose was hooked like the beak of an eagle and his bloodless mouth was thin-lipped and cruel. (Empey, "Ghost of the Black Wings" 23)

This horror announces himself as "the All Powerful, Emperor of the Skies." He is:

...Germany's most noted war scientist.... This inhuman monster—mad as a hatter—is responsible for poison gas, liquid fire and the rest of the hellish inventions. To him destroying enemy morale is the most potent factor in the winning of a war. (24)

Most of the "hellish inventions" are never explained. The one in the story is a terror that drops from the night sky without warning. Suddenly an enormous explosion tears apart the darkness. Immense destruction. Horrible loss of life. The cause unknown.

Fortunately O'Leary is around to defend the Allied war effort. Or rather, O'Leary would be around if he hadn't left the airfield. He's gone off to teach manners to an ace from another squadron — Peter Maher McGuffy. McGuffy has announced that he is the light-heavyweight champ of the air service. O'Leary disputes that — and is off to smack McGuffy flat.

So enters a character who remains with the series to its final paragraph. He is introduced as a neat fellow of the same size and build as O'Leary, with the same number of victories (thirty-two) and the Congressional Medal of Honor.

He and O'Leary snarl and fight, and sass each other, and later save each other's life, get drunk together, trick each other, all in the classic format laid down by *What Price Glory*? As you have already guessed, the pair of them get sent on a suicide mission to the Black Circus' aerodrome.

They are impersonating a pair of Austrian fliers who were captured before reaching their new assignment, the Black Circus. No one knows them but one fellow (added for suspense). And how is Count von Krassen to know who they are?

By a simple test. One of them can see pretty well in the dark.

And would you believe it, O'Leary has eyes like a cat. He can look down from the cockpit on a dead black night and see the trenches and guns and flowers, just as if it were day. It's a marvelous gift.

And so a new feature is added to the series. O'Leary's fabulous eyes bring victory during dozens of night combats in the next stories. Now, however, this unique ability merely confirms his identity as the remarkable Austrian.

After strenuous adventures at the Black Circus aerodrome, O'Leary and McGuffy end up in The Black Chamber, where men are driven mad, mad, mad, by darkness and lack of cognac. When they get out, a spy threatens to reveal O'Leary's true identity. So they kidnap von Krassen, steal a bomber, and attack a large black shed in which the secret weapon is concealed.

During the attack, the Roc is decapitated by machine gun fire which serves him right. The shed is blown up and the heroes escape.

After all these years, it may be revealed that the mystery weapon was an airplane full of explosives, operated by an automatic timer. At a preset time, the engine would shut off and the plane plunged like a V-1, blasting whatever was below. Between the effect and the explanation of how it was done is a distressing credibility gap. But that's how things are in this naughty world. If you're going to read literature about O'Leary and G-8, and such wonders, you have to get used to a sense of vague disappointment.

The next several stories are of the same antic frivolity. For reasons best known to himself, Empey now proceeds to change the scene. He does so thoroughly. The fury of the Black Circus and its terrible secret weapon is turned full on the Black Wings. With conclusive results.

The Squadron is destroyed. Except for Captain Wilkey, everyone is killed. Even Rags. Even Peter Maher McGuffy. (Empey will relent later.) All lie buried on the shattered site of the air field, done to death by the vile Huns. And O'Leary is soon to join them. As "O'Leary, Zeppelin Killer" (July 1934) opens, a grim plot unfolds. The Baron von Goelke, another upstanding, honorable German, has been blackmailed to crash his airplane into O'Leary's.

He does so.

The famous O'Leary, Sky Hawk, is dead.

Or so the Secret Service wishes it to be believed.

Planning to transfer O'Leary to the Secret Service, they take advantage of the murder attempt to change our hero's name to Patrick J. O'Hara and send him to London. There he will fight the Zeppelin menace.

Agent Zero-13 he is known as, a raw flying recruit by day and by night, "The Savior of London." That modest little title he thinks up all by himself.

Complications arrive at staggering speed. A reluctant German spy, Rita Wellington, is engaged to Lt. Aldrich. O'Leary/O'Hara is Aldrich's orderly. Rita is really Hudla von Goelke, sister of the Baron who is believed to have killed the Sky Hawk.

You got all this? There is more.

She feels that the Baron is a murderer. She wishes to break away from the German spy system. Yet she cannot. At the same time, Aldrich is trying to cure himself of cowardice. He isn't really a coward: he just can't stand loud noises, like shells going off and the corks coming out of champagne bottles.

While Aldrich and Rita/Hulda are attempting to straighten themselves out, the British are attempting to develop a disintegrating ray. They have outfitted O'Leary's Spad with two ray projectors and he hurtles forth, slaying fleets of Zeppelins and Gotha bombers.

Good God! He has just zapped a Zeppelin in which his good old pal, Reardon, is flying on an undercover mission. The Zeppelin is breaking up. The ray has paralyzed all within it. To save Reardon, O'Leary leaps into space, clutches the Zeppelin, tears his way inside, saves Reardon, and lands the Zeppelin.

He is then given the job of killing Rita, now discovered to be a spy. Instead, O'Leary takes it upon himself to fly her to Germany, where she will be protected by the anti- Kaiser party. This is because he realizes that she has sincerely reformed and it will tear up the Lieutenant if she dies. (The Lieutenant has discovered his courage, by the way, helped by an O'Leary trick.)

So all things come out wonderfully, and the ground work is in place for innumerable future complications.

The next half dozen issues include a pair of two-part serials and two short stories. Or that's one way of looking at them. Another way is to consider them parts of an episodic novel. Just where the novel begins is anybody's guess, since characters from one section wander over into the next, characters that once were dead live again, and confusion reigns.

In this morass we must grab for any solid point. Let's begin with O'Leary. He enjoyed many personalities since 1926. Now, in 1934, he is transformed to an Irish-flavored pulp magazine hero, along familiar lines and specifications:

Built like a panther and a full six feet high, a mop of tousled red hair topped a goodnatured, clean cut Irish face which was lighted by a habitual smile. Piercing steel-blue eyes, which when occasion demanded became hard as flint, added to the general picture. (Empey, "O'Leary the Devil's Darling" 16)

"O'Leary, the Devil's Darling" appears in two parts (September and October 1934). In brief, during the first part, O'Leary battles fiercely on ground and in the sky, but around him grows the deadly suspicion that he is a spy and traitor. Forged documents from Hulda von Goelke are discovered. He is arrested and sentenced to be shot. There is no escape.

During the second part, he escapes and clears his name. Repeatedly, ghosts of the Black Wings squadron appear to warn him of impending death. Repeatedly, blind luck comes to his rescue at the last possible second.

It keeps O'Leary stirred up, the reader emotionally exhausted, and enrages Baron Kofrank von Stoeffen who commands German espionage in London. From this point on, the Baron behaves like a madman out of G-8, sinister murder weapons whirling around him, a continuous slaughter of Allied troops and commanders roaring behind the paragraphs.

The Scarlet Death is the grisly weapon the Germans intend to use to slaughter all who live in Allied territories. The dread tale is told in "O'Leary Cracks the Crimson Legion" (two parts, November and December 1934).

(More exactly, the November-December parts cover the menace of the Scarlet Death. Later issues continue the story of how the Crimson Legion finally got obliterated. As mentioned earlier, these stories are so roped together that they'd float in a hurricane.)

The Scarlet Death is a vicious poison that can be concealed in fountain pens and cigars and whatnot. One touch destroys you. It destroys poor old Captain Wilkey, who endured so much.

O'Leary swears vengence. By accident, he gets hold of a fountain pen full of Scarlet Death. It is pure Irish luck.

Soon O'Leary falls into the power of Hauptman Karl von Essen, changed from a European gentleman to a ravening Prussian monster. This fiend plans to beat in O'Leary's brains with an iron bar, sink the corpse in deep water, then take O'Leary's identity and penetrate the US Air Force, learning every secret. But before the foundation of the Free World is shattered, von Essen accidentally uses the poisoned fountain pen and dies horribly.

Thereafter O'Leary escapes. Zeppelins are about to dump the Scarlet Death all over London. Instead, they meet O'Leary, howling mad. He shoots down one, crashes into another, and later is rescued from the Channel.

"O'Leary, the Devil's Undertaker" (January 1935) continues the story and the vendetta. In this adventure, O'Leary is considerably helped by Peter McGuffy, not dead after all, but alive, and violent, and swilling cognac by the bottle. O'Leary is now pretending to be von Essen and swaggers around German Headquarters, simply sopping up vital military information. But danger threatens. Hulda is the prisoner of the Great Master, another classy title for Fofrank von Stoeffen. She is tricked into identifying O'Leary as O'Leary, although she really believes him to be von Essen. That causes all manner of violence before O'Leary flies off to England with Hulda, carrying along von Stoeffen as prisoner. Then he returns to Germany to take the Great Master's place and destroy the threat of the Crimson Legion for good.

We have now come to one of those famous pulp magazine transformations which rose, without warning, like a whale in the bath tub. Equally without warning, the next issue of *War Birds*, March 1935, is *War Birds* no longer but *Terence X. O'Leary's War Birds*. Nor is the scene World War I. We have leaped ahead in time to about 1935. Captain O'Leary and Captain McGuffy are pilots in the US Air Force. And around them is about to explode a science-fiction menace that compares favorably with a lunatic's dream.

The fictional combination of aviation and science-fiction had begun, as so much else, in the 1890s dime novels, when airplanes themselves were no more than fantasy. *All Story* in the Teens and *Argosy All-Story Weekly* in the 1920s offered stories of very large flying machines full of very strange weapons that were used to seek gold, subjugate nations, or disguise murders. But it remained for *G-8 and His Battle Aces*, first issued dated October 1933, to fuse the World War I flying story and the Amazing Scientific Weapon in the Hands of German Monsters. This was science-fiction of a type—or at least fantasy fiction, since some minuscule morsel of science must be present to make it science-fiction. We have already seen that O'Leary was toying with disintegrator rays mounted on a Spad, while he was saving London from the Zeppelins. That was in mid-1934. Around the same time, the magazine *Dusty Ayres and his Battle Birds* appeared, replacing the older *Battle Birds* title and recounting the story of a war only slightly in the future.

Much the same thing happened with the O'Leary title. *War Birds*, a magazine with a good solid second class permit for mailing, more to be valued than gold, was converted to a future war epic. *Dusty Ayres* lasted twelve issues and was a respectable, hard action, sequential series. *O'Leary's War Birds* lasted three issues, and it too offered sequential hard action on every page. Unfortunately it also offered some of the worse prose in all the hero pulps. The prose must be experienced to be appreciated. Only the Gernsback publications came close to the purple ravings that Empey served forth to his fond readership:

A scowl of rage distorted [the villain's] repulsive features. Snarling like a beast he brought down his whip on the back of the navigator....

"You insolent dog," screamed the fiend. "How dare you defy my command...."

"You dirty murdering skunk," [the American] shouted. "Make us kill Americans will you? Look at me! Look at an American who has come into his own. Take that!"

Like a flash [the fiend] leaped back, side-stepped and drew a dagger from his red-feathered skirt.

Mouthing a demoniacal death-cry he sprang forward and stabbed with all the strength of his powerful arm.

The steel blade sank to its hilt into the jugular vein of the unsuspecting American. Down crumpled the victim of the thrust in a welter of blood.

The fiend threw himself on the dying man and stabbed and stabbed and stabbed, the while growling and snarling and cursing. (Empey, "O'Leary, Dyno-Blaster" 15)

All this in the language used by Keats, Thoreau, and Edgar Rice Burroughs.

The central idea of the series is that the remarkable scientist, Unuk, High Priest to the God of the Depths, has been alive for five hundred years and utterly crazy for most of these. He and his brilliant Under Priest, Alok, have taken over the island of Lataki in the Pacific. By chemical mind control, they dominate the brains of captured scientists, forcing them to construct an impressive collection of flying air fortresses, flying belts, death rays, beam weapons, magnetic projectors, force fields, ever- full beer steins, and similar apparatus, much of it leased from the Buck Rogers comic strip.

Unuk's purpose is nothing less than destruction of the United States, obliteration of England, then world domination, as as good a reason as any to launch a series.

Thus the premise of "O'Leary Fights the Golden Ray," *Terence X. O'Leary's War Birds*, March 1935.

Fortunately for humanity, the loyal activists of Latakia oppose this plot. They have never been able to convince the United States goverment that it is about to be crushed by science. However, the activists kidnap O'Leary and McGuffey to the island. There our heroes learn the truth.

Eventually O'Leary steals Unuk's giant air ship and flings away to save the United States from being pulverized by advanced missiles. The country is saved. Sort of.

General: "...Thousands of people killed and maimed. The Chicago debacle! The five battle-cruisers blasted into atoms. A large section of Washington destroyed! The Panama Canal practically wrecked! Minneapolis and St. Paul! El Paso!

Seattle! The Statue of Liberty demolished! And latest of all, more than half of Cincinnati laid waste by fire!" (Empey, "O'Leary Dyno-Blaster" 15)

These merry delights continue through the following novel, "O'Leary, Dyno-Blaster or Adventure of the Ageless Men" (April 1935).

The skies over the United States swarms with death-ray ships, destroying, searing, obliterating. Therefore O'Leary and McGuffey attack. Are shot down. Capture another vehicle. Are presumed destroyed. Plunge roaring from nowhere to smite the ungodly. Are nearly lost. Are saved.

This is no novel for those with high blood pressure or weak hearts. The action rages fantastically, O'Leary and McGuffey lost and mourned a dozen times and returned as often.

Finally Unuk is killed by a freak accident with a magnetic beam. Alok dies because O'Leary shot the fool out of him. And the fortress is blown to little small tiny bits.

Since the evil pair have died, the series must stagger along without them. In the next novel, "The Purple Warriors of Neptunia" (June 1935), even more appalling horrors confront O'Leary. Unuk and Alok to begin with. They are resurrected by Umgoop the Horrible, High Priest of the submerged kingdom of Neptunia.

Seems that Umgoop—what kind of a mind do you suppose thought up a villain named Umgoop?—has teamed up with the sinister High Priestess, Satania. Together they intend to:

1) destroy America

2) obliterate Ireland

3) conquer the world

To aid in this great project, they first use their advanced scientific knowledge to "reconstruct" the two dead crazies from the previous novels. Then off, around, over, under, bang, bang, bang. And bang. Both O'Leary and McGuffy get killed and both get reconstructed and the four wicked horrors get theirs, after about 32,000,000 killings.

If you judge the excellence of a novel by the number of casualties and destruction described, this is a great novel. Otherwise it is a terrible novel. But Lord have mercy, does it have narrative drive. (Madle, *Terence X* 5-8)[3]

With this issue, *Terence X. O'Leary's War Birds* comes to a sudden end, as if a Dyno-Blaster beam had played upon it. From the ruins, *War Birds* immediately rose, again alive, chastened and purified. As did O'Leary, abruptly returned to World War I, once more in full cry against the Crimson Legion and Ulrich von Bohne, The Red Destroyer.... October 1935, "The Sky Hawk Screams." It would be the final O'Leary in *War Birds*.

For all its weaknesses, the series had enjoyed a long run. O'Leary begins as an Irish goof; ends as a typical series hero. He never rose above stereotype, a fighting, bragging, swilling wonder who could be depended upon the blunder through to success, every time. He is delightful. He is amusing. He makes us laugh and admire; there is no need for belief. He is another in that long chain of Irishmen who laughed and fought through the pulps, vivid cartoons, all. Cartoons with vitality.

"Ah!" cries O'Leary, lifting the cognac bottle. "Never let it be said an O'Leary let dooty interfere with his drinking."

He got pretty much away from the bottle by the end of the series, even as the series got away from that troublesome subject, sex. (Virtually the only sensuous minx in the series is also a dead one.) O'Leary, however, is above sex as he is above death. He is a series hero, joyous and competent. Mankind's universal troubles are not his. If reality threatens, ever for an instant, he need only hurl the Spad into a twisting ascending "S" and trip the black machine guns, hosing a stream of bitter fire across the Fokker's fuselage.

However improbable, O'Leary's world attempts to impose fiction's order upon the remembered craziness of the Western Front. The Irishman, himself, part cartoon, part folk legend, reaffirms that the individual, so important to himself, is also important to the surrounding world. He influences that world in immediate and countable ways. Whether in the fiction of Talbot Mundy, Edgar Wallace, or the rude scribblings of Arthur Guy Empey, the individual, by force and personal worth, can alter the resistant stuff of the world. That is the most cherished convention in adventure fiction.

That convention carries a subordinate text, soon to be written large in the single-character magazines of the 1930s: The exceptional individual must face overwhelming hazards essentially alone. While aided by friends, he performs his feats as an individual. He alone accomplishes. He alone excels. No other individual is capable of standing alone before chaos and beating it to order.

This is not particularly realistic. Still, to the endangered reader of the Depression, surrounded by immense, inchoate forces, that iteration of personal worth might have offered temporary assurance. There might, after all, be a pathway through chaos.

The single-character pulp magazines of the 1930s offered many such pathways. To these magazines let us now turn, if briefly. While the subject bulks too large for a single chapter, we can glance across the next twenty years or so, meeting a few of the dominant characters, watching the single-character magazines rise gloriously, new redwoods in the forest of popular fiction.

# Chapter Ten
# The Children of Light

Once in Pittsburgh, you walked two blocks from Kaufman's Department Store, turned left and walked another block toward the Monongahela River. In 1940, failed businesses lined the street, their windows blank with dust or cancelled by boards nailed frame to frame. Broken glass glinted on the sidewalk.

In store windows along this street, handmade signs, curiously spelled, offered "Soup, Chop, Two Veg 20 cents," or second-hand clothing, or a dime haircut. Against brick walls, soiled by Pittsburgh air, hunched unshaven men in someone else's suit coat and ancient trousers. The men smoked in a kind of vacant confusion, their smeared eyes regarding the sidewalk as if to puzzle out its secret language.

Half way down the block, a doorway led into a small square room, smelling of cigarette smoke and a more somber odor, rancid and dark. At the back of the room, the wall was pierced by a door and a window through which you saw the cluttered cell in which the proprietor slept, cooked, and conducted whatever business came to him.

For this grimed place was a business. All around you piled second-hand pulp magazines, stacked and separated by title. On the tables filling the center of the room spread westerns and detective stories, *Argosy* in all conditions, *Short Stories*, love stories, adventure stories. In creating this swarm of used titles, monstrous printing presses in New York City and Chicago had gobbled immensities of paper and here the end product piled at last, read and discarded, offered for resale, five cents each—or two for a nickel, was the cover lacking.

On a low shelf along the left wall, other magazines waited in trued stacks, their spines giddy with promise. It was for these, the single-character magazines that you had traveled so far.

*G-8 and His Battle Aces*. The scarlet spined Spider, terror and death on every page. Three separate stacks of *Doc Savage*, orange spines spattered with white lettering. *The Phantom Detective, Bill Barnes, Operator 5*. A few *Pete Rice*, in which you had no interest. Fewer *Whisperers*, much battered. And The *Shadow Magazine*, a hundred more *Shadows*, including issues unbelievably old, rising towers of them showing the white spines of 1934 and earlier, the black spines of 1935, and the alternating blue and red of later years.

Here, in this unclean place, heaped magazines you had never expected to see, in quantities passing belief. Here piled novels with titles long praised in the magazine's letter column, till now unavailable as the sky: "Charg, Monster"—"Mox"—"Six Men of Evil"—"The Black Hush"—"The Grove of Doom."

Most used magazine stores rarely offered issues more than two years old. Only here, only in Pittsburgh, had you seen truly old magazines, legends of the remote past. Only here could you touch these fabulous creatures. You lift one from its pile. Grains of Pittsburgh soot scatter the cover illustration—The ominous figure of The Shadow caught in a flashlight beam as he picks the lock of a golden barred gate: "The Chain of Death."

Choice stuns you. So much is here. It is a library of the single-character pulp magazines that burst forth in 1931 and continued, issue on issue, an unending stream of delight, to this very day in 1940, so that *Shadow, Doc Savage, G-8, Spider, Phantom* could still be bought on news stands elsewhere in the city.

So much, here. So much. For twenty dollars, you could have bought and carried away every single-character magazine on the shelves. But twenty dollars! That unbelievable sum is money beyond understanding. Your infrequent coins are more copper than silver.

By the dimness of the front windows, cloaked in dirt, you select what you can afford. It is bitter labor. Each magazine discarded leaves a trickling wound. You yearn for them all, a hard, positive desire, more intense than hunger. But you select "The Seven Drops of Blood," "The Salamanders," "The Green Box," "The Chinese Discs," and finger the coins one by one into the patient hand of the business man, who is small and wide and smokes roll-your-owns, tilting his head to one side, so that the blue fumes slide past his narrowed eyes.

He wraps your four magazines in white paper and ties the package with string. You step into the hard light of the street, your body ringing with the tension of choice, already aching for what you could not afford.

Your mind leaps toward the future. Next year, when the family comes back to Pittsburgh.... Next year....

Next year, it is gone.

The shop remains, dirty windows and narrow doorway unchanged. But incredibly altered. Now used clothing piles the tables. "Any Dress 40 cts." "Mans Shoes." The air smells of unwashed cloth. No trace remains of the magazines, that rich ore which excited your mind for an entire year. Unendurable loss wrenches you. The stacks of Shadows erased completely. Vanished. Gone as utterly as the hour you stood, irresolute, before riches, slowly selecting four Shadows from those daunting stacks, feeling yourself tremble with exultation and regret.

The single-character magazine was a phenomena of the early 1930s. Other magazines offered fiction of mixed length, and one or more series characters, all published under such a general title as *Adventure, Dime Detective, Wild West Weekly*. The single-character magazine, however, devoted itself to the hero of its title and offered a monthly novel of his breathless adventures—or, in the case of *The Shadow*, a novel every two weeks. Nearly always, the novel was accompanied by a few short stories. These often featured additional series characters, some of whom conducted long careers in the back pages of another character's book. One or two departments, perhaps a club organized around the central character, rounded off the publication.

Since the time of the dime novel, no magazine had devoted the bulk of its pages to one continuing character. In truth, the single-character pulp was a contemporary dime novel, updated and expanded, containing more pages and innumerable illustrations. Like the dime novel, the pulp scintillated with dangers, fights, chases, hooded villains, death traps, luminous melodrama, and the miraculous exploits of the lead character, himself, around whom the fury of the narrative spun, as a hurricane whirls around its eye.

*The Shadow, A Detective Magazine*, was the first of the breed. Dated April-June 1931, the magazine began as a quarterly, proved hotly popular, soon became a monthly. So strong were sales that, as *The Shadow Magazine*, it shifted to twice-a-month publication, beginning with the October 15, 1932, issue.[1]

Thereafter the Heavens split wide.

Publishers, scenting a new trend, introduced six new single-character magazines in 1933 and five the following year. The competition between these specialized monthlies quickly saturated the market. For the next several years, other character magazines ventured forth, faces shining, hopes high, but with the life spans of a mayfly.

The Shadow, himself, that consummate figure, dominated the field. Through the lumbering prose (signed Maxwell Grant) glided a barely seen figure wrapped in black, laughing with cold menace, flaying gangsters with a pair of .45 caliber automatics. A gun-fighter, a brilliant detective, a master of disguise, armored by an invisible net of agents, The Shadow was incomparable.

You did not know then—how could you know, so young to history—that this extraordinary figure, novel beyond calculation, united disparate literary lines and visual images. His chilling laugh derived from a radio announcer's inspiration to characterize The Shadow, that weird voice of fate of Street & Smith's Detective Story radio program. It was an inspiration well crusted by age. Mysterious figures, laughing hollowly, had radiated menace since the gothic novels of 1795. As had mystery figures—creepy beings in cloak and slouch hat gliding, half seen, among the shadows, their eyes fiery points blazing beneath the black brim.[2]

Gothic novels, dime novels, mystery novels, pulp magazines, moving pictures, and stage productions all knew this figure well. The mystery figure was worn threadbare when Walter Gibson adopted it to flesh out that sinister radio voice.[3]

Swiftly The Shadow became more than a visual cliche. Each issue he displayed new abilities. He was fighter, magician, speaker of Chinese, justice figure, the hope of the police and despair of the underworld, reader of codes, inhabitant of a bizarre sanctum, who wore a Romanoff fire opal beneath his black glove, on occasion carried four to six .45 automatics. He was an escape expert, a ju jitsu master, sympathetic to those in distress, possessing searing intelligence and a prodigiously rapid mind. He was also a millionaire, and the world's foremost wall-climbing safe- cracker. He was aided—only that—by numerous idiosyncratic agents.

Through pages of astonished adulation The Shadow firmed. He made decisions. He forced action. Above all, he fought. Blood combat erupted with gratifying regularity. The prose crashes with gun fire, explosions, shrieking automobiles, howls of the wounded, all slashed across by the chilling mockery of The Shadow.

To oppose this extraordinary figure, Gibson blandly mated the 1914 underworld of Jimmie Dale with contemporary gangsters. It was a sort of literary shotgun wedding. Gangs of gun-mad thugs served the bidding of a criminal mastermind, a new one every issue. These masterminds echoed those similar figures of the dime novels and the early *Detective Story Magazine*—criminal geniuses who plan to steal the rainbow. We have met them before: Doctor Quartz, The Gray Phantom, Black Star, Trent, Mr. Chang, Rafferty, John Doe.... A glittering galaxy, certainly. All less murderous than the geniuses of death populating The Shadow and hacking through the novels of the Spider and The Phantom Detective.

Since he was one against multitudes, The Shadow evened odds by disguise. He was a disguise master, the latest of that improbable breed. The disguised detective seems to have originated in the fanciful *Memoirs of Vidocq* (1828-1829), becoming a convention in the pages of Old Sleuth, Nick Carter, and Old King Brady. In those more casual days, they pasted on false hair and drew charcoal wrinkles across their foreheads. Later characters grew increasingly deft. Cleek, for example, could twist his face (and underlying bone structure) until he resembled anyone. Colonel Clay obliterated his features with a rubbery compound, which he then tinted and shaped until he exactly resembled you or your mother's rich uncle.

For most of his career, The Shadow wore Lamont Cranston's face puttied over his own. This accounted for Cranston's well-known impassivity. Who would smile when his features might crack?

After the Shadow sparkled a succession of equally adept disguise masters: The Phantom Detective (1933), deft with wigs, greases, bits of wax and wire, and an automatic when disguise failed; G-8, the Flying Spy (1933), who relied on the artistry of Battle, his man servant, to disguise him as an arrogant Prussian, thus penetrating the secret laboratory where a German horror weapon fizzed; Secret Agent X (1934) who could impersonate anyone in the room and frequently did; The Avenger (1939) whose paralyzed face could be molded like clay.

(How easily they altered themselves, these disguise masters, and how poorly did the dime store disguise kits, sold at Halloween, serve the enterprising secret avenger, who gloomily discovered that crayons, paints, and fake mustaches produced nothing but a messy face.)

The Shadow's influence on later characters is so powerful that to assess him accurately is nearly as hard as slicing the ocean into equal pieces. By some odd twist of natural law, those who come first are generally loaded with garlands and praised for all the wonderful things that happened later. So *The Shadow, A Detective Magazine*, by initiating the single-character era, is often credited for reshaping the sprawling panorama of the 1930s pulp magazines.

But one volcano does not create a mountain range.

Other forces, hot and violent, rumbled beneath fiction's surface. As, for instance, Doc Savage's remarkable effect on later characters. The gradual domination of crime and mystery fiction (and much adventure fiction) by descendents of the hardboiled detective. The staggering popularity of secret-identity crime fighters and series characters. The unexpected success of weird menace magazines, *Terror Tales, Dime Mystery, Ace Mystery, Horror Stories*, filled with supernatural effects, sexually endangered women, and thinly disguised sadism.

Not the least among these influences, so furiously interacting, was one ill-appreciated, even today. It is represented by a scant stack of magazines from 1932 and 1933, half *Detective-Dragnet*, half *Ten Detective Aces*. (It is the same magazine retitled.)  In those issues, the decade-old clash between fantasy and realism once again erupted. The effect on the single-character magazines was powerful and immediate.

*Ten Detective Aces* began as *The Dragnet* (October 1928), one of Harold Hersey's publications that, as usual, was a good idea with a maggot gnawing its heart. *The Dragnet* specialized in crook stories, a genre of fake characters, fake situations, fake dialogue, and stories of colossal improbability. The magazine lumbered into 1930, a forlorn hulk, was sold to A. A. Wyn's Magazine Publishers group, and changed its name to *Detective-Dragnet Magazine*. After a year of detective and police stories, the magazine veered in a new direction—that of horror melodrama.

Which first flowered in Paul Chadwick's series about adventurer-criminologist Wade Hammond. The routine crimes Hammond investigated soon became anything but routine. Gradually they included such shining conceits as a poisoning ape, living skeletons, dried corpses wrapped in silk, a murdering horror gliding up skyscraper walls. It was wonderfully over-wrought stuff.

The horror melodrama was a tingling mixture, atmospheric as a haunted house. The form evolved during 1931-1932, in both *Dime Detective and Detective-Dragnet....* The story type combined violent action, multiple murder, weirdly horrible events, human scourges in prose that was never less than incandescent... (Sampson, *Ten Stories for Ten Cents* 11).

In March 1933, the magazine changed its title to *Ten Detective Aces*. Other writers now joined the carnival.

Lester Dent, already writing a monthly Doc Savage novel, introduced a gadget-oriented private investigator named Lee Nace. In his dangerous world, science-fiction married detection, and so men exploded, corpses sweated blood or became blue and pop-eyed, skulls peered from meteors, and crazies lined caves with human heads.

Norvel Page wrote equally bizarre stories. His wealthy private detective, Ken Carter, investigated dead men dangling by their necks from parachutes, bodies turned blue or turned to stone, Hell's music that killed, and such shards of chaos.

Snuggled next to these riotous melodramas were hardboiled stories of police and detectives or fairly conventional crime action stories. And the not so conventional Moonman stories by Frederick C. Davis, in which a costumed policeman, wearing a one-way glass bowl over his head, robbed criminals and gave the proceeds to the poor.

Obviously the fiction of *Ten Detective Aces* was of two separate species, like cats and plums. Ten years earlier, a similar fissure rent *Black Mask*. During the early 1920s, the Race Williams stories introduced the gun-hot crime fantasy, melodrama with all the hair on. At the same moment, Dashiell Hammett opened an alternate path by creating the realistic, hardboiled detective story. That division between realism and melodrama ran like an earth fault through the detective fiction of the 1920s and 1930s.

In *Ten Detective Aces* that difference was magnified. The earth fault became a Grand Canyon. The horror melodrama, untroubled by gravity, bounded wildly about, stuffed with nightmare images. Green lightning glared. The sky splintered. Adjectives, like ghouls, paraded the seething night. And action, like some frantic mechanism, pounded through frantic paragraphs.

For a few years.

Then horror melodrama abruptly vanished from the magazine. Other assignments had claimed the writers. Lester Dent churned out *Doc Savage*; Norvel Page began the odyssey of the *Spider*, to which Emile Tepperman would contribute much later. Paul Chadwick worked on *Secret Agent X*, as did G. T. Fleming-Roberts. Other writers, who had contributed to the odd flavor of *Ten Detective Aces*, now contributed to well known single-character series: *Operator 5* (Frederick C. Davis, Emile Tepperman), *The Phantom Detective* (Norman Daniels, W. T. Ballard), *Dr. Yen Sin* (Donald Keyhoe), *The Ghost and Captain Zero* (G. T. Fleming-Roberts), *G-Men* (Norman Daniels).

*Ten Detective Aces* continued as a conventional detective magazine, rather emphasizing the hardboiled side, until cancellation in 1949. Never again did it approach the loopy grandeur of those 1932-1933 issues.

Not that the horror melodrama dissipated into air. At the end of 1933, that high wild music merely shifted locales. It continued, more lunatic, more excessive, more ferocious than ever, through the pages of the *Spider, The Phantom Detective*, and *Secret Agent X*. In these magazines, cities crumbled. Populations died. Armies of costumed madmen cavorted as torture devices clamped soft white flesh and the streets swam red. Together with sidewalks, lobbies, and roofs.

Certain publishers specialized in this gaudy fiction. Standard Publications (under various other titles and masks) brought out *Thrilling Detective* and *Phantom Detective*, among hosts of others. At Popular Publications, home of the *Spider, Horror Stories, Dime Mystery, G-8, Operator 5*, and similar scarlet wonders, the horror melodrama, burnished bright, burnt across the years.

By contrast, Street & Smith magazines were cooler, less hysterical, less apt to favor story lines that required mounds of corpses to prove how terrible it all was.

At Street & Smith, the pace was equally ferocious, the criminal devices equally bizarre. Yet the iron sniff of sadism was absent, the maniacal masterminds less homicidal, the blood somehow less scarlet, and the heady whiff of sex did not trouble the pages. In a Street & Smith pulp, people got captured and escaped. They got chased and tumbled into death traps and tumbled out again. Many of the heroes would likely have taught Sunday School, if they could stop dodging bullets and knocking thugs on the head.

While *The Shadow* was Street & Smith's most popular single-character title, the *Doc Savage Magazine* pressed close behind.

That magazine was devoted to adventure, furious adventure in far places, heavily spiced with technology from next week and science from the next century. Through these stories raced Doc Savage and his five friends, geniuses all, spoken of in superlatives, The Greatest, The Best, The Most Distinguished.

How brightly they glittered, these hard, competent men, each a caricature. Monk Mayfair, chemist, looks like an ape, is immensely powerful, argues incessantly with Ham Brooks, lawyer and clothes-horse. Johnny Littlejohn, geologist, archaeologist, is lean, tall, with a mind-crushing vocabulary. Massive Renny Renwick, civil engineer, smashes doors with his immense bony fists. Long Tom Roberts, electrical engineer, is small, pallid, and ferocious. All are professional men, all tough as armor plate. And all are consumed by hunger for adventure, conflict, violence in its innumerable garish forms.

As is Pat Savage, Doc's cousin, a tall redhead whose smile numbs men in their tracks. She carries a frontier Colt .45 in her purse and horns into the adventures whenever she can.

No complexities here. The people you meet here are drawn in hard, clean line, their peculiarities enormously magnified, as if you saw them through a gigantic lens. In Doc Savage's world, exaggeration rules. Caricature and exaggeration, lightly frosted with humor, and wonderfully decked out in kindergarten's strong, bright colors.

Doc Savage, himself, is somewhat less simple, being, in equal proportions, wish fulfillment and myth figure. Tall, sun bronzed, powerful, relentlessly intelligent, he is a physician, surgeon, master of a battery of scientific and engineering disciplines, a supreme athlete, a millionaire, philanthropist, and executive. His reputation is international; his peers revere him. He can fight, fly, and speak thirty languages, and if his perfection is a dream beyond reach, it is one worth aspiring to. Even if requiring daily exercise and daily study.

The Shadow gave readers a figure to mystify and fascinate them; Doc Savage gave them a figure to admire and identify with. He is the sublime man, omitting only maturity's biting ambiguities and compromises. Late in the series, he becomes less confident, less omnipotent, and somehow less interesting. From the first page to the last, he was never entirely at ease with women, the only flaw in his smooth perfection. It was a flaw that linked him with every reader staggered by the mystery of the female.

What ultimately drew generations of adolescent boys and shapeless men to Doc Savage was not his intelligence or wealth, but the fabulous wonder of his physical strength. Most fictional heroes had a tendency to be slightly stronger than normal, able to lift more, strike harder, endure longer. Among these superior men, fiction threw forth, at long intervals, characters of even more astonishing superiority.

As Nick Carter, said to be stronger than any two men. As both The Night Wind and Polaris, each possessing truly abnormal physical strength and agility. Edgar Wallace's fantastically strong young man of The Iron Grip flipped davenports around, although mentally no greyhound. Tarzan was powerful enough to fight gorillas, and his influence predictably grins through certain of the Savage novels.

Of all these extraordinary figures, Clark Savage Jr. stands unique. His strength is simply inhuman. He lifts immense weights, tears apart chains, flings men about like balsa wood chips, carries people from danger, leaps shocking distances, runs all night, whips small armies.

After Doc Savage, characters great and small showed a decided tendency to demonstrate their astounding physical strength. Perhaps The Avenger did so most successfully. But they only reflected Savage's light. It is no wonder that the Bronze Man's most direct descendent is Superman. It could hardly be otherwise.

Savage and his friends are hardly realistic characters. Their world is the fantasy melodrama, that world Lester Dent exploited in the pages of Ten Detective Aces. It is a world ajitter with science-fictional devices — tidal wave generators, matter transmitters, magnetic weapons, mind-reading machines, devices to slow atomic vibration, chemical procedures to create invisibility.

Such inspired machinery is tightly harnessed to stories where one or more criminal gangs struggle for riches. From somewhere in the back chapters, a rich gleaming, light from an immensely valuable secret, illuminates frantic struggle as the criminals snarl and rend and the mastermind plots and the Doc Savage crew stand firm across their path.

Through the story wander men of eccentric habits and bodies like cartoons. Here glide women of shattering beauty, clutching secrets not yet to be told. Purple-faced industrialists, cranky inventors, adventurers with a knife down the back of their collar and shifty eyes, priests grown fanatic in their lost city, golden-skinned queens with dark eyes, rural sheriffs with goaty beards and brains like stone, helpful male secretaries, butlers with pistols bulging their formal dress, fat ladies with vacant smiles and a trained cobra in their candy box....

Fights erupt. Death traps whack shut. Doc's aides are captured. Once. More than once. Constantly. Doc is dead they saw him die disintegrated in the blast, gunned down in the sunlight, his airplane flaming, his car blasted.

Immediately he reappears, unscratched, aides rescued, a new clue snapped up. The action streaks wildly forward.

Around us rise ancient Mayan walls. English coastal marshes mist under the moon. On the window glass is etched the shadow of a human figure, huddled in terror. Dinosaurs pound through vine-choked jungle. Lost civilizations sprawl behind mountain walls, beneath the earth, down volcanic throats, on the sea bottom. Invisible men kill mercilessly. Living human skeletons lope toward you, guns in their claws. Low orbital space travel and pirate kings. Gangsters shout toward the treasure horde. Blue-white energy blasts out. The machine of eye-popping complexity. The mastermind revealed. Thick tendons on a cabled arm coated with skin like bronze lacquer....

Doc Savage is what every boy expected to be. And for the boys who had grown into men and disappointed themselves, Doc was the Shining Almost, the What Could Have Been, the gleaming being they felt inside. Only to have done a couple of things differently. You feel the possibility still within reach. Almost you can stretch out your hand, almost grope back through the confusions of your life to the turn you missed. Once found, to enter a world more warmly lighted in which success, admiration, excitement, effortless mastery is yours. As you always knew it would be.

Doc Savage is symbol of that world. The one so close. Which beckons you still. It tugs hypnotically, just around the corner. Only just out of reach. The way can still be found.

It can be found.

After The Shadow and Doc Savage, after The Phantom Detective and the Spider, Bill Barnes, G-8, and the other single-character magazines that flooded into the early 1930s after these, the torrent shrank to a trickle. Came Operator 5 and Secret Agent X in 1934. Then, at the middle of the decade, as the economy again dwindled and shrank, the heartbeat of new titles slowed and stuttered. Somehow new magazines could not endure. They flickered and were gone.

During 1935, an alternative form was tested—a single- character magazine in all but title, in this instance, *G-Men*, featuring that durable agent, Dan Fowler. The magazine caught on solidly, as did the 1939 *Jungle Stories*, with Ki- Gor (a Tarzan clone), and *Black Book Detective*, which interrupted a career of blameless mediocrity as a detective story magazine to offer a monthly novel about The Black Bat (July 1939), a costumed crime fighter with night vision.

Late in 1939, more formal single-character magazines returned to the newsstand, *The Avenger* (September 1939) being the first solid success. A brief, but intense, eruption of titles resulted. During 1940, about a dozen new single- character magazines boiled out, together with half a dozen others featuring major characters whose names never reached the mast head.

None of these endured. A year, perhaps two, saw their end.

Many silent reasons existed for this universal failure. The single-character formula established early in the 1930s, was wearing thin. Even established single characters, as they entered the war years, seemed strangely pallid. Long exposure had exhausted their hearts. Small wonder. The writers of these series also neared exhaustion; most had torrented out more than a million words a year for a decade, and the relentless monthly demand for new adventures, new excitements, had parched their imaginations.

It was, moreover, a time of wartime shortages. The cost of paper, staples, ink, color press work, salaries steadily inflated. The tiny profit generated by each magazine steadily eroded. Prices edged upward, eventually producing such anomalies as a *Dime Detective* for 15 cents.

As profits declined, distribution of the magazines became increasingly chancy. The distribution system reeled under wartime exigencies: loss of trained personnel, loss of rail capacity, inability to maintain schedules. Magazines were increasingly shipped late, or damaged, or lost in the churn between bindery and news stand.

There was another, more deadly change. The war first siphoned off readers, then returned them indifferent to the fictional blandishments of justice figures with disguised faces and secret identities blazing away at crime.

No wonder so many magazines failed during this period. The marvel was that so many survived.

No new single-character title would be issued until *Captain Zero* (November 1949), a crisp and rather sardonic look at superheroes through the medium of a newspaperman who periodically became invisible. The magazine lasted three issues.

That same year, Street & Smith cancelled both *The Shadow* and *Doc Savage*. Of the many character magazines birthed in 1933, only *The Phantom Detective* remained. That survivor, and a few western titles— *The Rio Kid Western, Texas Rangers, The Masked Rider Western*— continued the tradition of the single-character magazine into the 1950s.

*Hopalong Cassidy's Western Magazine* would become the last new single-character series magazine offered (three issues, Fall 1950-Spring 1951) (Drew, *Lous U Amour* 203). It was a curious coincidence that Cassidy should be featured, a case of the beginning showing up at the end, as if to demonstrate a cycle of something. For Cassidy had originally appeared in 1906 and was one of the key figures contributing to the convention of the roaming, gun-fighting cowboy.

Before Cassidy, such dime novel characters as Buffalo Bill and Young Wild West populated a hyper-active Western scene. As a class, these continuing heroes were physically powerful, uncompromising in character, experts with gun and lariat, and given to wandering with a close friend or so until they found violent adventure. All around them sprouted improbabilities, like lavender trees.

Cassidy was more realistic. As portrayed by Clarence Mulford, Hopalong worked and sweat. He also played cards, drank bar whiskey, chewed tobacco, and toward the end of his career was more inclined to think than to shoot.

Mulford's Cassidy was one of several important influences on western fiction characters. Another was Owen Wister's *The Virginian*, which contributed that memorable scene of two men stalking toward each other on a frontier street, hands hovering above weapons. The silent movies and their cowboy stars also played a part in defining the western story—as did the dozens of western melodramas played out on stages across the country. Scenes repeated a thousand times hardened to convention: furious rides, girls in peril, blistering gun fights, the outlawed hero, the robbed stage coach, the confrontation in the saloon, the villain and his disreputable horde, the agonizing beauty of the stark plains and mountains, the final fight, gun to gun.

All these matters, from dime novels and Zane Grey to B. M. Bowers and silent movies, combined to crystalize characters and situations in western fiction. Like all other conventions, once established, once accepted by writer, reader, and viewer, they inadvertently prevented development in other directions. It is always easier to walk a familiar road than cut new trails. Once accepted, the convention becomes an invisible wall. Only the ferociously creative recognize that a wall is there, let alone batter through it to the strangely colored fields beyond.

What other directions the western might have taken, we can hardly say. Enough that the path chosen, the conventions accepted, permitted nearly endless variation.

Writers fiddled endlessly with the story form, squeezing new juice from old rinds. Thus W. C. Tuttle transformed the western to farce in his Piperock series and tangled it with the mystery story in the Hashknife Hartley series. Jim Twin, the White Wolf, a reluctant outlaw fighting for justice, was cast in the bent hero mold, pioneered by Tom Mix movies and the Jimmie Dale magazine serials. Later The Lone Ranger, first on radio, then briefly in the pulps, emerged a formal justice figure inserted into a western story. And The Masked Rider, who first rode through a single-character magazine in 1934, adapted The Shadow to the western, becoming a cloaked mystery figure on horseback.

All these and more than a hundred others. Each with his own face, each stamped by all that had gone before. These continuing heroes wonderfully demonstrate the past's guidance and shaping force on the present.

The Shadow, Doc Savage, Hopalong Cassidy represent in miniature the sparkling complex of the 1930s series characters. Each stood unique and individual. But none of them flashed, uncompromisingly original, from the astonished air. They were the children of yesterday's light, and behind each lay a complex history extending through time. Through that extended history, character changed and interacted with other characters, other conventions.

Not many of these older influences are celebrated. While Tarzan and Sherlock Holmes still radiate powerfully, decades of lesser known characters have contributed their mite and melted into the tradition of popular fiction, as practiced during the Twentieth Century. Once each stood unique. Each was praised. Each brought variations and change and, to greater degree or less, altered the conventions of its form, as surely as the wagons of settlers, creeping one by one across the Great Plains, ground evidence of their passage into the rock.

Who among readers of the 1930s-1940s magazines realized that silent continuity? Among the mountains you cannot see more distant peaks. The magazines shone in your hand. The fiction within was crisply contemporary. Who thought of the past? You read in the clear bright present, and all was new. Amid the glories of the 1930s, the past kept its secrets. Even older readers, clinging passionately to their files of *Adventure* and *Argosy*, remained unaware of those vast, silent currents which had shaped their present reading. So the past concealed itself in the present, where it is always morning, and its offerings forever new.

Time slips away. Old loves grow hollow, old enthusiasms wear at last to gentle yawns. The store in Pittsburgh is fifty years gone, replaced by polished facades. The old magazines, once glorious in their millions, are also gone. They might never have been.

But fiction endures.

Fiction, that smiling spirit, has only changed her dress. Pulp magazines give way to the paperback and the ubiquitous television screen. Soon those too will yield to whatever new fictional form is presently incubating in tomorrow's surprised heart.

The medium changes. Styles change. Conventions alter. But fiction endures. And today's faces, shine forever new, new flowers on ancient vines.

# Notes

[1]Both the Lone Wolf and Jimmie Dale, the Gray Seal, are considered at length in *Glory Figures* (1983), the first volume of this series.

[2]An interesting discussion of the early Drummond and his influence on the English mystery adventure may be found in Chapter Three of William Vivian Butler's *The Durable Desperados* (London: McMillan, 1973).

[3]The information on the Drummond short stories is given by Jack Adrian in "The Exploits of Bulldog Drummond" (an introduction to the five stories), contained in *"Sapper": The Best Short Stories*, 133. All stories, Adrian points out, were published in the 1937 *Strand*, three of them after McNeile's death.

[4]Many of these characters are examined in *From the Dark Side* (1986), the third volume of this series.

## Chapter Two

[1]Considerable information about Frederic Van Rensselaer Dey is provided in J.R. Cox's bibliographic listings of the Nick Carter dime novels. In particular refer to "Nick Carter Stories, *Dime Novel Round-Up Bibliographic Listing #10*, Vol. number 4, Whole Number 526 (August 1977).

[2]By 1918, *The Cavalier* had been incorporated into the *All-Story Weekly. The Cavalier*, first issued dated October 1908, became *The Cavalier Weekly* with the January 6, 1912, issue and continued to May 19, 1914. It then became the *All-Story Cavalier Weekly* (May 16, 1914, through May 8, 1915). With the May 15, 1915 issue, the magazine was again retitled, becoming *All-Story Weekly* until July 1920, when it became *Argosy-All Story Weekly*.

[3]A biographical sketch of Johnston McCulley may be found in *Yesterday's Faces*, Vol. 3, "From the Dark Side," Popular Press (1987), 37-38.

[4]Quentin Reynold's *The Fiction Factory*, NY: Random (1955), 203, states that *"Complete Story Magazine* was merely *People's [Magazine]* with a new name." It is true that the format and fiction were similar and the editor (Archie Sessions) identical. They were, however, different magazines, each with separate volume numbers and separate second-class mailing privileges. *Complete Stories* did not absorb *People's* but merely occupied the niche left open when *People's* was cancelled, April 1922.

## Chapter Three

[1]William F. Nolan, "Behind the Mask: Erle Stanley Gardner," *The Black Mask Boys*, NY: Morrow (1985), 97. Nolan's biographical sketch of Gardner strongly brings to focus the man's personality and torrential energies.

[2]Many prominent hardboiled novels originated in this fashion, among them Dashiell Hammett's *Red Harvest, The Dain Curse,* and *The Maltese Falcon*;

Carroll John Daly's *The Tag Murders, Murder from the East, The Mystery of the Smoking Gun*; Raoul Whitefield's *Green Ice* and *Death in a Bowl*; and Paul Cain's *Fast One*.

[3]Gardner, "Getting Away with Murder," *Ellery Queen's Mystery Magazine* (reprinted from *The Atlantic Monthly*), 46:5, (November 1965). 46. In the course of this article, Gardner briefly discusses how Jenkins and Helen marry and how *Black Mask* editor Shaw's response to helen's dressless state led to her death. Gardner does not mention the difficulties a wife causes an action hero, which, we may assume, played a silent part in her demise.

[4]Robert Sampson, *Yesterday's Faces*, Vol. 4, "The Solvers," Bowling Green (1987), 149-151,discusses the X. Crook series.

[5]During this period, *Argosy*, companion magazine to *Detective Fiction*, underwent identical format changes.

[6]However Munsey continued to publish *Detective Fiction*, changing it to a monthly with the March 7, 1942, issue. The title was again changed to *Flynn's Detective* (July 1942 issue). Most of the fiction was dropped in favor of true crime. During this period, Gardner published nothing in the magazine.

[7]While dated January 1943, the magazine actually appeared on newstands as of November 20, 1942.

*Chapter Four*

[1]Additional biographical information about Bronson-Howard may be found in *Yesterday's Faces,* Vol. 5, "Dangerous Horizons," Popular Press (1991), 33.

[2]The heirarchy of British aristocracy begins with knight, and rises, step by wonderful step, to earl, baronet, baron, viscount, marquis, and duke.

[3]Clarence Herbert New, Chapter I. "The Mystery of the Free Lances," *The Unseen Hand,* NY: Caldwell (1918). This chapter provides elaborate detail about Grisscome, Trevor, and the creation of the Free-Lances. It would appear that the chapter was written especially for the book and had not received magazine publication. According to collector and bibliographer Diggs LaTouche, the balance of the book consists of stories published in *Blue Book* during 1916 and 1917. Chapter I contains much information that was never explained in the formal series. As, for example, that the names Trevor, Grisscome, Wray, Abdool, and the rest of the Free-Lance cast are pseudonyms, used by New to protect the identities of living people.

[4]Diggs LaTouche, letter to Robert Sampson, dated November 20, 1983.

[5]Frederick Lewis Allen, Chapter III, *Only Yesterday,* NY: Harper (1964), 46-49, discussing the Great Red Scare.

[6]The Doc Savage novel, *The Evil Gnome* (April 1940), is built around criminal use of a similar gas.

[7]Much of New's biographical was drawn from an obituary published in *Blue Book*, Vol. 56, No. 6 (April 1933), back of the front cover. This short article contains material quoted from an obituary published earlier int he *New York Times* (no date cited).

*Chapter Five*

[1]Bedford-Jones, "Post Mortem: H. Bedford-Jones," Introduced and edited by Michael Murphy (1980), 25. (This is a monograph comprised of two letter-essays written by Bedford-Jones to his friend, Vincent Starrett. A selection of Bedford-Jones to his friend, Vincent Starrett. A selection of Bedford-Jones/Starrett letters and editorial comments introduce the work. Both parts of the monograph offer loose autobiographical elements; both ramble among curiosities of book collecting, the publication of limited edition monographs, and a certain amount of personal history and fiction writing methods. During the first lettter, for reasons best known to himself, Bedford-Jones refers to himself as Henry James O'Brien. During the second letter, he discussed H. Bedford-Jones as if he were a separate personality. All useful information may be found in the second part. A copy of the document is filed at the University of Colorado Libraries, Boulder, Colorado.)

[2]Bedford-Jones, "Solomon's Submarine," *People's* Vol. XX, No. 2 (February 1916), 70-71. The Quoted scene has been heavily abridged.

[3]The magazine title was given on the spine as *Argosy-Allstory Weekly,* and on the cover as *Argosy All-Story Weekly. All-Story Weekly* soon appeared in reduced type that eventually shrank quietly away. A colored insert in the October 5, 1929, *Argosy* announces that the name of *Munsey's Magazine* will changed to *All-Story* and feature "The Best Fiction by the Best Writers." The incautious reader might fail to observe that the magazine would henceforth be dedicated to "Love Stories of Every Land," an extraordinary transformation fo the publication that had pioneered the scientific romance and featured such giants as Tarzan and John Carter of Mars.

*Chapter Six*

[1]For a more detailed examination of Mundy's early life, refer to "Willie—Rogue and Rebel" by Peter Berresford Ellis, 27-72, in Talbot Mundy: *Messenger of Destiny*, compiled by Donald M. Grant (Rhode Island: Grant, 1983).

[2]Robert Sampson, *Spider* (Bowling Green: Popular Press, 1987). This book discusses the character of Ram Singh, one of literature's great fighting men, and a continuation of that resplendent line which includes Narayan Singh.

[3]These adventuring women, and others, are discussed in the first volume of this series, "Glory Figures," *Yesterday's Faces*, Vol. 1 (Popular Press: 1983).

[4]The belief that the measurements and proportions of the Great Pyramid concealed secret information led to the founding of the Theosophical Society in 1875; they planned to look into the matter. Refer to Colin Wilson, *The Occult* (NY: Random House, 1971), 332.

[5]*Ibid*, 333. Wilson's discussion of Theosophy is considerably more detailed and considerably less frivolous than given here.

[6]A dug named "Soma" also crops up in Aldous Huxley's novel, *Brave New World,* published in 1932. The name is more likely suggested by a common source, such as an advertisement, than by a reading of *Jimgrim*. Still, more improbable things than that have happened.

*Chapter Seven*

[1]From September 1, 1917, through September 15, 1921, *Adventure* appeared twice a month. During the months of September and October of 1917, the magazines were dated as "First *Month*" for the first issue and "Mid-*Month*" for the second. The date of issuance appeared on the spine, front cover, table of contents, and first page of text. In November 1917, the dating abruptly became inconsistent. The "First" and "Mid" identification continued on the spine until October 10, 1921, when issuance increased to three times a month—the 10th, 20th, and 28th. The spine then duly reflected those dates. However, from the initial November 1917 issue, the dates on the magazine cover, table of contents, and first page became inconsistent with the spine. In those places, the date of the initial bi-monthly issue changed (for example) from "First Nov 1917" to "November 3, 1917." The second issue of the month became "November 18." These descrepancies remained unresolved until the October 10, 1921, issue. At that time, the spines became consistent with dates given elsewhere in the magazine. These variations are rarely explained in *Adventure* checklists and tend to puzzle those not familar with these irregularities. William J. Clark's Khlit checklist, which appears in *Xenophile*, #28, November/December 1976, p.73, dates the magazines appearing in the 1917-1921 period as either "3" or "18." In his *The Index to Adventure Magazine* (1990), Richard Bleiler simplifies this system, referring to the initial montly issue as "1" and the second as "15." Thus, "November 1, 1917." For purposes of this work, "First" and "Mid" are used where applicable.

[2]Mundy, as quoted in Talbot Mundy: *Messenger of Destiny*, 151-152.

[3]Elmer, Davis, letter in "The Camp-Fire," *Adventure*, 53:3 (June 30, 1925), 176-177. Only a few extracts are provided from this letter, which occupies two columns of small type and deals forcibly with various of Mundy's interpretations of history.

[4]Mundy, letter in "The Camp-Fire," *Adventure*, Vol. 54:2 (August 20, 1925), 174.

[5]Cleopatra was dark, as are many Mediterranean people, but her ancestry contained no trace of negroid blood, a few contemporary claims to the contrary. Refer to Michael Grant, *Cleopatra* (NY: Dorset, 1972), 171.

[6]Not only Cleopatra's personal description but her personality and motives differ radically from writer to writer. H. Rider Haggard's Cleopatra is not the same woman depicted by either Shakespeare or Bernard Shaw, and none agree with Mundy. Over the centuries, Cleopatra has become a canvas upon which authors render their versions of femininity.

[7]Arthur D. Howen Smith, *Grey Maiden* (NY: Centaur, 1974), 92. Throughout this book, "grey" is the designated spelling. In the original magazine stories, however, the word was spelled "gray" and is so used in this commentary.

[8]Everett Bleiler has advised that a Gray Maiden story may have later appeared in *Blue Book;* but that has not, so far, been traced.

*Chapter Eight*

[1]Bleiler, *op. cit.*, 261. See also the *Wilson Library Bulletin*, June 1954, 830.

[2]These six stories were incorporated in the 1927 Appleton hardcover, *A Helluva War.*

*Chapter Nine*

[1]Elliott White Springs (1896-1959) was an authentic combat pilot of the First World War. He flew with the 85th Squadron of the Royal Flying Corps and the 148th United States Air Service, destroying 11 enemy aircraft. Between 1927 and 1931, he wrote nine books, in addition to editing *War Birds*. He then worked himself up in textile manufacturing until he became a bank president and chief executive of a number of cotton mills. He served during the Second World War, retiring in 1942 as a Lieutenant Colonel.

[2]Sidney H. Bradd, "G-8, Flying Spy of the Pulps," *Xenophile* #11 (March 1975). This article discusses Robert Hogan's life and work, with particular reference to the writing of the G-8 series.

[3]For additional discussion of these three magazines, refer to Robert Madle's article, "Terence X. O'Leary's War Birds," in The Pulp Era, Issue No. 69 (January-February 1968), 5-8.

*Chapter Ten*

[1]Robert Sampson, *The Night Master,* Chicago: Pulp Press (1982), discusses the origins of the Shadow figure and the history of the magazine. A detailed discussion of the artists, writers, and editorial decisions producing the magazine may be found in *The Duende History of Shadow Magazine* by Will Murray, Odyssey (1980), and an *Addendum* to that *History,* dated March 3, 1980.

[2]Walter Gibson, The Shadow's creator, remarked that he had borrowed the image of his famous character from that of Bela Lugosa's stage portrayal of Dracula. Even that porttrayal was only another version of the mystery figure, already centuries old. Refer to the discussion of The Shadow's origins in *The Night Master*, Chapter III. "The Grand Tradition."

[3]To copyright The Shadow, Street & Smith decided to feature the character in a magazine novel. Walter Gibson was hired to transform the radio voice into a fictional character. Under the house name of Maxwell Grant, he did so for eighteen years. His work was supplemented by that of Theodore Tinsley, Bruce Elliott, and a single novel by Lester Dent.

[4]When Cassidy was revived in 1950, it was to exploit the popularity of the character as portrayed by television and moving pictures. Author Louis L'Amour repudiated his four Cassidy novels and refused to acknowledge authorship to his death. Refer to Bernard A. Drew, "Louis L'Amour's Hopalong Cassidy," *The Louis LAmour Companion* edited by Robert Weinberg, Kansas City: Andrews and McMeel (1992), 203.

# Works Cited

Albert, Walter A. *Detective and Mystery Fiction: An International Bibliography of Secondary Sources*. Madison: Brownstone, 1985.

Bedford-Jones, H(enry)." John Solomon's Biggest Game, Part 6." *Argosy*. 211:1 (22 Mar. 1930).

_____. "John Solomon—Supercargo." *Argosy* 76:4 (July 1914).

_____. "Post-Mortem."

_____. "Solomon's Submarine." *People'.'* 20:2 (Feb. 1916).

_____. "The Seal of John Solomon." *Argosy* 79:3 (June 1915).

Blackwood, Algernon. *Episodes Before Thirty*. NY: Dutton, 1924.

Bleiler, Richard. "A. History of the *Adventure* Magazine." Index to *Adventure Magazine*, Vols. 1 and 2. Starmont (1990).

Boggs, Redd. "I Remember Wild West Weekly." *The Pulp Western* (John A. Dinan). Borgo P, 1983.

Bradd, Sidney H. "G-8, Flying Spy of the Pulps." *Xenophile* #11 (Mar. 1975).

Bronson-Howard, George. "On the Night of the Charity Ball." *The Popular Magazine* 6:4 (Aug. 1906).

_____. "Behind the Green Lamps." *The Popular Magazine* 27:6 (1 Apr. 1913).

_____. "For the Good of the State." *The Popular Magazine* 5:6 (Oct. 1906).

_____. *Norroy, Diplomatic Agent*. NY: Saalfield, 1907.

_____. *Slaves of the Lamp*. NY: Watt, 1917.

_____. *The Black Book*. NY: Watt, 1920.

Buckley, Frederic Robert. "Cartel to William Shakespeare." *Adventure* 69:6 (20 Nov. 1924).

_____. "Concerning A Musician." *Adventure* 65:1 (15 Dec. 1927).

_____. "Deadly Weapons." *Adventure* 116:6 (Apr. 1947).

_____. "Of A Vanishment." *Adventure* 73:6 (1 Mar. 1930).

_____. "Of Chain Mail and Green Cheese." *Adventure* 111:5 (Sept.1944).

_____. "Of Education." *Adventure* 80:4 (1 Nov. 1931).

_____. "Of Glamour and Gunpowder." *Adventure* 110:6 (Apr. 1944).

_____. "Of Penitence." *Adventure* 105:2 (June 1941).

_____. "Of Vanity." *Adventure* 88:5 (15 May 1931).

Butler, William Vivian. *The Durable Desperados*. London: MacMillan, 1973.

Carr, Nick. *The Flying Spy*. Pulp Classic #18. Chicago: Weinberg, 1978.

_____. "A Man Called: Zorro." *The Pulp Collector* 4:3 (Spring 1989).

Charteris, Leslie. *Meet the Tiger*. NY: Sun Dial, 1940.

_____. *The Avenging Saint*. NY: Sun Dial, 1941.

_____. *Follow The Saint*. NY: Center, 1942.

Clark, William J. "H. Bedford-Jones in *People's*." *Xenophile* No.30. (March 1977).

Cook, Michael L., *Mystery, Detective, and Espionage Magazines*. Westport: Greenwood, 1983.

Cook, Michael L. and Stephen T. Miller, *Mystery, Detective, and Espionage Fiction: A Checklist of Fiction in U.S. Pulp Magazines, 1915-1974*. Vols. 1 and 2. NY: Garland, 1988.

Dinan, John A. *The Pulp Western*. Borgo, 1983.

Drew, Bernard A. "A Pulp Heroine." *Attic Revivals #2* (1980).

_____. "Herman Petersen, The Poolville Pulpster." *Attic Revivals* #2 (1980).

Dunning, Hal. "The Killer and the Kid." NY: *Complete Stories* 10:6 (July 1927).

_____. *White Wolf's Law*. Chelsea House 1928.

_____. "White Wolf Reaches Cactus Country." *Wild West Weekly*. 129:3 (1 July 1939).

Ellis, Edward Robb. *A Nation in Torment*. NY: Coward-McCann 1970.

Empey, Arthur Guy. "The Curse of the Iron Cross" *Battle Stories* 9:53 (Jan. 1932).

_____. "Ghost of the Black Wings." *War Birds*. 24:72 (Mar. 1934).

_____. "Hinky, Dinky, Parle Vous." *Battle Stories* 2:10 (June 1928).

_____. "O'Leary Carries On." *War Stories*. 34:100 (Nov. 1931).

_____. "O'Leary, the Devil's Darling." *War Birds* 26:78 (Sept. 1934).

_____. "O'Leary, Dyno-Blaster."*Terence X. O'Leary's War Birds*. Odyssey Publication #2, 1974.

_____. "O'Leary, Falconeer." *War Birds*. 23:68 (Nov. 1933).

_____. "O'Leary of the Rainbow Division." *Battle Stories* 7:39 (Nov. 1930).

_____. "Sgt. O'Leary's Tank Busters." *Battle Stories*11:62. (Dec. 1933).

_____. "Soldiers of Death." *War Stories* 1:1 (Feb. 1936).

_____. "The Men Who Make the Argosy." *Argosy* 239:1 (10 June 1933).

Gardner, Erle Stanley. "Cop Killers." *Black Mask* 17:1 (Mar. 1934).

_____. "Curse of the Killers." *Black Mask* 9:9 (Nov. 1928).

_____. "Getting Away with Murder." *Ellery Queen's Mystery Magazine* 46:5, Whole No. 264 (Nov. 1965).

_____. "Introductory Note." *Ellery Queen's Mystery Magazine* 15:78 (May 1950).

_____. "It's A Pipe." *Detective Fiction Weekly* 43:4 (10 Aug. 1929).

_____. "Laugh That Off." *Dead Men's Letters*. NY: Carroll & Graf, 1990.

_____. "Money, Marbles and Chalk." *Black Mask* 9:9 (Nov. 1926).

_____. "Promise To Pay." *Black Mask* 14:7 (Sept. 1931).

_____. "Red Jade." *Black Mask* 16:1 (March 1933).

_____. *The Amazing Adventures of Lester Leith*. Ellery Queen, ed. NY: Dial, 1980.

_____. *The Blond in Lower Six*. NY: Carroll & Graf, 1990.

_____. *The Blond in Lower Ten*. NY: Carroll & Graf, 1990.

_____. *The Case of the Crying Swallow*. NY: Morrow, undated.

_____. *The Case of the Murderer's Bride*. NY: Davis, 1969.

_____. "The Monkey Murder." *Detective Story Magazine* 157:3 (Jan. 1939).

_____. "The Painted Decoy." *Detective Fiction Weekly* 39:4 (23 Feb.1929).

Godfrey, Lydia S. "Pluck, Perseverance and Pressure." *Dime Novel Roundup* 54:2, Whole No. 572 (April 1985).

Goulart, Ron. *The Hardboiled Dicks*. Los Angeles: Sherbourne, 1965.

Graham, Sidney M. "U.S. Gold and Treachery." *People's* 21:6 (Dec. 1916).

Grant, Donald M., ed. *Talbot Mundy: Messenger of Destiny*. Rhode Island: Grant, 1983.

Grant, Michael. *Cleopatra*. NY: Dorset, 1992.

Grochowski, Mary Ann. "The Solution of 'The Elusive Vanardy'." *The Poisoned Pen* 2:5 (Sept./Oct. 1979).

Hagemann, E.R. *A Comprehensive Index to Black Mask, 1920-1951*. Bowling Green State University Popular Press, 1982.

Hawkwood, Allan. (H. Bedford-Jones) *Gentleman Solomon*. London: Hurst & Blackett, undated.

_____. *Solomon's Carpet*. London: Hurst & Blackett, undated.

_____. *Solomon's Quest*. London: Hurst & Blackett, undated.

Hersey, Harold. *Pulpwood Editor*. (p. 225).

Hogan, Robert J. "Wager Flight." *Air Trails* 6:5 (Aug. 1931).

Hughes, Dorothy B. *The Case of the Real Perry Mason*. NY: Morrow, 1978.

Kahn, Arthur D. *The Education of Julius Caesar*. NY: Schocken, 1986.

Kennicott, Donald. "Adventures In Editing." *Blue Book* 100:1 (Nov. 1954).

Lamb, Harold. *The Curved Saber*. NY: Doubleday, 1964.

_____. *The Mighty Manslayer*. NY: Modern Literary Editions, 1969.

Locke, John. *The Pulp Magazine Quick Reference Guide*. 1989.

McCulley, Johnston. *The Mark of Zorro*. NY: Dell, undated.

_____. "Zorro Rides Again." Bowling Green State University Popular Press, 1987.

McNeile, H. C. (Refer to "Sapper"). *Bulldog Drummond Strikes Back*. NY: Triangle, 1943.

_____. *Bull-Dog Drummond's Third Round*. NY: Doran, undated.

McSherry Jr., Frank D. "Captain of *Adventure*: Luigi Cardossa." *Pulp Vault* #6 (Nov. 1989).

Madle, Robert. "Terence X. O'Leary's War Birds." *The Pulp Era*. Issue Number 69 (Jan.-Feb. 1968).

Martyn, Wyndham. *Anthony Trent, Master Criminal*. London: Jenkins, 1922.

_____. *The Death Fear*. NY: McBride, 1929.

_____. *The Great Ling Plot*. London: Jenkins, 1933.

_____. *The Return of Anthony Trent*. NY: Grosset & Dunlap, 1925.

_____. *Trent Fights Again*. London: Jenkins, 1939.

_____. *Trent of the Lone Hand*. London: Jenkins, 1927.

Morland, Nigel. *Edgar Wallace News Letter #30* (May 1976).

Mott, Frank Luther. *A History of American Magazines, 1885-1905*. Vol. 4. Cambridge: Harvard UP, 1957.

_____. *A History of American Magazines, 1905-1930*. Vol. 5. Cambridge: Harvard UP, 1968.

Mundy, Talbot. *Jimgrim*. NY: Century, 1931.

_____. *Jimgrim and Allah's Peace*. NY: Appleton, 1936.

_____. *Jimgrim Sahib*. NY: Royal, undated.

_____. *The Devil's Guard*. Indianapolis: Bobbs-Merrill, 1926.

_____. *The Hundred Days and The Woman Ayisha*. NY: Century, undated.

_____. *The Lion of Petra*. NY: Appleton, 1933.

_____. *The Mystery of Khufu's Tomb*. NY: Appleton, 1935.

_____. *The Nine Unknown*. NY: Avon, 1968.

_____. *The Purple Pirate*. NY: Avon, 1970.

_____. *Queen Cleopatra*. NY: Ace, undated.

_____. *The Seventeen Thieves of El-Kalil*. London: Hutchison, undated.

_____. *Tros of Samothrace*. NY: Appleton, 1934.

Nevins, Francis M., Jr. "Aspects of the Unknown Gardner. Parts I and II." *The Mystery Readers Newsletter*. Vol. 5. Nos. 4 and 5 (1972).

New, Clarence Herbert. "Further Adventure of a Diplomatic Free Lance: No. 1, When the Fox Stole the Bait." *Blue Book* 12:6 (Apr. 1911).

_____. *The Unseen Hand*. NY: Caldwell, undated.

_____. "When China Fights." *Blue Book* 55:1 (May 1932).

Nolan, William F. *The Black Mask Boys* NY: Morrow, 1985.

O'Keefee, T.A.. "Where Is Mary Morell?" *Flynn's* 6:4 (9 May 1925).

Oppenheim, E. Phillips. *Mr. Laxworthy's Adventures*. London: Cassell, 1914.

_____. "The Peculiar Gifts of Mr. John T. Laxworthy: The Secret of the Magnifique.*" The Popular Magazine* 24:3 (15 May 1912).

_____. "The Debt Collector." *The Popular Magazine* 26:2 (1 Nov. 1912).

Queen, Ellery. "Erle Stanley Gardner: An Unorthodox Introduction." *The Case of the Murderer's Bride*. NY: Davis 1969.

Reynolds, Quentin. *The Fiction Factory*. NY: Random, 1955.

Robbins, Leonard A. *The Pulp Magazine Index (First Series, Vols. 1, 2, and 3)*. Starmont, 1989.

_____. *(Second Series)*. 1989.

_____. *(Third Series)*. 1990.

_____. *(Fourth Series)*. 1991.

Sampson, Robert. *The Night Master*. Chicago: Pulp Press, 1982.

_____. *Spider*. Bowling Green State University Popular Press, 1987.

_____. "Ten Stories for Ten Cents." *The Night Nemesis*. Vol. 1. Eds. Garyn G. Roberts and Gary Hoppenstand. Purple Prose, 1984.

_____. *Glory Figures. Yesterday's Faces*. Vol. 1. Bowling Green State University Popular Press, 1983.

_____. From the Dark Side: *Yesterday's Faces*. Vol. 3. Bowling Green State University Popular Press, 1986.

_____. The Solvers: *Yesterday's Faces*. Vol. 4. Bowling Green State University Popular Press, 1987.

_____. Dangerous Horizons: *Yesterday's Faces*. Vol. 5. Bowling Green State University Popular Press, 1991.

Sapper (Herman Cyril McNeile). *The Female of the Species*. London: Hodder and Stoughton, undated.

_____. *"Sapper": The Best Short Stories*. Intro. by Jack Adrian. London: Dent, 1984.

Smith, Arthur D. Howden. *Grey Maiden*. NY: Centaur, 1974.

Steeger, Henry. "An Interview with Henry Steeger." *Xenophile*. No. 33 (July 1977).

Surdez, Georges, "The Men Who Make the Argosy." *Argosy* 239:1 (June 10, 1933).

Swaim, John D. "The Doings of Dion, Part I: The Nest Egg." *Detective Story Magazine* 47:5 (18 March 1922).

_____. "Part III: Counting the Chickens." *Detective Story Magazine* 48:2 (8 April 1922).

Tompkins, Walker. "Confessions of a Pulp Western Hack." *Xenophile* #32 (May/June 1977).

Tonik, Albert, "Ramblings of a Perambulating Pulp Fan-Walker A. Tompkins." *The Pulp Collector* 2:4 (Spring 1987).

Vanardy, Varick (Frederic Van Rennselaer Dey). *Alias the Night Wind*. NY: Dillingham, 1913.

_____. *The Return of the Night Wind*. NY: Dillingham, 1914.

_____. *The Night Wind's Promise*. NY: Dillingham, 1914.

_____. *The Lady of the Night Wind*. NY: Macaulay, 1919.

Wallace, Edgar. "A Question of Rank."

_____. "Billy Best." *Everybody's* 40:1 (Jan. 1919).

_____. "Christmas At the China Dog." *The Stretelli Case*. Cleveland: International Fiction Library, 1930.

_____. "Hooky Patterson Dies Once."

_____. *People*. NY: Doubleday (1920).

_____. *Tam O'the Scoots*. NY: Burt, undated.

_____. "The Case of Lasky."

_____. "The Companions of the Ace High, II. Loving Heart and the Man with A Charmed Life." *The Popular Magazine* 52:1 (20 March 1919).

_____. *The Fighting Scouts*. London: Pearson, 1919.

_____. "The Last Load."

_____. "The Strafing of Muller."

_____. "V. Hooky Patterson Dies Once." *The Popular Magazine* 52:4 (7 May 1919).

Whitlock, Francis. "Tales of the Lost Legion: Anthony Atwater, Amateur Anarchist." *The Popular Magazine*. 10:4 (Feb. 1908).

Wilson, Colin. *The Occult*. NY: Random House, 1971.

Wirt, William. Autobiographical notes. "The Story-Tellers Circle: Jimmie Cordie and His Pals." *Short Stories*. Vol. 125, No. 1. Whole No. 547 (10 Oct. 1928).

_____. "He's My Meat." *Argosy* 217:5 (27 Dec. 1930).

_____. "I'm Shootin' Velly Good." *Argosy All-Story Weekly* 205:1 (13 July 1929).

_____. Letter in "Argonotes," *Argosy All-Story Weekly* 198:2 (Sept. 29, 1928).

_____. Letter "Flashes From Readers." *Detective Fiction Weekly* Vol. 47, No. 5 (1 Feb. 1930).

_____. "Private Property." *Short Stories*. (10 Oct. 1928).

_____. "The Devil's Tattoo." *Argosy* 234:1 (12 Nov. 1932).

_____. "The Story Tellers' Circle." *Short Stories*. 75:1 (10 Oct. 1928).

_____. "What Kept You?" *Argosy All-Story Weekly*. 206:6 (28 Sept. 1929).

Wood, S. Andrew. "The Golden Gambler." *Flynn's* 3:4 (3 Jan. 1925).

# Checklists of Magazine Appearances

The following checklists record magazine appearances of certain series characters discussed in this book. Not all listings are complete, since it has been impractical or impossible to access completely certain title runs. In four cases, published bibliographies have served as the basis of the checklist. These sources are acknowledged with appreciation and thanks: William J. Clark's Bedford Jones checklists, E. R. Hageman's Black Mask listings, Frank McSherry's Luigi Cardossa checklist, Ruth Moore's comprehensive bibliography of Erle Stanley Gardner, and the Zorro checklist of Edwin Murray and John McGeehan. In all cases, as many of these checklists were reconfirmed as possible and an occasional error corrected.

It is hardly possible to overstate the contributions made in these listings to Richard Bleiler, Randy Cox, Diggs LaTouche, Walker Martin, Steve Miller, and Will Murray. Without their help and constant support, drawing upon their collections of magazines, their extensive notes, and their equally extensive knowledge of these series, this book would have been far less comprehensive and this section far less detailed. Their generosity and kindness have supported this series since its inception and their aid sustains each page.

**BLACK BARR by Erle Stanley Gardner**
in *Black Mask*

| | | |
|---|---|---|
| 1925 | Nov | The Girl Goes with Me |
| 1926 | Oct | Buzzard Bait |
| 1927 | Jan | Whispering Sand |
| | Sept | Where the Buzzards Circle |
| 1928 | Aug | Fangs of Fate |
| | Sept | The Devil's Deputy |
| | Nov | Curse of the Killers |

**LUIGI CARADOSSO by F. R. Buckley**
in *Adventure*

| | | |
|---|---|---|
| 1924 | Nov 30 | Cartel to William Shakespeare |
| 1926 | Feb 10 | State Paper |
| 1927 | Aug 1 | Death Warrant |
| | Dec 15 | Concerning a Musician |
| 1928 | Jan 1 | Of Gallantry |
| | Mar 15 | Of a New Life |

|      |         |                                    |
|------|---------|------------------------------------|
|      | Jul 15  | Of Resolution                      |
|      | Nov 15  | Postscriptum                       |
|      | Dec 1   | Of Moonsickness                    |
| 1930 | Mar 1   | Of a Vanishment                    |
|      | May 15  | Of Animal Musick                   |
|      | June 15 | Of Diversion                       |
|      | Oct 1   | Of Possession                      |
| 1931 | May 15  | Of Vanity                          |
|      | Nov 1   | Of Education                       |
| 1932 | May 15  | Of Prophecy                        |
| 1933 | Jan 15  | Of Slander                         |
| 1934 | Mar     | Of the Meek                        |
|      | Aug     | Of High Command                    |
| 1940 | May     | Captain of the Guard               |
|      | Jul     | Red Is the Blade                   |
|      | Oct     | Teacher of Sword-play              |
|      | Dec     | Gold Ball and Chain                |
| 1941 | Jun     | Of Penitence                       |
|      | Sept    | Single Combat                      |
| 1943 | Feb     | Of Sorcery and Swordplay           |
| 1944 | Apr     | Of Glamour and Gunpowder           |
|      | Jun     | Of Treachery                       |
|      | Sept    | Of Chain Mail and Green Cheese     |
| 1947 | Apr     | Of Deadly Weapons                  |
|      | Jul     | Of Blood and Booty                 |
|      | Dec     | Of Treachery and Tradesmen         |
| 1948 | Mar     | Of Blood and Brothers              |
|      | Sept    | Of Vice and Virtue                 |
|      | Dec     | Of Lords and Lunatics              |
| 1949 | Jun     | Of Wine, Women, and Wickedness     |
| 1951 | Feb     | Captain of the Guard (reprint)     |
|      | May     | Red Is the Blade (reprint)         |
| 1952 | May     | Red Runs My Blade                  |
| 1953 | Mar     | Gateway To Treason                 |

in *World Wide Adventure #4*

| 1968 | Fall | Of Moonsickness |
|------|------|-----------------|

JIM CLAVERING by Walter Archer Frost
In *Flynn's* (Series title: "The Admirable Crimes of Captain Clavering"):

| 1926 | Apr 17 | Mrs. Ralston's Pearls     |
|------|--------|---------------------------|
|      | Apr 24 | The Ruby Buckle           |
|      | May 1  | The Delancy Diamonds      |
|      | May 8  | The McCallister Carbuncle |
|      | May 15 | The Laidlaw Pendant       |
|      | May 22 | The Alton Ruby            |

in *Flynn's Weekly*:

|        |                         |
|--------|-------------------------|
| May 29 | The Morton Diamond      |
| Jun  5 | The Carrington Sapphires |
| Jun 12 | The Ashford Necklace    |
| Jun 19 | Mrs. Amory's Diamond    |

COMPANIONS OF THE ACE HIGH by Edgar Wallace
in *The Popular Magazine*

| 1919 | Mar 7  | I: The Woman of the Lorelei |
|------|--------|------------------------------|
|      | Mar 20 | II: Loving Heart and The Man with a Charmed Life |
|      | Apr 7  | III: The Kurt of Honor |
|      | Apr 20 | IV: Hooky Who Played with the Germans |
|      | May 7  | V: Hooky Patterson Dies Once |
|      | May 20 | VI: The Man Who Shelled Open Boats |

JIMMIE CORDIE by W(illiam) Wirt (partial listing)
in *Short Stories*:

| 1928 | Oct 10 | Private Property |
|------|--------|------------------|
| 1935 | Jan 10 | Thy Son Grows Cold |
|      | May 25 | How Do You Spoke A Gun? |

in *Frontier*:

| 1928 | Nov | When Tigers Are Hunting |
|------|-----|--------------------------|
| 1929 | Jan | That Fish Thing |
|      | Apr | Right Smack At You |

in *Argosy All-Story Weekly*:

| 1929 | Jul 13  | "I'm Shootin' Velly Good" |
|------|---------|----------------------------|
|      | Aug 17  | The River Lies in Front |
|      | Sept 28 | "What Kept You?" |

in *Argosy*:

| 1930 | May 10      | The Death Spell of Nong Chik |
|------|-------------|-------------------------------|
|      | Oct 4, 11, 18 | The Nine Red Gods Decide (3-part serial) |
|      | Dec 20,27   | "He's My Meat!" (2-part serial) |
| 1931 | Mar 28      | Jades and Afghans |
|      | Dec 5       | Aztec Treasure |
| 1932 | Aug 6       | War Dragons |
|      | Nov 12      | The Devil's Tattoo |
| 1933 | Jan 21,28   | A Manchu Robin Hood (2-part serial) |
|      | Apr 29      | The Face in the Rock |
|      | Sept 16     | Ammunition Up |
|      | Dec 9       | The White War Lords |
| 1934 | Jul 7       | The Mad Monks |

1934    Sept 15
         thru 29         The Assassin (3-part serial)

DION by John D. Swaim
in *Detective Story Magazine* (7-part series titled "The Doings of Dion"):

| 1922 | Mar 18 | The Nest Egg |
| | Mar 25 | Hiding the Shells |
| | Apr 8 | Counting the Chickens |
| | Apr 15 | Robbing the Roost |
| | Apr 22 | Sleeping Dogs |
| | Apr 29 | The Inside Job |
| | May 27 | Au Revoir |

BULLDOG DRUMMOND by "Sapper" (H. C. McNeile)
in *The Popular Magazine*:

1925    Oct 7        The Nameless Terror (retitling of The Final Count)

in Detective Fiction Weekly:

1929    Jun 15
         thru Jul 13    The Masked Strangler (retitling of Temple Tower) 7-part serial

1931    Feb 12
         thru Mar 21   The Island of No Return (5-part serial)

1937    Mar 13
         thru Apr 24   Bulldog Drummond's Challenge (7-part serial)
         Sept 4       Lonely Inn
         Nov 20      Wheels Within Wheels
         Dec 25      The Oriental Mind

1938    Jan 1       Thirteen Lead Soldiers

in *Detective Fiction Weekly* by Gerald Fairlie

1938    Jun 11
         thru Jul 16    Bulldog Drummond on Dartmoor (6-part serial)

in *Mystery Novels Magazine Quarterly* by "Sapper"
1933    Summer     Bulldog Drummond Strikes Back

in *Popular Detective* by "Sapper"
1937    Jul         The Mystery Tour

GREY MAIDEN by Arthur D. Howden Smith
in *Adventure*
1926    Jun 23      The Forging
         Jul 23       The Slave of Marathon

|      | Aug 23 | *A Trooper of the Thessalians |
|------|--------|-------------------------------|
|      | Nov 8  | *Hanno's Sword                |
|      | Dec 31 | *The Last Legion              |
| 1927 | Feb 15 | *The Rider from the Desert    |
|      | Apr 15 | Thord's Wooing                |

* Appears in *Grey Maiden* (1974)

ED JENKINS, The Phantom Crook, by Erle Stanley Gardner
in *Black Mask*

| 1925 | Jan  | Beyond the Law                 |
|------|------|--------------------------------|
|      | Mar  | Hard As Nails                  |
|      | Jun  | Not So Darned Bad              |
|      | Jul  | Three O'Clock in the Morning   |
|      | Dec  | The Triple Cross               |
| 1926 | Jan  | According To Law               |
|      | Apr  | Register Rage                  |
|      | May  | ThisissoSudden                 |
|      | Jun  | Forget 'Em All                 |
|      | Sept | Laugh That Off (2)             |
|      | Nov  | Money, Marbles and Chalk       |
|      | Dec  | Dead Men's Letters (2)         |
| 1927 | Feb  | The Cat-Woman (2)              |
|      | Mar  | This Way Out (2)               |
|      | Apr  | Come and Get It (2)            |
|      | May  | In Full of Account (2)         |
|      | Nov  | The Wax Dragon (1)             |
|      | Dec  | Grinning Gods (1)              |
| 1928 | Feb  | Yellow Shadows (1)             |
|      | Mar  | Whispering Feet                |
|      | Apr  | Snow Bird                      |
|      | May  | Out of the Shadows             |
|      | Dec  | The Next Stiff                 |
| 1929 | Jan  | One Crook To Another           |
|      | Feb  | Bracelets for Two              |
|      | Mar  | Hooking the Crooks             |
|      | Apr  | No Questions Asked             |
|      | Oct  | Straight from the Shoulder     |
|      | Nov  | Brass Tacks                    |
|      | Dec  | Triple Treachery               |
| 1930 | Jan  | Double Or Quits                |
|      | May  | The Crime Crusher              |
|      | Jun  | Hell's Kettle (3)              |
|      | Jul  | Big Shot                       |
| 1931 | Jul  | Tommy Talk                     |
|      | Aug  | Hairy Hands                    |
|      | Sept | Promise To Pay                 |

| | | |
|---|---|---|
| | Oct | The Hot Squat |
| | Dec | Strictly Personal |
| 1932 | Jan | Face Up |
| | Mar | Feet First |
| | Apr | Straight Crooks |
| | May | Under the Guns |
| | Jun | Cooking Crooks |
| | Jul | Rough Stuff |
| | Sept | Black and White |
| 1933 | Feb | The Hour of the Rat |
| | Mar | Red Jade |
| | Apr | Chinatown Murder |
| | May | The Weapons of a Crook |
| | Sept | Whispering Justice |
| | Oct | The Murder Push |
| | Dec | Dead Men's Shoes |
| 1934 | Jan | A Guest of the House |
| | Mar | Cop Killers |
| | Apr | New Twenties |
| | Jun | Burnt Fingers |
| | Sept | The Heavenly Rat |
| | Nov | Hot Cash |
| 1935 | May | A Chance To Cheat |
| | Oct | Crash and Carry |
| | Dec | Above the Law |
| 1936 | May | Beating the Bulls |
| 1937 | Mar | This Way Out |
| 1938 | Apr | Muscle Out |
| 1939 | Sept | Dark Alleys |
| 1940 | Jun | Tong Trouble |
| | Dec | Jade Sanctuary |
| 1941 | May | Chinese People |
| | Dec | Rain Check |
| 1942 | Apr | Two Dead Hands |
| 1943 | Mar | The Incredible Mister Smith |
| | Sept | The Gong of Vengence |

in *Argosy*

| | | |
|---|---|---|
| 1961 | Sept | The Blond In Lower Six (novel) (1) |

Stories have been reprinted in the following collections:

(1) *The Blond in Lower 10* (1990)
(2) *Dead Men's Letters* (1990)
(3) *The Black Mask Boys* (1985)

*JIMGRIM* by Talbot Mundy
in *Adventure*:

| 1921 | Nov 10 | The Adventure at El-Kerak (1) |
| | Dec 10 | Under the Dome of the Rock(1) |
| 1922 | Jan 10 | The "Iblis" at Ludd |
| | Feb 20 | The Seventeen Thieves of El-Kalil |
| | Mar 10 | The Lion of Petra |
| | Apr 20 | The Woman Ayisha (2) |
| | May 30 | The Lost Trooper |
| | Jul 10 | The King in Check |
| | Aug 10 | A Secret Society |
| | Sept 10 | Moses and Mrs. Aintree |
| | Oct 10 | Khufu's Real Tomb (3) |
| 1923 | Mar 20 thru | |
| | Apr 30 | The Nine Unknown (5-part serial) |
| | Dec 10 | Mohammad's Tooth (4) |
| 1926 | Jun 8 thru | |
| | Aug 8 | Ramsden (5-part serial) (5) |
| 1930 | Nov 15 thru | |
| | Feb 15, 1931 | King of the World (7-part serial) (6) |

   (1) Included in the volume *Jimgrim and Allah's Peace*
   (2) Included in the volume *The One Hundred Days* and *The Woman Ayisha*
   (3) Book publication as *The Mystery of Khufu's Tomb*
   (4) Published as "The Hundred Days" in book *The Hundred Days* and *The Woman Ayisha*
   (5) Book publication both as *Ramsden* and *The Devil's Guard*
   (6) Book publication as *Jimgrim* and *Jimgrim Sahib*

*KHLIT* by Harold A. Lamb
in *Adventure*:

| 1917 | First Nov | Khlit (1) |
| 1918 | First Jan | Wolf's War (1) |
| | Mid-Feb | Tal Taulai Khan (1) |
| | First Aug | Alamut (2) |
| | Mid-Oct | The Mighty Manslayer (2) |
| | Mid-Dec | The White Khan (1) |
| 1919 | First Feb | Changa Nor (2) |
| | Mid-Apr | Roof of the World (2) |
| | Mid-Jul | The Star of Evil Omen (2) |
| | Mid-Sept | The Rider of the Gray Horse (2) |
| 1920 | First Jun | The Lion Cub (2) |
| | Mid-Jul | Law of Fire |
| | First Aug | The Bride of Jagannath (2) |
| | Mid-Sept | The Masterpiece of Death |

|      | First Nov    | The Curved Sword                 |
|------|--------------|----------------------------------|
| 1925 | Sept 30      | Bogatyr (2)                      |
|      | Nov 30 thru  |                                  |
|      | Dec 20       | White Falcon (3-part serial) (3) |
| 1926 | Jan 10       | The Winged Rider (1)             |
|      | Dec 8        | The Wolf Master                  |

1) Included in the volume, *The Mighty Manslayer* (1969)
2) Included in the volume, *The Curved Saber* (1964)
3) Published as *The White Falcon* (1926)

JOHN T. LAXWORTHY by E. Phillips Oppenheim
in *The Popular Magazine* (12-part series titled "The Peculiar
    Gifts of Mr. John T. Laxworthy"):

| 1912 | May 15  | The Secret of the *Magnifique*                  |
|------|---------|-------------------------------------------------|
|      | Jun 1   | The Tragedy of the Flower Farm                  |
|      | Jun 15  | The House of the Woman of Death                 |
|      | July 1  | The Strange Meeting at the Villa De Cap Frinet  |
|      | Jul 15  | The Vageries of the Prince of Liguria           |
|      | Aug 1   | Mystery House                                   |
|      | Aug 15  | The Flowers of Death                            |
|      | Sept 1  | The Deserted Hotel                              |
|      | Sept 15 | The Stetson Affair                              |
|      | Oct 1   | A Little Matter of Forty Thousand Pounds        |
|      | Oct 15  | The Disappearance of Mr. Colshaw                |
|      | Nov 1   | The Debt Collector                              |

LESTER LEITH by Erle Stanley Gardner
in *Detective Fiction Weekly*

| 1929 | Feb 23  | The Painted Decoy               |
|------|---------|---------------------------------|
|      | Mar 2   | A Tip from Scuttle              |
|      | Mar 23  | The Dummy Murder                |
|      | Apr 6   | The Case of the Fugitive Corpse |
|      | Apr 27  | The Pay-Off                     |
|      | May 11  | A Hot Tip                       |
|      | Jul 20  | A Peach of a Scheme             |
|      | Aug 3   | Even Money                      |
|      | Aug 10  | It's a Pipe!                    |
|      | Aug 31  | Faster Than Forty               |
|      | Sept 21 | Double Shadows                  |
|      | Oct 26  | The Artistic Touch              |
|      | Nov 23  | Lester Takes the Cake           |
| 1930 | Jan 11  | The Doubtful Egg                |
|      | May 3   | Both Ends Against the Middle    |
|      | Jun 7   | Put It In Writing!              |

|      |         |                                                              |
|------|---------|--------------------------------------------------------------|
|      | Jul 26  | Hot Dollars                                                  |
|      | Aug 23  | In Round Figures (1)                                         |
|      | Sept 27 | The Man on the End                                           |
|      | Dec 13  | Lester Frames A Fence                                        |
| 1931 | Jan 24  | Cold Clews                                                   |
|      | Mar 14  | The Candy Kid (2 & 3)                                        |
|      | Apr 18  | Big Money                                                    |
|      | May 23  | Hot Cash                                                     |
|      | Jun 27  | Not So Dumb                                                  |
|      | Jul 11  | The Girl with the Diamond Legs                              |
|      | Sept 26 | The Gold Magnet                                              |
|      | Nov 7   | The Crimson Mask                                             |
|      | Nov 21  | Rolling Stones                                               |
|      | Dec 26  | Red Herring                                                  |
| 1932 | Feb 27  | The Play's the Thing                                        |
|      | Apr 9   | The Bird in the Hand (1 & 4)                                 |
|      | Jun 4   | Thieves' Kitchen                                            |
|      | Jul 9   | Closer Than a Brother                                       |
|      | Jul 30  | A Deal in Cement                                             |
|      | Nov 5   | False Alarm                                                  |
|      | Dec 24  | Juggled Gems                                                 |
| 1933 | Feb 4   | One Jump Ahead                                               |
|      | Apr 1   | The Radio Ruse                                               |
|      | Jun 10  | Thin Ice                                                     |
|      | Jul 8   | Crooks' Vacation                                            |
|      | Dec 2   | The Burden of Proof                                          |
| 1934 | Feb 24  | Lost, Strayed and Stolen                                     |
|      | Jun 2   | Dead To Rights                                               |
|      | Jun 30  | Crocodile Tears                                              |
| 1935 | Jan 26  | Queens Wild                                                  |
|      | Nov 2   | Screaming Sirens                                             |
| 1936 | Mar 21  | Bald-Headed Row                                              |
| 1939 | Sept 16 | Lester Leith, Magician (1: retitled "The Hand Is Quicker Than the Eye") |
|      | Oct 28  | A Thousand To One (1)                                        |
|      | Nov 18  | Fair Exchange                                                |
| 1940 | Jan 20  | Sugar                                                        |
|      | Mar 16  | Monkeyshine                                                  |
| 1941 | Mar 29  | The Exact Opposite (1)                                       |
|      | Nov 29  | A Sugar Coating                                              |

in *Detective Story*

|      |      |                            |
|------|------|----------------------------|
| 1938 | Dec  | Planted Planets            |
| 1939 | Jan  | The Monkey Murder          |
|      | Feb  | The Seven Sinister Sombreros |
|      | Mar  | The Fourth Musketeer       |

|       | Apr  | With Rhyme and Reason |
|-------|------|------------------------|
|       | May  | The Queen of Shanghai Night |
|       | Aug  | The Ring of Fiery Eyes |

in *Flynn's Detective Fiction*

| 1943 | Jan | Something Like A Pelican |
|------|-----|---------------------------|
|      | Jul | The Black Feather |

in *Ellery Queen's Mystery Magazine* (all reprints)

| 1950 | May | Lester Leith, Impersonator (retitling of "A Thousand To One") |
|------|-----|----------------------------------------------------------------|
|      | Nov | Lester Leith, Financier (retitling of "Something Like a Pelican") |
| 1951 | Oct | The Exact Opposite |
| 1952 | Jul | In Round Figures |
| 1953 | Dec | The Bird in the Hand |
| 1954 | Nov | The Candy Kid |
| 1955 | Jul | The Hand Is Quicker Than the Eye (retitling of "Lester Leith, Magician") |

(1)  *The Amazing Adventures of Lester Leith* (1980)
(2)  *The Case of the Crying Swallow* (undated)
(3)  *The Case of the Murderer's Bride* (1969)
(4)  *The Hardboiled Dicks* (1965)

NORROY, DIPLOMATIC AGENT by George Bronson-Howard
in *The Popular Magazine*:

| 1905 |      | (First Series: "Norroy, Diplomatic Agent") |
|------|------|---------------------------------------------|
|      | Apr  | I. How Norroy Created a New Republic |
|      | May  | II. A Tilt with the Muscovite |
|      | Jun  | III. The Isle of St. Anthony |
|      | Jul  | IV. The Eagle's Eyrie |
|      | Aug  | V. A Yankee Knight Errant |
|      | Sept | VI. The Honor of the Ambassador |
|      | Oct  | VII. The Friend of the Chief Executive |
| 1906 |      | (Second Series: "Norroy, Diplomatic Agent") |
|      | Jun  | I. The Editor and the Diplomat |
|      | Jul  | II. A Prince for a Pawn |
|      | Aug  | III. On the Night of the Charity Ball |
|      | Sept | IV. By Aid of an Anachronism |
|      | Oct  | V. For the Good of the State |
| 1907 | Oct  | An Alias from Burke's |
|      | Dec  | The Brotherhood of Suppression |
| 1908 | Oct  | The Return of Norroy |
| 1911 | Feb 1 | The Code Book (novel) |

| 1912 | | ("The Further Chronicles of Norroy, Diplomatic Agent") |
|---|---|---|
| | Nov 15 | The First Round |
| | Dec 1 | The Kidnapping of Norroy |
| | Dec 15 | The Curio Collector |
| 1913 | Jan 1 & 15 | The Green Hour (2-part serial) |
| | Feb 1 | The Secret Stairway |
| | Feb 15 & Mar 1 | The Green Finch (2-part serial) |
| | Mar 15 & Apr 1 | Behind the Green Lamps (2-part serial) |
| 1918 | May 20 | I. The Book of the Betrayers |
| | Jun 7 | II. An Enemy to the Emperor |
| | Jun 20 | III. The Bureau of Missing Articles |
| | Jul 7 | IV. His Country or His Life |
| | Jul 20 | V. A Leaf from the Kaiser's Book |
| 1920 | Oct 7 to Nov 20 | The Devil's Chaplain (4-part serial) |
| 1923 | Feb 7 | The Lady of the Lost Garments |

(NOTE  An associated series featuring Baedeker Bok, who become one of Norroy's agents, also appeared in The *Popular Magazine*. The following stories are Bok adventures; all mention Norroy.)

| 1911 | Jul 1 | Baedeker Bok |
|---|---|---|
| | Aug 15 | The Night of a Million Candles |
| | Sept 1 | Milady of the Millionaires |

*T. X. O'LEARY* by Arthur Guy Empey
*in War Stories*:

| 1926 | Dec | Under Three Flags |
|---|---|---|
| 1927 | Jan | O'Leary Saves the Sector |
| | Feb | O'Leary Proves His Courage |
| | Mar | O'Leary on Liason |
| | Apr | O'Leary Holds the Trench |
| | May | O'Leary Consults the Stars |
| 1931 | Nov | O'Leary Carries On |
| 1932 | Apr | O'Leary, Wagon Soldier |
| | Jun | O'Leary, Secret Service |

in *War Stories* (Second Series)

| 1936 | Feb | Soldiers of Death in *Battle Stories* |
|---|---|---|

NOTE:  Issues to 1932 are identified by date, volume, and whole numbers.  From 1933 through 1936, the date was dropped and the magazine identified only by the volume number, which was then used as a whole number, the magazine having become an unannounced annual.

| | | Whole # | |
|---|---|---|---|
| 1928 | Feb thru Jun | 6-10 | Hinky, Dinky, Parle Vous (5-part serial) |
| | Jul 11 | | O'Leary Signs the Armistice |
| 1930 | Sept thru Dec | 37-40 | Terrence X. O'Leary of the Rainbow Division (4-part serial) |
| 1932 | Jan | 53 | Curse of the Iron Cross |
| | Apr | 55 | O'Leary's Rough Riders |
| | Jun | 56 | The Y.M.C.A. Goes Over the Top |
| | Jul | 57 | That Fightin' Irish Son-of-a-Gun |
| 1933 | | 62 | Sgt. O'Leary's Tank Busters |
| 1935 | | 65 | O'Leary Tames the Boche |
| 1936 | | 66 | Terence X. O'Leary in Ethopia |

in *War Birds*:

| | | |
|---|---|---|
| 1933 | Jul | O'Leary, Sky Hawk |
| | Aug | O'Leary Flies a Ghost |
| | Nov | O'Leary, Falconeer |
| | Dec | Suicide Wings |
| 1934 | Jan | O'Leary Paints the Eagle |
| | Mar | Ghost of the Black Wings |
| | Apr | O'Leary Rides with Death |
| | Jun | O'Leary's Last Supper |
| | Jul | O'Leary, Zeppelin Killer |
| | Sept & Oct | O'Leary, the Devil's Darling (2-part serial) |
| | Nov & Dec | O'Leary Cracks the Crimson Legion (2-part serial) |
| 1935 | Jan | O'Leary, the Devil's Undertaker |
| | Feb | O'Leary, Hell's Thunderbolt (magazine retitled *Terence X. O'Leary's War Birds*) |
| | Mar | O'Leary Fights the Golden Ray |
| | Apr | O'Leary, Dyno-Blaster, or The Adventure of the Ageless Men |
| | Jun | The Purple Warriors of Neptunia (magazine retitled *War Birds*) |
| | Oct | The Sky Hawk Screams |

JOHN SOLOMON by H. Bedford-Jones
in *The Argosy:*

| | | |
|---|---|---|
| 1914 | Jan-Feb | The Gate of Farewell (2-part serial) |
| | Jul | John Solomon — Supercargo |
| 1915 | Jun | The Seal of John Solomon |

in *Argosy*

| 1930 | Jan 25 | The Mysterious John Solomon |
|---|---|---|
|  | Feb 15 to | John Solomon's Biggest Game |
|  | Mar 22 | (6-part serial) |
| 1931 | Aug 15 to | Solomon's Caves |
|  | Sept 5 | (4-part serial) |
| 1932 | Feb 13 | Solomon Settles Accounts |
| 1933 | May 20 | Solomon in the Catacombs |
|  | Dec 2 to | The Terror of Algiers |
|  | 23 | (4-part serial) |
| 1934 | Jun 9 | John Solomon of Limehouse |
| 1935 | Jan 5 | The Case of the Kidnapped Duchess |
|  | Feb 9 | The Case of the Deadly Barque |

in Far East Adventure Stories:

| 1931 | Feb to Nov | Gold of Ishmael (six-part serial: Feb, Mar, Apr, Jul, Sept, Nov) |
|---|---|---|

in *People's Magazine*:

| 1915 | Mar | Solomon's Quest* |
|---|---|---|
|  | Jun | Gentleman Solomon* |
|  | Oct | Solomon's Carpet* |
| 1916 | Feb | Solomon's Submarine |
|  | Aug | John Solomon, Argnaut |
| 1917 | Jan | The Shawl of Solomon* |
|  | Jul | Pilgrim Solomon |
|  | Dec 10 | John Solomon, Retired |
| 1918 | Jun 25 | John Solomon's Son |
| 1921 | Jul | John Solomon |
|  | Oct 25 to | John Solomon — Incognito* |
|  | Dec 10 | (4-part serial) |

* These novels—and it is believed others not identified—were published in English cloth-bound editions. The author's name was given as Allan Hawkwood.

TAM O'THE SCOOTS by Edgar Wallace

in *Everybody's*

| 1917 | Nov | I. The Case of Lasky | (1) |
|---|---|---|---|
|  |  | II. Puppies of the Pack | (1) |
|  | Dec | I. The Coming of Muller (Story is numbered I rather than III.) | (1) |
|  |  | IV. The Strafing of Muller | (1) |

(NOTE: Subsequent stories are not identified by number.)

| 1918 | Feb | Annie — the Gun | (1) |
|---|---|---|---|
|  | Mar | The Law-Breaker and Frightfulness | (1) |
|  | Apr | The Man Behind the Circus | (1) |
|  | May | A Question of Rank | (1) |

|      | Jun  | A Reprisal Raid                          | (1) |
|------|------|------------------------------------------|-----|
|      | Jul  | The Last Load                            | (1) |
|      | Aug  | The Gentlemen from Indiana               | (2) |
|      | Sept | The Duke's Museum                        | (2) |
|      | Oct  | The Man Called McGinnice                 |     |
|      | Nov  | The Cloud Fishers                        | (2) |
|      | Dec  | The Kindergarten                         | (2) |
| 1919 | Jan  | Billy Best                               | (2) |
|      | Feb  | The Wager of Rittmeister von Haarden     | (2) |
|      | Mar  | A Day with von Tirpitz                   |     |
|      | Apr  | The Debut of William Best                | (2) |
|      | May  | The Woman in the Story                   | (2) |
|      | Jun  | The Infant Samuel                        | (2) |

NOTE  A final Tam story appeared as "Christmas Eve At The China Dog" in *The Stretelli Case*.

1. Included in volume *Tam O'The Scoots*
2. Included in volume *The Fighting Scouts*


*Tros of Samothrace* by Talbot Mundy
in *Adventure*:

| 1925 |          |                              | reprinted in (1)            |
|------|----------|------------------------------|-----------------------------|
|      | Feb 10   | Tros of Samothrace (2)       | Lud of Lunden               |
|      | Apr 10   | The Enemy of Rome            | Lud of Lunden               |
|      | Jun 10   | Prisoners of War             | Lud of Lunden               |
|      |          |                              | Chapters 1-7)               |
|      |          |                              | Avenging Liafail,           |
|      |          |                              | (Chapters 8-11)             |
|      |          |                              | Helma                       |
|      | Aug 20   | Hostages to Luck             | Avenging Liafail            |
|      |          |                              | Helma                       |
|      | Oct 10   | Admiral of Caesar's Fleet    | Avenging Liafail,           |
|      |          |                              | (Chapters 1-12)             |
|      |          |                              | Liafail                     |
|      |          |                              | Praetor's Dungeon           |
|      | Dec 10   | The Dancing Girl of Gades    | Liafail                     |
|      |          |                              | Praetor's Dungeon           |
| 1926 | Feb 10,  | The Messenger of Destiny     | Helen                       |
|      | 20,28    | (3-part serial)              | Praetor's Dungeon           |
| 1935 | May 1    | Battle Stations!             | Purple Pirate               |
|      | Jun 15   | Cleopatra's Promise          | Purple Pirate               |
|      | Aug 15   | The Purple Pirate            | Purple Pirate               |
|      | Oct 1    | Fleets of Fire               | Purple Pirate               |

NOTE:  Tros also appears in the novel, *Queen Cleopatra* (1929); this did not receive magazine publication.

1. Reprint information is as cited in Donald M. Grant's *Talbot Mundy —
Messenger of Destiny*, "Books," (1983).
2. All 1925-1926 stories appear in the volume *Tros of Samothrace*
(1934), containing ninety-six chapters, each headed by a quotation.
Titles of the original magazine novels are not given. Those titles and
their corresponding chapters in Tros are as follows:

| *Magazine Title* | *Chapters* |
|---|---|
| "Tros of Samothrace" | I through XIV |
| "The Enemy of Rome" | XV through XXVI |
| "Prisoners of War" | XXVII through XXXVII |
| "Hostages to Luck" | XXXVIII through LI |
| "Admiral of Caesar's Fleet" | LII through LXVII |
| "The Dancing Girl of Gades" | LXVIII through LXXXI |
| "The Messenger of Destiny" | LXXXII through XCVI |

*The White Wolf* (Jim-twin Allen) by Hal Dunning
in *Complete Stories*:

| 1927 | Feb | The White Wolf |
|---|---|---|
| | March | Jim Allen Rides To Town |
| | Apr | Nemesis of the Range (novel) |
| | May | The Outlaw Sheriff |
| | Jul | The Killer and the Kid |
| | Sept | Wolf's Law |
| | Nov | Jim-twin Allen Drops In |
| | Dec | Jim-twin Allen Comes To Town |
| 1928 | | |
| | Feb | The Wolf Rides Again |
| | Mar | The House of Sinister Men |
| | May | Outlaw's Law |
| | Jun | Son of a Fightin' Fool |
| | Jul | Buzzards' Meat |
| | Aug | Judgment of the Desert |
| | Sept | Nothin' But a Rope |
| | Oct 15 | The Wolf Makes His Kill |
| | Dec 15 | No Trespass |
| 1929 | Jan 15 | Jim Allen, Gentleman |
| | Feb 1 | For the Last Time |
| | Mar 15 | The Tiger of the Border |
| | May 15 | The Blood Trail |
| | Jun 15 | The Ranger and the Rose |
| | Jul 15 | Bread on the Waters |
| | Aug 1 | An Even Chance |
| | Sept 1 | The Ghost of the Wolf |
| | Oct 1 | Not Worth Killin' |

|      |         |                                 |
|------|---------|---------------------------------|
|      | Oct 15  | "Regular an' Lawful"            |
|      | Nov 1   | Just a Man                      |
|      | Nov 15  | The Lion and the Mouse          |
|      | Dec 1   | Two of a Kind                   |
|      | Dec 15  | A Case of Psychology            |
| 1930 | Jan 1   | In His Own Web                  |
|      | Jan 15  | The Word of the Wolf            |
|      | Feb 1   | A Man's Country                 |
|      | Feb 15  | Wolf Poison                     |
|      | Mar 1   | Horseshoes for Luck             |
|      | Mar 15  | The Wolf Pays a Debt            |
|      | Apr 1   | The Left-Handed Shooter         |
|      | Apr 15  | The Last Gamble                 |
|      | May 1   | A Pat Hand                      |
|      | May 15  | The Long Trail                  |
|      | Jun 1   | The Wolf Goes North             |
|      | Jun 15  | As a Man Sows                   |
|      | Jul 1   | Runt Justice                    |
|      | Jul 15  | Lower Than a Snake              |
|      | Aug 1   | Counterfeit Hero                |
|      | Aug 15  | Two Innocents in Hurricane Gap  |
|      | Sept 1  | Not Guilty                      |
|      | Oct 1   | A Real Horse                    |
|      | Nov 1   | Boomerang                       |
|      | Nov 15  | Of Their Own Will               |
|      | Dec 1   | The Miracle                     |
| 1931 | Jan 1   | In Their Own Coin               |
|      | Jan 15  | The Outlaw Legion               |
|      | Feb 15  | Charge of the Ancients          |
|      | Mar 15  | With His Own Weapons            |
|      | May 1   | Outlaws Ain't So Bad            |
|      | May 15  | Devil's Brew                    |
|      | Jun 15  | Plum Legal                      |
|      | Jul 1   | The Perfect Alibi               |
|      | Jul 15  | You Got To Be Hard              |
|      | Aug 1   | It'll Be Justice                |
|      | Sept 1  | The Cheater Pays                |
|      | Sept 15 | Tiny Tim Wins His Spurs         |
|      | Oct 15  | Magnificent Fools               |
|      | Nov 15  | Tinhorn                         |
| 1932 | May 1   | Accordin' To the Book           |
|      | May 15  | Ranger King                     |
|      | Jun 1   | Absentee Justice                |
|      | Jul 1   | Hangman's Hickory               |
|      | Jul 15  | No Rangers Wanted               |
|      | Aug 1   | Wolves Can Climb                |

|      |            |                                  |
|------|------------|----------------------------------|
|      | Aug 15     | Once an Outlaw                   |
|      | Sept 1     | Coyotes Reward                   |
|      | Sept 15    | Quicksand                        |
|      | Oct 1      | "Women Is Sure Peculiar"         |
|      | Oct 15     | Gents Use Guns                   |
|      | Nov 1      | Battle Cry                       |
|      | Nov 15     | Left-Handed Law                  |
|      | Dec 1      | Outlaw Island                    |
|      | Dec 15     | The Christmas of a Wolf          |
| 1933 | Jan 1      | Hell's Acres                     |
|      | Jan 15     | Two-Spots Can't Win              |
|      | Feb 1      | Found Gold                       |
|      | Feb 15     | Pardner's Honor                  |
|      | March 1    | Destroying Angel                 |
|      | March 15   | There's Always Wolves            |
|      | Apr 1      | For a Friend                     |
|      | Apr 15     | Guns Talk Last                   |
|      | May 15     | Hostage Trail                    |
| 1934 | Feb 15     | High-Water Cache                 |
|      | Apr 30     | Colts Alter Cases                |
|      | Jul 1      | Golden Pelts                     |
|      | Jul 22     | Wolf's Clothing                  |
|      | Sept 24    | Hard To Hit                      |

in *Wild West Weekly* (signed Hal Dunning; written by Walker A. Tompkins, except as indicated)

|      |             |                                              |
|------|-------------|----------------------------------------------|
| 1938 | Nov 19      | Fangs of the White Wolf                      |
|      | Dec 17      | The White Wolf Leads a Pack                  |
| 1939 | Jan 14      | Deputy Sheriff White Wolf                    |
|      | Mar 4       | White Wolf's Outlaw Pack                     |
|      | Jul 1       | White Wolf Reaches Cactus Country            |
|      | Sept 2      | A Trap for White Wolf                        |
|      | Sept 30     | Sonny Tabor Tracks the White Wolf            |
|      |             | (Ward M. Stevens — pseudonym for Paul S.     |
|      |             | Powers—and Hal Dunning)                      |
|      | Nov 4       | White Wolf At Ghost Mine                     |
|      | Dec 30      | White Wolf's Six-gun New Year                |
| 1940 | Mar 30      | White Wolf's Snake-Fang Clue                 |
|      | May 25      | Twin of the White Wolf                       |
|      | Nov 30      | White Wolf Talks Turkey                      |
| 1941 | March 15 &  |                                              |
|      | 22          | Gun-Mad Masquerade (2-part serial)           |
|      | Jun 28      | White Wolf's Outlaw Loot                     |
| 1942 | Mar 21      | White Wolf's Law                             |
|      | May 2       | Renegade Reward                              |
|      | Aug 1       | Wolf Tracks West                             |

|      | Sept 12 | Bonanza Bullion |
|      | Oct 31  | Hot-Lead Homecoming |
|      | Dec 26  | Substitute SHeriff |
| 1943 | Mar 13  | Blizzard Buscaderp |
|      | Jun 19  | Trigger Twins |

The preceding checklist consolidates and supplements information provided by William J. Clark, J.A>Hickey, Jack Irwin, and Harvey King in Xenophile Nos. 24 (July 1976, pps. 38-39), 28 (Nov/Dec 76, p. 71, and 30 (March 1977, p. 138.)

ZORRO by Johnston McCulley
in *All-Story Weekly*:

| 1919 | Aug 9 thru | The Curse of Capistrano (5-part serial) |
|      | Sept 6     | Published as The Mark of Zorro (1924) |

in *Argosy-AllStory Weekly*:

| 1922 | May 6 thru | |
|      | Jun 10     | The Further Adventures of Zorro (6-part serial) |

*in Argosy*

| 1931 | Oct 3 thru 24 | Zorro Rides Again (4-part serial) |
| 1932 | Nov 12        | Zorro Saves a Friend |
| 1933 | Apr 22        | Zorro Hunts a Jackal (retitled and reprinted in Cavalier Classics, Sept 1940) |
| 1934 | Aug 18        | Zorro Deals With Treason (reprinted in Cavalier Classics, July 1940, and in the Argosy Bicentennial Issue, 1976.) |
| 1935 | Sept 21 & 28  | Mysterious Don Miguel (2-part serial) |
| 1941 | Jan 25 thru   | The Sign of Zorro (5-part serial) in |
|      | Feb 22        | Cavalier Classics |
| 1940 | Jul           | Zorro Deals With Treason |
|      | Sept          | Zorro Hunts By Night in Max Brand Western |
| 1954 | May           | Zorro Rides the Trail in Short Stories |
| 1959 | Apr           | The Mask of Zorro in West |
| 1944 | Jul           | Zorro Draws His Blade |
|      | Sept          | Zorro Upsets a Plot |
|      | Nov           | Zorro Strikes Again |
| 1945 | Jan           | Zorro Saves a Herd |
|      | Mar           | Zorro Runs the Gauntlet |
|      | May           | Zorro Fights a Duel |
|      | Jul           | Zorro Opens as Cage |
|      | Sept          | Zorro Prevents a War |
|      | Oct           | Zorro Fights a Friend |
|      | Nov           | Zorro's Hour of Peril |
|      | Dec           | Zorro Lays a Ghost |

| 1946 | Jan | Zorro Frees Some Slaves |
| | Feb | Zorro's Double Danger |
| | Mar | Zorro's Masquerade |
| | Apr | Zorro Stops a Panic |
| | May | Zorro's Twin Perils |
| | Jun | Zorro Plucks a Pigeon |
| | Jul | Zorro Rides At Dawn |
| | Aug | Zorro Takes the Bait |
| | Oct | Zorro Raids a Caravan |
| 1947 | Jan | Zorro's Moment of Fear |
| | Feb | Zorro Saves His Honor |
| | Mar | Zorro and the Pirate |
| | Apr | Zorro Beats a Drum |
| | May | Zorro's Strange Duel |
| | Jun | A Task for Zorro (short novel) |
| | Jul | Zorro's Masked Menace |
| | Aug | Zorro Aids an Invalid |
| | Sept | Zorro Saves an American |
| | Oct | Zorro Meets a Rogue |
| | Nov | Zorro Races with Death |
| | Dec | Zorro Fights for Peace |
| 1948 | Feb | Zorro Serenades a Siren |
| | Mar | Zorro Meets a Wizard |
| | Apr | Zorro Fights With Fire |
| | May | Gold for a Tyrant |
| | Jul | The Hide Hunter |
| | Sept | Zorro Shears Some Wolves |
| | Nov | The Face Behind the Mask |
| 1949 | Jan | Zorro Starts the New Year |
| | Mar | Hangnoose Reward |
| | May | Zorro's Hostile Friends |
| | Jul | Zorro's Hot Tortillas |
| | Sept | An Ambush for Zorro |
| | Nov | Zorro Gives Evidence |
| 1950 | Jan | Ranch Marauders |
| | Mar | Zorro's Stolen Steed |
| | Sept | Zorro Curbs a Riot |
| | Nov | The Three Strange Peons |
| 1951 | Jan | Zorro Nabs a Cutthroat |
| | Mar | Zorro Gathers Taxes |
| | Jul | Zorro's Fight for Life (short novel) |

ABB-1348

11/1/93

PS
374
A35
S2
1983
─────
V.6

0 00 02 0579751 7
MIDDLEBURY COLLEGE